Jewitt's Ceramic Art of Great Britain 1800–1900

Jewitt's
Ceramic Art of Great Britain
1800–1900

by Geoffrey A. Godden F.R.S.A.

being a revised and expanded edition of
those parts of
The Ceramic Art of Great Britain
by Llewellynn Jewitt, F.S.A.
dealing with the nineteenth century

BARRIE & JENKINS
LONDON

Books by Geoffrey A. Godden
Victorian Porcelain
British Pottery and Porcelain, 1780–1850
Encyclopaedia of British Pottery and
    Porcelain Marks
Antique China and Glass under £5
An Illustrated Encyclopaedia of British
    Pottery and Porcelain
The Handbook of British Pottery and
    Porcelain Marks
Minton Pottery and Porcelain of the First
    Period
Caughley and Worcester Porcelains,
    1775–1800
The Illustrated Guide to Lowestoft Porcelain
Coalport and Coalbrookdale Porcelains
Stevengraphs and Other Victorian Silk
    Pictures
The Illustrated Guide to Mason's Patent
    Ironstone China

Edited by Geoffrey A. Godden
Revised 15th Edition of William Chaffers'
*Marks and Monograms on European and Oriental
Pottery and Porcelain* (British Section) *Pencillings
by the Way* by Thomas E. Beaumont: A 'con-
stitutional' Voyage Round the World: 1870 and
1871

In Preparation
The Illustrated Guide to Ridgway Porcelain
The Illustrated Guide to Daniel Porcelain
Chamberlain's Worcester Porcelain

The Ceramic Art of Great Britain by
Llewellynn Jewitt was first published in 1878,
with a revised edition in 1883, by Virtue & Co.
Ltd., London.
This edition first published 1972 by
Barrie & Jenkins Limited,
2, Clement's Inn, London, W.C.2.
© Geoffrey A. Godden 1972
Designed by Michael R. Carter
Photoset in Malta by St Paul's Press Ltd
Printed in Great Britain by
Butler & Tanner Ltd,
Frome and London
ISBN 0 214 65350 1

... Mr. Jewitt's work is a perfect encyclopaedia
of British pottery, and must henceforth take its
place as the text book of Ceramic Art in England.

The Art-Journal, 1878.

Opposite

Title page of the first edition

THE
CERAMIC ART

OF

GREAT BRITAIN

FROM PRE-HISTORIC TIMES DOWN TO THE PRESENT DAY

BEING A HISTORY OF THE ANCIENT AND MODERN

POTTERY AND PORCELAIN WORKS

OF THE KINGDOM

AND OF THEIR PRODUCTIONS OF EVERY CLASS

BY

LLEWELLYNN JEWITT, F.S.A.

LOCAL SECRETARY OF THE SOCIETY OF ANTIQUARIES OF LONDON ;
HON. AND ACTUAL MEMBER OF THE RUSSIAN IMPERIAL ARCHÆOLOGICAL COMMISSION, AND STATISTICAL
COMMITTEE, PSKOV ;
MEMBER OF THE ROYAL ARCHÆOLOGICAL INSTITUTE OF GREAT BRITAIN AND IRELAND ;
ASSOCIATE OF THE BRITISH ARCHÆOLOGICAL ASSOCIATION ;
HON. MEMBER OF THE ESSEX ARCHÆOLOGICAL SOCIETY AND OF THE MANX SOCIETY, ETC.;
COR. MEMBER OF THE ROYAL HISTORICAL SOCIETY,
ETC. ETC. ETC.

ILLUSTRATED WITH NEARLY TWO THOUSAND ENGRAVINGS

IN TWO VOLUMES.—I.

LONDON
VIRTUE AND CO., Limited, 26, IVY LANE
PATERNOSTER ROW
1878

Note on Illustrations

Reproductions of 54 engravings and numerous factory marks are incorporated in the text. There are also 116 black and white plates and 10 colour plates. Reference to all illustrations is made in the index.

CONTENTS

LLEWELLYNN JEWITTS INTRODUCTION TO THE FIRST EDITION, 1878

In issuing my present work I have two distinct personal duties to perform, and I hasten, in these brief lines of introduction, to discharge them. First, I earnestly desire to ask indulgence from my readers for any shortcomings which may be apparent in its contents; and next, I desire emphatically to express my thanks to all who have in any way, or even to the smallest extent, assisted me in my labours. The preparation of the work has extended over a considerable period of time, and I have had many difficulties to contend with that are, and must necessarily be, wholly unknown to any but myself – hard literary digging to get at facts and to verify dates, that is not understood, and would scarce be believed in, by the reader who turns to my pages – and hence errors of omission and of commission may have, nay, doubtless have, crept in, and may in some places, to a greater or less extent, have marred the accuracy of the page whereon they have occurred. I can honestly say I have left nothing undone, no source untried, and no trouble untaken to secure perfect accuracy in all I have written, and yet I am painfully aware that shortcomings may, and doubtless will, be laid to my charge; for these, wherever they occur, I ask, and indeed claim indulgence. I believe in *work*, in hard unceasing labour, in patient and painstaking research, in untiring searchings, and in diligent collection and arrangement of facts – to make time and labour and money subservient to the end in view, rather than that the end in view, and the time and labour and money expended, should bend and bow and ultimately break before *time*. Thus it is that my 'Ceramic Art' has been so long in progress, and thus it is that many changes have occurred during the time it has been passing through the press which it has been manifestly impossible to chronicle.

I have the proud satisfaction, however, of knowing that my work is the only one of its kind yet attempted, and I feel a confident hope that it will fill a gap that has long wanted filling, and will be found alike useful to the manufacturer, the china collector, and the general reader.

When, some twenty years ago, [in the 1850s] at the instance of my dear friend Mr. S. C. Hall, I began my series of papers in *The Art Journal* upon the various famous earthenware and porcelain works of the kingdom, but little had been done in that direction, and the information I got together from time to time had to be procured from original sources, by prolonged visits to the places themselves, and by numberless applications to all sorts of people from whom even scraps of reliable matter could be obtained. Books on the subject were not many, and the information they contained on English Ceramics was meagre in the extreme. Since then numerous workers have sprung up, and their published volumes – many of them sumptuous and truly valuable works – attest strongly to the interest and pains they have taken in the subject. To all these, whoever they may be, the world owes a debt of gratitude for devoting their time and their talents to so important a branch of study. To each of them I tender my own thanks for having devoted themselves to the elucidation of one of my favourite pursuits, and for having given to the world the result of their labours. No work has, however, until now been entirely devoted to the one subject of British Ceramics, and I feel therefore that in presenting my present volumes to the public I am only carrying out the plan I at first laid down, and am not even in the slightest degree encroaching on the province of any other writer.

I think I may safely say there is scarcely a manufacturer – even if there be one at all – in the length and breadth of the kingdom with whom I have not frequently communicated in the progress of this work. Except in some few solitary instances I have received the information I have sought, and my inquiries have met with the most cordial and ready response.

To all those who have thus assisted me with information or otherwise, and especially to my friend Mr. Goss, who has greatly assisted me over the onerous task of some of the Staffordshire potteries, I offer my warmest thanks; and to those few others, who from inattention, short-sightedness, or other cause, have not responded to my inquiries, I would express my sorrow if, through that inattention on their part, I have been unable to give as full particulars regarding their potteries as I could have wished. To thank by name those who have assisted me with information would require a long list indeed; I therefore tender my acknowledgments to all in the one emphatic good old English expression – 'Thank you!'

Llewellynn Jewitt.

Winster Hall, Derbyshire,
November, 1877

EDITOR'S INTRODUCTION TO THIS EDITION

In 1878 Llewellynn Jewitt published the two volumes of his *The Ceramic Art of Great Britain from pre-historic times down to the present day*. Work on the preparation of this book had extended over the previous twenty years and the result must be acknowledged as the first serious study of the history of British ceramics.

Today, the undoubted value of Jewitt's book results from his wide coverage of nineteenth-century ware and the incorporation of much first-hand information on the manufacturers of this period. The extent of his research on the smaller nineteenth-century manufacturers may be seen by comparing the 1878 edition with the revised 1883 edition. In these five years, Jewitt amended and brought up to date the histories of hundreds of factories of which one can search in vain for even the briefest mention in any other reference book.

In revising this Victorian work over some ten years, I have omitted all reference to pre-1800 ware (as this period is now better covered by modern works of reference) and brought Jewitt's detailed history of our nineteenth-century ceramic art up to the year 1900. The additional material is, like Jewitt's, largely gathered from contemporary sources – rate books and Victorian journals or trade magazines, such as the *Pottery Gazette*. Much information will be found on the smaller manufacturers and on the utilitarian ware of the period. It is interesting to see the extent to which our nineteenth-century pottery was exported all over the world, for Jewitt lists the markets each firm supplied.

Jewitt's original editions were illustrated exclusively from nearly two thousand line engravings. For reasons of space, many of these have had to be omitted. The examples retained relate to nineteenth-century products and have been chosen to illustrate interesting documentary exhibition pieces or the ware of some of the lesser known manufacturers; to these has been added a selection of one hundred and twenty photographs and a selection of contemporary illustrated advertisements. The advertisements have been chosen to show typical examples of the period and not unique 'museum' pieces.

In the earlier editions of this history, the accounts of the various manufactories appeared within their geographical section but in no specific order. In an attempt to facilitate the use of this revised edition as a reference book, I have therefore rearranged the material. To this end, Part One – which is preceded by my own pictorial glossary – is devoted to the Staffordshire Potteries, with the main towns appearing in their alphabetical sequence. Part Two deals with the non-Staffordshire producers of pottery and porcelain, listed in alphabetical order of the places where they worked.

When setting out to prepare this edition, I had first intended to find a means of indicating to the reader where textual changes had been made and where new matter had been written in. In practice, however, it soon become clear that to do so throughout would be impractical without obliging the reader to pick his way through a maze of square brackets, elipses and editorial notes. I therefore decided to risk the displeasure of textual purists and present a revised text directly, even where this involved occasional paraphrasing of the original. The reader may be assured, however, that such liberties as I have permitted myself in this respect have been modest. As will be obvious, I have changed the tense of passages where Jewitt was referring to contemporary events and incorporated my own account of events occurring later than the date at which he was writing.

Before progressing to Jewitt's work, it is fitting to give a few basic facts about this ceramic historian to whom all twentieth-century collectors are deeply indebted. Firstly, it would be well to point out that the author spelt his first name with two 'n's – Llwellynn – although most later writers have failed to follow his example.

Llewellynn Jewitt was born at Kimberworth, near Rotherham, on 24th November 1816. He was the seventeenth child of Arthur and Martha Jewitt, his father then being a master at the local school. Young Llewellynn must have gained his love of research and writing from his father, for not only did Arthur Jewitt establish a Yorkshire magazine, the *Northern Star*, but he was also the author of *History of Lincoln, Lincolnshire Cabinet, Panorama of the Peaks* and several handbooks. All Llewellynn Jewitt's schooling was gained directly from his father, who was his sole tutor.

Llewellynn closely followed the pattern of his father's life. He was extremely studious and showed an early interest in archaeology. In 1853, he established the *Derby Telegraph* – the first penny paper in the country. Seven years later, he founded a national magazine, *The Reliquary*, and acted as its editor until his death in 1886. Jewitt also regularly contributed to *The Art-Journal* and was the author of over twenty books, including *The Stately Homes of England* and *The Mountain, River, Lake and Landscape Scenery of Great Britain* – two- and three-volume works respectively.

It is a source of wonder that Jewitt found time to prepare his *Ceramic Art of Great Britain*, which was first published in 1878; but the research was carried out over a long period and the book really arose from the success of a series of articles published in *The Art-Journal* magazine. His first article appeared in the January 1862 issue and was entitled 'Old

Derby China, a history of the Derby Porcelain Works'. Having lived in that city, Jewitt had gained much local knowledge; but when writing of other works, he had all the groundwork to cover. Following on from Derby, Jewitt next wrote of Worcester porcelain (*The Art-Journal*, February 1863) and, as a natural progression, he then turned to Coalport and the Salopian wares. His diary gives numerous references to his quest for information.

It is interesting to follow the diary entries to see the work involved in preparing the Coalport article for *The Art-Journal* – an account which later was to be enlarged and brought up to date for the *Ceramic Art of Great Britain*. The relevant diary entries start on New Year's Eve, 1861:

Sent to *Art Journal* by book-post my MS. of the 'History of the Worcester Porcelain Works' ... Wrote to Messrs. Rose & Co., Coalbrookdale, and to Mr. R. Thursfield, of Broseley, asking information about Salopian china.

4th January 1862.
... Wrote to Mr. Maw, on Salopian China. Heard from Mr. Rose, of the Coalbrookdale China Works, wishing me to go over ...

7th January 1862.
... Mr. Maw, R.S.A., of Benthall Hall, Broseley, wrote to invite me to stay with him on my visit to Shropshire. Mr. Thursfield of Broseley also wrote to invite me.

13th January 1862.
Started for Shropshire at 7.20 in the morning. Went by rail to Wolverhampton, thence by another line to Shiffnal Station, where I arrived at 11.30. Mr. and Mrs. Rose, who had been staying at Birmingham, came by same train, so as to be ready to receive me. The carriage was waiting for us at Shiffnal, and Mrs. Rose drove us to Rock House, Coalport. After dinner we went to his China Works, and remained till dusk. Spent the evening chatting. No people could be more kind if they had known me all their life.

14th January 1862.

After breakfast went to the Works, where I remained till dinner. After dinner went again and remained till dusk, examining the goods and catechising the workpeople. Mr. R. Thursfield of Broseley called to see me. Mr. Rose invited Mr. Abraham, his principal painter, to tea with us, and we spent a most delightful evening. I made great progress with my notes on the works during the day and examined a large number of the old copper-plates.

15th January 1862.

...at ten drove to Broseley in Mr. Rose's carriage, to Mr. Thursfield. Saw his pottery. Arranged with him to write me a history of tobacco pipes for *Reliquary*. He gave me a Caughley cup and saucer. Thence to Mr. Maw's Works. Saw his tessellated pave-ments...After dinner went through a pipe factory, and returned to the Works...

16th January 1862.

...Returned to Maw's Works, thence to the Hall to dinner. After dinner Mr. G. Maw drove me to Wroxeter (Uniconium)...

17th January 1862.

...After breakfast at the (Coalport) works till two p.m. Mr. Rose made me a present of a splendid tea service, panorama painted. Finished my notes. Mr. Rose invited Mr. Abraham to dine with me...

21st January 1862.

Writing history of the Salopian China Works for *Art Journal*, wrote twelve folios...

25th January 1862.

...Received a box of old Coalport china from Mr. Rose, for examination. Among the rest the 'Benbow' Mug.

27th January 1862.

Sent remainder of Coalport MS. to Mr. Rose, at 4 Newcastle Street, Strand. Sent the draw-ing of the Coalport works to S. C. Hall, to have engraved.

28th January 1862.

Drawing (The Benbow) mug and marks, Coalport China, for *Art Journal*.

Jewitt's 1878 edition of his *Ceramic Art of Great Britain* was published in two volumes and was prepared over several years. Pen was first put to paper on 17th February 1869. By January 1876, work was drawing to a close and he wrote in his diary:

...I am anxious to get all my notes to-gether now, rapidly, for the first volume is done, and the second far advanced – and the Staffordshire Chapters are what I am hard at now...

It would appear that much of the information contained in these Staffordshire chapters was arrived at by the simple expedient of writing to the various manufacturers. In a letter dated 30th March 1876, he had cause to complain of their lack of co-operation:

... Unfortunately I find some – nay many – of the manufacturers who are too blind, or too lazy, or too ignorant to reply to any enquiries. So, from many, although I write twenty letters to one firm perhaps, I really can get no res-ponse. It arises, surely, from a want of atten-tion, but it is very awkward, and makes it difficult to get all houses in ...

Fortunately, Jewitt's good friend (and bio-grapher) William Henry Goss – himself a noted Stoke manufacturer – was able to carry out local research and fill in some of the gaps. And in June 1877 Jewitt wrote to thank Goss for the supply of missing material, some five months before the completion of his work in November 1877:

...It is very kind of you to take so much trouble as to go to Longton, but I am, in truth, ashamed to put you to so much trouble. You have no idea of the trouble I have had with some of the manufacturers ...

Jewitt seems to have been unduly pessimistic, for by one means or another, and with the local help of Goss, he was able to publish a unique record of the Staffordshire potters of his period.

To this superb coverage, I have presumed, humbly, to bring the details up to the end of the century and to add some new information and fresh illustrations.

When Llewellynn Jewitt died, at twenty past nine on the morning of 4th March 1886, students of British ceramic art lost their guiding star – one whose work has survived to lead countless later devotees through the intricate maze of nineteenth-century manufacturers. And it was not only to students and collectors that Jewitt performed a great service. The names and works of many potters are remembered today only because of Llewellynn Jewitt and his famous book.

To readers requiring fuller details of the original author, I recommend *The Life and Death of Llewellynn Jewitt* by William Henry Goss (published by Henry Gray, London, 1889) – a lengthy but interesting book from which these notes have been gleaned.

Geoffrey A. Godden

17 Crescent Road,
Worthing, Sx., England.
October, 1971

ACKNOWLEDGMENTS

First and foremost, acknowledgment must be made to Llewellynn Jewitt, who died in 1886, on whose painstaking research and original work the present volume is based.

Sincere acknowledgment must also be made to the original research carried out by the late Alfred Meigh (1869–1951) on the numerous Staffordshire manufacturers. The very many dates added to names and firms mentioned in the Staffordshire section of this work are in nearly all cases from Alfred Meigh's manuscripts and copies of rate records now in my possession.

I should also like to thank the many librarians and museum curators who have come to my aid so readily in supplying information on their local potteries.

The nineteenth-century issues of *The Pottery Gazette* have proved an invaluable source of information, and several old advertisements from this journal have been reproduced. I would like to express my gratitude to the former publishers of the magazine, Messrs. Scott, Greenwood & Son Ltd., for permission to use this material. Illustrations have been supplied by Mr. & Mrs. Boas of Kenway Antiques, London (No. 37); Mr. & Mrs. Breeze (No. 109); the Brighton Museum (No. 19); the Conservatoire National des Arts et Metiers, Paris, (Nos. 62 and 63); Messrs Doulton's (Nos. 98 and 101); Sir Arthur Elton (No. 86); Dr. Pitman (No. 83); Messrs Sotheby & Co. (Nos. 72 and 93); the City Museum and Art Gallery, Stoke-on-Trent (No. 71); the Sunderland Museum (No. 107); the Victoria and Albert Museum (Nos. 35, 52, 70, 85, 97 and 106); and the Worcester Works Museum (the Dyson Perrins Museum) (No. 115). To the officers of these museums or firms I am greatly indebted. Other illustrations are from my own collection or from the stock of Messrs. Godden of Worthing Ltd.

GLOSSARY

Plate 1.

I have prepared this brief glossary of the technical terms used in this book in the hope that it will be helpful to those readers who may be unfamiliar with them.

G. G.

BASALT

A hard, black, unglazed body introduced by Josiah Wedgwood in the 1760s. At first, this standard body was termed 'Egyptian Black'. The name 'Basaltes' appears to have been first used in Wedgwood's 1773 catalogue for his re-

xvi

fined and improved Egyptian black body. Fine ornamental vases as well as useful teaware were produced in the basalt body by Wedgwood and by a host of other eighteenth-century potters. The easily moulded body remained very popular into the early years of the nineteenth century.

The standard work on this ware is *The Makers of Black Basaltes* by M. H. Grant (William Blackwood & Sons, 1910). Several marked examples from different firms will also be found featured in *The Illustrated Encyclopaedia of British Pottery and Porcelain*, G. A. Godden (Herbert Jenkins London, 1966). See Plate 1.

Plate 2.

BAT-PRINTING (Plate 2, above)

This form of printing was introduced in about 1800. The basic design was engraved, or punched, into the flat copper-plate by means of dots (rather than lines) of varying depths and degrees of closeness to form the required light and shade. On to this completed "copper" was pressed a pliable glue, or gelatine, slab which transferred an oily impression on to the ware. Ceramic pigment was subsequently dusted on to the oil, the colour being fixed by the firing process. The general effect of bat-printed designs was far more effective and delicate than the line-engraved type (see Plate 12).

BISCUIT, BISCUIT-KILN

Biscuit ware is that which has undergone the first firing but has not yet been glazed. In most cases, biscuit ware is but half finished; under-glaze blue decoration would be applied at this stage. Some objects were, however, intended to be marketed in this unglazed state – the white Derby biscuit figures and groups are a case in point.

The biscuit kiln was that used for the important first firing. In most cases, the ware was fired to its highest temperature in this kiln, the subsequent firings being at progressively lower temperatures.

BLUE AND WHITE, see 'Underglaze blue'.

CERAMIC

'Ceramic' is the group name for fired clays, embracing all types of pottery and porcelain. This name is generally pronounced with a soft 'c' (seramic), but several authorities favour the old spelling 'keramic', with a consequent hard 'c' pronunciation.

Plate 3.

CREAMWARE

As the name suggests, this is a cream-coloured earthenware. It is normally associated with Josiah Wedgwood's name, and he certainly perfected this body and popularised it so that it became *the* standard eighteenth-century body. However, creamware was made by most English potters from the 1770s onwards. It was seldom over-decorated, often being quite plain or having only an enamelled border design. It was especially popular on account of its clean-looking appearance, closely rivalling the more expensive porcelain. It was also inexpensive and its light weight made it cheap to ship to the export markets. It 'flooded' Europe to such an extent that numerous manufacturers of Continental tin-glazed faience were forced to imitate the new English ware or close. After patronage by Queen Charlotte, Wedgwood introduced the term 'Queensware', by which name it is often known. Most nineteenth-century earthenware of this type is 'Pearlware' rather than creamware (see page xxiv).

The reader is referred to *English Cream-coloured Earthenware* by D. C. Towner (Faber & Faber, London, 1957) – a work which, in the main, is concerned with eighteenth-century creamware. The dish shown in Plate 3 is also an eighteenth-century example, transfer-printed in Liverpool.

Plate 4.

GLOST KILN

The kiln in which the glazed ware receives its second firing, to mature the glaze. This firing is less severe than the first biscuit firing (see page xvii).

GRANITE WARE

A name used from the 1840s onwards for a hard, durable, ironstone-type body. This was much used for dinner services and other useful ware. It was very popular in the export markets for its strength and low cost, being closely akin to Ironstone-china. The name 'Granite' linked with other terms such as 'china' or 'ware' is found incorporated in many factory trade marks from the 1840s onwards (see Plate 80).

IRONSTONE CHINA

A heavy, strong and extremely durable earthenware body patented by Charles J. Mason in 1813 (see page 103). A huge range of utilitarian as well as decorative ware was made by the Mason family as well as by other potters who subsequently manufactured 'Ironstone China'. The name is incorporated in several different trade marks from 1813 onwards – although some potters used other names, such as 'Granite China', for ware basically similar to Ironstone. The reader is referred to *The Illustrated Guide to Mason's Patent Ironstone China* by G. A. Godden (Barrie & Jenkins, London, 1971). See Plate 4.

Plate 5.

JAPAN PATTERNS

The general description 'Japan pattern' is applied to gay designs having areas of underglaze blue in conjunction with overglaze enamels and, often, gilding. Most traditional Derby designs are of the Japan-type, as are those shown in Plate 5. However, it must be clearly understood that by no means all Japan patterns are of Derby origin, for most post-1800 porcelain and pottery manufacturers produced these designs. They were inexpensive to produce, being repetitive bold designs suitable for apprentice painters to carry out (often on slightly faulty ware); and yet the public found them gay and colourful, and they were universally popular

xx

Plate 6.

Plate 7.

JASPER

A fine stoneware body, usually unglazed, and coloured with various materials to form a hard, coloured body. Blue jasper is that most often met with, but various different colours were made. Wedgwood's perfected Jasper in about 1775, and subsequently this firm and others produced a wide range of objects in it – from jewellery and small portrait medallions to fireplace plaques and large vases. Wedgwood's still produce their celebrated Jasper ware.

A range of various Jasper ware is featured in *The Illustrated Encyclopaedia of British Pottery and Porcelain*, by G. A. Godden (Herbert Jenkins, London, 1966).

JET

A glossy black body much favoured by smaller manufacturers in the later part of the nineteenth century for teapots, etc. (see advertisement reproduced on page 28). Similar but earlier ware is often termed 'Jackfield', although it was often made in the Staffordshire Potteries and not in Shropshire.

LUSTRE

A shiny surface in imitation of silver, copper, etc., produced by thin metallic films. Various other interesting effects were produced – resist or stencilled patterns, Sunderland type 'Splash' lustre (Plate 7), etc. See W. D. John and W. Baker's *Old English Lustre Pottery* (Ceramic Book Co., Newport, Mon., 1951) and an article by G. B. Hughes in *Country Life Annual*, 1955. A special type of Wedgwood mottled pink (or Moonlight) lustre is featured in W. D. John and J. Simcox's *Early Wedgwood Lustre Wares* (Ceramic Book Co., Newport, Mon., 1963).

Plate 8.

Plate 9.

MAJOLICA

A tin-glazed earthenware (in imitation of Italian Maiolica ware) introduced by Minton's in 1850 and taken up by most manufacturers of the period. It has since come to mean any form of earthenware decorated with semi-translucent coloured glazes, such as the tea set shown in Plate 8, a design registered by George Jones (see page 126) of Stoke in April 1873.

MOCHA DECORATION

A type of tree-like decoration on earthenware – banded mugs, jugs, etc. – produced by a simple chemical reaction of an added acid liquid applied to a special alkaline ground. C. T. Maling's advertisement (page 212) includes a jug of this type. Made by many potters over a long period.

Plate 10.

PARIAN

A white (normally unglazed) body introduced in the 1840s for the reproduction of marble statues, etc. Capable of being moulded into intricate shapes. Also much used for jugs, etc. See *The Illustrated Guide to Victorian Parian China* by C. & D. Shinn (Barrie & Jenkins, London, 1971).

Plate 11.

PEARL-WARE

A variation of the well known creamware body but whiter in hue, often due to the use of a covering glaze slightly tinted with blue. Much English pottery from c.1780 onwards should correctly be termed 'Pearl-ware', but it is often called creamware in error. Production continued into the nineteenth century, its use being mainly confined to tableware. Interesting facts on this type of ware are incorporated in two articles by Ivor Noel-Hume in the American magazine *Antiques* of March and December 1969. Pearl-ware is nearer in general appearance and whiteness to porcelain than is creamware.

POTTERY

Pottery or earthenware is fired clay, or clay with other materials – the finished article being opaque. Being fired at a lower temperature than stoneware or porcelain, it often emits a rather dull ring when tapped.

PORCELAIN

Clay with other materials (soaprock, bone-ash, feldspar, etc.) fired to a degree at which it partly melts to form a translucent body. Translucency is the standard test for porcelain. But

Plate 12.

PÂTE-SUR-PÂTE

A form of ceramic cameo in which the white relief design is built up by hand over a darker body. This was an expensive and painstaking process introduced at the Sèvres factory in France and brought to Minton's in England by M. L. Solon (see page 122). Various other firms also employed this technique from the 1870s (see Plates 11, 74).

The reader is referred to Chapter 8 of *Victorian Porcelain* by G. A. Godden (Herbert Jenkins, London, 1961).

very thick or under-fired porcelain can, in extreme cases, be opaque; and some bodies that we do not normally term porcelain, such as jasper, can in some cases be translucent to a slight degree. Porcelain is normally white and gives a clear mellow ring when tapped, unless the object is cracked.

PRINTING

The printing of ceramics dates back to the middle of the eighteenth century, and it has been continued ever since. The basic technique involves the skilled engraving (or etching) of the design on to a flat sheet of copper in such a way that the recessed lines will hold pigment. For the different components of a tea service, for example, many different-sized copper-plates would be required, although the design on each piece might be the same. Once a copper-plate is engraved and ready for use, however, it has to be warmed, and a ceramic pigment (normally blue) is rubbed into the recessed

design. Surplus pigment is wiped from the surface, and a sheet of tissue-like paper is applied and pressed on to the engraved copper to pick up the pigment from the engraved lines. The charged paper, after trimming, is then applied to the ware (normally before it is glazed), so transferring the design. The paper is subsequently soaked off, the oil burnt from the pigment and the covering glaze applied. The object is then fired once more to mature the glaze.

The process sounds complicated but, in fact, it is simple and inexpensive – for cheap labour was employed to carry out the repetitive processes. The willow pattern is the most famous of the underglaze blue printed designs. Plate 12 shows an engraved copper-plate – one of hundreds employed by numerous firms to produce willow-pattern dessert services and other objects. In this case, the engraved copper is for a dinner plate. During the nineteenth century,

Plate 13.

Plate 14.

many designs consisted of an overglaze printed outline which was subsequently coloured-in – again by inexpensive, often child, labour. See also 'Bat-printing'.

QUEENSWARE, see Creamware.

REGISTERED DESIGNS AND NUMBERS

Thousands of shapes and patterns were registered at the Patent Office so that they could not be copied by other manufacturers. An Act of 1842 enabled any shape or added design to be so registered, and registered ware bore a diamond-shaped device to show that the object was so protected. A typical diamond-shaped registration mark is shown under the upturned cup in Plate 13. This design was registered by Messrs. Brown-Westhead, Moore & Co. (page 64) on 1st February 1869. The letters and numerals in the corners vary with each design and enable the date of registration to be decoded. The key to this coding is given on page 258,

xxvi

with further information on the subject.

In January 1884, a new system was introduced, replacing the diamond-shaped device with progressive numbers which were usually prefixed with the abbreviation 'R^d No.' for Registered Number. This system has continued to the present time. The key to dating these numbers is given on page 259.

ROCKINGHAM GLAZE

A rich purple brown glaze, favoured at the Rockingham works early in the nineteenth century and subsequently taken up by other manufacturers, including Wedgwood. Many firms advertised 'Rockingham' ware during the second half of the century, but these descriptions relate to the type of coloured glaze and not to the place of manufacture. The lidless Cadogan-type teapot shown in Plate 14 is, however, a true example of Rockingham or Brameld earthenware (see page 231). This coloured glazed earthenware is quite different from the famous Rockingham porcelain.

SAGGER

Protective fireproof earthenware container in which ware is fired in the kiln.

SGRAFFITO

A traditional form of decoration in which the design is incised through a contrasting slip or glaze exposing another colour or the clay body. Hannah Barlow's work for Doulton's (Plate 99) is a form of sgraffito, but here the incised pattern is accentuated with added colour. Various spellings – 'Sgraffiato', etc. – have been used.

SLIP-WARE

A traditional form of pottery decoration in which a whitish or coloured cream-like 'slip' is trailed over a clay-coloured object. The famous Toft ware dates back to the seventeenth century, but the method of decoration was also widely employed in the nineteenth century – mainly by the country potters. This ware can look considerably earlier than its true date of manufacture.

SPONGED WARE

A cheap type of earthenware decorated with simple patterns by means of a sponge cut to a given shape – a star, for example. Several Scottish potters produced such ware, which has a primitive charm.

STONE CHINA

A hard, durable type of earthenware, related to Ironstone china. In fact, the difference between the two relates only to the name given to the ware by different manufacturers. The name 'Stone China' appears in several trade-marks of the 1820–50 period.

STONEWARE

One of the earliest forms of ceramic material – in the main, any suitable natural clay which has been fired to a high temperature (about 1,300°C) so as to become partly vitrified. Decoration is mainly confined to the pure shape, or simple incised patterns, or 'sprigged' motifs – the last being separately moulded relief designs which are applied or 'sprigged' on to the object. The

Plate 15.

jug shown in Plate 15 is of this type and is fitted with a silver cover bearing a year mark of 1835. Much stoneware is of eighteenth-century date, but traditional types were produced well into the nineteenth century and these might often appear to be of an earlier date than they really are.

The surface glaze is often slightly pitted, due to the introduction of salt into the kiln. The salt formed sodium oxide and hydrochloric acid, which settled on the ware in vapour form. This combined with the alumina and silica in the clay to form a remarkably hard, durable glaze – one that has not yet been bettered for utilitarian ceramics such as sewer or water pipes.

TERRA-COTTA

Red unglazed refined earthenware. Figures, vases and the like were produced in this type of body as well as useful ware; but because it is slightly porous, the insides of jugs and the like have to be glazed.

UNDERGLAZE BLUE

This term applies where the blue portion of the decoration has been applied to the biscuit body before glazing. Most eighteenth-century porcelain factories produced blue and white designs, hand-painted or transfer printed, under the glaze; and in the nineteenth century, a vast quantity of inexpensive useful earthenware was printed in underglaze blue. The large firms, such as Spode, produced very fine quality blue-printed designs (see Colour Plate V). Several firms engraved special designs for their export markets, many depicting North American views; but the majority of blue-printed ware was of ordinary stock patterns, such as the well known willow pattern (see Plate 12).

YELLOW WARE

A yellow or cane coloured earthenware produced in the Burton-on-Trent district for utilitarian objects. Also known as 'Derbyshire Ironstone'. Kitchen ware, such as mixing bowls, was often in this material.

Jewitt's Ceramic Art of Great Britain 1800–1900

PART I
THE STAFFORDSHIRE
POTTERIES

INTRODUCTION

The large and commercially important, as well as thickly populated, district known as the 'Staffordshire Potteries', or simply 'the Potteries', comprises a number of towns, and places adjoining them. The main towns or districts are: BURSLEM, COBRIDGE, ETRURIA, FENTON, HANLEY, LANE END, LONGTON, STOKE AND TUNSTALL.

The general picture of the Potteries may be clouded by the image of the larger firms, such as Copeland, Minton and Wedgwood, with their continuous history; but in fact, as the following pages well illustrate, the Staffordshire Potteries were, in the main, made up of hundreds of relatively small potteries (hardly factories in the accepted sense of the word) situated in narrow streets.

These countless small potteries changed ownership at frequent intervals as the trade was highly competitive and profit margins were cut to unrealistic levels. This fact is underlined in page after page of this work, where the several changes of ownership or partnership are recorded.

These smaller potteries were mainly concerned with producing ordinary domestic earthenware, decorated with printed designs – inexpensive ware which was shipped in large quantities to the many export markets which were rapidly developing and which offered a large market for almost any type of useful pottery.

Apart from utilitarian table ware, with its willow-pattern-type blue prints, the Staffordshire Potteries are famous for their naive but charming figures or animals – models which graced the mantel or window-sill of thousands upon thousands of often humble homes, not only in the country of their origin but also throughout the world. These Staffordshire figures were made by many different potters (who did not normally mark their figures with a name), some of whom are listed on pages 72, 91, 102, with typical specimens being shown in Plates 24, 44, 46 and 58.

An interesting account of the Staffordshire Potteries in the early 1850s is contained in the weekly magazine *The Leisure Hour – A Journal of instruction and recreation* of 2nd June 1853. The following quotations from this journal help to set the scene before we move on to list the different manufacturers who made the district internationally famous:

. . . The Potteries consist of a number of small towns lying pretty closely together, and mostly, if not entirely, comprised within the borough of Stoke-upon-Trent. Stoke itself stands about twenty-five miles north of Stafford, and something like double that distance south of Manchester. It is rather centrally situated with respect to the neighbouring towns and hamlets which make up the borough, the principal of which are, Burslem, Etruria, Fenton, Hanley and Shelton, Longton, or Lane End, Newcastle-under-Lyme, Tunstall, and a few minor hamlets and villages . . .

Stoke (see pages 108–137) is a place of considerable antiquity, and is indirectly noticed in Domesday-book . . . The aspect of the streets and thoroughfares of Stoke is anyting but attractive to a stranger, presenting more the appearance of a fourth-rate London suburb than a town of business. Rows of small brick-built houses, rarely more than two stories in height, are broken into by huge brick-built factories covering whole acres in extent; monstrous cones of solid brick lift their peaked heads above the roofs of the houses, and here and there their burly basements bulge forth into the street and shoulder the passenger out of the direct path. Tall chimneys of brick soar up into the sky and spread their clouds of smoke through the sooty air; and beneath your feet a pavement of brick borders either side of the muddy road . . .

The preceding description of Stoke is in some degree applicable to most of the towns in the Potteries, though each would afford some very marked differences, a few of which we proceed to specify. Thus Burslem, which stands upon a somewhat lofty eminence, has the advantage of a picturesque site, which Stoke, lying in a comparative hollow, cannot boast. Burslem, which lies about three miles to the north, when approached from the railway, which runs within a mile of it, presents a fine subject for the pencil of the artist; there are deep dells and abrupt declivities, surmounted by irregular buildings and pyramidal kilns of the Hill Pottery (see page 20), which crowns the ridge of the rising ground . . . On entering Burslem the stranger will find it a large and really handsome market-town adorned with capital buildings, and supplied with handsome and well-furnished shops and good hotels . . .

Hanley (page 55) is also a handsome market-town pleasantly situated, hardly more than a mile distant from Burslem, and two from Stoke. It has the advantage of being placed upon high ground, is large, and apparently very populous, and, standing about the centre of the district, is considered by some as the capital of the Potteries. It is joined to Shelton, which stretches down the hill to within a mile of Stoke, Hanley and Shelton being spoken of as one town; and within them, or in their immediate neighbourhood, some of the most extensive manufactories are to be found . . .

Longton, or Lane End (pages 82, 85) . . . is perhaps the most characteristic town in the whole of the Pottery district. It is, as the name implies, a very long town, and is undoubtedly the most crowded, and if we are to judge from outward demonstrations, the least polished locality in the whole borough. It is a place, however, where a vast deal of business is done, and abounds in manufactories, some of considerable extent, which do a large trade. A great many of these are in the hands of men of limited capital, not a few of whom produce an inferior kind of ware suited for a cheap market. It is by the exertions of the Longton potters that the working-man and the cottages are enabled to set a china tea-service on their tables, brilliant in colours and gold, at a cost we must not name, but which the humblest house-keeper can contrive to pay. An immense quantity of the low-priced English china, as well for exportation as for home consumption, is here manufactured weekly, as well as earthenwares of all kinds, and toys consisting of images in gold and colours of men and women and rustic groups, and dogs and cats, and Swiss cottages, and Bonapartes, Victorias, Great Moguls, Dukes of Wellington, Tom Thumbs, shepherds, dairymaids, cows, John Bulls and John Wesleys, etc., etc., as the advertisements say, 'too numerous to mention'. (For these Staffordshire figures, see pages 72, 91, 102.) Here, too, is the chief stronghold and refuge of the old willow-pattern plates and dishes . . .

Longton has two churches . . . the town is crossed near the market-place by the railway on a viaduct twenty or more feet above the road, the cheap fares and short stages on which are a source of great convenience to the dwellers in the Potteries. Longton, which is three miles from Stoke, extends into the town of Fenton (page 48) and Fenton is a long straggling village made up principally of numerous pot-

ters' establishments, that line the road on either side of the way, and the humble dwellings of the work-people . . .

The town of Tunstall (page 138) is situated about four miles from Stoke, upon the turnpike road leading from Liverpool to London; it is altogether a town of modern erection, and has doubled its population several times within the last half century. It contains a large number of thriving manufactories, producing the coarser sort of ware, to the establishment and prosperity of which there is no doubt that its abnormal increase is due. Of all the pottery towns, Tunstall is the most regularly built . . . The population of Tunstall at the present time [that is, June 1853] cannot, it is supposed, be very far short of nine thousand; three score years ago it was little more than an insignificant hamlet, forming one of the eight small townships comprised in the north side of Wolstanton parish . . .

A pleasant walk of about a mile along the towing path of the canal westward from Stoke, brings the visitor to the neat little village of Etruria (page 39), which is entirely the creation of the late celebrated Josiah Wedgwood, being built by him for the purpose of carrying out his improvements in the pottery manufacture. It consists of the mansion called Etruria Hall, still occupied by his descendants, the extensive manufactory covering many acres of ground on the western bank of the canal, branches of which are carried into the manufactory itself, and a wide brick-built street of workmen's dwellings sloping down the hill towards the railway, which has a station on the spot; to these have lately been added a number of houses of a better class, probably the abodes of clerks, foremen, and directors in the works.

. . . The manufactory contains every imaginable convenience for carrying on the numerous operations of the potter, and is abundantly supplied with the various mechanical contrivances which experience has suggested for abbreviating and facilitating his labours . . .

. . . The following is a statement of the probable annual consumption of articles in the Staffordshire Potteries:

Ball Clay, from Devon and Dorset	45,000 tons per year
China Clay (Cornish)	15,000 tons per year
Cornish Stone and flint	24,000 tons per year
Straw, for packing	16,000 tons per year

The population in 1851 was reckoned at 90,000; but from the rapid increase by immigration it is supposed now to exceed 100,000.

The coals consumed annually in manufactures amount to no less than 468,000 tons, some of the pot-works consuming as much as sixty tons a day each; the consumption in collieries and mills is not less than 282,000 tons; making altogether 750,000 tons of coals per annum used for pottery purposes. The mills supply the smaller establishments with materials ready ground and fit for use, as only the larger manufacturers grind their own. Every potter, however, prepares his own glazes, which, if he choose, he can have ground at the public mills.

The entire value of the goods made annually in the potteries is estimated at £1,700,000; of this the large amount of £1,300,000 represents the value of the exports, leaving goods to the amount of £400,000 for home consumption. The value of the gold annually consumed in the ornamentation of china and earthenware is about £36,000.

Of the pottery of Staffordshire which is exported, more than one-third goes to the United States; and the rest finds its way in various bottoms to the following places – Canada, British North American Colonies, Brazil, East Indies, West Indies, Germany, Holland, Denmark, Russia, Italy and the Italian islands, Spain and the Balearic islands, Turkey, Foreign West Indies, West Africa, Cape of Good Hope, Sumatra and the Eastern Archipelago, Australia, etc. etc.

In the 1880s, some fifty thousand persons were employed in (or were dependent upon) the manufacture of china and earthenware in the Staffordshire Potteries. In 1910, the various towns were merged to form the present city of Stoke-on-Trent, although the old districts still retain much of their individuality.

We can now proceed to discuss the towns, in their alphabetical sequence, and the many manufactories and their products.

BURSLEM

Dr. Plot, writing in 1686, says 'The greatest pottery they have in this country is carried on at Burslem, near Newcastle-under-Lyme, where for making their different sorts of pots they have as many different sorts of clay, which they dig round about the towne, all within halfe a mile's distance, the best being found nearest the coale.' The town has earned for itself the name of 'mother of the potteries'.

Moving forward into the nineteenth century, we find that in the early 1840s[1] there were the following potters working in Burslem:

Enoch Wood & Sons; S. Alcock & Co; Machin & Potts; Mellor, Venables & Co; T. Godwin; John Wedge Wood; Barker, Sutton & Till; Peter Hopkin; Wm. Pointon; S. Mayer & Co; J. Hawley; Maddock & Seddon; J. Vernon & Co; J. & T. Edwards; Cork & Cundliffe; Nehemiah Massey; Ann Holland; Daniel Edge and Jones & Bell.

We can now profitably follow the changing fortunes of these and other potters who have practised their craft in the town of Burslem.

Enoch Wood

Enoch Wood, the son of the celebrated Ralph Wood, was born in January 1759. He started modelling at an early age and was a very good practical potter (he was also historian and collector of Staffordshire earthenware) and had been apprenticed under Wedgwood.

[1] According to *The Borough of Stoke-upon-Trent* by John Ward, W. Lewis & Son, 1843.

In 1781, Enoch Wood modelled the celebrated bust of John Wesley. From 1795 to July 1818, Enoch was in partnership with James Caldwell using the style Wood & Caldwell.

Wood & Caldwell

This firm (Enoch Wood and James Caldwell) produced eathenware of superior character, both in services and ordinary articles. Some of their teapots were of admirable design and excellent workmanship. Busts and small statuettes were also extensively made, as were highly ornamental candlesticks. The usual impressed marks are:

WOOD & CALDWELL
    BURSLEM   or
STAFFORDSHIRE
                WOOD & CALDWELL

Messrs. Wood & Caldwell worked in the period 1795 to July 1818. From July 1818 to 1846, the firm traded under the style Enoch Wood & Sons. Much fine earthenware was produced in this period (Plate 16) – a good deal for the American market – and some rare porcelain was produced. This, with some of the earthenware, is sometimes marked Wxxx, impressed into the article.

The Churchyard Works

The Churchyard Works, at the house adjoining which Josiah Wedgwood was born and where he was apprenticed to his brother Thomas, formed the north-east boundary of the churchyard of the old church at Burslem. The works were occupied by various members of the Wedgwood family until they were sold to Thomas Green in 1795. Mr. Green manufactured earthenware at these works and for some time resided at the house near the works, which had been built by one of the Wedgwood family. The property remained in Thomas Green's hands until his bankruptcy in 1811, when it appears to have been purchased by a manufacturer named Joynson, from whom it passed to John Moseley or Mosley (1812–22), subsequently J. & J. Jackson. The pot-works were then held by various tenants and, until about 1858, were let off in small holdings to different potters. About that period, Jesse Bridgwood of Tunstall became the tenant of the premises as a general earthenware manufacturer, and was soon afterwards joined in partnership by Edward Clarke, whose practical experience greatly increased the reputation of the works. The firm, having taken a lease of

the premises, remodelled many of the buildings, erected others, and greatly improved the whole place by bringing to bear many improvements in body unknown to, and unthought of by, their predecessors.

After Mr. Bridgwood's decease in 1864, these works (and the large establishment at Tunstall) were carried on by the surviving partner, Edward Clarke, until, after a short time, he ceased working them, when they passed into other hands as his tenants. The manufactory was afterwards again carried on by Mr. Clarke in partnership with Josiah Wood under the style of Wood & Clarke during the period 1871–2. The productions of the Churchyard Works, while carried on by Mr. Clarke, were opaque porcelain or 'white granite' for the American market; ordinary earthenware in the usual services; artists' goods (palettes, tiles, slabs, saucers, etc.); and door furniture. The impressed mark was 'Bridgwood & Clarke', and the printed mark a royal arms, with the words 'Porcelain Opaque, B & C, Burslem.'

Plate 16. Representative parts of a lengthy printed earthenware dinner service by E. Wood & Sons. Printed name mark, c.1825.
Godden of Worthing Ltd.

In 1873, Mr. W. E. Withinshaw entered upon the Churchyard Works, and produced dinner, tea, toilet, and other services; vases, jugs, tea-pots, kettles, and jug stands; trinket and fancy articles; candlesticks, and all the usual varieties of useful and ornamental goods, both plain, printed, painted, enamelled, and gilt. In toilet services, he introduced many designs of novel character. In vases, also, Mr. Withinshaw pro-duced some good designs, and the decoration was judiciously arranged. In jet ware, all the usual articles – teapots, kettles, jugs, spill-cases, etc. – were made. The impressed mark was W.E. WITHINSHAW; and on the dinner ware was printed the name of the pattern, with the initials W.E.W.

Mr. Withinshaw's connection with the Church-yard Works ceased in 1878, when he was suc-ceeded by Francis Joseph Emery, who continued the manufactory until 1880, when it again re-verted to Edward Clarke who, having relin-quished his large works at Tunstall, removed hither and continued the production of the white granite ware for the American markets. In addition to this white granite, which was pro-duced in large quantities and of the very highest quality of body, Mr. Clarke made a distinct class of fine white earthenware called 'Royal Semi-Porcelain', which was specially adapted for retail trade in the United States. These goods are of a vitreous body, and in colour and richness of glazing strongly resemble French china; they have a fine and effective appearance with enamel decorations. In addition to these, Mr. Clarke produced ordinary earthenware ser-vices and the usual classes of articles of various degrees of decoration in printing, underglaze painting, and gilding. In 1887, Messrs. A. J. Wilkinson took the Churchyard Works from Edward Clarke, and continued into the twentieth century. This firm subsequently worked the Royal Staffordshire Pottery, Burslem.

The Bell (or Brickhouse) Works

The Bell Works were, at the time when the great Josiah Wedgwood entered on their occu-pancy, the property of William Adams, who

took possession for himself in 1770; but he relet them in 1774. Later, the works passed to John Adams, of Cobridge, and in 1847 again passed by will to Isaac Hitchen of Alsager. They were occupied by Joseph Wedgwood until his re-moval to Etruria, after which William Bourne, an earthenware manufacturer, held them for some years and was tenant in 1809. In about 1822, he entered into partnership with a potter named Cormie, and carried on the business under the style of Bourne & Cormie. In 1836, the works, having then remained for some time unoccupied, were divided. One portion was taken by Beech & Jones as an earthenware manufactory; another portion was taken away for the building of the Independent chapel, which was erected on its site in the following year; and other parts were let off to various holders for different purposes apart from the pot trade.

In 1839, Beech & Jones dissolved partnership, the former alone continuing the concern for the production of china and earthenware figures. In 1846, William Beech became tenant of the remaining premises and in 1853 took into partnership Mr. Brock, which firm, however, only lasted until 1855, from which date William Beech carried on the manufactory until his death in 1864, when he was succeeded by Jane Beech, during the period 1866–73, and then Beech & Podmore. In 1876, a part of the pre-mises was purchased by the Board of Health for the purpose of building a covered market on the site, and the remainder was taken down. Jane Beech (and formerly William Beech) produced a large number of Staffordshire earthenware figures of the type shown in Plate 44, and also the popular chicken boxes.

Waterloo Potteries

These works were carried on in the latter part of the eighteenth century by Walter Daniel, who was succeeded by Timothy and John Lockett, the manufacture at that time being principally salt-glazed ware. About 1809, the premises were purchased by Joseph Machin and Jacob Baggaley, and carried on by them for the making of china and ordinary earthenware. In 1831, Mr.

Fig. 1. Messrs. Boote's productions, 1851 Exhibition

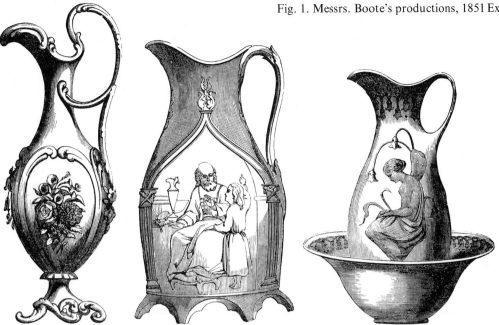

Machin died and was succeeded by his son, William Machin, and partners. The works next passed into the hands of Richard Daniel, next to Thomas Edwards, and in 1850 were purchased by T. & R. Boote. In 1853, Messrs. Boote took out a patent for 'Certain improvements in pottery and mosaic work'. These consisted in producing 'coloured designs on grounds of different colours, as black on white or white on black. First, the designs are made from a mould, as in figuring, and laid on the moulds for making the ware; the ground colour is then put on. Second, the design, cut in paper, parchment, etc. is laid in the moulds and the halves fastened together, the colour to form the ground is poured in, after which the paper, etc. are removed and other colour poured in to fill its place. Third, producing different coloured raised surfaces. The figures in low relief in the inside of the moulds are filled with a composition, the halves of the moulds fastened together, and the slip poured in to form a thin coating, which is then supplemented with an inner lining of a cheaper material to form a substratum, thus producing mosaic and other elaborate designs. In this process the excess of liquid is withdrawn when the necessary thickness is attained.'

Parian was also produced in vases, jugs, groups, and other objects. One of the most effective groups was that of 'Repentance, Faith, and Resignation', modelled by Gillard.

Among the Parian vases some, the body of which was buff and the raised flowers white, had a pleasing and softened effect. All these decorative classes of goods were discontinued by Messrs. Boote in about 1865, and the firm then confined itself to the production of the ordinary white granite ware for the American markets, and encaustic and other glazed and unglazed pavement-tiles. For these latter, the firm was patentee of a process for inlaying encaustic tiles with clay dust – a process which was also adopted for the manufacture of dishes and other articles in earthenware in what this firm called 'Royal Patent Ironstone' and by which, by means of one press alone, as many as a hundred dozen plates or small dishes could be made in a day.

The marks used on the white granite were the impressed initials T & R B printed in black and another bearing the crest and a greyhound couchant, collared and slipped, between two laurel wreaths. Another mark comprises the royal arms over the wording ROYAL PATENT

11

IRONSTONE T & R BOOTE. On the tiles, the name T & R BOOTE appears in raised letters. The firm continued into the twentieth century as tile manufacturers.

Washington Works

The business carried on at this manufactory originated experimentally in King Street, Burslem, where, in about 1838, William Sadler Kennedy commenced the production of palettes and other requisites for artists' use. Shortly afterwards, removing to a pottery in Bourne's Bank, he added the manufacture of door-furniture, letters for signs etc., in which, in conjunction with William Maddock, great improvements were made. In about 1847, the manufacture was removed to the Washington Works.

In 1852, Mr. Kennedy was joined in partnership by his brother-in-law, James Macintyre, who shortly afterwards became sole proprietor of the works. In 1863, James Macintyre patented methods of producing oval, reeded, octagon and other forms by the lathe and succeeded in producing a rich, cream-coloured body which, under the name of 'Ivory China', held a high reputation. So far as can be ascertained, the successful application to door-furniture of the earlier invention of the beautiful black, which was produced by dipping the brownish red bisque in a rich cobalt glaze, also originated at these works. This 'jet', produced in great perfection, was applied in plain and also with richly gilt and enamelled ornamentation, not only to door-furniture but also to inkstands and similar goods. James Macintyre died in 1868, having previously taken into partnership his manager, Thomas Hulme, and his son-in-law, William Woodall. In 1880, Thomas Hulme retired from the concern and was succeeded in the partnership by Mr. Wiltshaw. The business is still carried on under the old style of James Macintyre & Co. (Ltd.); but in the twentieth century, production has been confined to electrical fittings.

Nile Street Works

That these works were built upon the site of an early pottery is evidenced by fragments of pitchers, 'porringers', and other salt-glazed domestic vessels of 'red and yellow clay marbled together', being exhumed at one time or other during the alterations. Messrs. Riley, who removed from here to the Hill Works, were succeeded by James Cormie, uncle of Thomas Pinder, who traded under the style of Pinder, Bourne & Co. China was at one time made here, but then only printed, enamelled, and gilt earthenware, fine red-ware, jet-ware, and sanitary goods. The red-ware or terra-cotta of Pinder, Bourne & Co. was of fine, hard and durable quality; and the vases, spillcases, and other articles richly enamelled and gilt in arabesque and other patterns were remarkably good. Among other specialities were flower-vases and jardinières skilfully painted in birds, flowers, etc. The firm patented improvements in ovens and in steam printing-presses; but the latter, having excited the hostility of the workmen at the time of the riots in 1842, were abandoned. The firm received medals at the London and Paris Exhibitions of 1851, 1855 and 1867.

The marks were a garter with the name of the pattern and initials P.B. & Co. surmounted by a crown and encompassed with a wreath of laurel,

and the triangle-shaped mark reproduced. Messrs. Pinder, Bourne & Co. were of the period 1862–82. Plate 17 shows part of a tasteful Pinder, Bourne & Co. earthenware dessert service, made in February 1877.

After the works passed into the hands of Messrs. Doulton, in 1882, immense strides in improvements in every department were made, and the productions rank with the very best. This is especially noticeable in the body of the finest earthenware, which arrived at a state of perfection. As a rule, earthenware is, by the generality of people, looked upon as inferior in every way to china and as unworthy of the high artistic treatment lavished upon that favoured body. This, however, is a mistake, and Messrs. Doulton wisely directed their energies not only to its improvement but its *Perfection*. In this they

Colour Plate 1. Superb Royal Doulton porcelain
dessert ware painted by David Dewsberry. Date
marks for 1907.   *Editor's collection.*

Plate 17. Pinder, Bourne & Co. earthenware dessert service, name mark impressed, with potting numerals for February 1877.

Godden of Worthing Ltd.

were successful, and the result is that their earthenware has all the fineness and beauty, the artistic treatment, and the exquisite finish of the best classes of porcelain with, in addition, a softness of surface and a delicious creaminess of tone.

Messrs. Doulton employed a large number of first-class artists in the decoration of the ware, and new studios were fitted up to meet the requirements of the increased demand that sprung up for high-class art-productions. In 1884, Doulton's Burslem factory commenced the manufacture of fine porcelain, a product for which they are now internationally famous.

The artists include P. Curnock, D. Dewsbury (see Colour Plate I), F. Hancock, H. Mitchell, E. Raby and G. White.

Messrs. Doulton's continue to the present day, and their Burslem products (including many figures and groups) have won world-wide fame. Nineteenth-century marks include:

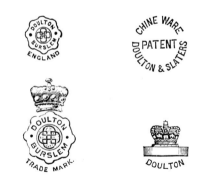

or 'Doulton' impressed.

The Newport Pottery

Established at the close of the eighteenth century by Walter Daniel, it passed, in about 1810, into the hands of John Davenport; afterwards to Cork & Edge (1846–60); Cork, Edge & Malkin (1860–70); and was then continued by Edge, Malkin & Co. (1870–1902).

13

Fig. 2. Cork & Edge's Exhibits in 1851. Some designs were lustred.

Cork & Edge, in their ordinary earthenware, introduced a process of inlaying patterns in the ground-body, but of different colours. These were intended for the cheapest markets but were produced in good taste. Two tea-pots and a ewer, shown at the Great Exhibition in 1851, are reproduced in Figure 2 from an engraving. The productions of the firm were dinner ware and jet, enamelled lustre, and other fancy goods; and all the ordinary ware for the home and foreign markets. Messrs. Edge, Malkin & Co. (Ltd.) continued to 1902.

Dale Hall

The extensive works at Dale Hall (or Dale Hole, as it used to be written), founded in 1790, originally belonged to Joseph Stubbs – a successful manufacturer of earthenware during the

1822–5 period, who, having retired from business, died in 1836. He was succeeded in about 1843 by Messrs. Thomas, John and Joshua Mayer, who from 1855 traded as Mayer Brothers & Elliot, and from them the works passed successively through the firms of Mayer & Elliot, Liddle, Elliot, & Co., Bates, Elliot & Co., Bates, Walker & Co., and Bates, Gildea, & Walker to the firm of Gildea & Walker during the 1881–6 period. By the earlier firms ordinary earthenware was produced, but under Messrs. Mayer – who came from Stoke to Dale Hall – many important improvements were effected.

Messrs. Mayer were probably from the manufactory at Cliff Bank previously worked by Daniel Bird. Shaw says that these works were had by T. Mayer in 1829, and continues: 'We shall just notice here that Mr. T. Mayer has succeeded in a chef-d'oeuvre of the Art of Pottery, by many considered as the best Specimen of Solid Earthenware hitherto produced.

It is an Earthenware Table, of truly elegant workmanship, thirty-two inches diameter, on an elegant pedestal of proportionate dimensions, ornamented in a very chaste style with subject from National History.' Messrs. Mayer were exceedingly clever potters – especially Joseph Mayer, who died prematurely through excessive study and application to his art. They introduced many important improvements in manufacture and decoration, especially in the beautiful polychromatic bisque printing (in the Pratt manner) which was continued by their successors and other firms.

Besides ordinary earthenware, this firm produced stoneware of a highly vitreous quality; Parian of an improved body; a fine caneware, in which some remarkably good jugs (notably the 'oak' pattern) were made; and other ware. In the stoneware, besides many well-modelled jugs and other articles, they made tea-urns (which they were the first to introduce) of excellent design and admirable finish. The peculiar body of the stoneware of which these were made was capable of withstanding the variations of temperature to which vessels of this kind, usually formed of metal, are liable. These were not made to any extent by Messrs. Mayer, but were later reproduced by Gildea & Walker.

Messrs. T. J. & J. Mayer (1843–55) also produced some admirable designs in vases, decorated with a profusion of exquisitely modelled raised flowers. Two 1851 Exhibition examples are shown in Figure 3. The dinner-plates, dishes, &c. of Messrs. T. J. & J. Mayer were characterised by an excellent 'fit' in nesting, lightness of body, and neatness of finish. In 1851, they received a medal for their exhibits.

The firm of Gildea & Walker, from 1881 to 1886, produced in earthenware every variety of

Fig. 3. Messrs. T.J.&J. Mayer's Vases, 1851 Exhibition.

dinner, tea, toilet and other service from the plain white and ordinary printed to the most elaborately enamelled, painted and gilt patterns. The jugs, too, were a speciality; of these, there was an immense variety of excellent shapes. The same remark will apply to the toilet services which were, as a rule, characterised by good form and artistic decoration. Among other articles in earthenware, the richly ornamented spirit-barrels formed a distinct feature. In stoneware, well designed and sharply executed patterns in jugs, tea-pots and other articles were made in great variety; in terra-cotta, statuary groups, figures and busts were made. In this stoneware material – a clay found on their own works – the firm produced a large variety of subjects, and a selection of these formed a notable figure in the Philadelphia Exhibition of 1876.

Another speciality of the firm they named their 'Turner Jasper Ware'. This consisted of a terra-cotta body with a slip of various colours – green, blue, chocolate, buff, etc. – decorated with bas-reliefs, many of which are Flaxman's designs, as used by Turner in the eighteenth century. A large number of Turner's moulds belonged to the firm. The body, however, lacks the fineness, hardness, and compact character of the old Turner ware.

Another speciality of Gildea & Walker was a process by which printing in from two to five colours was successfully transferred on to the ware in its unglazed state. By this process – the invention of the Mayer Brothers – vases, dinner and other services, pot lids[1] and other articles were decorated in good taste. As the entire pattern was transferred in one operation from the coloured print, they were produced at a comparatively moderate cost.

A special feature of Gildea & Walker's fabrique was their assortment of 'dips' or coloured clays, embracing a great variety of shades. In using these dips, the firm did not ignore the traditions of its predecessors, for this clay

[1]See *Antique China and Glass under £5*, G. A. Godden, Arthur Barker Ltd, London, 1966, Chapter VI.

decoration was potting in its purest form. Instead of the pigments being applied to the bisque body, or burnt into the glaze in the form of an enamel, the colour is inseparable from the body – in fact, *is* the body of the ware – and cannot be removed or affected by any chemical action. Another speciality of the firm was a process of printing in gold, which it developed and perfected. The effect of some of the patterns printed in gold on the quiet but decorative tones of the dips is rich and chaste.

The marks of Messrs. Mayer were T.J.&J. MAYER: MAYER BROS, etc. Those of the later firms were BATES, WALKER & Co. PATENTEES (or other successive changes), on an oval ribbon, with date, etc., of registration inside; and a nude figure kneeling and holding

a ewer in front of him, on a tablet with the date 1790. This device was introduced in a variety of ways, with the initials B.W. & CO., B.G. & W., or G. & W., LATE MAYERS, and the name of the pattern, etc. On some, the device is surrounded by a circular ribbon; on others by a triangular one. Messrs. Gildea & Walker continued to 1886. The Dale Hall Works were subsequently worked by Keeling & Co. (Ltd.) from 1886 to 1936. They used the above mark with the initials K & Co. B.

The Dale Hall Pottery

The Dale Hall Pottery was the oldest existing works in Dale Hall. It belonged to the brothers John and George Rogers until 1815, when the latter died. Spencer Rogers having joined his father, the business was carried on under the style of John Rogers & Son. In 1816, John Rogers died, but the firm continued as John Rogers & Son until 1842, when the manufactory was purchased by James Edwards, formerly of the firm of James and Thomas Edwards of the Kiln-Croft Works. Messrs. Rogers produced tableware of a higher and better quality than most of their contemporaries, and were especially famed for their light blue 'Broseley' or 'Willow' pattern services. The early mark used by them was simply the name ROGERS impressed in or printed on the ware, sometimes with the addition of the sign of Mars or Iron:

o→

ROGERS

James Edwards was an entirely self-made man. Commencing as a thrower at Messrs. Rogers', he became a manager at Philips' of Longport, and at John Alcock's of Cobridge. Then he commenced business in partnership with John Maddock; afterwards with his brother Thomas Edwards, and carried on business in Sylvester Square, Burslem; and next in partnership with John Maddock in the same town. In 1842, he purchased the manufactory of Rogers & Son, and commenced entirely on his own account. To him the white granite ware which became so important a feature in the Pottery district mainly owes its excellence. In 1851, a medal, with an additional certificate of merit for beauty of form and excellence of goods exhibited, was awarded to Mr. Edwards.

James Edwards, who had taken his son Richard into partnership in 1851, retired from the concern ten years later and died in 1867, one of his last acts of thoughtful benevolence being that of (only a few days before his death) sending to a number of his old workpeople at the manufactory cheques varying in amount from £20 to £100 each, according to each one's length of service. The works were continued by Richard Edwards under the style of James Edwards & Son until 1882, when they passed into the hands of Knapper & Blackhurst, who continued for a few years. The marks used were the royal arms above the name; the same, with the

STONE CHINA
JAMES EDWARDS & SON   *J E & S*
DALE HALL

addition beneath of the trade-mark, a dolphin entwined round an anchor; the initials in writing letters, surrounded by a circular garter bearing

the words IRONSTONE CHINA; the name J. EDWARDS. & SON DALE HALL surrounded by an oval garter bearing the words IRONSTONE CHINA; and DALEHALL surrounded by a similar oval garter bearing the name JAMES EDWARDS & SON. An impressed mark of EDWARDS D. H. was also used.

Albert Street Works

Established by John Hawthorne in 1854 and continued by him until 1869, when they were taken by Wiltshaw, Wood & Co., and from 1877 carried on by William Wood & Co. They were among the earliest in this branch of trade. The goods made were door-plates, lock-furniture, etc. in white, black, gilt and painted; drawer, shutter and other knobs in oak, white black, etc.; bedstead vases; caster bowls; umbrella, walking-stick, sewing-machine, closet and other handles; ink-stands, bottles and wells; highly-decorated jam-pots and biscuit-jars for the table; match-pots; tea-pot and urn stands of various degrees of decoration, painted, gilt and enamelled; and every description of china used by brassfounders, tin-plate workers, japanners, etc. The mark used was W W & Co. This firm continued to about 1932.

The Mersey Pottery

Established in 1850 by Anthony Shaw, and from 1882 carried on as Anthony Shaw & Sons. Goods specially adapted for the various American markets were made, the specialities being white graniteware and cream-coloured ware for the United States; the same with the addition of printed, lustred and painted goods for South America, and printed for the colonies. In 1855, Anthony Shaw was awarded a medal at the Paris Exhibition.

The mark formerly used was the royal arms, with ribbon bearing the words STONE CHINA, and beneath, in three lines, WARRANTED ANTHONY SHAW BURSLEM. That used from 1882 has the words WARRANTED ANTHONY SHAW & SON'S Opaque Stone

Plate 18. A selection of typical earthenware figures made by John Walton of Burslem, c.1815–25. Name mark on scroll.

Victoria & Albert Museum (Crown copyright).

China ENGLAND. This firm was taken over by A. J. Wilkinson Ltd. in about 1900.

John Walton

Pottery figures may be found bearing the name WALTON, in a scroll, on the back of the base. Such figures, normally with a tree background, were made by John Walton at his works in Navigation Road, Burslem, from about 1806 (the first Directory entry is 1822) to about 1835. Walton's pottery was taken over by George Hood, who produced similar but unmarked pottery figures at Burslem, Hanley and Tunstall. Similar figures were made by Ralph Salt of Hanley during the 1828–46 period, and by Charles Tittensor.

For detailed information on John Walton, and on the many other manufacturers of Staf-fordshire figures, the reader is referred to R. G. Haggar's *Staffordshire Chimney Ornaments* (Phoenix House Ltd., London, 1955). See Plate 18 for typical examples; but the reader is warned that fakes with the 'Walton' mark have been produced in the twentieth century.

Obadiah Sherratt

Obadiah Sherratt is credited with a decorative and colourful class of Staffordshire earthenware groups (see Plate 19) mounted on feet instead of the normal flat base. He started potting at Hot Lane in about 1815 and in 1828 moved to Waterloo Road. Obadiah Sherratt died in 1841, but his son Hamlet continued the pottery to about 1854.

For further information on the Sherratt family and their groups, see R. G. Haggar's *Staffordshire Chimney Ornaments* (Phoenix House Ltd., London, 1955).

John Maddock & Son

Manufactured, in the nineteenth century, white granite ware for the American markets. The firm claim establishment in 1830, and continue to the present day. The marks are self-explanatory. The style J. & J. Maddock was also used.

New Wharf Pottery – (Hollinshad & Kirkham, late J. Daniel & Co).

Printed ware of the kind made for the home, Russian, Italian and French markets, and all the usual kinds of painted and Paris white ware suitable for the African, Australian and American trades were produced. Messrs. Hollinshad & Kirkham worked the New Wharf Pottery from 1872 to 1876 and subsequently moved to Tunstall.

The Overhouse Works – Wedgwood Place.

In 1787, the record runs, 'Thomas Wedgwood, Manufacturer of Cream-coloured Ware and

China glazed Ware, painted with blue' worked the Overhouse Pottery at Burslem. The old works were situated at the back and side of the Overhouse, with entrance in Wedgwood Place, where that street joined Scotia Road.

Early in the nineteenth century, the Overhouse Works were occupied by Goodfellow & Bathwell, who were succeeded in 1819 by Edward Challinor, and from about 1828 by William Pointon. In 1856, they passed to Morgan, Williams & Co., afterwards to Morgan, Wood & Co. who, in 1861, were succeeded by Allman, Broughton & Co., and later by Robinson, Kirkham & Co. In 1869, the old works were entirely taken down and a new and extensive manufactory was erected with all the latest improvements of machinery and appliances, the jiggers all being driven by steam-power and the drying stoves heated by exhaust steam. The rebuilding, after half a century of active occupation by one person, was thus commemorated in ornamental scroll stonework over the entrance: 'Edward Challinor commenced business here A.D. 1819, and rebuilt the premises A.D. 1869.' The new manufactory was opened in 1870 by Ralph Hammersley, who removed here from the

Plate 19. Two Staffordshire earthenware groups of the type, on footed bases, attributed to Obediah Sherratt of Burslem, c.1820–30. Large group, 12¼ inches high.   *Brighton Museum & Art Gallery.*

Church Bank Pottery at Tunstall and who had previously been engaged for twenty years with Mr. Challinor. In 1833, the firm's style was changed to Ralph Hammersley & Sons and as such remained until sold in 1905 to T. Gater. Twentieth-century owners include Gater, Hall & Co., King & Barratt, and Barratts of Staffordshire Ltd.

The goods produced by Hammersley were the ordinary description earthenware in services of various kinds and the usual classes of useful articles which (besides a good home trade) were shipped in large quantities to the United States, Canada and Sweden. Stoneware jugs were also produced. The mark was the initials R.H. & S. in various forms until 1905.

The Hill Top Pottery or Hill Pottery

These works, formerly belonging to Ralph Wood, were for many years – from about 1828 to 1859 – carried on by Samuel Alcock & Co., by whom they were rebuilt and enlarged in 1839, their rearranged manufactory comprising the works of J. & R. Riley (working period 1802–28), John Robinson & Sons, and William Taylor, which were all taken down for the purpose. The productions of Alcock & Co. were

porcelain, Parian, and the finer descriptions of earthenware – one of their specialities being semi-porcelain of fine and durable quality. The marks include: ALCOCK & Co. or S. ALCOCK & Co.

HILL POTTERY
BURSLEM

either printed along with the name of the pattern, or some device, or impressed in the ware. The fine early porcelain is unmarked and is often mistaken for Rockingham. Many finely modelled Parian jugs, etc., were made by Alcock's. Alcock ware is now little known, but it is of fine quality. The reader is referred to G. Godden's *British Pottery and Porcelain, 1780–1850* (Arthur Barker, London, 1963) and *Antiques* magazine, April, 1952. In 1860, the works and general estate were purchased by Sir James Duke and Nephews and continued by them until 1863, when they sold it to Thomas Ford, who in 1864 sold it to the Earthenware and Porcelain Company, by whom (under the management of Richard Daniel, once a noted china manufacturer at Stoke, Hanley and Burslem) it was carried on under the style of the Hill Pottery Company, Limited, late S. Alcock & Co.

The productions of Sir James Duke and Nephews were earthenware services, both white and cream-coloured, and china and Etruscan

Fig. 4. Hill Pottery (Sir James Duke & Nephews) exhibits in 1862.

Plate 20. Porcelain dessert service of patterns registered by E. J. D. Bodley in June 1876.
Godden of Worthing Ltd.

ware – some of which is shown in the contemporary engraving (Fig. 4). The operations of the Hill Pottery Company were of short duration, for in 1867 it was put into liquidation and sold up, when the property again came into the hands of Thomas Ford. In the same year, the works were divided – the china department being taken by Alcock & Diggory and the earthenware part by Burgess & Leigh (late S. Alcock & Co.), who manufactured the ordinary as well as the higher and more artistic classes of earthenware goods, both for the home and foreign markets. The firm produced all the usual services, and useful as well as many highly ornamental articles. The mark used by the firm was a beehive on a stand, with bees, a rose-bush on either side, and a ribbon bearing the name of the pattern ('Kensington', for instance) beneath, and under this the initials of the firm, B.L. & Co. Messrs. Burgess, Leigh & Co. worked the Hill Pottery to

1899 and then this firm continued at the Middleport Pottery, Burslem.

The Hill Pottery China Works

On the division of the Hill Pottery Company manufactory in 1867, part was carried on by Alcock, Diggory & Co. In 1870, the firm became Bodley & Diggory; but in the following year, Mr. Diggory having retired, the manufactory was continued by Edward F. Bodley. In 1874, the style was again changed to Bodley & Son, and in 1875 to that of Edwin J. D. Bodley. The productions formerly embraced china, earthenware and Parian, but from the 1870s were confined to china. A speciality of Mr. Bodley's productions was that of pans and vases for chandeliers and lamps. These were made in

21

various forms, and more or less highly decorated. They formed an important branch of manufacture. Services of all the usual kinds, some elaborately decorated, were also made. A Bodley porcelain dessert service design, registered in 1876, is shown in Plate 20. E. J. D. Bodley continued to 1892. Messrs. A. Heath & Co. were at the Hill Pottery from 1895 to 1897.

Crown Works

Established in about 1867 by Lea, Smith & Bolton, who were succeeded by W. E. Withinshaw, and next by Gaskell, Son & Co. In 1882, the works were rebuilt by Edwin J. D. Bodley, by whom they were carried on in conjunction with the Hill Pottery. The productions were china door-furniture and similar goods, including finger-plates, knobs, escutcheons, roses, caster-bowls and other fittings; scale plates and weights; stands and bases for lamps; and an infinite variety of articles for fittings of many kinds – white, coloured, black, enamelled and gilt – while the imitations of marbles, malachites and other stones were remarkably clever. From about 1889 to 1898, Messrs. Plant Bros. were at the Crown Works.

Queen Street Pottery

Messrs. Tinsley & Bourne entered on these works – which were formerly occupied by Joseph Edge and others – in 1874, and were succeeded in 1882 by Mr. W. H. Adams, who continued to about 1885.

Scotia Works

This manufactory was originally the parish workhouse of Burslem. It was then, in 1857, converted into a manufactory by James Vernon who, in 1862, was succeeded by the firm of Bodley & Harrold and shortly afterwards Edward F. Bodley & Co., who in 1880 changed to Edward F. Bodley & Sons and in 1881 removed to the New Bridge Pottery, Longport. At these works, the usual descriptions of earthenware, printed, enamelled and gilt, and 'ironstone china', for steamship and hotel use, were made. The bodies and glazes were considerably improved by the manager, Edward Beardmore.

The mark was the Staffordshire knot, with the words SCOTIA WORKS. This firm ceased in 1898.

The Hill Works

On the opposite side of the road to the Hill Pottery already described. The Hill Works were of old foundation and were, I am informed, worked by Enoch Wood.

After Wood's time, the works were carried on by Mr. Taylor, and next by John and Richard Riley (who removed to them from the Nile Street Works), by whom they were rebuilt in 1814 and who produced china, earthenware and Egyptian black ware. They next passed to Alcock & Keeling and, on the retirement of the latter, to S. Alcock & Co. who, having rebuilt and enlarged the Hill Pottery, removed there as already detailed. In about 1851, Barker & Son took The Hill Works for the production of goods for the home and foreign markets. On their failure, they were, in 1860, succeeded by Morgan, Wood & Co., which firm was from 1870 to 1880 altered to Wood & Baggaley and then to Jacob Baggaley, who ceased in 1886. The goods, which were mostly for the home market, comprised printed and decorated dinner, toilet, tea and breakfast services, and green-glazed dessert ware. The mark used by the firm was a bee with wings expanded, beneath which is a ribbon with the initials M W & CO, or W & B, or J B. From 1886, the works were taken by Messrs. Dunn Bennett & Co.

Swan Bank Pottery

These works – after having passed successively through the hands of Thomas Edwards; Pinder, Bourne & Co.; Beech & Hancock (later of Tunstall); and Hancock, Whittingham & Hancock (later of Stoke) – in 1873 came into the hands of Tundley, Rhodes & Procter, and so continued until the death of Mr. Tundley in 1883, when the style changed to Rhodes & Procter. The goods produced were printed, enamelled and gilt earthenware of the useful classes, in all the usual services, etc., for the home, Russian and South American markets. The mark is T.R. & P. or R. & P. beneath the

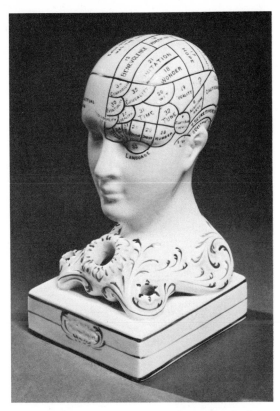

Plate 21. An earthenware phrenological head of the type made by Charles Collinson, c.1860. 5 inches high. *Godden of Worthing Ltd.*

name of pattern. The works were taken over by Keeling & Co. in 1886.

Collinson

Charles Collinson & Son were potting at Fountain Place, Burslem, from 1851 to 1873. This firm produced mainly sanitary ware but also possessed some of Enoch Wood's moulds and made some of the popular phrenological heads in earthenware (Plate 21).

Sylvester Pottery

In Nile Street, formerly belonging to Charles G. Baker, the Sylvester Pottery passed by purchase in 1876 to the firm of Holmes, Plant & Madew who, in addition to ironstone china and porcelain, produced door-furniture and brass-founders' sundries in china. The mark is the initials H.P. & M. Messrs. Holmes, Plant &

Madew were succeeded in 1886 by Holmes & Plant (also listed as Holmes, Plant & Co.). The works were subsequently made part of Doulton's Nile Street factory.

High Street Pottery

This manufactory, also known as Union Bank through its having been for some time worked by the Potters' Trades Union, belonged at one time to a family named Marsh and was also carried on by Whittingham, Ford & Co. from about 1868 to 1873, from whom it passed to Buckley, Wood & Co., who produced ordinary earthenware for the home trade. The mark is the initials B W & Co., used to 1885, when Buckley Heath & Co. succeeded. This firm continued to 1890. In 1892, the owners were Buckley Heath & Greatbatch; and J. Wade & Co. from 1892 to 1927.

Sneyd Pottery

In Albert Street, these works – formerly carried on for the production of ordinary earthenware by Messrs. Bennett – came, in about 1867, into the hands of Williams, Oakes & Co., which firm was in 1876 altered to Oakes, Clare & Chadwick and continued to 1894. Rockingham, jet, majolica, and common earthenware of the ordinary classes were produced, as were chests-of-drawers' feet in large numbers and other fittings of various designs.

Hadderidge Pottery

These works, carried on by Thomas Heath – and afterwards, successively, by John Wedgwood, Mr. Phillips, and W. & G. Harding – came into the hands of Heath & Blackhurst in 1859, who were succeeded by Blackhurst & Tunnicliffe, and then in 1880 by Blackhurst & Bourne, by whom they were continued for middle-class quality earthenware, plain and decorated, for the home trade. In this class, all the usual table, toilet, tea and other services and a variety of other articles were made. The mark is a garter, encircling the initials H & B., B & T., or B & B. Messrs. Blackhurst & Bourne continued to 1892. From 1895 to 1904, Messrs. W. Edwards & Sons worked the Hadderidge Pottery.

528
14—11—8 inches

374
14—11—8 inches

369
12½ inches only

554
14—11—8 inches

529
14—11—8 inches

372
14—11—8 inches

376
14—11—8 inches

555
14—11—8 inches

556
14—11—8 inches

443
13 inches high

526
12½ inches only

527
14—11—8 inches

Navigation Road

The works of Edward Corn were erected in about 1853, on what was a timber-yard, and carried on by W. & E. Corn – who were, from 1864, exclusively devoted to the production of white granite ware for the United States and other foreign markets. W. & E. Corn continued at Navigation Road until 1891, when they moved to Top Bridge Works, Longport. A W. & E. Corn advertisement of 1895 is reproduced in Plate 22.

Bleak Hill Works

These works formerly belonged to Moore Brothers, who produced white granite ware for the American markets, then successively to M. Isaacs & Son, Beech & Podmore (who removed here from the Bell works in 1876), and Podmore alone who, in 1880, was succeeded by Francis Joseph Emery of the Churchyard Works. The goods produced were the higher and better classes of services for exportation to the United States; and in these, through the soundness of body and superior quality of glaze, Mr. Emery was able to produce a better and more artistic phase of underglaze colouring than that attained by other firms. He also, with marked success, introduced etching in its varied forms of 'point', 'aquatint', and a modification of mezzotint, as well as photographic processes for decoration. F. J. Emery's 'Pint Imperial Measure' tankards design was registered in 1881. He continued at the Bleak Hill Works until 1894.

Sytch Pottery

Of very old foundation. In the nineteenth century, the Sytch Pottery passed successively into the hands of J. & R. Hall (1802–22) and then J. Hall & Sons. In about 1832, Barker, Sutton & Till took to the works; but at subsequent periods, Mr. Barker and Mr. Sutton withdrew from the partnership. From 1850, it remained in the hands of Thomas Till, who joined in partnership with his sons and the firm became Thomas

Plate 22 (facing). An advertisement for W. & E. Corn's 'Royal Art Pottery' vases, showing typical shapes of the 1890s. Reproduced from *Pottery Gazette*, April 1895.

Till & Sons. The ware produced was good middle-class earthenware. Besides earthenware of the usual average quality – in which services and innumerable useful articles were made by them – Messrs. Till produced coloured bodies of various kinds (cane, sage, drab and lilac); stoneware of a hard and durable kind for jugs, etc.; jet glazed ware; terra-cotta; enamelled ware; and various coloured lustres. These were principally intended for the home trade. At the Paris Exhibition of 1855, the firm received a certificate of merit. The mark used was the name of the firm in various forms. Messrs. Thomas Till & Sons (Ltd.) continued to 1928.

Kiln Croft Works

These works were of old establishment. In or about 1820, they were carried on by James and Thomas Handley; and in 1825 by James and Thomas Edwards, who were succeeded in about 1835 by Willett & Marsh. They were then continued by Mr. Marsh alone, and next by T. & R. Boote, who were succeeded in 1864 by Henry Burgess. The goods were the usual quality of white graniteware in services and various articles for the United States and Canadian markets. The mark was the royal arms, with the name or initials of the firm. Henry Burgess continued to 1892.

Wellington Street Works (Staffordshire Figures)

John Parr was producing Staffordshire earthenware figures, hen boxes ('nest eggs'), etc., at Wellington Street from about 1870 to the 1880s. In 1880, he was joined by Mr. Kent and the style became Kent & Parr. An interesting advertisement of 1881 (which claims the firm's establishment in the year 1814) reads: 'KENT & PARR . . . MANUFACTURERS OF ALL KINDS OF EARTHENWARE FIGURES AND ORNAMENTS, comprising centre pieces, Dogs, White & Gold, Black & White, Red & White; Hounds, standing, Sitting and Lying; Poodle Dogs all in several sizes; Watch stands; Hens and a very large assortment of GROSS figures; carpet Balls, number Balls, Nest Eggs, Bird cisterns . . . Special attention to Carpet Balls and Nest Eggs for Export.' Dogs of the above type are shown in Plate 23, and Staffordshire cottages of the type made by many different potters are shown in Colour Plate II.

In 1894, the firm became William Kent and the works were named the Novelty Works. The same type of Staffordshire earthenware figures and animals were produced into the twentieth century. An advertisement of 1904 reads: '... SPECIALITIES: OLD STAFFORDSHIRE FIGURES. SPECIAL LINES IN TOBY JUGS, SPANIEL DOGS, POODLES, HOUNDS, COLLIES, PUGS, HORSEMEN, COWS, &c. &c. ...' A page from a twentieth-century Kent catalogue showing typical models is reproduced in Plate 24. It includes several that are reissues of late eighteenth- and early nineteenth-century figures. These Kent "Staffordshire" figures are unmarked.

The Albert Pottery

Built in 1860 by William Smith, of Tunstall, on whose failure in 1862 it was taken by Dix & Tundley for the production of foreign-trade goods. In 1864, the works were purchased by Charles Hobson. After his death, in 1875, they were continued by his two sons, George and John Hobson. By Charles Hobson the works were considerably enlarged. New ovens were added, and flint and colour mills, a steam slip-house, pug mills, and a sagger-makers' mill were built. The productions were confined to the home trade and consisted of the usual services and other articles in earthenware – white, printed, lined, enamelled and gilt. This firm continued to 1901 and subsequently (to 1924) was carried on by George Hobson. The pottery was called the Sneyd Pottery from 1906.

Plate 23. Two typical Staffordshire earthenware dogs of a traditional form made by Kent & Parr, as well as by many other firms, in the second half of the nineteenth century. Copies are still being made.
Editor's collection.

Colour Plate II. A selection of Staffordshire
earthenware cottage and castle ornaments,
c.1850–70.   *Godden of Worthing Ltd.*

Waterloo Pottery

These works were established in about 1846 by James Vernon, continued from 1875 under the style of James Vernon & Sons and James Vernon, jun., and then carried on by J. & G. Vernon Brothers from 1880 to 1889 for the manufacture of ordinary earthenware for the South American, West Indian and Mediterranean markets.

Central Pottery

This old established pottery was formerly worked successively by Hopkin & Vernon, Hulme & Booth, Thomas Hulme, and Burgess & Leigh, who were succeeded in 1870 by Richard Alcock, by whom the works were considerably enlarged, rebuilt and remodelled. At Mr. Alcock's death, in 1881, the works passed into the hands of Wilkinson & Hulme and then, in 1885, to Arthur J. Wilkinson. Earthenware for the home markets was formerly made, but the operations were afterwards confined to white graniteware for the United States. In addition to this, Mr. Wilkinson introduced with considerable success gold lustres on the graniteware. The mark was the royal arms surmounted by the words ROYAL PATENT IRONSTONE and beneath, in three lines, ARTHUR J. WILKINSON, LATE R. ALCOCK, BURSLEM, ENGLAND.

In about 1896, Messrs. A. J. Wilkinson took the *Royal Staffordshire Pottery*, Burslem and have continued there until the present day. This firm took over many famous pottery firms and also worked the Churchyard Pottery, Burslem.

WILLIAM KENT, Novelty Works, Wellington St., BURSLEM

Plate 24. A page from a Kent catalogue of 'Staffordshire figures', showing typical models that have been produced for very many years.

H. J. Wood.

Henry James Wood established a small pottery in Chapel Lane in about 1884. After about four years, he moved to the larger Alexander Pottery in Navigation Road. Jet and Rockingham glazed earthenware was at first produced; later, general earthenware. The firm continues today.

Gibson & Sons (formerly Gibson, Sudlow & Co. during the period 1875–84).

This firm took the Albany Pottery in Moorland Road in 1885. Messrs. Gibson & Sons specialised in the production of jet and other earthenware teapots. An advertisement of 1888 shows a selection of 'jet' teapots (Plate 25). The firm became a limited liability company in 1905 and trades to this day as Gibson & Sons Ltd.

27

Most of these are
REGISTERED
Shapes and Designs.

Worcester Shape,
3 1 3.

Chelsea Shape,
3 4 2.

Chelsea Shape,
3 3 6.

Grecian Shape,
3 4 4.

Princess Shape,
3 0 6.

Queen Shape,
2 5 0.

Portland Shape,
3 7 0.

NOTE.

Any of these Patterns can be had in
Sugars & Creams, Kettles, Coffee Pots,
Jugs, Open & Mounted.
Kettle, Jug and Teapot Stands.

Silver Shape,
3 0 4.

Silver Shape,
3 6 5.

Plate 25. An advertisement for Gibson & Sons' 'jet'
(page xxi) teapots. Reproduced from the *Pottery
Gazette Diary* of 1888.

Other Burslem firms working in Burslem in 1890 and not previously listed include:

Baker & Roycroft
B. Benson
Joseph Clews
Dean Bros.
Edwards & Goodwin
Ford & Riley
New Wharf Pottery Co.
W. E. Oulsnam & Sons
R. Rhodes & Co.
J. Robinson
Shaw & Ridge
Smith, Ford & Jones
Robert Sudlow
Thomas Wood & Co.

And in 1900:

C. F. Bailey
Joseph Barber
Edwards Bros.
Ford & Sons
Hollinshead & Griffiths
William Hulme
Samuel Johnson
King & Barratt
A. J. Mountford
Enoch Plant
Price Bros.
J. Sadler & Sons
Robert Sudlow & Sons
Tilstone Bros.
Wooldridge & Walley
Wood & Barker Ltd.
Wood & Hulme
Wood and Son
W. Wood & Co.

COBRIDGE
AND
LONGPORT

Clews

Ralph & James Clews were well known earthenware manufacturers at Cobridge from about 1818 to about 1835. Good blue printed ware was produced and much was exported to America. Name marks occur on some specimens.

Cobridge Works

The manufactory of W. Brownfield & Son was erected in 1808 and worked by Stevenson & Bucknall, and from 1816 to 1836 by Andrew Stevenson alone.[1]

[1]For information on the Stevenson family of Staffordshire potters, the reader is referred to *Antiques* magazine, June 1955 – an article by N. Emery.

In 1836, the premises were opened by Robinson, Wood & Brownfield and, after Mr. Robinson's death in the same year, were continued by Wood & Brownfield until 1850. In 1850, Mr. Wood retired and the business was continued solely by William Brownfield until 1871, when he was joined in partnership by his eldest son, William Etches Brownfield, and from that time it was carried on as W. Brownfield & Sons. The goods produced during the earlier period of the works were the ordinary white, blue-printed, and sponged varieties of earthenware.

Plate 26. Brownfield earthenware dessert ware – the shapes registered in June 1860, the printed pattern in March 1862. *Private collection.*

Plate 27. A typical W. Brownfield moulded jug – a design called 'International', registered in January 1862. *Editor's collection.*

From 1850, rapid strides were made in the improvement of the ware, and under W. Brownfield & Sons they became equal to any others produced. In earthenware, they made white, printed, enamelled and gilt ware, from the simplest to the more elaborate and costly patterns, in table, toilet, and dessert services and all the usual articles for household use. Many of the printed patterns are well designed; and in the better classes of goods, the enamelling and gilding are very effective. The shapes shown in Plate 26 were registered in June 1860. The printed design is coloured-over by hand.

The stoneware and Parian jugs produced were a speciality of this firm. The typical jug form shown in Plate 27 was registered in January 1862. Tea services, tea-kettles, tea-pots, flower-pots, vases, jardinieres, trinket services and

other goods were also produced in earthenware, in every style of decoration.

In 1871, the manufacture of china was added to that of earthenware, new buildings being specially erected for the purpose; and the productions in this department made rapid strides towards perfection. In china were produced dinner, tea, breakfast, dessert and other services, jugs, and a variety of useful articles, as well as vases and other fancy goods. Messrs. Brownfield & Sons in this branch produced some novel and very effective designs in dessert-services, centre-pieces, fern and flower-stands, etc. Notable among these is a pair of magnificent vases, exquisitely painted with Etty-like subjects of 'Morning' and 'Midday'. Among the minor pieces was an oviform vase representing the hatching of an egg: the body of the vase is true to nature in colour – that of a sea-bird's egg. Services with centrepieces were also made. These were produced in the very finest porcelain, and the figures – representing the seasons with their attributes – were modelled by Hughes Protat.

Majolica was another of the specialities of Brownfield's manufacture; this had a good body, a firm glaze and brilliant colours. In this material, the firm manufactured all the usual ornamental and useful articles known to the trade.

In Parian, too, a large percentage of figures, groups, busts, vases, and all the usual – and many unusual – elegancies of home life were made. The body is of good quality.

The mark of the firm upon the printed goods was formerly W & B, W B, or W B & S in addition to the name of the pattern. The later mark on both earthenware and porcelain was the double globe device reproduced here. The

Fig. 5. Brownfield's goods at the Exhibition of 1862.

impressed mark is the Staffordshire knot enclosing the initials W B. The name BROWNFIELD was also employed impressed into the body. The firm enjoyed a large home trade, as well as an export one to Denmark, France, Germany, Holland, Russia, Italy, Spain, Portugal and the United States. The manufactory was very extensive, upwards of six hundred persons being employed in the 1880s. In 1893 or 1894, the Brownfield's Guild Pottery Society Ltd. was formed. It continued until 1900, when the old works were demolished. Messrs. Myott rebuilt on the site in 1901.

The reader is referred to G. W. & F. A. Rhead's *Staffordshire Pots and Potters* (Hutchinson & Co., London, 1906) for an account of the Brownfields.

T. Furnival & Sons

Established in 1851, T. Furnival & Sons occupied two old Cobridge manufactories, one

formerly belonging to Adams and the other to Blackwell, and ranked high as manufacturers of white granite and vitrified ironstone and decorated toilet ware for the United States, Canadian, and Continental markets. For the home trade, they produced 'patent ironstone' dinner and other services in various styles of decoration. Among their specialities were dinner services, etc., of Italian design, in plain, white ware, the ornamentation on which was indented from an embossed mould, the lines being as fine and delicate as if cut in by the graver so as to have the appearance of chasing; and the lines being filled with glaze, the surface was still even. Another noticeable feature was the clever combination of transfer-printing, hand-painting, enamelling, and gilding, which characterise some of the services. Figure 7

Plate 28 (facing). A Brownfield & Sons advertisement showing typical shapes of the mid-1880s. Reproduced from the *Pottery Gazette*, 1886.

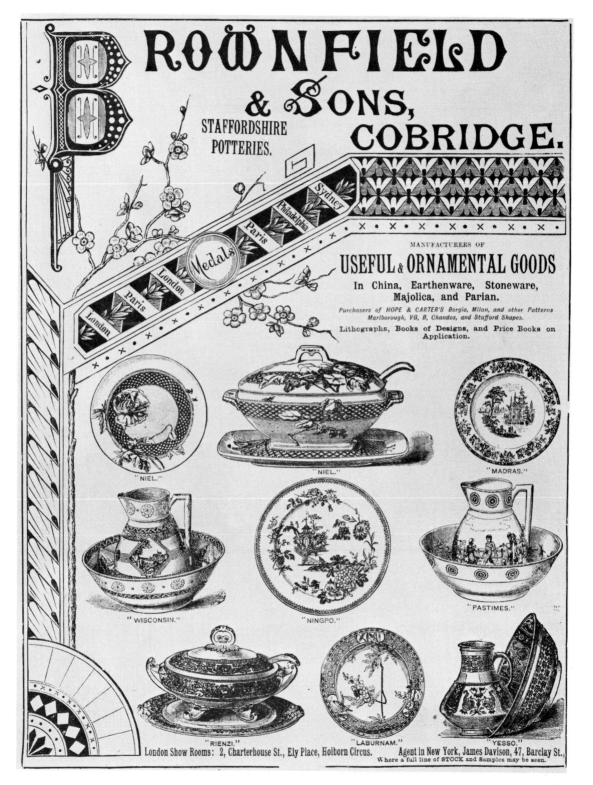

Fig. 6. Brownfield & Sons' Centrepieces. Modelled
by Carrier Belleuse. 1876 Exhibition.

shows a group of Furnival's general goods from
the 1862 Exhibition.

Among the most successful of their toilet
services were the 'Swan' and 'Nautilus',
which were of great beauty. These were produced in white, heightened with gold, and enamelled in colours. The early mark of the firm
was simply FURNIVAL impressed in the ware.
From 1890, many printed name or initial marks
were used.

In connection with these works, Mr. F. J.
Emery of the Bleak Hill Works introduced in
about 1865 a method of crayon drawing and
painting on the unglazed surface of earthenware
and china, which came much in repute, and
drawings were made in it by some of the artists
as well as by lady and other amateurs. The unglazed articles and prepared crayons and colours were supplied by Mr. Emery, who afterwards became a partner with Edward Clarke at
Longport, and proprietor of the Bleak Hill

Works. Thomas Furnival & Sons continued under the style Furnivals (1913) Ltd. until the 1960s.

Lincoln Pottery (Sneyd Green, Cobridge)

A pottery formerly managed by John and Robert Godwin from 1834 until 1866. From 1868, Bates & Bennett were manufacturers here of general earthenware of ordinary quality, the principal productions being what was called 'Imperial measure ware' for the home markets, and also Egyptian black ware and mortars and pestles. Messrs. Bates & Bennett worked until about 1895.

Abbey Pottery

At these Cobridge works – established, it is said, in 1703 – Messrs. Wood & Hawthorne, who succeeded H. Meakin in 1879, manufactured white graniteware for the American markets only. (The pottery was formerly carried on by Edward Pearson, from 1853 until 1873). The mark was the royal arms, with the words IRONSTONE CHINA, WOOD & HAWTHORNE, ENGLAND. Messrs. Wood

Fig. 7. Furnival's general goods, 1862 Exhibition.

& Hawthorne continued to 1887 and were succeeded in that year by Messrs. Sant & Vodrey – a partnership which continued until 1893.

Villa Pottery

At the beginning of the nineteenth century, this pottery belonged to Mr. Warburton. From about 1835 to 1845, it was carried on by Jones & Walley. A typical marked Jones & Walley moulded jug is shown in Plate 29.

From 1845 until 1865, Edward Walley continued the Villa Pottery, after which it passed into the hands of Wood, Son & Co., afterwards Wood & Dunn. In 1879, it passed to William Edward Cartlidge, who removed here from Bourne's Bank. Formerly, white graniteware for the American markets was made; then Britannia-metal-mounted goods, ordinary earthenware, jet figures, Rockingham, and majolica were produced. W. E. Cartlidge continued until about 1892.

Cobridge Works

Established in 1834 by Harding & Cockson, who produced china goods. From the death of Mr. Harding, in 1856, the business was continued until 1861 by his sons, in partnership with

Mr. Cockson; from 1862 to 1865 by Charles Cockson alone (during the whole of which time china was produced); and from 1866, when Elijah and David Chetwynd became partners, the firm was continued by Messrs. Cockson & Chetwynd. In 1873, Charles Cockson died; and in 1876 the firm became Cockson & Seddon, succeeded in the following year by Birks Brothers & Seddon. In 1866, the making of china was discontinued and the manufacture of white graniteware for the American trade was substituted. The mark is the royal arms and the name IMPERIAL IRONSTONE CHINA, COCKSON & CHETWYND, or COCKSON & SEDDON, or BIRKS BROTHERS & SEDDON, who continued to 1888.

Cobridge Pottery

At these extensive works, which were enlarged in 1880, Henry Alcock & Co. manufactured white graniteware, under the names of "Ironstone china" and "Parisian porcelain", exclusively for the American markets, and also the common descriptions of printed ware. This firm continued into the twentieth century. "Ltd" was added to the title in 1900, and the works renamed the Elder Pottery.

Plate 29. A Jones & Walley moulded stoneware jug of a design first published in July 1842, and later copied by other manufacturers. *Editor's collection.*

Elder Road Works

This pottery, worked by Meakin & Co. from 1865 till 1882, was capable of turning out about 2,500 crates of white graniteware annually for the United States. It passed, in 1882, into the hands of the Crystal Porcelain Pottery Co. Limited, whose speciality was the production of hard porcelain tiles and plaques, and telegraphic and chemical ware. The mark was the crest – a dove holding a palm-branch. This firm continued, at the above address, until 1886. A later firm, the Porcelain Tile Company, then operated these works.

Prospect Pottery

Ernest Pidduck started at this Cobridge pottery in about 1899. Jet and Rockingham earthenware was produced. The firm was Pidduck, Rushton & Co. from 1900 to 1903.

Stevenson

There was more than one firm of potters of this name in Staffordshire. Some were of Cobridge. Ralph Stevenson used an oval-shaped mark bearing a three-masted ship with the name 'Stevenson' above it impressed in the ware. Another used a crown within a circle, on which was A. STEVENSON, WARRANTED, STAFFORDSHIRE; and another impressed mark of the period 1816–36 was the name STEVENSON. Good blue printed ware was exported to America in quantity.

Lincoln Pottery

From 1882 to 1885, Messrs. Beech & Tellwright manufactured here ordinary earthenware, majolica, etc., for both home and foreign markets. From 1885 to 1890, Frederick Beech & Co. produced similar ware at the Lincoln Pottery.

Sneyd Green Pottery

Thomas Cartwright (& Sons) produced ordinary earthenware here in the 1860s. Their lustre teapots were noteworthy.

LONGPORT

Davenport's

In 1773, a manufactory was erected at Longport by John Brindley (brother of the celebrated James Brindley, the engineer), who also built for himself a handsome residence near at hand. Shortly after 1773, Edward Bourne built another manufactory; and this was followed by a third, erected by Robert Williamson.

In 1793, the first-named manufactories passed into the hands of John Davenport, who, in 1797, added to his other operations 'the chemical preparation of litharge and white lead for the use of potters', which, however, was afterwards discontinued. In 1801, the business of glass-making was added. In about 1830, Mr. Davenport retired from active business and chiefly resided at Westwood Hall, near Leek, where he died in 1848. The business, after his retirement in 1830, was carried on by his second son, Henry Davenport (who died in 1835), and the youngest son, William Davenport. Henry Davenport purchased the manufactory of Robert Williamson, and added to his other works. After the death of Henry Davenport, the manufactories were carried on by his youngest brother, William Davenport, under the style of W. Davenport & Co. He died in 1869 and the entire business was carried on by his son, Henry Davenport, until September 1881, when he converted it into a private company – Davenport's Ltd.

In 1806, the Prince of Wales (afterwards George IV) and the Duke of Clarence (afterwards William IV) visited Davenport's works. On the accession to the throne of William IV in 1830, the King gave the order to this firm to manufacture for him the service to be used at his coronation banquet. This superb royal service was completed in a very satisfactory manner and was the subject of high commendation from the King. On this 1830 service, the crown was first used by the firm in its mark.

In the earlier years of the Longport manufactory under Brindley, earthenware alone was produced. No marked pieces are known. Mr. Davenport at first confined his operations to the manufacture of white, cream-coloured, and blue-printed ware, and these were of good substantial quality. Later on, china was commenced, and formed an equally extensive branch with the earthenware. In both of these, all the usual services and miscellaneous articles were produced, from the plain to the most elaborately decorated, for the home and foreign markets. The china is of remarkably fine and good quality in body, in glaze, and in make; and in all these particulars, it ranks among the best produced in the district. The tea and dessert ware is of extreme excellence and many of the patterns are unsurpassed for richness of colouring and gilding.

Among their specialities were adaptations of the finest Japanese and Chinese patterns in the Derby tradition. The deep blues, the rich gradations of red and the other colours employed were, in some of the patterns, laid on with a lavish richness; and being combined with the most elaborate and delicate as well as massive gilding, they produced intricate patterns of sumptuous appearance. Some of the cups (notably those with sunk panels and others which are bowl-shaped and supported upon gilt feet) are of elegant form, and those in blue and white are highly successful. In celadon and 'Rose du Barry' they produced charming but simple services, as they did also in white.

In stone china, dinner and dessert services – as well as jugs and other articles – were produced in all styles of decoration. The services in ordinary earthenware were also extremely varied in pattern, decoration, and variety of shapes.

The marks used by Davenport's have been various, the anchor being the distinguishing characteristic.

 Printed c.1805–20.

Impressed mark. c.1790–1820

 Printed on porcelain in blue. c.1850–70.

DAVENPORT
LONGPORT
STAFFORDSHIRE

c.1870–87.

Many other marks were employed. The third mark was employed c.1815–25 printed in black, not blue. Production ceased (after some years of trouble) in 1887, and the works were purchased by Thomas Hughes. A good selection of Davenport ware is shown in *The Illustrated Encyclopaedia of British Pottery and Porcelain* by G. A. Godden (Herbert Jenkins, London, 1966, Plates 190–200).

New Bridge Works, Longport

This manufactory, previously carried on by W. Davenport & Son, passed in 1877 into the hands of Edward Clarke, of the Churchyard Works at Burslem, and intermediately of the Phoenix Works, Tunstall, who moved here from the last-named place and took into partnership Mr. F. J. Emery, the inventor of the process of crayon drawing and printing on the bisque surface referred to on page 25. The mark was EDWARD CLARKE & CO.

In 1881, the manufactory was purchased by Edward F. Bodley & Son, of the Scotia Works, who removed to it in that year, Mr. Bodley dying between the time of purchase and removal. The goods produced were 'Genuine Ironstone China' and earthenware in all classes, of which the usual services and other domestic articles were made. The mark is the Staffordshire knot enclosing within its loop the words NEW BRIDGE POTTERY. E. F. Bodley & Son continued at the New Bridge Works until 1898.

Waterloo Road Works

Established in 1820 by Thomas Hughes, and carried on by him and his successors, Stephen Hughes & Co., till about 1856, from which time until 1881 they were continued by Thomas Hughes, grandson of the first-named, by whom the whole place was enlarged, improved and modernised. In 1881, Mr. Hughes removed to Top Bridge Works, Longport, and was succeeded, in 1883, by Mellor, Taylor & Co., who continued to produce the usual articles in hard durable granite or ironstone china for the American markets up to 1904. Goods were also, to some extent, produced for the home trade. The former mark, stamped on the ware, was THOMAS HUGHES IRONSTONE CHINA. That of the later firm was the royal arms in plain shield, with crown and wreath, exactly copied from the reverse of the half-crown of Queen Victoria, surrounded by the words MELLOR, TAYLOR & CO., ENGLAND. WARRANTED STONE CHINA.

ETRURIA

Wedgwood

The name Etruria will always be linked with Messrs. Wedgwood's, for it was here that most of Josiah Wedgwood's celebrated ware was made. For the early history of the Wedgwoods, the reader is referred to W. B. Honey's *Wedgwood Ware* (Faber & Faber, London, 1948). The following notes start with the 1790 period.

In 1790, Wedgwood took into partnership his three sons, John, Josiah, and Thomas, and his nephew, Thomas Byerley – the style of the firm being Josiah Wedgwood, Sons, and Byerley. In 1793, John Wedgwood retired from the concern, and the style was then altered to Josiah Wedgwood, Son, and Byerley. In 1794, Josiah Wedgwood was seized with his last illness, and on the 3rd January 1795 he died and was, on the 6th, buried in the churchyard at Stoke-on-Trent.

For a time after Josiah Wedgwood's death, the management of the business devolved on Mr. Byerley. In 1800, the partners were the brothers Josiah and John Wedgwood and Thomas Byerley, and so continued until Byerley's death in 1810. Thomas Wedgwood, who suffered constant ill-health, took no part in the management of the business.

After the death of Byerley, the business was carried on by the second Josiah Wedgwood alone until November 1823, when he took his eldest son Josiah (the third of that name) into partnership under the style of Josiah Wedgwood & Son. In 1827, when another son, Francis, was taken into partnership it became Josiah Wedgwood & Sons. In 1841, Josiah Wedgwood, senior, retired from the business, and it was carried on by his sons until the following April, when Josiah Wedgwood, junior, also retired.

The mark remained simply WEDGWOOD despite the above changes in the firm's title.

The manufacture of china, which had never been attempted by the first Josiah, was commenced at Etruria in about 1812 but was discontinued in 1822. In 1879, the manufacture of porcelain was again introduced and has since become one of the marked successes of the firm. The first china was of very good quality in texture of body, colour, glaze, and decoration. The mark is the name WEDGWOOD, printed in red, gold, or blue. Stone china was also made at Etruria from about 1820 to about 1861. This type of earthenware is normally marked WEDGWOOD'S STONE CHINA, printed in two lines.

The classes of goods manufactured by the Messrs. Wedgwood in the 1870s were much as they were in the time of the great Josiah. The same block moulds were used; the same principles were acted upon and carried out; the same mixture of bodies and glazes, with certain modifications, were in daily use; the same varieties of goods were manufactured; and thus many of his vases, medallions and other goods were still produced in all their original beauty. And although the ornamental goods then produced had not quite the charm of super-excellence which, in the eyes of a collector, age gives to those made in the days of the first Josiah, Messrs. Wedgwood's jasper and other ornamental goods stood as far in advance of their competitors of the day as did those of the great Josiah in relation to the competitors of his own time. They were simply unsurpassable, both in design and execution. It must be remembered that in the days of the first Josiah Wedgwood there was

39

little competition in other branches of the potter's art, and the great care, skill, and labour he bestowed upon his purely ornamental pieces was, there can be no doubt, amply repaid in the high prices he could obtain for them. This was not so in the 1870s; for at that time productions of attractive and showy character were so extensively made, and so readily purchasable at a low rate, that the quiet, unobtrusive but truly lovely bas-reliefs originated by Wedgwood only commanded a limited sale – and even then at such prices as would not admit of the same scrupulous attention being paid to their production as in the earlier days.

The firm still produced jasper, basaltes, red,

Fig. 8. Wedgwood three-colour Jasper vase.

cream-coloured, and other ware. The jasper goods were still, as they had ever been since the first production of that marvellous body, the great speciality of their works. In this, since the days of Turner, although they had many imitators, they had never even been approached, and their goods still maintained their old and high reputation. All the famous works of the olden time were still made in all their beauty, with the addition of many new and ever-varying designs and combinations. The jasper was produced in dark and in light blue of various shades (with, of course, the raised figures and ornaments in white), in sage-green, in pink and in other tints. It was also produced both in 'solid jasper' – that is, the body coloured throughout – and in 'jasper dip', which was a white jasper body with the colour laid on the surface. The 'solid jasper' was reintroduced in 1856. The manufacture of majolica was commenced at Etruria in 1860. With regard to this it is necessary to state that the true Italian majolica, as well as Minton's reproductions, were made with a coarse cane-coloured body and decorated with opaque enamel colours; but Wedgwood's were the first to use a white body and semi-transparent coloured glazes. By this process, much greater brilliancy of effect was produced than by the use of enamel colours. In majolica, all the usual classes of goods, including umbrella-stands, vases, etc., were made.

In malachite, mottled, agate and other ware, dessert, toilet, and trinket services, and a variety of both useful and ornamental articles, were made. Parian busts and figures of good quality were made in about 1848 or 1849. Another variety of ornamental work was the 'inlaid' ware, in which the effect was much the same as the wood 'Tunbridge ware'. It was made by the same process as the famous 'Henri Deux' ware – an impress from a metal runner being filled up with a different coloured clay and afterwards turned or scraped level on the surface. In this ware, a magnificent and highly appropriate chess-table was produced to use with the celebrated Flaxman chessmen.

Cream-coloured ware, the veritable 'Queen's

Colour Plate III. A fine quality Wedgwood jasper-
ware ornamental plate with typical white relief
motifs, c.1850. Diameter, $8\frac{3}{4}$ inches.
                              Godden of Worthing.

Fig. 9. Wedgwood Jasper wares, 1851 Exhibition.

ware' of the olden time, was still extensively made. Of a delicate creamy whiteness in colour, light and pleasant to the touch, true and close-fitting in the potting, and covered with a faultless glaze, this ware still held its own and maintained its wonted supremacy. In it, services and every variety of useful articles were made, and it is pleasant to add that the pieces were still made in the old moulds used in the great Josiah's time, with only such modifications as fitted them for more modern notions. In the pearl body, which was of great hardness and durability and of a pearly whiteness, services and useful goods were manufactured in plain white, printed, and decorated varieties. In Rockingham ware, tea-pots, coffee-pots, services (the cups white inside), and other articles were made, as were

also 'porous ware' water-bottles, butter-coolers, etc., and 'mortar ware'. In the red ware – a rich colour and fine body – services and a large number of other articles were produced, and were frequently ornamented with raised figures, etc. in black, with good and striking effect. Blue printing had been introduced at Etruria at an early date and was, with black, etc., continued under the third Josiah Wedgwood. The firm had, some time before, introduced a process by which photographs of the original drawings, in colours, were produced on ware by the same method as the auto-type process (Plate 30). This formed a notable feature of progress in scientific decoration, and it was only right that, as photography itself was the undoubted discovery of a Wedgwood, its development as an aid to ceramic decoration should have been left to his successors.

Fig. 10. Wedgwood 1862 Exhibition pieces.

Another feature was the revival of the old imitations of porphyry, agate, pebble and Aberdeen granite – the latter being made by encrusting the pliant clay of the vase with innumerable small fragments of various coloured clays before firing. In this chaste style, the 'Leda Vase' is a notable example. Among the more beautiful of their achievements in jasper were a pair of exquisite Renaissance ewers, with bas-reliefs of 'Peace' and 'War'; a large plaque of the 'Seven Ages', modelled after a design by Walter Crane; and a series of subjects from Chaucer, Shakespeare, and Milton. In porcelain were, notably, a pair of vases, 2 feet 6 inches high, painted with subjects of nymphs and amorini by T. Allen for the Paris Exhibition, 1878, where the firm obtained a gold medal.

One of the then most recent additions to the productions of these works was a new method of impressed decoration of tiles, patented by Mr. Marsden, which was adopted and perfected by Messrs. Wedgwood. The process had many advantages, foremost of which was the easy manner of exact reproduction of special designs at no additional cost over that of stock patterns. The principal charm in these tiles was the harmony of colour in conjunction with softness of tone, arrived at by the method of impressing the colours. [This 'Email Ombrant' style of intaglio decoration, which was filled with a coloured glaze, was mainly used for dessert services in the 1870s.]

The principal painter at Etruria for many years was the late gifted M. Emile Lessore, an artist of more than European reputation, who took rank above all others in that exquisite style for which he was so famous. As M. Lessore and his works were so closely identified with Etruria, a few words on his career cannot but be interesting. He was born in 1805, his father being a notary, for which profession the son was at first intended. Giving up law for art, he entered for a short time the studio of Ingres. In 1831, he exhibited his first picture, 'Le Frère Malade', in the Salon at Paris, and from that time until 1850 continued to exhibit both oil and water-colour pictures which were always eagerly sought for and purchased at high prices. In 1851, Lessore was induced, through offers made to him by the Sèvres china manufactory, to turn his attention to china painting. He attempted to introduce a more artistic feeling at Sèvres, and succeeded notably. A pair of large vases decorated by him, which were exhibited in Paris in 1853, were purchased by the Emperor of Russia for a thousand guineas. The originality of

Fig. 11. 1871 Exhibition vase in three-colour jasper ware.

Plate 30. An oval Wedgwood tray decorated by H. Hope Crealocke's photographic process, and a pair of vases painted by H. Brownsword, c. 1873–6. Vases, 6 inches high.   *Editor's collection.*

Fig. 12. Painted by Lessore. 1862 exhibition.

Lessore's work caused a division amongst the artists at Sèvres, and the partisans of the two camps were so virulently wearisome in their disputes that in 1858 he abandoned Sèvres and came to England, where – after being employed for a short time by Minton's – he joined Messrs. Wedgwood, who thoroughly appreciated his talents and his loyal sympathetic character. The most remarkable of his works were shown in the Exhibition of 1862, the Paris Exhibition of 1867, and at Vienna in 1873, and medals were awarded to him in all countries.

The climate of England, especially Staffordshire, not suiting him, he returned to France, living at Marlotte, near Fontainebleau, where he still continued his connection with the Wedgwoods, painting pieces and sending them to be fired at Etruria. There is little doubt that Emile Lessore was one of the first artists in England to revolutionise the decoration of pottery, and some of his pieces were unmistakably more artistic than was usually produced in faience (see Plate 31). The drawing, without being laboured, was true to nature; the colouring, as a rule, was subdued and delicate, and the master hand was apparent in every touch. During the seige of Paris, many of Lessore's finest works were concealed by him in the cellars of his cottage and afterwards preserved by Messrs. Wedgwood. He was the first to employ the freedom of the artist's brush to the decoration of pottery, which previously had been painted with the finished and stippled perfection of the miniature painter but without the imagination and freshness of an artist's sketch. M. Lessore died in 1876, and soon afterwards his remaining works were sold by Messrs. Wedgwood to Mr. Mortlock, by whom they were exhibited in London (see *The Studio*, July 1960).

In 1878, Messrs. Wedgwood's reintroduced a fine quality bone-china. Many finely painted services and other examples will be found bearing tasteful hand-painted designs. For this new porcelain, a printed mark incorporating the Portland vase was used. For the remainder of the century, Wedgwood's continued to produce their traditional ware – jaspers, basalte and creamware. These nineteenth-century examples all bear the impressed 'Wedgwood' mark. From 1860, a three-letter system of dating was

Plate 31. A selection of Wedgwood creamware
painted by the Sèvres-trained artist Emile Lessore
between 1859 and 1876. Large dish, diameter $14\frac{3}{4}$
inches. *Editor's collection.*

Plate 32. A selection of Wedgwood jasper ware of the late Victorian period, with the word 'England' added to the standard name-mark 'Wedgwood'.
Godden of Worthing Ltd.

employed (see page 47). From 1891, 'England' occurs impressed on some ware. 'Made in England' is of twentieth-century dating. 'Victorian Wedgwood' is discussed and illustrated in *Country Life*, October 13th, 1960.

Typical late 'England' marked jasper ware is illustrated in Plate 32.

Since the end of the Second World War, the Wedgwood works has been situated in a new factory in a country setting, at Barlaston, close by Stoke-on-Trent. These new works rightly attract many persons who wish to see the various manufacturing processes, as well as the works collection of former products.

WEDGWOOD'S IMPRESSED
YEAR LETTERS

Occuring in sets of three (from 1860), the *last* shows
the year of manufacture

O	=	1860	O	=	1886	
P	=	1861	P	=	1887	
Q	=	1862	Q	=	1888	
R	=	1863	R	=	1889	
S	=	1864	S	=	1890	
T	=	1865	T	=	1891*	From 1886 to 1897 the
U	=	1866	U	=	1892	earlier (1860–1871) letters
V	=	1867	V	=	1893	are repeated
W	=	1868	W	=	1894	
X	=	1869	X	=	1895	*From 1891
Y	=	1870	Y	=	1896	'ENGLAND'
Z	=	1871	Z	=	1897	should occur on specimens
A	=	1872				
B	=	1873				
C	=	1874				
D	=	1875				
E	=	1876				
F	=	1877	A	=	1898	
G	=	1878	B	=	1899	
H	=	1879	C	=	1900	From 1898 to 1906 the
I	=	1880	D	=	1901	letters used from 1872 to
J	=	1881	E	=	1902	1880 re-occur, but
K	=	1882	F	=	1903	'ENGLAND'
L	=	1883	G	=	1904	should also appear.
M	=	1884	H	=	1905	
N	=	1885	I	=	1906	

From 1907 the sequence was continued, but a '3' replaces the first letter. From 1924 a '4' replaces the '3'. After 1930 the month is numbered in sequence and the last two numbers of the year are given, i.e. 1A 32 = January 1932, 'A' being the workman's mark.

FENTON

Minerva Works

In 1812, these works (which were established in 1801) were held by Charles James Mason & Co., the producers of the famous Patent Ironstone China (page 62) and from them passed to Pratt & Co., who were succeeded by Mr. Gerard (or Jerrad) and then by Richard Hassall. In about 1833, Mr. Hassall was joined in partnership by Thomas Green, son of Thomas Green of the Churchyard Works, Burslem. Shortly afterwards, Richard Hassall retired and Thomas Green was joined in partnership by Mr. W. Richards, of Great Fenton, and the business was continued by Green & Richards until 1847, when the latter withdrew. The business was then continued by Thomas Green alone until his decease in 1859, and from 1859 to 1876 was carried on under the trading style of Green & Co.

The ware made by the earlier firms was the commonest kind of blue printed, white and gold, and lustre. During the partnership with Mr. Richards, a variety of ornaments, small ewers and basins, toy mugs and jugs were extensively made. This trade, however, was checked by the introduction of a similar but cheaper class of goods from France. This had a good effect on the firm, for it induced attention to be turned to a better class of productions – and this again was more decisively done in 1851, when goods of a highly creditable character were made. The productions were china tea, breakfast, dessert, trinket and other services; toy sets, jugs, mugs, feeders, wheel-barrow and spade salts; and a large variety of other articles, both for home and foreign markets.

From 1876 to 1889, the style was T. A. & S. Green, and from then to 1948 the firm was Crown Staffordshire Porcelain & Co. The present title is The Crown Staffordshire China Co. Ltd.

For illustrations of early twentieth-century 'Crown Staffordshire' reproductions of earlier ware, the reader is referred to J. F. Blacker's *The ABC of XIX Century English Ceramic Art* (Stanley Paul & Co., c. 1911, not dated).

Victoria Works

For many years, from about 1811 to 1843, this manufactory was carried on by S. Ginder & Co., and was then held by James Reeves (from 1870), who produced the more ordinary qualities of earthenware. This firm continued to 1948.

Fenton Potteries (W. Baker & Co)

The goods produced here were of the ordinary class of printed, sponged, and pearl-white granite ware suitable for the British North American, United States, West Indian, African, and Indian markets. Messrs. W. Baker & Co. started in High Street, Fenton, in 1839. In 1868, they moved to the Fenton Potteries and continued to 1932. Their name occurs in full in various printed marks.

Fenton Pottery

This was established in 1825 by C. J. & G. M. Mason for the manufacture of their famous Ironstone China ware (page xix and Plate 4).

The works of C. J. Mason & Co., says John Ward,[1] in 1843, 'standing obliquely to two turnpile-roads, and on the line of the Canal Company's railway, present an extensive front of four stories in height, inscribed in large letters "Patent Ironstone China Manufactory". For this article of trade, which Messrs. G. & C.J. Mason introduced some years ago, they obtained extensive public favour, and an almost exclusive sale, on account of its resemblance to porcelain, and its very superior hardness and durability'. Messrs. Mason were succeeded by Samuel Boyle in 1849, from whom the works passed, in 1862, into the hands of E. & C. Challinor, formerly E. Challinor & Co (1853–62) of Sandyford and Tunstall. The goods produced were white granite, printed, sponged, and common earthenware for the American, Australian and other foreign and colonial markets. In these, tea, coffee, breakfast, dinner, toilet and other services, and all the usual useful articles, were produced. In jugs, Messrs. Challinor produced the 'Ceres' or 'Wheat', 'Paris', 'Garland', 'Barbery', 'Lily', 'Missouri', 'Florence', 'Versailles', 'Lotus' or 'Cora', and other shapes, both plain and embossed. The earthenware was of ordinary quality, specially designed and well adapted for the various markets to which

it was sent. The marks are the Staffordshire knot impressed in the ware, with or without the words:

E & C CHALLINOR
FENTON

E & C CHALLINOR

IRONSTONE
CHINA
E & C CHALLINOR

within an ornamental border, surmounted by

[1]*The Borough of Stoke-upon-Trent* by John Ward (W. Lewis & Son, 1843).

the royal arms, also impressed in the ware, and the following printed on the surface: the royal arms with crown supporters, motto, etc., and, beneath, a ribbon with IRONSTONE CHINA, E & C CHALLINOR FENTON; the name of the pattern, i.e. 'Australia', 'Gothic', 'Portland', etc., within various borders and the name E & C CHALLINOR, or E & C C. Messrs. E. & C. Challinor continued to 1891.

Fenton Potteries

These works were in the hands of Messrs. Pratt from the commencement of the nineteenth century. The style of the firm was F. & R. Pratt & Co. and they produced all the ordinary classes of earthenware goods in services, and the usual useful and ornamental articles. They were large makers of druggists' sundries and of articles in a compact, vitreous terra-cotta. Another speciality was underglaze multi-colour printing, for which they received special mention by the Jury at the 1851 Exhibition. A silver medal was also awarded to them by the Society of Arts for a pair of the largest Etruscan-style vases up to that time produced; they were exhibited in 1851 and were purchased by the Prince Consort.

Messrs. F. R. Pratt & Co. produced most (but not all) of the well known and decorative colour-printed 'Pot Lids'. Dessert and tea services were also made in this style. A selection of typical Pratt ware is shown in Plate 33. Many Etruscan-style vases were also made. The firm continued into the twentieth century and was subsequently merged with the Cauldon Potteries Ltd. Pratt multi-colour printed ware is discussed and illustrated in *The Pictorial Pot Lid Book* by H. G. Clarke (Courier Press, London, 1970) and *Antique China and Glass under £5* by G. A. Godden (Arthur Barker, London, 1966).

Opal China Works

Messrs. E. Hughes & Co. established this works in 1889 and produced a good range of china tea-sets, jugs, etc. The firm continued into the twentieth century.

Plate 33. A selection of Pratt earthenware, mostly
decorated by the multi-colour printing technique.
The large dish represents a design shown at the 1851
Exhibition. Diameter, 12¾ inches.

Godden of Worthing Ltd.

High Street

Samuel Radford established a pottery in the High Street in about 1885 (he had earlier worked at Longton). Good quality china ware was produced and marketed under the trade name RADFORDIAN. The first continued to 1957.

Sutherland Pottery

Messrs. Thomas Forester, Son & Co. started potting at the Sutherland Works in about 1884. They produced china and earthenware dinner, tea, dessert and toilet sets. An advertisement of 1885 is reproduced in Figure 13. In 1885, they were succeeded by Messrs. Forester & Hulme and by Hulme & Christie from 1893 to 1902.

Fig. 13. Thomas Forester, Son & Co's ware, advertised in 1885.

Heron Cross Pottery

Messrs. Hines Brothers built this pottery in 1886. Good quality 'Opaque Porcelain' and 'Ivory' ware was produced into the twentieth century. The firm was taken over by Grimwade's in 1908.

Portland Pottery

James Broadhurst established these works in 1872 (he had earlier worked at Longton). A wide range of good quality earthenware was produced. In 1897, '& Sons' was added to the style and the firm continues today as James Broadhurst & Sons Ltd.

Grosvenor Works

In Foley Place, this manufactory was established in about 1850 by Till, Bourne, & Brown. Since their time, the successive changes in the proprietorship have been Bourne & Brown; Charles Brown alone; Jackson & Brown (1865);

51

Fig. 14. Messrs. Jackson & Gosling's china, c. 1881.

and Jackson & Gosling, who did a large home and foreign trade from 1866 to 1908. The manufactures were confined to china, in which tea, breakfast, and dessert services were produced. Messrs. Jackson & Gosling continued at Fenton to 1908 and then at Longton.

Lane Delph Pottery

Gimson Wallis & Co. produced earthenware of the ordinary class, chiefly for the foreign markets, from 1883 to 1890. The works were

52

formerly managed by John Pratt & Co. during the period 1851 to 1878.

Park Works, Market Street.

Messrs. Ralph Malkin (& Sons) manufactured here the ordinary classes of earthenware goods from about 1865 to 1894.

Foley Pottery

This is one of the oldest works in the district. It was originally occupied by Samuel Spode, who lived in a large house adjoining. It was afterwards occupied by Charles Bourne (1807–30). The porcelain produced by Charles Bourne is very good quality, similar in many respects to the Spode ware. Bourne porcelain bears the initials C.B., placed above the pattern number, in fractional form. See *Collectors' Guide* magazine, May 1967. The Foley Pottery was later in the possession of Hawley & Co., manufacturers of earthenware during the 1842–93 period.

Salopian Works

William Morley, of the Baltimore Works, having erected a new manufactory here, in the 1880–3 period, removed to the new premises in 1883 and continued to 1906. Earthenware, often in colourful 'Old Derby' patterns, was produced.

The Foley Potteries

These potteries take their name from the Foley family, who owned property in the neighbourhood. They were built by John Smith of Fenton Hall in about 1827, the first firm by whom they were worked being Elkin, Knight & Bridgwood, who made the better classes of 'Willow Pattern' and other blue printed services. On the retirement of Bridgwood, in about 1840, the style was changed to Knight & Elkin; and subsequently, on the retirement of Mr. Elkin, in 1846, it was changed to J. K. Knight alone. In 1853, when he was joined in partnership by Henry Wileman (wholesale china dealer, of London) the style became Knight & Wileman. On the retirement of Mr. Knight, in 1856, Mr. Wileman carried on the works alone till 1864, when his two sons succeeded him as J. Wileman

& Co. In 1868, the partnership was dissolved, and from that time till 1892 the business belonged to James F. Wileman.

From 1892 to 1925, the style was Wileman & Co. The goods produced were the usual granite ware, printed ware, lustres, Egyptian and shining blacks, and cream-coloured ware. All of these were of the ordinary classes for household use; and the great bulk of the trade was export to the United States, Panama, Australia, South Africa, Ceylon, Java and India. The Foley China Works were built in 1860 by Henry Wileman, and both the old and the new works were continued – the old for earthenware, the new for china.

King Street Works

These works were established in the latter part of the eighteenth century by Thomas

Shelley, who was succeeded by Jacob Marsh, from whom they passed to T. & J. Carey in about 1840. The productions were ordinary Rockingham ware and earthenware. Messrs. Carey also occupied two other manufactories at Longton. King Street Works were next held by a company, and in about 1853 they passed into the hands of John Edwards. The goods produced were semi-porcelain and white granite for the American markets. Until 1856, Mr. Edwards produced china in addition, but this was discontinued. The firm was subsequently John Edwards & Co. (Ltd.) and ceased about 1900.

The Foley (In King Street)

Messrs. Robinson & Co. produced china of the usual classes both for home and export trades from 1873 to 1888.

Miles Mason

A leading manufacturer in the latter part of the eighteenth century. An invoice of his of

Plate 34. A selection of Miles Mason porcelain teaware of pattern number 91. Impressed mark M. MASON, c.1805–10.   *Godden of Worthing Ltd.*

1797 enumerates blue dessert sets, each consisting of '1 centre piece, 4 shells, 2 hearts, two cucum. tureens, dishes & stands, and 24 dessert plates'; 'melon shapes', 'squares', oval and round baking dishes, oval and square salad dishes, 'Nankeen spitting pots', basins and egg-cups. Such ware would probably have been made at Liverpool, where Miles Mason also had a pottery, not at Staffordshire.

Miles Mason was the father of George Miles Mason, Charles James Mason – of 'Ironstone china' celebrity (see page 103) – and William Mason. Miles Mason went to London and established a shop for the sale of Chinese porcelain in the 1780s. He afterwards was a partner in a manufactory at Liverpool. He started potting in Staffordshire in about 1800. By 1805, he had built up a large trade in good quality porcelain and moved to the Minerva Works at Fenton. In June 1813, his sons George M. Mason and Charles J. Mason succeeded him and produced their 'Mason's Ironstone' (Plate 4).

Miles Mason's mark on porcelain was his initial and name, impressed into the ware – M. MASON. The teaware shown in Plate 34 bears this impressed mark M. MASON. Other Mason's porcelain is featured in *The Illustrated Guide to Mason's Patent Ironstone China* by G. Godden (Barrie & Jenkins, London, 1971).

Between 1890 and 1900, the following firms were established at Fenton:
H. K. Barker
Gilmore Bros.
W. H. Sharpe
J. Wilson & Sons
Rubian Art Pottery
Fountain Place Works
Canning Street Works
Park Works.

HANLEY
AND
SHELTON

Wilson

Robert Wilson, the successor to Neale & Wilson, devoted himself mainly to the production of cream-coloured earthenware, plain or decorated in the Wedgwood manner. His name is occasionally met with simply as WILSON impressed in the body of the ware, and occasionally in connection with a crown

C
WILSON

and the distinctive mark C as shown here. After the retirement or death of Robert Wilson, his brother David carried on the works from 1802 until 1815. It was afterwards D. Wilson & Sons; then Assignees of Wilson; then Phillips & Bagster (c.1820–33). The Phillips of this firm was Jacob, brother to Jonathan Phillips, the retailer of Oxford Street, London. The manufactory and house adjoining, where Bagster had resided, came on to the market and were purchased by Joseph Mayer, son of and successor to Elijah Mayer. The Church Works were then, in about 1832, rented by William Ridgway & Co., Mr. Ridgway being Joseph Mayer's cousin. Joseph Mayer had in his employ a clever modeller, Leonard James Abington, who was also a chemist, and he placed him in partnership with William Ridgway, thus making the '& Co'.

When Joseph Mayer ceased potting and let the best part of his works to W. Ridgway & Co. in 1832, he retained an oven and other parts of the works, as well as some warehouses and stabling adjoining his residence, and had these crammed with some of the best of his stock – Egyptian black, cane, chocolate brown, and Queen's ware, some of the latter elaborately perforated and painted – an indescribable jumble of most beautiful pottery; and there it remained, locked up, until his death in 1860.

To return to the Church Works: the next addition to the firm, as soon as he was old enough to enter it, was William Ridgway's son Edward John, the title of the firm being changed to William Ridgway, Son & Co. In course of time, William Ridgway retiring, the two manufactories were carried on by Edward John Ridgway and L. J. Abington. The firm was styled Ridgway & Abington during the 1848–60 period. It was ultimately Edward John Ridgway alone; and from 1866 to 1878, it was Powell & Bishop. In 1878, this firm became Powell, Bishop & Stonier, which in 1891 became Bishop & Stonier – a well-known twentieth-century firm.

The New Hall Works

Historically interesting. The company consisted of Samuel Hollins of Shelton, Anthony Keeling of Tunstall, John Turner of Lane End, Jacob Warburton of Hot Lane, William Clowes of Port Hill, and Charles Bagnall of Shelton. The company traded under various styles: Hollins, Warburton, Daniel & Co., etc. Of the six persons concerned, the following are brief details:

Samuel Hollins, a maker of fine red-ware teapots, etc. (from the clay at Bradwell previously worked by the brothers Elers) at Shelton, was the son of Mr. Hollins of the Upper Green, Hanley. He was an excellent practical potter who made many improvements in his art. He was afterwards one of the partners of the New Hall China Works. His successors in the Hollins manufactory were his sons, trading as Messrs. T. & J. Hollins during the 1795–1820 period.

Anthony Keeling, of Tunstall, was son-in-law of the celebrated potter Enoch Booth, having married his daughter Ann. Keeling succeeded Enoch Booth in his business, which he carried on successfully for many years. He erected a large house near the works. In 1810, he retired to Liverpool, where he died.

John Turner, first of Stoke and then of Lane End, father of John and William Turner, was one of the cleverest and most successful potters Staffordshire ever produced. In 1762, he commenced manufacturing at Lane End and made many improvements in the art. By the discovery of a vein of fine clay at Dock Green, he was enabled to compete successfully not only with other potters but also with Wedgwood himself. Many of his productions in black and in jasper, etc. equal those of Wedgwood and are sometimes mistaken for them. Turner's creamware and stoneware (of which his jugs are best known to collectors) rank high in excellence of both design and manipulation.

Jacob Warburton of Hot, or Holt, Lane – a man highly respected by every class, and who lived until the year 1826 – was born in 1740 and passed his long and useful life as a potter, in which art he rose to considerable eminence.

William Clowes of Port Hill, was, it is said, only a sleeping partner in the concern. In 1787, Clowes & Williamson were "potters" at Fenton.

Charles Bagnall, of Shelton, who had previously been with Joshua Heath, was a potter of considerable experience in the middle of the eighteenth century. He was probably a son of the potter of the same name who was a maker of butter-pots in Burslem in about 1710. The family has been connected with Staffordshire for many generations.

The New Hall Company, being thus formed, purchased the patent-rights for hard-paste por-

celain from Richard Champion of Bristol. The first operations were conducted at the works of one of the partners, Anthony Keeling, at Tunstall, which was then a mere small street, or rather roadway, with only a few houses – probably not more than a score – scattered about it and the lanes leading to Chatterley and Red Street. To accommodate the new branch of manufacture at Keeling's pot-works some alterations became necessary, and thus it was some little time before the partners had the satisfaction of seeing anything produced under their patent-right. Disagreements also arose, which ended in Turner and Keeling withdrawing from the concern; and, in about 1780, Keeling is said to have removed to London.

The remaining partners removed their work from Keeling's premises and took a house in Shelton, known as Shelton Hall – afterwards the New Hall in contradistinction to the Old Hall. At this time, Shelton Hall, which had been purchased in 1773 by Humphrey Palmer, was occupied by his son, Thomas Palmer, as a pot-works. In 1777, Humphrey Palmer, intending a second marriage – with Hannah Ashwin of Stratford-on-Avon – gave a rent charge of £30 on the Hall and pot-works and a life interest in the rest of the estate as a dower to that lady, reserving the right for his son, Thomas Palmer the potter, to get clay and marl from any part of the estate for his own use. In 1789, Humphrey Palmer and his wife being both dead, the estate passed to their infant and only child, Mary Palmer, of whose successor's executors, after some uninteresting changes, it was ultimately purchased by the china manufacturers. At this time, the works had been considerably increased; and they grew gradually larger, till, in 1802, they are described as three messuages, three pot-works, one garden, fifty acres of land, thirty acres of meadow, and forty acres of pasture.

Fairly settled at New Hall, the company (Hollins, Warburton & Co.) took as their manager John Daniel, who afterwards became a partner. A considerable quantity of china was produced under the patent, but the most extensive and profitable branch of the New Hall business was reputedly the making and vending

Plate 35. A New Hall porcelain teapot, of typical form, bearing the date 1803. 6 inches high.
Victoria & Albert Museum (Crown copyright)

of glaze (or body) called 'composition', made according to Champion's specification and supplied by the New Hall firm to the potters of the neighbourhood, and even sent to other localities, at a highly remunerative price. In 1810, the firm (Samuel Hollins of Shelton; Peter Warburton, son of Jacob Warburton of Cobridge; John Daniel of Hanley; and William Clowes of Port Hill) purchased the New Hall estate for £6,800. In 1813, Peter Warburton died, leaving his share in the works to his father (Jacob Warburton) and John Daniel as trustees under his will. In 1821, John Daniel died, and two years afterwards Clowes also died.

Hard-paste porcelain continued to be made at New Hall until about 1812, when bone paste – which had been gradually making its way in the district – finally superseded it; and the company continued their works on the newer system. In 1835, the entire stock of the concern,

which had for a short time been carried on for the firm by a Mr. Tittensor, was sold off and the manufacture of china entirely ceased at New Hall.

The early specimens of New Hall porcelain are mainly unmarked or bear only the painted pattern number prefixed by 'N' or 'No'; but of course, other firms also marked their ware in a similar fashion. The body is of good colour and clear, and the decorations, especially the flowered examples, are remarkable for the brightness of their colours. The printed mark used with the pattern number – and this was not, it appears, adopted until about 1812 – is the one shown here. But printing was practised at New Hall and some remarkably good examples have come under my notice, both on the earlier hard paste and on bone china.

The reader is referred to G. E. Stringer's *New Hall Porcelain* (Art Trade Press Ltd., London,

1949) for a detailed history of the works and illustrations of typical specimens. A more recent work is D. Holgate's *New Hall Porcelain and its Imitators* (Faber & Faber, London, 1971).

The works, after having been closed for a short time, were opened by William Ratcliffe, who for a few years made the commoner description of white and printed earthenware for ordinary home consumption. In 1842, they passed into the hands of W. Hackwood & Son, who removed from their works near Joiner Square (later called the Eastwood Pottery); and in 1849, Mr. Hackwood senior having died, they were continued by his son, Thomas Hackwood. The goods were various descriptions of earthenware, principally for Continental markets, and bore the name HACKWOOD impressed.

In 1856, the works passed into the hands of Cockson & Harding, who manufactured the same kind of goods, using the mark C & H, LATE HACKWOOD impressed on the bottom. In 1862, Mr. Cockson having retired from the concern, the works were carried on by the remaining partners – the brothers W. & J. Harding who, besides an extensive trade with Holland and Italy in cream-coloured printed ware, produced druggists' fittings as well as Egyptian black, Rockingham and tinted ware. In 1869, Messrs. Harding gave up the business, when John Aynsley, china manufacturer of Longton, purchased the back portion of the works and let it to Thomas Booth & Sons. The entire front of the New Hall works was purchased by Henry Hall, metal mounter of jugs, teapots, etc., so that the manufactory became divided into two distinct properties. The portion occupied by Messrs. Booth, having been burnt down, was rebuilt. Their productions were the usual classes of ordinary earthenware in printed, painted, enamelled, and gilt services; stoneware, in which a large variety of jugs and teapots were made; and jasper ware. They were succeeded in their business in about 1870 by Ambrose Bevington & Co., who continued the manufacture to about 1890.

From 1892 to 1899, Messrs. Plant & Gilmore were working the New Hall factory. From 1900 to 1957, the New Hall Pottery Co. Ltd. produced a wide range of earthenware including many old patterns and styles.

Market Street

Joseph Glass was a potter in Hanley in the middle of the seventeenth century. His works are stated to have been still carried on by him or his son, Joseph Glass, in the beginning of the eighteenth century. From 1822 to 1838, the works were carried on by John Glass. From him they passed, in 1840, to Samuel Keeling & Co., then in 1852 to J. & G. Meakin, and lastly to Taylor Brothers (1862–71). The works, situated in Market Street, were then pulled down.

Old Hall Works

The Old Hall Works are among the most historically interesting of any in the district, being built on the site of or quite closely adjoining the Old Hall or Manor House of the Colclough family. The works were built in about 1770 by Job Meigh, on what I believe was for a time previously a salt-glaze white-stoneware pottery carried on by a Mr. Whitehead. From 1770 until 1861, the works were uninterruptedly carried on by Job Meigh, his son, and his grandson (Charles Meigh) successively. In 1861, Charles Meigh transferred the business to a limited liability company called The Old Hall Earthenware Company Ltd., by whom it was carried on until 1886, when it became The Old Hall Porcelain Co. Ltd. and as such continued to 1901. The productions included every variety of earthenware, from the most highly decorated to the ordinary blue printed and plain white ware, stoneware, jet ware, and Parian. In earthenware, all the usual dinner, tea, breakfast, dessert, toilet and other services and all other articles were made. In these, the body is of the finest quality, hard, and of remarkable durability, and the glaze hard and clear. Many of the patterns of dinner services are of great beauty and elegance. The form of the covered dishes is chaste and remarkably effective.

Among the patterns produced by the staff of artists employed were many others of great beauty – the excellence of the painting, the gilding, the jewelling, and the enamelling being

Fig. 15. 1851 Exhibits of C. Meigh, Old Hall Works.

very apparent in all, and the combination of printing and hand-painting carried to great perfection. Dessert services made in every style of decoration, the richer and more costly varieties being equal to any produced by other firms in quality of body, in shape, in pattern, and in artistic treatment. Toilet services formed an extensive branch of the productions. In stoneware; jugs and other articles were produced and many bear the manufacturer's name and date of registration of the design; in black ware: water-bottles, elegant little tea-kettles, spill-cases, vases, and other articles were made, and effectively decorated with matt and burnished gilding, enamelling, etc. In Parian: vases, groups, busts, figures and other ornamental articles were produced. The body was of good quality and the modelling and finish excellent.

Some of the marks are the following:

In 1851, medals were awarded to Charles Meigh, who had also received medals from the Society of Arts. Many finely modelled jugs were made in the 1840s and 1850s (Plate 36). Charles Meigh was one of the foremost manufacturers of the day. In contrast to the utilitarian jugs, the reader may refer to the fine vases shown in Plate 37 – a pair of vases first shown at the 1851 Exhibition and now housed in the Victoria & Albert Museum.

Plate 36. A fine and typical Meigh stoneware
moulded jug of a form registered in September 1844.
10 inches high.   *Editor's collection.*

Plate 37. A fine pair of Meigh earthenware vases shown at the 1851 Exhibition. 40 inches high. These vases are now on display in the Victoria and Albert Museum.

Mr. & Mrs. Boas, Kenway Antiques, London.

Birch

Edmund John Birch produced Egyptian black (basalt) articles of good quality from about 1796 to 1813 at Albion Street, Shelton. His mark was the name BIRCH impressed in the ware. Examples can be seen in Plates 57 and 58 in G. Godden's *The Illustrated Encyclopaedia of British Pottery and Porcelain* (Herbert Jenkins, London, 1966).

Shorthose & Co.

The marks SHORTHOSE & CO., SHORT–HOSE, Shorthose & Co. and Shorthose are found on a variety of ware, including ordinary cream-coloured services, white and printed goods, and Egyptian black (basalt) and other articles. John Shorthose worked at Hanley from about 1807 to 1823.

W. Baddeley

William Baddeley produced earthenware and basaltes at Eastwood, Hanley, from 1802 to about 1822. His mark was the word EAST-WOOD impressed. EAST is often poorly impressed, so the mark at first sight might appear to be WEDGWOOD.

61

Plate 38. Representative pieces from a Hicks, Meigh
& Johnson earthenware dinner service of c.1825.
Initial mark H. M. & I. Tureen, 11¼ inches high.
Godden of Worthing Ltd.

Broad Street Works

These works are interesting as being the
place where the celebrated Mason's Patent
Ironstone China, in addition to most varieties
of useful earthenware, was made. Charles James
Mason, the inventor of the famous Mason's
Patent Ironstone China, was a potter of great
skill at Lane Delph. In 1813, he took out a patent
for his process (page 103). The manufacture
was carried on under the styles of G. & C.
Mason and C. J. Mason & Co., the partners
being Charles James Mason and his brother
George Miles Mason. After a time, G. M. Mason
withdrew from the concern, which was then

continued by C. J. Mason. For want of capital and other causes, however, it gradually dwindled; and in 1848, Mason became bankrupt.

Francis Morley purchased many of the moulds and copper-plates, and removed the whole of his manufactory. Mr. Morley, who married a daughter of William Ridgway and was a partner in the firm of Morley, Wear & Co., succeeded to the old-established concern of Hicks, Meigh & Johnson, which he carried on for a time under the style of Ridgway & Co., and afterwards as F. Morley & Co. This manufactory was one of the oldest in the Potteries. Hicks, Meigh & Johnson were among the most successful of the manufacturers in the district and produced, among other ware, a remarkably good quality 'Stone china'. They were also large manufacturers of earthenware of the ordinary and finer kinds (Plate 38), and of china. From 1857 to 1862, Morley was in partnership with George Ashworth. On Morley's retirement, the original Mason moulds passed to the brothers George L. and Taylor Ashworth, who continued the manufacture of Patent Ironstone China (which they and their predecessors sometimes termed 'Real Ironstone China' on their marks) and produced all Mason's best patterns in services, vases, etc., made from his original models. They also manufactured Meigh's stoneware from his old moulds.

Messrs. Ashworth, besides these features of their trade, made table, toilet, dessert and other services, and ornamental goods of the best quality, in every description of general earthenware. In vases and jugs, the handles are usually dragons and other grotesque animals. The vases are of bold form and design, rich in their colours and massive in gilding. The basic marks used by Mason were principally the following:

MASON'S PATENT
IRONSTONE CHINA

or

PATENT IRONSTONE CHINA.

Impressed prior to 1825 in
line or circular form.

Printed 1825+

The reader is referred to R. G. Haggar's *The Masons of Lane Delph* (Lund Humphries, London, 1951) and G. Godden's *The Illustrated Guide to Mason's Patent Ironstone China* (Barrie & Jenkins London, 1971) for a detailed study of the Mason story. The Masons worked several factories during the first half of the nineteenth century.

After the patent passed out of Mason's hands into those of Morley & Co., the principal mark was impressed in the ware,

REAL
IRONSTONE
CHINA

and the royal arms, with supporters, crest, motto, etc., above the words IRONSTONE CHINA was printed on the bottom of the goods. The later marks are on a garter. 'Real Ironstone China' enclosing the royal arms and G. L. Ashworth & Bros. Hanley; Mason's mark with the addition of ASHWORTHS; a crown with the words ASHWORTH BRO[s] above, and a ribbon bearing the words REAL IRONSTONE CHINA beneath it; and the royal arms, with supporters, crest, motto, etc. and the words IRONSTONE CHINA. The Ashworth marks are after 1862.

ASHWORTHS
REAL
IRONSTONE
CHINA

Cauldon Place

These works were founded in about 1802 by Job Ridgway (who had formerly been in partnership with his brother George at the Bell Works, c.1782–1802). Job died in 1814. His two sons, John and William Ridgway, carried on as J. & W. Ridgway. In 1830, a dissolution of partnership took place, John Ridgway continuing the Cauldon Place Works and William removing to

Plate 39. A Ridgway 'Stone China' ewer and basin of pattern number 1362 with pre-1830 initial mark J. W. R., for the brothers John and William Ridgway. Ewer, 10¼ inches high.

Godden of Worthing Ltd.

a new manufactory which he had erected. John Ridgway ware is often unmarked, but it was of very fine quality – in porcelain (Colour Plate IV) as well as in the various types of earthenware. The water-jug and basin shown in Plate 39 are in the durable 'Stone-china' body, and are of the 1820–30 period. A contemporary engraving of 1851 Exhibition pieces is also reproduced in Plate 40.

John Ridgway continued, with various changes of partners, under the style of John Ridgway (& Co.) until 1855, when the Cauldon Place business traded as J. Ridgway, Bates & Co. and then Bates, Brown-Westhead & Co. (1858–61). In 1862, the trading style became T. C. Brown-Westhead, Moore, & Co. Mr. W. Moore, who had for many years been a valuable assistant to Mr. Ridgway, died in 1866, and his brother James Moore – succeeding to the management of the potting – was admitted into partnership in 1875. James Moore died in 1881, and his nephew, Mr. F. T. Moore, took the entire management of the potting department. In 1882, Mr. T. C. Brown-Westhead died, and

William B. Moore, the elder son of William Moore (unitedly with his brother, Mr. Frederick T. Moore) took the entire management of the business. Extensive additions were made to the manufactory in a long range of new buildings, giving increased warehouse accommodation, with rooms for artists, designers, modellers and engravers, and a new show-room. The entire premises were considerably enlarged, and the Royal Victoria Works were added. Over one thousand people were employed by this firm.

The goods produced at Cauldon Place embraced almost every description of ceramics. In earthenware, all the usual table and toilet services and useful and ornamental articles of every class were made. In china, which was of high quality, an immense variety of services and articles were produced, the ground colours being of a remarkable purity and evenness; the gilding, both matt and burnished, was of unusual solidity, and the painting was of the most exquisite character. The same remarks apply with equal force to the dessert ware. Vases of pure and severe taste in form, and displaying great skill and judgment in decoration, were

Plate 40. John Ridgway & Co's porcelain services, reproduced from engravings in the 1851 Exhibition catalogue.

Colour Plate IV. A selection of Ridgway porcelain
teaware of the 1820 period. Pattern number $\frac{2}{825}$
Teapot, $6\frac{1}{2}$ inches high. *Godden of Worthing Ltd.*

Ridgway & Co.'s Table Service.

Ridgway & Co.'s Tea and Coffee Service.

Ridgway & Co.'s Dessert Service.

also produced. In floral encrusted ware, the Cauldon Place works was paramount. In tea services, several novel ideas were introduced. One service has the handle of the cup formed of a cord, doubled and passed through a loop, and either tied around the rim or formed into four knots as feet (Plate 13). The 'egg-shell' china, white body, lined with Rose du Barry, is finer and of higher class than that usually produced; and the floral decorations, in raised gold, silver, and colour, are perfection itself, both in design and in manipulation.

In dinner services, too, the firm took first rank – the patterns being unapproached by any other we have seen in the delicacy of grounding; the richness, clearness and beauty of the matt and burnished, raised and flat gilding; the softness and masterly touch of the painting; the effective admixture of silver with the gold and colours; and the purity of the art-feeling that pervades the whole.

In the 1876–7 period, Messrs. Brown-Westhead, Moore & Co. manufactured for the Prince of Wales a splendid and costly china dessert service decorated with finely-painted hunting subjects, no two pieces being alike. They also made for the Imperial family of Russia richly decorated dinner, tea, dessert and breakfast services, all of which orders were obtained in competition with the Sèvres, Dresden, and other Continental manufactories; and also services for the Emperor of Morocco, including punch-bowls of extraordinary largeness.

The firm also introduced improvements in druggists' and perfumery goods, anti-corrosive taps, etc. The highest class of Parian was also produced. The firm had some years before experimented in the application of photography to the decoration of porcelain, and had produced some interesting specimens. It was not, however, sufficiently successful to be continued. The basic marks used by the Cauldon Place Works were the following, of which many variations occur:

Fig. 16. Messrs. Brown-Westhead, Moore & Co's exhibit at Philadelphia in 1876.

J.W.R. or J & W.R.
Marks c. 1814–30.

J R or J R & Co.
Marks 1830–55.

B W M & Co.
Marks c. 1862–1904.

From 1904, the title became Cauldon Ltd. and, subsequently, Cauldon Potteries Ltd. The trade mark Cauldon occurs as the mark.

The Trent Works

In Joiner Square, the works were built by Stanway, Horne & Adams in 1859. From 1880 to 1885, they were carried on by the surviving partner, Thomas Adams. They were established for the production of ornamental goods in Parian, and useful goods of an improved design in stoneware and ordinary earthenware. Their great speciality was cheap ornamental Parian, in which jugs of various kinds, vases, figures, groups, busts and a large number of other articles were made – no less than 460,000 pieces of these alone being made and disposed of during one year. Notable among the designs for jugs and cream ewers were the Indian corn, pineapple, shell, and dolphin patterns. Classical statuettes, groups and busts in Parian were made a prominent feature of the works. The aim of the Trent Works was the production of good average designs in Parian at a cheap rate,

so as to place them within the reach of all. In this, they were eminently successful. Stoneware, lustre ware, and terra-cotta was also produced. The markets supplied were the home, United States, the Continent, etc. No mark was used. From 1887 to 1900, Messrs. Edwards & Son manufactured Parian and majolica at the Trent Works.

Keeling

In 1796, James Keeling patented improvements in decorative and glazing processes, and, in conjunction with Valentine Close, some improvements in ovens, kilns, and processes of firing. His ware was of remarkably good quality, and some of the services were decorated with series of scenes and views. He continued at New Street until 1831.

Stafford Street Works

This manufactory was originally occupied by Reuben Johnson & Co., from 1817 to 1823, who produced the ordinary classes of earthenware and stoneware. From them, it passed to Thomas Furnival jun & Co., in about 1840, and Furnival & Clark, by whom it was continued until 1851, when it was taken by Livesley, Powell and Co. In 1866, Mr. Livesley went out of the concern, and the firm changed its name to Powell & Bishop, by which it continued till 1878 when, John Stonier of Liverpool having joined the concern, it changed to Powell, Bishop & Stonier. The firm owned two other manufactories – the Church Works for white granite, and the Waterloo Works for china (see page 69).

At Stafford Street, earthenware alone was produced – but this was of the finest quality and in every style of decoration, for the home, French, Australian and other markets. The body was extremely hard, compact and durable, and, whether in pure white or of the rich, deep and full creamy tint of their 'Oriental Ivory' body, was clear in colour. The decoration of the dinner services, which were a speciality of these works, ranges from the plain white and printed goods up to the most elaborately and gorgeously enamelled, painted and gilt varieties; and in each of these stages, the decorations –

Plate 41. A Powell & Bishop earthenware toilet set, the design registered in March 1878. Jug, 13½ inches high.　　　　　　　　　　*Private collection.*

whether simple or complicated – are characterised by the most artistic feeling. In toilet services, a number of effective and well-conceived designs were produced in transfer printing, lustred, enamelled, painted, and gilt varieties. The ewers are, in shape and decoration, of unusually good designs. A part toilet set of a design registered in 1878 is shown in Plate 41.

Dinner, tea, and dessert services were also made in the finest earthenware, and of considerable variety and beauty in design. The firm, besides reproducing in all its softness and delicacy of tint and evenness of surface the famous old ivory or cream-coloured ware of Josiah Wedgwood, introduced a beautiful ware which they called 'Oriental Ivory'. In this, dinner, tea, dessert and toilet services and ornamental were made. The firm received medals from the Exhibition in 1862, and were large exhibitors at Philadelphia in 1876.

The marks used by the firm have been the words $\begin{smallmatrix} \text{BEST} \\ \text{P \& B} \end{smallmatrix}$ and a triangle enclosing a circle, impressed in the ware; and the initials P & B, or P B & S, in addition to the name of the pattern, printed on the surface. The trade mark, adopted in about 1875, was the Caduceus, impressed in the body or printed on the surface of the best goods; the special mark for the 'Oriental Ivory' being a Chinese man seated on the ground, holding over his head an umbrella bearing the words ORIENTAL IVORY. The 'London' services have a banner bearing the words LONDON P B & S.

Messrs. Powell, Bishop & Stonier continued to 1891, when they were succeeded by Messrs. Bishop & Stonier – who continued to the 1930s. Similar marks to the above were used.

Waterloo Works

In about 1875, these works were erected for the manufacture of china by Powell, Bishop & Stonier, in place of one formerly occupied by them but removed for town improvements. At this manufactory, china of the finest quality was made in the white – the whole of the decoration being accomplished at their principal works in Stafford Street (see preceding entry). In china, the firm produced all the usual services and miscellaneous articles in every variety of decoration. In dessert services this firm ranked high, not only for the quality of the body and glaze and beauty of their designs but also for the artistic feeling and excellent finish which characterise their best productions. In these, and in tea services, they introduced with excellent effect a species of decoration which may be said to give the appearance to the various articles of being inlaid with ormolu.

Plate 42. John Bevington's porcelain in the Dresden-style. Crossed-swords mark with J. B. monogram below. c.1880. Candlesticks, 8¼ inches high.
Godden of Worthing Ltd.

They also introduced a new china body of the most delicate green tint, in which they produced a variety of articles – notably the 'Dovedale' tea set and 'Victoria' dessert service – which were chastely decorated and became very popular.

Kensington Works

Established by Wilkinson & Rickuss in about 1856, who were succeeded in 1862 by Wilkinson & Sons, and next by Bailey & Bevington. Mr. Bailey having retired in 1872, the works were carried on by John Bevington, who produced ordinary earthenware, ornamental china, Parian and stoneware – the speciality being imitation Dresden for home, United States and Australian markets. In the 1880s, John Bevington advertised 'Reproductions of the Old Dresden, Derby, Chelsea, and Worcester patterns, in figures, vases, candelabra (1, 2, 3, 4 & 5 lights) baskets, etc.'. Many of the items bear a blue mark of the crossed swords (of Dresden) with the monogram J.B. A pair of marked figure-candlesticks of this type are shown in

Plate 42. John Bevington continued at the Kensington Works until his death in 1892.

Burton Place Works

This manufactory was worked by Thomas Bevington (1877–90), whose family had held it since 1862. The productions were china, in which all the usual useful and ornamental classes of goods were made for the home markets, fancy ivory earthenware, gold-thread ware, and a patent 'Victorian Ware' in which the surface is covered with felspar crystals, decorated with veins of gold to represent gold-bearing quartz. The mark is the royal arms and BY ROYAL LETTERS PATENT. The ordinary mark is the double triangle, between the initials T.B., enclosing a crown in its centre. Formerly, Parian statuettes and majolica goods were made, but these were discontinued in about 1870. The gold-thread ware has the surface covered and matted with fine threads in the most intricate manner, and these are gilt and form a ground upon which well-modelled flowers are added. In china, imitations of the old Crown Derby patterns were produced to a considerable extent and with success. The patterns, colours and gilding are all in good style, and the quality of the china body is excellent. Thomas Bevington succeeded J. & T. Bevington from 1867 to 1877.

Clarence Street Works

Here, from 1874 to 1879, Ambrose Bevington produced the usual classes of earthenware and china. In 1880, he removed to the New Hall Works, and was succeeded by the Crystal Porcelain Company, and then in 1882 by C. Littler & Co., who were extensive manufacturers of high-class earthenware. In this, all the usual dinner, breakfast, tea, toilet and dessert services were made in all the most popular styles of decoration. C. Littler & Co. continued to 1884.

Nelson Place

Commenced in 1850 by John Bamford, these works produced ordinary stoneware and Parian until 1883.

Phoenix and Bell Works

These manufactories in Broad Street were both worked by Clementson Brothers, who made white granite and common painted ware for America and Canada. For the latter market, they also produced some good decorated ware. The back part of the Phoenix Works was originally part of John and Edward Baddeley's Broad Street Works (later taken by the Ashworth Brothers), which it adjoined.

In 1832, the Clementson business was started by Reed & Clementson, but Joseph Clementson shortly after became sole proprietor and, in 1845, enlarged the works. In 1856, he purchased the Bell Works on the other side of the road, opposite the Phoenix, formerly William Ridgway's. In 1867, he retired from business, leaving it to his four sons, who continued under the title Clementson Bros until 1916. An attractively printed Clementson plate bearing the date 1839 is shown in Plate 43.

The Bedford Works

These works at Shelton were built by Edward John Ridgway, son of William Ridgway, in 1866, and to them he removed from the Church Works, High Street, where he had carried on business in partnership with Mr. Abington during the 1848–60 period. In 1870, Mr. Ridgway took his sons into partnership, and the concern was carried on as E. J. Ridgway & Sons. In 1872, he retired in favour of his two sons, John and Edward Ackroyd Ridgway, who were joined in partnership by Joseph Sparks and continued the business as Ridgway, Sparks & Ridgway until 1879. Their productions included all classes of fine useful earthenware, jet, stone, terracotta, and jasper, of very superior bodies and decoration, for the home, American and Continental markets.

One of the great specialities of the firm was their jet ware, highly decorated in raised enamel, after the Limoges ware. In these, a remarkable richness, beauty, and delicacy was obtained; and the designs, as well as the treatment of the foliage and figures, were artistic and well considered for effect. Another speciality was relief decoration on various stoneware bodies. Jasper

Plate 43. A Joseph Clementson printed earthenware plate dated 1839. Printed name and address mark.
Editor's collection.

teapots and other articles were produced. Mosaic and inlaid decoration was also successfully carried out by the firm, and their ordinary stoneware jugs and other articles are remarkable for purity of design, the high relief of their ornament and the hardness and compactness of their body. The mark is the Staffordshire knot, enclosing the letters R.S.R. From 1879, the Bedford Works have been part of Messrs. Ridgway's, later to become Ridgway's (Bedford Works) Ltd. and today Ridgway Potteries Ltd.

Mayer Street Works

In about 1877, Samuel Lear erected a small china works on part of the site of the old manufactory, which included as warerooms and offices the residence of the Mayers. Mr. Lear produced domestic china and, in addition, decorated all kinds of earthenware made by other manufacturers – a speciality being spirit-kegs. He added to his Mayer Street works a new manufactory, built by himself in 1882, in the High Street and there carried on a successful manufacture of ordinary china, majolica, ivory body earthenware, and Wedgwood-type jasper ware. Samuel Lear fell on bad times in 1886 and his creditors closed the works.

Cannon Street

These works, dating back to the beginning of the nineteenth century, were for many years carried on by Thomas Ford (and T. & C. Ford) who here commenced business and later built a larger manufactory in the same street. From 1875, the business was carried on by Edward Steele, who produced earthenware of the more ordinary qualities, stoneware of good useful character, majolica, and Parian. In stoneware, all the usual useful classes of goods were made, and many of the designs and workmanship were of good character. In majolica, both useful and

71

ornamental goods were produced. Parian statuary – one of the specialities of the firm – was extensively made, some hundreds of different single figures, groups, busts, and animals, besides numbers of ornamental articles, being issued. Edward Steele continued to 1900. He did not mark his products.

Percy Street

It was recorded in 1878 and again in 1883 that William Machin made ordinary earthenware and common coloured figures at Percy Street. This simple statement is important as it is one of the very few contemporary references to Victorian Staffordshire figures (see Plate 44) and their manufacturers. From 1875 to 1884, William Machin worked at Percy Street; and from 1884 to 1912, he worked at the Dresden Works, George Street, Hanley. William Machin is recorded as one of the producers of Staffordshire dogs (Plate 23) in 1890.

Eastwood Vale

Taylor, Tunnicliffe & Co., who formerly manufactured in Broad Street very excellent door-furniture and other fittings for Birmingham houses, built more commodious works here in 1876. They continue to the present day as manufacturers of porcelain for electrical purposes.

Albion Works

At these works in Stafford Street, John Dimmock & Co. were large producers of earthenware of superior quality and finish from about 1862 to 1878. The old-established firm of Thomas Dimmock & Co., when John Ward's *History of Stoke-on-Trent* was published in 1843, held three manufactories: one 'in Hanley, adjoining the New Market house, formerly

Plate 44. Three typical Staffordshire earthenware figures of the type made by William Machin and other Staffordshire manufacturers, c.1860.
Private collection.

James Whitehead's, afterwards J. & W. Handley's; another on the upper end of Shelton, formerly of Edmund John Birch, afterwards of Christopher Whitehead; and an enamelling and gilding establishment adjoining the King's Head at Shelton'. J. Dimmock & Co. were succeeded in 1878 by W. D. Cliff, who continued to 1904, but the old title John Dimmock & Co. was retained.

Hope Street Works

Established in 1800. In 1838, James Dudson entered upon the works and carried them on till his death in 1882. They were then continued by his son. At one time, ornamental china figures, vases, and services were made. The productions were later white and coloured stoneware jugs, tea and coffee pots, sugar-boxes, etc., metal-mounted goods, flower-pots,

Plate 45. A selection of Dudson Brothers' jasper ware in the Wedgwood style. This ware was made in dark blue, dark green, sage green, light blue and brown grounds. Reproduced from a *Pottery Gazette* advertisement of 1898.

Trent Pottery

Established at Eastwood in 1867 by Livesley & Davis, the style was, on the retirement of Mr. Livesley in 1871, changed to J. H. & J. Davis. In 1875, J. Davis retired, and then the concern was carried on by J. H. Davis alone in 1891. Until about 1870, the productions were confined to white granite-ware for the United States, but dinner, toilet, and tea services, and other articles, both for the home and foreign markets were later added. He was also an extensive maker of sanitary ware.

Brewery Works

From 1871 to 1879, Robert Cook made Parian goods in large quantities, for the American market, at the Brewery Works.

candlesticks, etc. Among the registered designs for jugs were the 'Fern', 'Argyle', 'Barley', 'Vine-border', 'Pineapple', and 'Wheatsheaf' patterns, which were produced in a variety of colours. Wedgwood-type jasper ware in brown, green or blue was also produced in quantity (Plate 45). In mosaic ware, Mr. Dudson made a variety of articles in white, drab, blue, and other bodies inlaid with a variety of colours. These included tea and coffee-pots, sugar-bowls, jugs, etc., of different shapes. James Dudson, who received 'honourable mention' in the Exhibitions of 1851 and 1862, supplied both home and foreign markets. Some ware, including jugs and rare hen boxes, is impressed-marked DUDSON. Messrs. Dudson Brothers Ltd. continue at Hope Street, Hanley, to the present day.

Victoria Works

At these works in St. James Street, the productions of Adams & Bromley, carried on until 1873 as John Adams & Co., were majolica and jasper ware of high class, both in quality and design. Parian portrait busts were produced, and were remarkable for their truthfulness and artistic treatment. In jasper, besides vases and candlesticks, tea and other services, tea and coffee-pots, table-kettles, fruit-bowls, jugs and a variety of other decorative and useful articles, cameos and medallions for inlaying and other ornamental purposes were made to a large extent and of satisfactory quality. The jasper is, in quality and in general character of ornamentation and colour, a very close imitation of the Wedgwood ware; and the shapes of many of the articles evince good taste in design. In majolica, bread-trays, cheese-trays, candlesticks, flower-pots, vases, garden-seats, jardinieres, figures, and a very large variety of useful and ornamental goods were produced. The quality of the majolica was far above the average; the workmanship in all cases was skilful and good. Notable among these are a large flower-vase, some four feet in height, with a well modelled Cupid supporting the bowl; a flower vase on mask feet and surrounded by a wreath of oak-leaves; another large vase in which the handles are formed of Cupids; water-lily and other well conceived dessert pieces, etc. Green-glazed dessert ware was also extensively made. The mark is the name ADAMS & CO., or ADAMS & BROMLEY, or A. & B. Messrs. Adams & Bromley continued to 1894.

Charles Street Works

This manufactory, which was carried on by J. W. Pankhurst (& Co.), is one of the oldest in Hanley. In the 1880s, it was owned and worked by Charles Mellor. Mr. Mellor made Egyptian black ware for the Dutch markets, as did his successors, Toft & Keeling, who also produced other varieties of earthenware. It was next carried on by Toft & May in the 1825 to 1833 period, and then by Robert May, who was succeeded by William Ridgway, who changed the manufacture to that of white

granite goods for the American markets and was succeeded by J. W. Pankhurst & Co. in about 1850. They continued (at Old Hall Street) until 1883. The mark used by the firm was the royal arms and name, printed in black, on the ware.

Cobden Works, High Street

These works formed a part of those founded in the latter part of the eighteenth century by Elijah Mayer, who in about 1805 took his son into partnership under the style of Elijah Mayer & Son (1805–34). It was afterwards Joseph Mayer and Joseph Mayer & Co. Elijah Mayer was a potter of considerable eminence, and he produced an extensive variety of goods. His Egyptian black or basalt ware was, in quality of body, nearly equal to that of Wedgwood, and the ornamentation was sharp and well defined; in this, he produced teapots, cream-ewers, bowls, and other articles. In cream-coloured ware, services and all the usual useful articles were made, and were of unusually good style and quality. For these and his 'brown line' patterns he was noted. His cane-coloured or drab unglazed goods were another of his famous productions. Elijah Mayer produced a service commemorative of Nelson's Trafalgar and Nile victories which became very popular. His mark was 'E.Mayer' impressed in the ware, and afterwards 'E.Mayer & Son'. Of the later firm, some examples with the name Joseph Mayer & Co. are recorded.

In 1867, the premises were purchased by Gelson Brothers, who in 1876 dissolved partnership, the business being conducted by Thomas Gelson & Co., who in 1881 were succeeded by James Bevington (previously of J. & T. Bevington), who produced to a large extent and in great variety all the usual classes of decorated china and fancy goods. James Bevington continued to 1885.

Messrs. Gelson & Co., who originally made white granite-ware for the American markets, abandoned that branch and confined themselves to the production of the highest classes of useful goods for the home trade. In this, they made dinner, tea, breakfast, toilet and other services in every variety of printed, enamelled, and gilt patterns. One of their specialities was the successful imitation of the old Dresden style. Another of their decorative ideas was the introduction of Anglo-Saxon and early Irish interlaced ornaments in bands encircling mouthewers and other articles.

Eagle Works

This business, commenced at Longton in 1845, was removed to Hanley in 1848 by James Meakin. In 1852, he retired and was succeeded by two of his sons, James and George Meakin. In 1859, the business having considerably increased, the Eagle Works were erected, and in 1868 were considerably enlarged. The firm had also branch works at Cobridge and Burslem, and were large producers of earthenware, the

IRONSTONE CHINA.
J. & G. MEAKIN.

speciality being white granite-ware in imitation of French china. The mark is J. & G. MEAKIN, stamped in the ware and printed in black.

Pearl Pottery

These works, in Brook Street, were established by Ralph Salt (worked 1820–43, died 1846) and he and his successors, Richard Booth and Williams & Willet, manufactured painted earthenware figures. In 1860, the works passed into the hands of William Taylor, who commenced making white granite and common coloured and painted ware. But this he discontinued, and confined himself to white granite-ware for the United States and Canadian markets, of both qualities – the bluish tinted for the provinces, and the purer white for the city trade. He was succeeded in 1881 by Wood, Hines & Winkle, who produced 'opaque porcelain' in all the usual services for dinner, tea, breakfast and toilet; a large number of specialities in dejeuner, five o'clock tea, trinket, and beer sets; vases, plaques, cruets, and other useful and ornamental articles up to 1885. From 1885 to 1889, Messrs. Winkle & Wood worked the Pearl Pottery; and from about 1892, it was worked by Messrs. Wood & Bennett. A Wood, Hines & Winkle advertisement of 1884 is reproduced in Figure 17.

Cannon Street

Charles Ford (formerly Thomas & Charles Ford, 1854–74) manufactured here the best class of china in tea, breakfast, dessert, and table services for the home markets. Charles Ford built up a large trade from 1874 and continued to about 1904. His mark is a monogram of the initials C.F., often placed inside the outline of a swan.

Norfolk Street Works

These works in Cauldon Place, established by R. G. Scrivener and Thomas Bourne (R. G. Scrivener & Co.) in 1870, were situated about midway between Stoke and Hanley. The productions were good quality, decorative china tea, breakfast, dessert and other services and fancy articles, and earthenware toilet and other services of a more than average degree of artistic decoration. They exported considerably to the colonies, and also supplied the home markets. The mark is the initials $\begin{smallmatrix} R.G.S. \\ \& Co. \end{smallmatrix}$ impressed. They continued to 1883.

Broad Street

The old established works formerly occupied by George Ash, from 1865 to 1882, as a Parian and majolica manufactory were carried on by Grove & Cope from 1883 for the production of fancy china ornaments. Mr. Grove continued alone to 1885. George Ash was a noted manufacturer of Parian and earthenware teapots and jugs with metal covers.

Eastwood Pottery

Here, William Stubbs manufactured china and earthenware services of the commoner kinds, lustres, stoneware jugs, black teapots, etc., and the smaller and commoner classes of earthenware toys and ornaments.

Fig. 17. Wood, Hines & Winkle advertisement of 1884.

This is another interesting contemporary reference to the manufacturers of unmarked Staffordshire earthenware figures ('toys') of the type shown in Plate 46, although these models cannot be identified with this one manufacturer.

William Stubbs was at the Eastwood Pottery from 1862 to 1897. He started in about 1847 at the Waterloo Works, Hanley. Lustre earthenware was extensively made here.

Ranelagh Works

Established in 1846 by Mr. Stephenson, these works were successively occupied by James Oldham, Oldham & Co., T. R. Hindle, and Hollinshead & Stonier, and from 1875 to 1885

by Jones & Hopkinson, who produced all the commoner classes of earthenware and stoneware services and general articles. From 1886 to 1892, these works were occupied by Messrs. Jones, Hopkinson & Sherwin.

Swan Works

In Elm Street, established by Samuel Bevington as Parian works and afterwards carried on by his son, John Bevington, Swan Works passed in 1866 into the hands of W. L. Evans & Co., and in 1871 to Neale, Harrison & Co., who gave up the manufacturing and confined themselves to decoration only. They were succeeded by T. A. Simpson, who continued to about 1887. This firm continued at the separate Cliff Bank

76

Plate 46. A selection of Staffordshire earthenware
figures of the general type made by William Stubbs
and other manufacturers, c.1840–70. Large three-
dog group, 9½ inches high. *Godden of Worthing Ltd.*

Works and in the twentieth century produce tiles, under the style T. A. Simpson & Co. Ltd., at Burslem and at Stoke.

Brook Street Works

These works were under the partnership of Worthington & Green from 1844 to 1864. Messrs. Worthington & Son continued until 1893 and produced earthenware and stoneware, both for home and foreign markets.

Dresden Works

In 1843, Edward Raby produced at these works in Tinkersclough china ornaments with raised or 'Dresden' flowers. From 1856 until 1864, they were carried on by John Worthington and William Harrop; from that time until 1875 by Thomas Worthington and William Harrop under the style Worthington & Harrop; and from that time by William Harrop alone. The productions were the cheaper classes of Parian goods and fancy jugs in stoneware and ordinary earthenware, of good middle-class quality, all of which were supplied both to the home and American markets. From 1880 to 1894, the firm was William Harrop & Co.

The works were situated at what was called Tinkersclough – a place whose name is said to be 'derived from the fact of its being frequented in the olden times as a place of rendezvous by gipsies and travelling tinkers'.

Excelsior Works

These works in New Street were established in 1873 by Banks & Thorley, who, having removed to new premises, were succeeded by Dean, Capper & Dean, who manufactured jet, china and earthenware from about 1882 to 1885.

Waterloo Works

In Lower Charles Street, these were old-established works which had been occupied by W. Stubbs, Thomas Booth & Son, Holmes & Plant, Pugh & Glover, Beech & Morgan (1880–

2) and G. & B. Burton. The higher and better classes of china and earthenware in toilet and other services – painted, enamelled, and grounded – stoneware jugs, teapots, and jet and other ware were largely made and had all the usual classes of decoration, both for home and foreign markets. The 'milk sets' or 'beer sets' are good in form of tray, jug, and horns, and are the most artistic of any produced; as are also their Stilton cheese-tubs and egg-frames, the body of which is of the purest ivory colour. In 1889, G. & B. Burton (Burton Bros.) moved to Stoke.

Boston Works

Messrs. Banks & Thorley (est. 1875), having for the purpose erected a new manufactory, removed to the Boston Works, High Street, in 1879 from their works in New Street. Their productions were majolica, terra-cotta, jet, and stoneware, and these they produced for both home and foreign markets. In terra-cotta, water-bottles of porous body unglazed, of elegant forms and of a more or less highly decorated character, with stoppers and stands; water-goblets, tobacco-jars, etc., were made in great variety. These porous goods were of three distinct kinds – a clear full red, a buff, and a purplish white. They were printed, painted, enamelled, and gilt in encircling borders, wreaths, etc., in groups of flowers and ferns, or in Japanese figure subjects, and were of excellent shape and workmanship. In majolica, cheese-stands, bread-trays, dessert services, jugs, egg-holders, jardinieres, flower-pots, tea-pots, ladies' work-baskets, water-bottles and an infinitely wide variety of ornamental articles were made. Notable among the dessert services in majolica is one with a rich chocolate-coloured ground, which throws out, with a strikingly beautiful and rich effect, a naturally arranged group of ivy, ferns and anemones. Besides these, green glaze dessert services and a large variety of other articles, both useful and ornamental, were made. Banks & Thorley became Banks & Co. in 1887 and Edward Banks from 1888 to 1889.

New Street

Messrs. J. & R. Hammersley (who also had works in Nelson Place) had here an establishment for decorating china of all descriptions. Their name occurs in Patent Office records in 1887. This firm continued to 1917.

Castle Field Pottery

These works, discontinued in about 1880, were at one time carried on by Mr. Ball, who distinguished himself as the first to bring out hollow and glazed bricks, and these he made for Prince Albert's model cottages. They were from his works at Poole, in Dorsetshire, and matured at Etruria. In 1860, Davenport, Banks & Co. established themselves here, and manufactured fancy goods until 1873, when Mr. Banks retired and was succeeded by Mr. Beck

Plate 47. A pair of black-ground gold-printed earthenware vases by Davenport, Beck & Co. (initial mark), c.1873–80. 10½ inches high.
Private collection.

as Davenport, Beck & Co. until 1880. The principal productions were fancy antique goods, majolica in all its varieties, porous goods, terra-cotta water-bottles, etc., jet ware, and the ordinary earthenware. The mark was a castle and the letters D.B. & CO. ETRURIA within an oval garter bearing the words TRADE MARK. A pair of gold decorated Davenport, Beck & Co. vases of the 1873–80 period are shown in Plate 47.

Henry Venables

The Etruria Road Works, established in 1860, manufactured Etruscan-red porous goods, black basalt ware, jet glazed ware, and blue and other coloured jaspers. In these, Henry Venables produced a large variety of vases, as well as other ornamental and useful goods, until about 1869.

Boothen Works

Messrs. Dunn, Bennett & Co. here manufactured earthenware and ironstone china in all the usual services, both for the home and American markets. Their productions were of a high quality; and having retail establishments both in London and New York, they were in a position to cater successfully for both countries. Messrs. Dunn, Bennett & Co. were at the Boothen Works from 1878 to 1887 and subsequently at Burslem.

Pelham Street Pottery

These works were built in 1877 by the firm of Pugh & Glover, of the Waterloo Works, from which in that year they removed. They produced all the usual services and articles in ordinary earthenware and in every style of decoration, as well as stoneware jugs and other articles for both home and foreign markets. From 1887 to 1892, Messrs. Pugh & Hackney were at the Pelham Street Works.

Pelham Street Works

Built in 1881 by Alfred Bullock & Co. for the manufacture of majolica and jet ware, both of which they produced in large quantities and of great excellence in body and decoration.

From 1887 to 1893, Messrs. Bullock & Cornes were at Pelham Street; and then Messrs. Bullock & Bennett, from 1894 to 1902.

Upper Hanley Works

In 1875, Messrs. Hollinshead & Stonier, at that time of the Ranelagh Works, were joined in partnership by Mr. Holmes and removed to this manufactory in the High Street, where they carried on the business under the style of Holmes, Stonier & Hollinshead until 1882, when it was changed to Stonier, Hollinshead & Oliver. Their productions were the useful classes of earthenware and white granite for the home, American, South African and Australian markets. This firm continued to 1891.

Hallfield Pottery

Built in 1882 by Messrs. Whittaker, Edge & Co., who made a fair quality of general earthenware for all markets until 1886. Whittaker & Co. continued to 1892, and Whittaker Heath & Co. from 1892 to 1898.

Havelock Works

At these works in Broad Street, Mrs. J. Massey, formerly of Mayer Street, made earthenware jugs, teapots and general majolica in about 1882.

Falcon Pottery

Messrs. J. H. Weatherby & Sons established a small works at Tunstall in 1891. In the following year, they moved to the larger Falcon Pottery in the High Street at Hanley. Good quality earthenware tableware has been produced up to the present time. The marks include the initials J H W & Sons or the name 'Weatherby'.

Marlborough Works

Messrs. Mountford & Thomas made majolica of good quality at these works in Union Street.

Dessert sets, baskets, tea-sets, garden seats, etc. from 1881 to 1888.

Union Street Works

H. Shenton made common general earthenware from about 1881 to 1902.

Providence Pottery

Elijah Rigby jun. produced common earthenware from 1882 to 1889 at this pottery in Chell Street.

Pyenest Street Works

Messrs. J. & J. Snow (also of Albert Works, Stoke) produced terra-cotta, jet, and ordinary earthenware here from 1877 to 1907.

Eastwood Pottery

Charles Meakin had a manufactory for American granite-ware at the Eastwood Pottery, Lichfield Street, from 1883 to 1889.

In 1829, the Hanley manufactories named by Simeon Shaw were E. Mayer & Son; Job Meigh & Son (Old Hall); Dimmock & Co; Toft & May; J. Keeling; W. Hackwood; T. Taylor; J. Glass; J. & W. Ridgway; Hicks, Meigh & Johnson; H. Daniel & Sons; J. Yates; and Hollins, Warburton, Daniel & Co. (The New Hall Company).

Those enumerated by John Ward in 1843 are the Old Hall Works. the New Hall Works; Cauldon Place Works; William Ridgway and partners (six manufactories); Thomas Dimmock & Co. (four manufactories); Samuel Keeling & Co; William Hackwood; Samuel and John Burton; Samuel Mayer; Thomas Furnival, junior & Co; George Lomas; Joseph Clementson; Yates & May, formerly John and William Yates, successors to their father; William Dudson; William White; Henry Mills, then newly erected; and other smaller factories. Edward Phillips was also a manufacturer, and used his name in full 'Edward

Phillips, Shelton, Staffordshire' on his goods. Other names are J. Sneyd, Toft & May, and T. Taylor.

Hanley potters working in 1900 and not previously listed include:
Art Pottery Company
Bennett & Shenton
W. Bennett
A. Bullock & Co.
Cartlidge & Matthias
E. Cotton
M. Dean
Gray & Co.
A. G. Hackney
Hanley China Co.

J. Howlett & Co.
Kirkland & Co.
Lancaster & Sons
W. Moore & Co.
Morris & Co.
J. Peake
Pearl Pottery Co.
Pointon & Co. Ltd.
Rigby & Stevenson
W. Sandland
Sherwin & Cotton
Smith & Co.
U. Thomas & Co.
Upper Hanley Pottery Co.
Victoria Pottery Co.
Wardle & Co.

LANE END

Turner

William and John Turner, whose manufactory was in the High Street, have been previously referred to in this work (page 56). They were among the best and most successful potters at the end of the eighteenth century and early part of the nineteenth century. In about 1756, John Turner and Mr. Banks made white stoneware at Stoke; but in 1762, Turner removed to Lane End, 'where he manufactured every kind of pottery then in demand, and also introduced some other kinds not previously known'. In about 1780, he discovered a valuable vein of fine clay at Green Dock, from which he 'obtained all his supplies for manufacturing his beautiful and excellent stoneware pottery of a cane colour, which he formed into very beautiful jugs, with ornamental designs, and the most tasteful articles of domestic use' (see an article by E.N.Stretton in *Apollo* magazine of October 1958). Turner produced 'a shining blue glazed pottery similar to that of the Japanese porcelain', as well as making many other improvements in the art.

He died in 1786 and was succeeded by his sons, William and John Turner, who became, as above mentioned, among the best potters of the day, equalling in many respects Josiah Wedgwood himself. In jasper ware, Egyptian black, and other finer ware there is little choice between Turner and Wedgwood, although the composition of each firm's bodies was not the same and had been obtained by different processes. In 1800, Messrs. Turner took out a patent for a new method of manufacturing porcelain

and earthenware by the introduction of 'Tabberners Mine Rock' ('Little Mine Rock' or 'New Rock'). The works were closed in about 1805.

TURNER.

The mark used by the Turners was simply the name TURNER, impressed on the jasper and other bodies. On their blue-bordered and printed ware they sometimes used the Prince of Wales' feathers, with the name 'Turner' beneath. On rare ware, often with Japan-style patterns (see Plate 48) produced under the 1800 patent, the written mark 'Turner's Patent' occurs. From about 1803 to 1805 or 1806 the style was Turner & Co. Mr. Bevis Hillier's book *Master Potters of the Industrial Revolution – The Turners of Lane End* (Cory, Adams & Mackay, London 1965) is a mine of information on the Turners.

C. Heathcote & Co.

The Heathcotes were potters in Lane End from about 1815 to 1824. The ware produced was good quality blue-printed, painted, and gilt services, and ornamental goods. The mark

was the Prince of Wales' feathers with the name C.HEATHCOTE & CO. above and, on a ribbon beneath, the name of the pattern – such as CAMBRIA.

Plate 48. Typical specimens of 'Turner's Patent' ware of the 1800 period. Covered cup, 5½ inches high. *Godden of Worthing Ltd.*

Myatt

'At the southern extremity of Foley,' wrote Shaw in 1829, 'are the house and factory of the late Mr. Myatt, one of the first persons who received the Wesleyan and Methodist preachers, and in whose parlour Wesley stood, while from the window he preached to a vast congregation when last he passed through Staffordshire only a few months prior to his decease.' Myatt produced ordinary white and printed earthenware and red-ware in about 1802. His mark was his name, impressed: MYATT.

It should be noted that other, and later, potters used this mark.

Harley

Thomas Harley, a manufacturer at Lane End, produced some good earthenware services, jugs, and other articles during the period 1805 to 1812. He sometimes marked with his name in full in writing letters *T. Harley, Laneend,* and at other times HARLEY, impressed.

Bailey & Batkin

This firm made a fine quality of silver lustre. There was in the Mayer collection a service of it, and one large piece with BAILEY & BATKIN, SOLE PATENTEES running round a central band (Plate 49). Messrs. Bailey & Batkin worked from 1814 to about 1822. Records indicate that this firm produced unmarked lustre tea-sets, etc., for the American market.

Mayer & Newbold

This firm produced excellent porcelain and earthenware from about 1817 to 1833. One of their marks was

and another 'Mayer & Newbold' in full. At other times, the initials M & N were used. Examples are rare. Richard Newbold continued from 1833 to 1837.

Plate 49. A rare silver-lustre 'Perdifume', bearing the moulded name of the patentees, Messrs. Bailey & Batkin of Lane End, c.1820. 8½ inches high.

Godden of Worthing Ltd.

LONGTON

Sutherland Road Works

These works were commenced in 1862 by Messrs. Adams, Scrivener & Co. Mr. Scrivener having a few years afterwards retired from the business, Mr. Adams was joined by Titus Hammersley and the concern was carried on by them under the style of Harvey Adams & Co. until the death of Mr. Hammersley in 1875, when he was succeeded by his son George Harris Hammersley, the style of the firm remaining as before. The productions comprised china, semi-china, and fine stoneware. In earthenware, toilet and all the usual table services, and numberless useful articles of the best designs and highest finish were made. In stoneware, jugs, teapots, and other articles were produced, as was also in china, tea, breakfast, dinner, dessert, trinket, toilet and other services, jugs of various kinds, vases, and an endless variety of ornamental and highly decorated goods. The quality of the china was remarkably fine and good, and the glaze of more than average excellence.

In tea and breakfast services, many novel but at the same time chastely beautiful designs were introduced by this firm, who have also the credit of being the first to make and introduce 'moustache cups' – an invention that became so popular as to be adopted by many other firms. These services made by Harvey, Adams & Co. were in every style, from the simple white and gold to the most richly, even gorgeously-painted, gilt, enamelled, and jewelled varieties. In some services – both tea and dessert – what may be called an ormolu decoration was introduced. It gave a richness and a

solidity to the patterns which could not otherwise be easily obtained. The jewelling – especially the pearl borders – was admirably executed, and with marked effect.

Two important features in the productions of these works were the introduction of silver, both as a ground and as a heightening, and of embossed leaf decoration of a peculiar and artistic character. In like manner with gold, the silver is introduced both matt and burnished and forms a pleasing and marvellously rich combination with gold and colour. It was introduced on tea services in bands upon wreaths of flowers, and other decorations are painted with marked effect. One of the finest and most chastely beautiful of the ceramic productions is an open-work plate in which solid silver forms the ground for the centre. On this silver ground is painted, with all the skill that art is capable of, a group of flowers. The richness and delicacy of the colouring are 'thrown-up' and a finer and more exquisitely beautiful effect is produced by this ground than could by any other means have been effected. The open-rim work, with its interlaced ribbon, and the whole of the subordinate decorations, is in excellent keeping and harmony with the central group.

In leaf-decoration, Harvey Adams & Co. introduced 'shamrock' tea and breakfast sets, which became deservedly popular; embossed foliage dessert services; fern and foliage tea and dessert services. A plate and a footed comport of a design registered in 1870 are shown in Plate 50. The firm also introduced the primrose on tea, breakfast, and dessert services. The leaves and flowers of the primrose are in relief and are beautifully painted and tinted from nature. They are also finished in various styles, but always in strict accordance with the simplicity of the original design.

Messrs. Harvey Adams & Co. also entered very largely into the work of ornamental flowering in relief à la Dresden, and brought out a number of good shapes in vases, jardinieres, and other articles, with flowers and plants modelled on the ware and painted true to nature. In this and in other departments of the art-manufactory, they secured the services of several well-known artists – among them Henry Mitchell, medallist of the Paris and Vienna Exhibitions celebrated as an animal, landscape and figure painter, and whose works are remarkable for their finish, their modelling, and their delicacy of treatment, and whose greys and flesh tints are of peculiar purity and beauty; Mr. Swan, and Mr. Longmore – the former a clever flower-painter, and the latter highly skilled in this artistic treatment of birds.

The firm also brought out in great variety a series of designs of the Chinese, Japanese, and Persian style, consisting of figure and floral decoration, and adapted them to tea, breakfast, and dessert services, and ornamental goods – the cobalt blue, introduced largely in these patterns, being of a specially pure and rich colour. And while many of these are for the general buyer, a very large number are of a high class character. In these, Mr. Slater (who left the firm in 1881) happily realised the full force of the special characteristics of this ancient style of art and produced works admirably drawn and exquisitely coloured. He was succeeded as art-director by John Marshall (a talented flower-painter), who ably maintained the reputation of the firm, evincing great taste and experience in the production of new shapes and designs of the Persian, Chinese, and Japanese schools, which commanded heavy sales in the home, American and Australian markets. In 1885, Mr. Harvey Adams retired and G. Hammersley continued as Hammersley & Co. into the twentieth century. The present firm is Hammersley & Co (Longton) Ltd., of the Alsager Pottery, Longton.

Plate 50. Porcelain ware of a design registered in January 1870 by Harvey Adams & Co. of Longton.
Godden of Worthing Ltd.

Market Street Works

These are said to be the oldest works in Longton and to be contemporaneous with those of Wedgwood at Etruria. They were originally carried on by Cyples, afterwards by Cyples & Barker (1846), who were succeeded by Thomas Barlow. For many years, Egyptian black and other tinted bodies only were made, but these were of a fine and very superior character. Lustre ware was also produced, and some of this was marked with a large letter B impressed in the body. Later on, china for foreign markets was produced of good average quality both in body and glaze. Mr. Thomas Barlow successfully turned his attention to the production of the most costly classes of decorated goods for the home markets in about 1870, and these have an excellent body and glaze.

In 1871, Mr. Barlow exhibited some of his productions, which attracted much attention; some of these are shown in Figure 18. Tea, breakfast, dessert, and dejeuner services, and a number of ornamental articles in every style of decoration, were made. Many of Mr. Barlow's designs and patterns were original and worthy of commendation. Thomas Barlow ceased potting at Market Street in about 1883.

Coronation Works

Messrs. Waterhouse Barlow produced earthenware at these works in Commerce Street in all the usual varieties for the South American, African and Indian markets from about 1860 to 1882, when '& Son' was added to the title; and as such, the firm continued into the twentieth century.

Carlisle Works

This manufactory in the High Street, formerly belonged to the Bridgwoods, then to Cyples & Ball during 1847 and 1848, and from 1850 to Adams & Cooper. From 1881, it was carried on by R. H. Plant & Co. Formerly, Egyptian black, brown and lustre ware, as well as china, was made, but china was later the exclusive product. R. H. Plant & Co.

Fig. 18. Barlow's tea services, 1871 Exhibition.

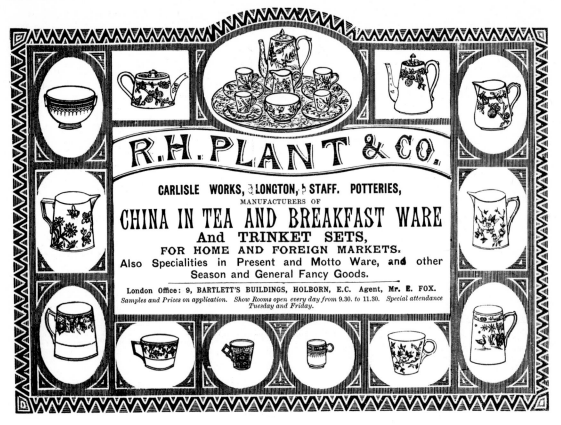

Fig. 19. R. H. Plant & Co.'s advertisement of 1885.

continued to 1898. From 1898 to the present day, the firm has been R. H. & S. L. Plant (Ltd) of the Tuscan Works, Longton. An advertisement of 1885 is reproduced.

Park Works

At these works in the High Street, Charles Allerton & Sons manufactured both earthenware and china in the usual varieties, as well as good gold and silver lustre ware, both for home markets and export. The works were established in 1831. In 1912, the firm became Allertons Ltd. Nineteenth-century ware was seldom marked. J. F. Blacker, in his *The ABC of XIX Century English Ceramic Art* (Stanley Paul & Co, London, c.1911), illustrates a selection of Allerton ware of the 1900 period and includes an interesting letter from the firm.

Sheridan Works

Built in 1858 by John Sheridan, the works passed into the hands of George Edwards & Co. in 1866 and were then carried on by George Edwards alone. In about 1840, the business of Mr. Edwards was commenced in Market Street by Thomas Cope and James Edwards, and after the death of the former was continued by Mr. Edwards, who died in 1873 at the age of seventy-nine. His son, George, continued to 1904.

The productions were china tea, breakfast, and dessert services, in plain white and in every style of decoration, both for the home and foreign markets. Among the specialities were small cans and saucers, richly and elaborately decorated in gold and colours, in 'Japan work', for Morocco, Gibraltar, and the Turkish markets; and tea-sets, tea-jars, kettles, etc., decorated in an immense variety of patterns, in imitation of old Japanese examples, for the Dutch trade.

Plate 51. A John Tams advertisement showing typical products. Reproduced from a *Pottery Gazette* of 1886.

Commerce Street

Messrs. H. Aynsley & Co. (the managing partner being Oswald Deakin) manufactured all the usual varieties of lustre, Egyptian black, drab, turquoise, and painted ware, as well as stoneware mortars. The works were originally carried on by Wooley, and afterwards by Chetham & Robinson during the 1822–37 period. After remaining for half a century in the family of Chetham, they passed into the hands of H. Aynsley & Co. in 1873. Messrs. H. Aynsley & Co. Ltd. continue at the Commerce Works today.

Crown Pottery

John Tams manufactured the usual classes of earthenware at this pottery in Stafford Street and specialised in the manufacture of government measures, mugs and jugs. This firm, which continues to the present day, was established early in the nineteenth century. An advertisement of 1886 is reproduced in Plate 51.

Crown Works

Thomas Bettany produced china tea, dessert and other services at these works from 1859 to 1870. From 1870 to 1887, Messrs. Collingwood & Greatbatch continued; and from 1887 to 1947, these works were worked by Collingwood Bros. (Ltd).

Stafford Street Works

These works, amongst the oldest in Longton, were occupied from about 1822 to 1833 by John & Charles Harvey, who were succeeded by Hulme & Hawley, from whom they repassed into the hands of the former family, being carried on from 1835 to 1853 by Charles and W. K. Harvey, sons of Charles Harvey of the original firm. In 1841, these gentlemen worked three manufactories in Longton. In 1853, C. & W. K. Harvey were succeeded by Holland & Green, who continued to 1882. By the first two firms useful earthenware was made, and this was continued by C. & W. K. Harvey, who added china to the productions and also, to a large extent, gold lustre ware. Later on, these were discontinued, and the firm devoted themselves to printed goods and white granite-ware, chiefly for the North and South American and Continental markets.

The greater portion of the buildings was taken down in 1882 for the erection on their site of a row of shops. A part of the manufactory was carried on by Green, Clark & Clay from 1882 to 1885, and continued as Green & Clay to 1891. The mark was the name of the pattern or body, the royal arms, and the name or initials of the firm, i.e. H. & G. for Holland & Green, during the period 1852–82.

IRONSTONE

HOLLAND & GREEN.

H. & G.

The toilet services produced by this firm were of superior quality. The ground colours – rose-du-Barry and Brunswick green – especially were of great clearness and beauty, and the gilding rich and elaborate.

Peel Pottery

These works, originally belonging to Thomas Stirrup, were continued by Bell, Deakin & Proctor; Webb & Walters (1865–7); S. Webb & Co. (1868–72); and John Green, at whose death they passed into the hands of Thomas Hulse (1880–2), and from him to Hulme & Massey (1882–9). The first three firms originally produced common classes of earthenware. China was added by Webb & Walters, and later made alone. It was of more than average excellence in body, and of various styles of decoration. Many were richly gilt, and the floral and other decorations carefully painted. In 1887, the works passed into the hands of R. V. Wildblood; and in 1888, the style was Wildblood & Heath. From 1899 to 1927, the title was Wildblood, Heath & Sons (Ltd).

King Street and Market Street

At these works, John Lockett manufactured the usual varieties of earthenware, china, stoneware, lustre, Egyptian black, drab, and other

ware from 1851 to 1879. In 1862, he produced special examples for the exhibition of that year. Some are shown in Figure 20. After his death, the premises – after being unoccupied for some time – were held by Taylor, Waine & Bates from 1879 to 1882, then by Charles Glover, and then by Bradbury & Son; but they were vacant in 1883.

Florence Works

Messrs. Taylor & Kent were established at the Florence Works in 1867. They produced a wide range of attractive china and majolica ware. Nineteenth-century marks include the initials T & K, and L for Longton. Messrs. Taylor & Kent Ltd. are today important manufacturers of bone china.

King Street

Mr. Lockett, nephew of the John Lockett of King Street and Market Street, continued his uncle's business in King Street; but in 1883 he moved to works in Chancery Lane, Longton, trading under the title J. Lockett & Co. As such, the works continued to 1960 and subsequently at Burslem.

Fig. 20. Messrs. Lockett's 1862 Exhibition products.

Chancery Lane

Taylor, Hudson, & Middleton – who here produced, between 1870 and 1877, all the ordinary varieties of china ware – dissolved partnership, Mr. Taylor joining his son-in-law, Mr. Rent, in new works in High Street, and the other partners removing to the Alma Works and Bagnall Street. They were succeeded by Maddox & Ridge to 1882 and continued by Mr. Ridge (formerly of the firm of Ridge, Meigh & Co) from 1883 to 1892 as Ridge & Sons.

High Street

Established in about 1840 by Thomas Cooper, these works were carried on by Keeling & Walker from 1856 to 1872, the latter of whom, John Walker, continued to 1880. He manufactured the ordinary classes of earthenware, gold and silver lustre and figures. The mention of figures is an interesting contemporary (in 1878 and 1883) reference to a manufacturer of the unmarked Victorian Staffordshire earthenware figures of the type shown in Plate 46.

Plate 52. A camel-shaped teapot – a design by
Messrs. Moore of Longton in 1874. 7½ inches high.
Victoria & Albert Museum (*Crown copyright*).

St. Mary's Works

This manufactory in Mount Pleasant was
carried on from about 1841 by Hamilton &
Moore and so continued until 1859, when
Samuel Moore became sole owner. In 1862, he
built the St. Mary's Works; and in 1870 he was
succeeded by his two sons, Bernard and Samuel
Moore, who from 1872 carried on the business
under the style of Moore Brothers. The productions were, from the first, china of a good
quality, in which all the usual breakfast, tea,
dinner, dessert, dejeuner and other services
were made; but in addition to this, attention
was given, with marked success, to the development of the strictly ornamental departments.
A camel teapot – the Arab tying on the bale
forming an excellent handle, and the neck and
head on the camel an admirable spout – is a well
conceived design and is powerfully and cleverly
modelled (Plate 52).

For table decoration, the firm produced many
good designs in centrepieces, lamps, baskets,
etc. incorporating well-modelled Cupids. The

Persian turquoise glaze made by the firm was
remarkably clear and brilliant in colour, and
not surpassed by other houses. In enamelling,
Moore Brothers made much progress, some of
their designs in cloissonne enamelling being
highly effective both in form of vessel and in
arrangement of colour. Notably among these
are 'pilgrims' bottles', the rich and massive
gilding of which throws out and relieves the enamelling in a very marked and effective manner.
In china, and also in majolica, Japanese reproductions were made. Pâte-sur-pâte ware
was also produced in about 1878. Good painted
decoration was carried out under the art director Richard Pilsbury. Mirror frames of large size
were also a speciality of these works.

Messrs. Moore Brothers' operations were
principally confined to the home markets, a
large proportion of their goods bearing the
name of the dealers, such as 'T. Goode & Co.
London'. The colourful begging-dog basket
ornament shown in Plate 53 bears the mark of
this leading London retailer as well as the impressed name-mark MOORE.

The mark of the makers is either the name
MOORE or, from 1880, Moore Bros. impressed

or incised in the body of the ware. MOORE BROS. painted on the surface, or a printed globe mark, dates from about 1880.

The works were continued by Moore Brothers to 1905, when Bernard Moore moved to Wolfe Street, Stoke, and produced some wonderful glaze effects such as 'sang de boeuf'. The St. Mary's Works were purchased by Messrs. Thomas Wild & Co. in 1905.

Talbot Works

These works in Commerce Street, carried on by Thomas Walters from 1879 to 1913, were established by Riddle & Lightfoot in about 1835 and continued to 1851. The productions were china of ordinary quality for both home and export markets.

New Town Pottery

Erected in 1845 by James Meakin, who continued it until 1850, it passed to Stanley & Lambert, who in 1855 were succeeded by J. & H. Procter & Co., who produced common earthenware in the usual cream-colour, printed, painted, and lustred varieties. The mark was a crown upon a ribbon, bearing the word WARRANTED; over the crown STAFFORDSHIRE, and beneath the ribbon, P for Procter. In 1876, the

works passed into the hands of Dale, Page & Goodwin, of the Church Street Works. These works were established in the latter half of the eighteenth century and, in 1780, were carried on by John Forrester, who was succeeded in about 1811 by Hilditch & Sons, who in their productions followed closely in the wake of Josiah Spode and Thomas Minton, at which time most of the processes here were carried out by female hands. In 1830, the firm changed to Hilditch & Hopwood, who at the exhibition of 1851 sent up some notable examples of their productions, one of which was a dessert service decorated in the Renaissance style, in gold, with landscape and figure vignettes, mainly illustrative of Scott's 'Marmion' Messrs. Hilditch & Hopwood's products were not marked with their name, but some shapes registered under this name bear witness to the high standard of their porcelain. The tea-set shown in Plate 54 illustrates shapes registered in April 1844.

The tea services exhibited at the same time were remarkable for their excellent body, the design and execution of the painted decoration, the high class of the ground colours, and the massiveness of the gilding. One example, with raised antique foliage in gold on the fine old 'Derby blue' ground, was especially good,

Plate 53. A well modelled Moore Brothers porcelain basket, one of a pair. Impressed name-mark. c.1885. 11 inches high. *Godden of Worthing Ltd.*

Plate 54. A Hilditch & Hopwood porcelain tea
service, showing shapes registered in April 1844.
Godden of Worthing Ltd.

while the painting of others, with small landscapes in medallions, and wreaths of flowers, was far beyond average merit.

In 1858, on the death of William Hopwood, the works were continued by the trustees till May 1867, when the business, stock, and plant – including the moulds and copper-plates – were sold to Dale, Page & Goodwin, who in 1876 removed to the larger premises called New Town Works, and continued to 1892. The productions of the firm consisted of all the usual services in china, and were of a better class than those of many other houses. In tea and breakfast services, the firm was particularly successful in designs where leaves, accurately copied from nature, were carelessly thrown on grounds of various tints. Other designs with wreaths of roses on the same ground, and others again closely diapered with burnished gold, were among their more successful patterns. Their productions also included dessert services with fruit, flowers, and landscapes, with richly designed festoons, borders, and gilding; dinner services, richly gilt and enamelled; jet ware, etc. Majolica was added to the other productions of the firm in the 1870s. The New Town Pottery was subsequently known as the Blythe Works.

Church Street Majolica Works

In 1877, Thomas Forester commenced business at a small manufactory in High Street; and as his business rapidly increased, he took additional premises in Church Street. These he shortly afterwards took down, and built upon their site a new manufactory – the Phoenix Works – which he completed in 1879. The new premises gave him greater scope for his enterprise and, extending his connection, they were soon found to be too small for his requirements. He therefore purchased the adjoining china manufactory and completed his enterprise by joining the two works together, thus making one factory with six large ovens and every other possible convenience and appliance. The works enlarged with the business, and the business with the works, till Mr. Forester's manufactory ranked among the most important pottery establishments of the locality. Certainly no other instance is on record in which, in six years only, so much was done single-handed by any manufacturer. A trade advertisement of the 1881–2 period is reproduced in Plate 55.

In the beginning of 1883, Thomas Forester took his sons into partnership and the business was carried on under the style of Forester & Sons. Upwards of four hundred hands were employed. The goods produced were of a varied character in both useful and ornamental classes, and included vases of unique design and of various sizes. Flowering 'à la Barbotin' was carried on to a large extent. Mr. Forester also introduced various articles of cabinet ware in vases, jardinieres, etc. made with Barbotin flowerwork on tortoiseshell and marble grounds, some cornucopias upwards of thirty-six inches high giving evidence of considerable skill. One of the productions of merit is the life-size St. Bernard's dog on a large pedestal, three feet six inches in height, which was modelled by Gallimore from a prize dog. The quality of Messrs. Forester's majolica was remarkably firm and good in body, the colouring well managed and the glaze very satisfactory, as was the modelling of the floral decorations.

Messrs. Thomas Forester & Sons (Ltd.) continued to 1959. The basic marks incorporate the Phoenix and the initials T.F. & S. Ltd.

Borough Pottery

These works, established in 1869 by Cartwright & Edwards, were extensive and built as a 'model factory'. The ovens were on the down-draught system. The clay – both the blunging, sifting, and other processes – was prepared by machinery; the water was taken out by pressure; the throwing-wheels and jiggers were turned by steam-power; and the workshops were fitted with steam drying-stoves, so that no fires were used in drying the goods. The goods produced in the nineteenth century were the normal classes of earthenware. Messrs. Cartwright & Edwards (Ltd.) continue to the present day and, during the twentieth century, manufacture bone-china as well as earthenware. They have occupied various works other than the

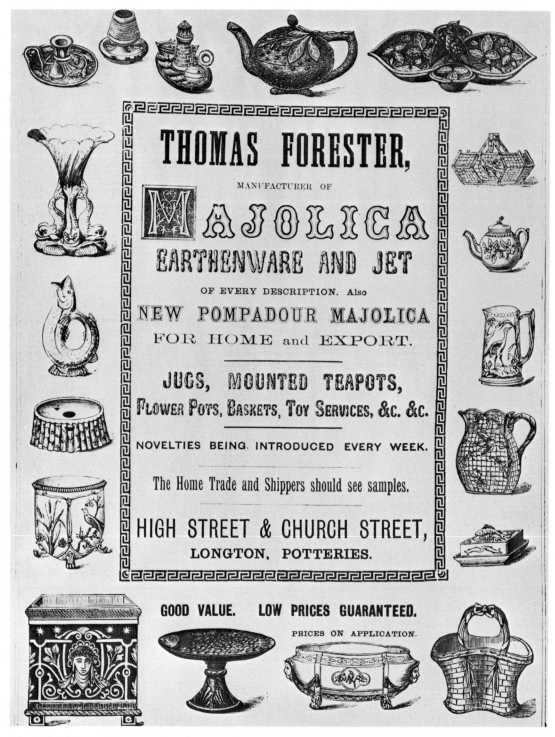

Plate 55. A Thomas Forester advertisement of 1882, showing typical low-priced majolica ware of the period. Reproduced from *Pottery Gazette*.

Borough Pottery. The standard marks incorporate the initials C & E.

Mount Pleasant Works

These works in High Street, formerly occupied by Thomas Birks & Co. and then, from 1880 to 1884, by Hallam & Day, were then carried on by J. Day & Co., who produced china, earthenware, and gold and silver lustre of the more ordinary qualities.

New Street

Messrs. Cooper & Kent (formerly Cooper, Till & Co.) produced china goods of the more ordinary qualities from 1882 to 1892.

Prince of Wales's Pottery

These works, in Sutherland Road, were established by Benjamin Shirley of Bangor, Wales, on the day of the marriage of H.R.H. the Prince of Wales – 10th March 1863 – and were, in honour of that event, named the Prince of Wales's Works. They were carried on for a time by Benjamin Shirley and Walter Freeman under the style of Shirley & Freeman (late of the Sheridan Works). On the death of the former, in 1864, Titus Hammersley became a partner with Mr. Freeman. In 1866, Edward Asbury joined the firm, which was carried on as Hammersley, Freeman & Co. In 1870, Mr. Freeman retired from the concern, and the style at that time was Hammersley & Asbury. After the death of Mr. Hammersley, in 1875, the works were continued by Mr. Asbury alone under the style of Edward Asbury & Co.

The goods produced were china, tea, coffee, dessert, and trinket services – a special feature being articles bearing local views in colour, for sale at watering-place – principally for the home markets; but goods were also shipped to Australia and the United States. The mark used was the Prince of Wales' feathers, with the letters H & A in a garter, or A. & Co. Edward Asbury & Co. continued to 1925.

High Street Works and Willow Street Works

Walter Freeman, just spoken of as a proprietor successively of the Sheridan and the Prince of Wales's Works, withdrew from the latter in 1870 and entered on this manufactory, which he continued till his death in 1882. After that time, they were carried on by Boughey, Shaw & Martin to 1887. The productions were confined to china, in which were produced tea, breakfast, trinket, and dessert services in great variety of style, and other articles for the home, American and Australian markets. Messrs. Boughey, Shaw & Martin worked the Willow Street Pottery from 1883 to 1887 and were succeeded in 1887 by Matthew Boughey and in 1897 by M. Boughey & Co., who continued to 1901.

Newmarket Works

These works in Market Street were among the oldest in Longton. They were occupied by Martin & Shaw, between 1816 and 1824, for the manufacture of lustre ware and china. Martin & Shaw were succeeded by Abel Booth, and after other changes the manufactory came into the hands of Messrs. Glover, Colclough & Townsend, who were extensively engaged in ware for the Eastern markets. From this firm, the works passed in 1868 to Messrs. Skelson & Plant and from them, in 1879, to Messrs. Radford & Co. The productions were china tea, breakfast, and dessert services, etc., chiefly for the home trade. From 1885 to 1894, Messrs. Radford & Ward were at the Newmarket Works.

Alma Works

Messrs. Middleton & Hudson (formerly Copestake & Allen) produced at these works in High Street the ordinary services, etc., in china from about 1881 to 1888. From 1889, the firm was continued at the Delphine Pottery, Bagnall Street, as J. H. Middleton, and from 1912 '& Co.' was added to the title. Since 1941, the title has been Hudson & Middleton Ltd.

Market Street

These works, successively held by Knight & Rowley from 1873 to 1878, Messrs. Colclough, Trubshaw & Co., and W. Jones, were carried on from 1883 by Jones & Howson, who produced the usual classes of china goods in tea, breakfast, and dessert services for the home and foreign markets. Many of their shapes and patterns were of great beauty, and the quality of the body was good. It was here that Sampson Bridgwood made his first start and laid the foundation of his ultimate success. Messrs. Jones & Howson continued to 1896.

Victoria Works

These were built by Ralph Shaw in about 1828. In about 1858, they were taken by Joseph Finney, who carried on the business to 1899. For the first fifteen years of Mr. Shaw's working, earthenware was manufactured; but it was then converted into china works, and so continued to 1899. The goods produced by Messrs. J. Finney & Co. were the usual classes of tea, breakfast, and dessert services, and fancy goods of average quality in body and decoration for home and foreign markets.

Stanley Pottery

James Dawson occupied these works in Stafford Street from 1875 to 1893 and produced ordinary earthenware of the usual classes.

Russell Street

William Edwards manufactured ordinary earthenware here from 1875 to 1902.

Gladstone Works

Messrs. Richard Hodson & Co. produced china services of the ordinary quality from 1879 to 1885 at these works in High Street.

British Anchor Works

At these works in Anchor Road, occupied by J. T. Hudden, earthenware only was made. J. T. Hudden established a factory in Stafford Street in 1859 and was an important manufacturer until 1885.

Royal Porcelain Works

These works in Forrester Street, Anchor Road, which belonged to David Chapman, formerly Robinson & Chapman (1872–3), were

built as a 'model factory' and were much enlarged. All the throwing-wheels and jiggers were turned by steam-power, and many other operations which under the old system were done by manual labour were here carried on by the aid of steam. China of a superior quality and style of decoration was produced. David Chapman worked from 1882 to 1889. From 1889 to 1895, the style was David Chapman & Sons. The firm then moved to the Atlas Works.

Gladstone Pottery

Messrs. Procter, Mayer & Wooley, who succeeded Hudson & Son in 1883, produced ordinary china services at this Stafford Street pottery. They continued to 1892, when they were succeeded at the Gladstone Pottery by George Procter & Co., who continued into the twentieth century.

St. Gregory's Pottery

In High Street, established in 1794 by Mr. G. Barnes and successively held by Barnes & Wood, Wood & Blood, William Chesworth, Beardmore & Birks, and G. Townsend, this pottery passed in 1864 to Tams & Lowe, and in 1875 to William Lowe. The goods produced comprised all the usual varieties of articles in useful ordinary earthenware, and in china of an average quality – for which new works were specially built. In the former, dinner, tea, toilet and other services were made in white, printed, coloured, and gilt varieties; in the latter, only the ordinary common classes were made, principally for the home trade. Mosaic jugs and teapots, mounted and otherwise, were well formed and decorated. The usual mark is a garter, with the words STAFFORDSHIRE IMPROVED, enclosing the name of the pattern and the Staffordshire knot. The ribbon is surmounted by a crown, and beneath are the initials of the firm – T. & L., or otherwise. William Lowe continued to about 1930 at the Sydney Works.

Gold Street Works

From 1882, these were the works of Messrs. Lowe, Ratcliffe & Co. (formerly Barker Brothers, 1872–82). This is one of the oldest manufactories in Longton, historically interesting from the fact of gold lustre having been, reputedly, here first discovered and applied for decorative purposes. The earthenware was of the ordinary medium quality, both for home and for foreign markets, and consisted of cream-coloured, white, fancy sponged, painted, and printed, enamelled, and other descriptions, in toilet, dinner, breakfast, and tea services and other articles. Lowe, Ratcliffe & Co. worked from 1882 to 1892.

Wellington Works

Established in Stafford Street in 1862 by G. L. Robinson & W. Cooper and afterwards carried on by G. L. Robinson under the style of Robinson & Son, and later, in 1871, by G. A. Robinson and others as Robinson, Repton, & Robinson, the works passed into the hands of Warrilow & Cope in 1880. The goods principally produced were tea, breakfast, dessert, and other services; also toilet trinket-ware, vases, centrepieces, and a large variety of ornamental china goblets, fruit and other baskets, open-work (or pierced) compots and moustache-cups. Majolica was introduced by Warrilow & Cope with good artistic and commercial results. This firm continued to 1894.

Heathcote Works

Established in 1854 by William Brammall and John Dent, Heathcote Works passed to William Brammall (1859–64), then in 1865 to Edwin Brammall & Repton. From 1876, the manufactory was carried on by W. H. Derbyshire & Co. The manufactures consisted of china, tea, breakfast, and other services, and all the usual useful articles in that material suitable for the home trade.

St. Gregory's Pottery

In 1883, James Wilson having erected these new works in March Street, transferred to them his Parian works, formerly in High Street, and added the manufacture of china to his other business. James Wilson started at High Street in 1879 and continued at Marsh Street to about 1897.

Green Dock Works

Established in 1846. Mr. F. D. Bradley (formerly Hampson Brothers, 1854–70, and Cooper, Till & Co., 1875–6) manufactured improved stoneware, ordinary earthenware and lustres for the home, American, Australian and other markets. From 1876 to 1896, F. D. Bradley worked several potteries in London. Many examples are in the well-known style of Moore Brothers. An 1889 advertisement lists 'table decorations, time pieces, candelabras, lamps, tazzas, fruit and flower bowls, centres, etc.' This porcelain, such as the pieces shown in Plate 56, bears the impressed mark BRADLEY.

Chadwick Street

At these works, Frederick Jones & Co. manufactured ordinary earthenware from about 1880 to 1886.

23 High Street

J. L. Johnson produced, in about 1875, all the usual services, etc., in the commoner classes of china.

Baddeley

In about 1720, William Baddeley (an old name in the district) commenced making brown ware at Eastwood, Hanley. In about 1740, having invented an 'engine-lathe', he began to make turned articles in cane and brown ware. He was succeeded in the pottery by his son, William Baddeley.

This second William Baddeley (worked from 1802 to 1822) made many improvements in the ware and attempted, both by an imitation of body of his vitreous ware and by his mark, to palm off some of his goods as Wedgwood's. His mark was the word EASTWOOD impressed on the ware, but he contrived to have the EAST indistinct and the WOOD clear, thus hoping to catch the unwary by the latter syllable. He died at an advanced age. The works at Eastwood having been sold, his son, William Baddeley, commenced in Queen Street, Hanley, for the manufacture of terra-cotta articles; and a large trade was carried on in earthenware knobs for tin and japanned tea and coffee-pots. He also

Plate 56. Two porcelain ornaments of Moore
Brothers type but bearing the impressed name-mark
'Bradley', c.1880. Vase, 8 inches high.
Godden of Worthing Ltd.

made fancy pipes, japanned terra-cotta, and
other goods. At the Market Lane Works, he was
the first to make telegraph insulators in iron
moulds with screw and lever pressure.

In 1846, the works were removed to Longton
(Wharf Street), and here the manufacture of
imitation stag, buck, and buffalo-horn and bone
handles for knives and forks for the Sheffield
trade was first introduced. In this branch, a very
good trade was done, but the working handlers
of Sheffield refused to work them up, and threats
were sent to several masters that if they did not
give up the terra-cotta knife-handle trade their
works would be blown up. The masters, thus
intimidated, gave up the use of these handles,
and on Mr. Baddeley visiting Sheffield an attack
was made on his life. Letters were sent to him on
his return threatening that, if he did not give up
making the handles, he and his works 'would be

done for'. The manufacture was then discontinued.

Mr. Baddeley, who died in 1864, held the St.
Martin's Lane Works, and his widow carried on
business in Commerce Street from 1864 to 1875.
Their son, William Baddeley, commenced
manufacturing in the Normacott Road in 1862
and continued to 1875. His productions were
rustic terra-cotta articles for floral, horticultural, useful and decorative purposes – the
principal articles being fern-stands, vases,
flower-stands, hyacinth pots, flower-pots,
garden seats, flower-baskets, crocus pots, globe-
stands, brackets and inkstands. The designs
were all taken from nature, and appropriate to
to the intended use of the vessel. His imitations
of bark, and of various woods and plants, was
remarkably good.

Waterloo Works

Built in Stafford Street in 1815, the year of the
Battle of Waterloo, and in honour of that event
named the Waterloo Works. At these works,

which were large and commodious, were produced by Brough & Blackhurst the ordinary classes of earthenware, enamelled and gilt services and the like, suitable both for the home and foreign markets. Messrs. Brough & Blackhurst worked the Waterloo pottery from 1872 to 1895.

Heathcote Road Pottery

Messrs. J. & H. Procter removed here in 1876 from the New Town Pottery. The productions were common earthenware in the usual cream-colour, printed, painted, and lustred varieties. The mark was a crown upon a ribbon, bearing the word WARRANTED; over the crown is STAFFORDSHIRE, and beneath the ribbon P for Procter. Messrs. J. & H. Procter started in c.1857, and '& Co.' was added in 1859. They continued to 1884.

Sutherland Pottery

Established at Daisy Bank in 1870 by Joseph Holdcroft for the manufacture of majolica, Parian, and silver lustre ware for the home, Continental, South American and Australian markets. Mr. Holdcroft, who for eighteen years was in the employment of Minton & Co., commenced business in another manufactory in Longton, which he left on the erection of his Sutherland Pottery. His majolica productions were of a high class, both in design and in workmanship. A 'Wren Vase', with well-modelled birds and flowers, was a speciality of his works. His mark was his initials impressed in the ware.

J. Holdcroft continued to 1906 when the firm became Holdcrofts Ltd, a firm that continued until the 1920s.

Church Street

These works, for the production of Parian, jasper, and majolica ware, belonging to G. A. Robinson, were pulled down in 1876 for town improvements, Mr. Robinson erecting new works in Sutherland Road and using the style Robinson & Co. until 1886.

Cornhill Works

Poole & Unwin entered on these works, which had previously been carried on as general earthenware works by others, in 1871. The productions were middle-class earthenware, stoneware jugs and other utilitarian items chiefly intended for the home market. Gold and silver lustres of the ordinary kind and rustic majolica were also at one time made. The mark of the firm was P & U, in a diamond-shaped outline,

impressed in the body of the ware, from 1871 to about 1876. Very rare Staffordshire figures occur with this mark or with the name UNWIN. Joseph Unwin continued the Cornhill Works under his own name to 1890, and to 1926 as Joseph Unwin & Co.

Sutherland Pottery

These works in Normacott Road were established in about 1873 by Skelson & Plant, who were previously in the New Market Works, Chancery Lane, Longton, and the Heathcote Road Pottery of which they were also proprietors. These latter were established by Thomas Beardmore in 1864 and much enlarged by Stubbs & Bridgwood before they came into the hands of Skelson & Plant. At these works, china was made in all the usual useful services until the closure in 1892.

St. James's Place

The St. James's Place works were established by William Bradshaw in about 1822 and afterwards occupied by John Gerrard, Jesse Cope & Co., and Baggaley & Ball. In 1831, they were taken by Robert Gallimore, who was joined in partnership by George Shubotham in about 1840. In 1842, Gallimore retired from the concern and the business was then continued by George Shubotham and William Webberley under the style of Shubotham & Webberley. In 1847, Mr. Shubotham died and the works were carried on by William Webberley alone. In 1858, this gentleman purchased the premises and soon afterwards pulled down the old buildings and

Plate 57. Two Staffordshire earthenware figures
bearing the relief-moulded 'S. Smith' name-mark,
c.1880. 11 inches high.   *Editor's collection.*

erected a new commodious 'four-oven' manufactory.

Originally, lustre ware only was produced,
but china was added by Mr. Gallimore. In 1844,
lustre was entirely abandoned, and from that
time china alone was made. This was produced
in all the usual services for the home, Dutch and
Australian markets until about 1892. No mark
was used.

The Sutherland Works

These works were established in Barker Street
in about 1860 by Sampson Smith, at whose death
they passed into the hands of John Adderley,
who continued the production of china tea and
other services, silver and gold lustre, and china
figures and ornaments, using the old style of
Sampson Smith. Sampson Smith established
his first works in the High Street in c.1846. He
must be regarded as one of the largest producers
of Staffordshire earthenware figures and dogs.
An advertisement of 1883 reads: 'Figures, all
kinds and sizes. Dogs, white and gold, black
and gold, red and white, and black and white.
Jet and gold tea pots and kettles, silver lustre
tea pots, etc. etc.' This nineteenth-century

102

Smith ware is very rarely marked. The firm continued into the twentieth century and became a
limited company in 1918. In about 1934, they
moved to the Wetley Works.

Rare examples of Sampson Smith's figures
bear a relief-moulded name mark. Two such
marked examples are shown in Plate 57. However, most figures were not marked. A page
from a twentieth-century Sampson Smith catalogue is shown in Plate 58.

Daisy Bank

These historically interesting works were built
in the latter part of the eighteenth century by a
Mr. Hughes, and passed successively through
the firms of Drury, Ray & Tideswell, and Ray &
Wynne, to Charles James Mason & Co., who

Plate 58. A page from a Sampson Smith catalogue
of c.1900. Most of these figures will not bear a
name mark.

succeeded the latter firm. It was in these works that Mr. Mason produced his famous 'Ironstone china' (Plate 4), the firm at that time being George Miles Mason and Charles James Mason, and subsequently C. J. Mason only. The patent taken out by C. J. Mason in 1813 was for 'a process for the improvement of the manufacture of English porcelain', the process, according to the specification, consisting 'in using scoria or slag of ironstone pounded and ground in water, in certain proportions, with flint, Cornwall stone, and clay, and blue oxide cobalt'. It should also be added that the name 'Ironstone' was simply a combination of 'iron' and 'stone', used to denote the extreme hardness of the body as combining the strength of both. From various causes the manufactory after some years, though a great artistic and manipulative success, became a commercial failure.[1]

In 1853, the lease (afterwards the freehold) of the premises was sold to Hulse, Nixon and Adderley. In 1869, Mr. Nixon died and the firm's style was changed to Hulse & Adderley, and so continued until 1874 when (Mr. Hulse having died in the preceding year) it was altered to William A. Adderley. Since Mason's time, the premises have been very considerably enlarged and improved.

The productions were good quality china and earthenware for the home, foreign and Continental markets. W. A. Adderley continued to 1905 (& Co. was added to the firm's style from 1886), and from then onwards the style has been Adderleys Ltd.

Cobden Works

In 1880, Thomas Poole took the Cobden Works in Edensor Road. China and majolica useful ware was produced for the home, colonial and foreign markets. The firm continued as Thomas Poole until about 1925, when the style was changed to Thomas Poole (Longton) Ltd.

[1]The full history of Mason's Ironstone china is given in Geoffrey Godden's *The Illustrated Guide to Mason's Patent Ironstone China*, Barrie & Jenkins, London, 1971.

Albert Works

Messrs. T. Wild & Co. established the Albert Works in the High Street at Longton in about 1894. A good range of high quality china was produced. The intitial C was added to the style in 1903, and from this period the initials T.C.W. occur in most marks. The firm today is Messrs. Thomas C. Wild & Sons Ltd. of St. Mary's China Works, Longton.

Crown Pottery

Messrs. Broadhurst & Sons commenced potting at the Crown Pottery in Stafford Street in about 1855. By 1864, James Broadhurst was in sole charge. Productions of this period included a good range of gold and silver lustre earthenware. In 1872, James Broadhurst moved to the Portland Pottery at Fenton, where the present firm – James Broadhurst & Sons Ltd. – continue today.

Park Hall Street

Daniel Sutherland & Sons entered on these works in 1863, and they were carried on by the sons under the same style until about 1875. The productions were majolica jugs, vases, tripods, flower-holders; bread, cheese and fruit dishes; water-bottles, tea and coffee pots, kettles and other articles; and in Parian groups, figures, busts, jugs, brooches, crosses and trinkets. Stoneware jugs, teapots, etc., were also made. The mark of the firm was S & S, but was rarely used.

Viaduct Works

Established in Caroline Street in about 1836. This manufactory passed into the hands of Cooper, Nixon & Co. in 1863, and to Cooper & Dethick in 1876. They produced plain and printed earthenware of the ordinary kinds, and drab and other coloured bodies, both for the home and foreign markets. The mark is the initials of the firm (C & D), who continued to 1888 and were succeeded by William Cooper & Sons from 1888 to 1891.

High Street and Sutherland Road

Messrs. James Beech & Son opened these works in about 1846. After the death of Mr. Beech and his son, they passed to Stephen Mear, by whom they were carried on under the old title until about 1895. All the usual tea, breakfast, and dessert services in china of good quality and in various style of decoration were made.

King Street

These works were established in 1875, being opened on March 25th of that year by Bridgett, Bates & Beech. After the death of Mr. Beech, in 1882, they were continued by Bridgett & Bates. They manufactured china only, but in this were produced all the usual services in every variety of style, both for the home and foreign markets. Messrs. Bridgett & Bates continued until about 1915.

Anchor Pottery

Sampson Bridgwood & Son, who were extensive manufacturers, first carried on business in the Market Street Works, and next for many years at a manufactory in Stafford Street, originally occupied by G. Forrester, which was purchased by the Commissioners of Longton and pulled down for the erection of the market buildings. They then removed to the Anchor Pottery (in about 1853), where they produced both china and earthenware. In china, all the usual tea, breakfast, and dessert services were made – partly for the home, but principally for the United States and Canadian markets. An advertisement of 1896 is reproduced in Plate 59. In earthenware, white granite was made for the United States, Australian and Canadian trades. The speciality was what was technically called 'Parisian granite' (stamped 'Limoges'), which has a fine hard durable body and excellent glaze.

The nineteenth-century mark used on china was an impressed stamp of the name S. BRIDG-WOOD & SON. The Parisian granite bears the impressed stamp, an oval with the word LIMOGES and, in the centre, P.G. (for Parisian granite). It also bears the printed mark of an elaborate shield of arms with mantling, sceptres, etc., and the words PORCELAIN OPAQUE,

BRIDGWOOD & SON.

As Messrs. Sampson Bridgwood & Son Ltd. the firm continues to the present day.

Beaconsfield Pottery

Messrs. Blair & Co. occupied the new manufactory erected in Anchor Road in 1880 as china works. From 1912 to 1923, the style was Blairs Ltd.; and from 1923 to 1930, Blairs (Longton) Ltd.

Old Foley Pottery

Messrs. Moore & Co., late Samuel Bridgwood, produced white granite ware of the ordinary character, for the American markets, from 1872 to 1892, and were succeeded during the 1892–6 period by Moore, Leason & Co.

Anchor Works

These works in Market Street were carried on by T. & J. Carey from about 1823 until about 1843, when they came into the possession of John Ashwell, who occupied them for about thirteen years. They were afterwards carried on by William Green, from whom they passed in about 1860 to Copestake Brothers and were from 1871 occupied by George Copestake, who produced china of the usual varieties for both the home and foreign markets until 1889.

Edensor Road

Messrs. Aidney & Griffiths erected here a new china works and produced all the usual classes of services from 1882 to 1895. The firm is also listed as Aidney, Griffiths & Co.

Edensor Road China Works

These works were erected by Johnson & Poole in 1878. They continued to 1883.

Edensor Road

Mr. F. D. Bradley had his 'Elkin' china manufactory next to the above from 1876 to 1883. He subsequently worked the Flaxman Pottery in Sutherland Road, Longton, from 1887 to 1896.

Plate 59. A Bridgwood & Son advertisement of 1896 showing typical products of the period. Reproduced from *Pottery Gazette*.

S. BRIDGWOOD & SON,

Manufacturers of Dinner, Toilet, and Fancy Ware
FOR ALL MARKETS,
Anchor Pottery, LONGTON.

Dresden Works

Established in Normacott Road by John Procter in about 1843. These works, after being worked successively by Glover & Colclough and Goodwin & Bullock (1852–8), came into the hands of the firm of Mason, Holt & Co. in 1858, after which time they were much enlarged. All the usual tea, breakfast, dessert and other services, in china of excellent commercial quality, were made until 1884.

Dresden Works

These china works in Stafford Street, established by John Ferneyhough, passed in 1858 into the hands of Shelley & Hartshorne, who were succeeded by Adams & Scrivener in 1861, who in turn were succeeded in 1866 by John Ferneyhough, who continued to 1892.

Palissy Works

These works in Chancery Lane were erected in 1862 by Richard H. Grove for the purpose of decorating, not manufacturing, china ware. In 1867, he retired and was succeeded by his son, Frederick Wedgwood Grove, and his partner, John Stark. They commenced manufacturing their own ware having increased the premises for the purpose and erected the necessary kilns and machinery. They manufactured earthenware only. In this, all the usual dinner, dessert, toilet and other services and domestic articles were produced, of all degrees of decoration – from plain and printed to enamelled and gilt varieties. Spirit and wine show-barrels or casks were also specialities. Messrs. Grove & Stark continued to 1885. F. W. Grove continued to 1889, the firm subsequently becoming Grove & Oliver (1889–94), Grove & Prowse (1895–8), then Grove & Co. to about 1904.

Potters working at Longton in 1890 and not previously listed include:

R. S. Adams
Adderley & Lawson
J. Amison
Anderson & Copestake
J. Ball
Barker Bros.
Barker & Batty
Blackhurst & Hulme
J. Bradbury
R. Bridgwood
British Anchor Pottery Co. Ltd.
Cartlidge & Allen
J. H. Cope & Co.
R. J. Edwards & Co.
J. Finney
Hammonds & Buckley
Hawley & Co.
J. Heath
Jones & Co.
Jones & Hulme
Massey Wildblood
Middleton & Hudson
E. J. Pugh & Co.
Robinson & Son
Rowley & Co.
Shaw & Ridge
T. Sutherland
Taylor & Forester
J. Unwin
Waine & Bates
H. M. Williamson & Sons

Longton potters of the 1900 period not mentioned in the main list include:

C. Amison
Arrowsmith & Co.
Barker Bros.
Barkers & Kent Ltd.
T. W. Barlow & Son
G. L. Bentley & Co.
Beresford Bros.
J. W. Beswick
Blackhurst & Hulme
Boulton & Co.
R. Bridgwood
British Anchor Pottery Co. Ltd.
F. Cartlidge & Co.
Colclough & Co.
T. Cone
J. H. Cope & Co.
Dresden Porcelain Co.
Hawley Webberley & Co.
T. Heath
Hill & Co.

Holmes & Son
A. B. Jones & Sons
T. Lawrence
T. Ledgar
Longton Porcelain Co.
A. Machin & Co.
A. Mackee
McNeal & Co.
J. H. Middleton
T. Morris
A. Plant & Sons
Ratcliffe & Co.
Redfern & Drakeford
Rowley & Newton
J. Shore & Co.
Star China Co.
J. Unwin & Co.
C. Waine
G. Warrilow & Sons
Wileman & Co.
H. M. Williamson & Sons
J. B. Wood

STOKE-UPON -TRENT

Spode – Copeland

The first notice of the name of Spode that I have met with in connection with potting is the entry of the 'hiring' of Josiah Spode by Thomas Whieldon in 1749. The entry is of considerable historical interest as being the first hiring of Josiah Spode, who – being born in 1733, he would at that time have been sixteen years of age – was the founder of the family which subsequently rose to such eminence in the art. The 'hiring' being for three years, and at wages ranging from 2s. 3d to 3s. 3d per week while other men were at the same time being paid 5s. 3d to 7s. per week, would appear to have been a kind of apprenticeship, or, at all events, a 'finishing touch to the learning of the trade. From April till Martinmas, which is the great time for all hirings in the pottery trade, the payment was to be 2s. 3d per week 'or 2s. 6d if he deserves it', with the prospect of a rise of sixpence per week in successive years.

He appears to have fully worked out his time, and to have been found deserving, for in 1752 his 'hiring' was raised to 7s a week with 5s. 'earnest'; and in 1754 to 7s. 6d weekly with £1. 11. 6d 'earnest'. At this time he must have been married, for in the same year, 1754, it appears that the second Josiah Spode was born. But little is known of the early life of this second Josiah Spode. The probability, however, is that his father, after leaving Whieldon's service, commenced a small manufactory on his own account and that he learned the business with him.

In about 1770, Spode the son, being at that time about sixteen years old, is stated to have taken the works at Stoke previously carried on by Turner, or Turner & Banks. He is said also to have introduced, in about 1784, transfer printing into Stoke. Early products include very good basalt ware.

In the early 1790s[1], Mr. Spode commenced making porcelain in addition to earthenware and was the first to introduce felspar into its composition. The early porcelain normally bears only a painted pattern number and *very* rarely the **impressed** mark SPODE. In 1805, he introduced a strong new body known as 'Stone China', which he manufactured to a large extent and exported to France and other countries. In 1806, H.R.H. the Prince of Wales visited the works, and Mr. Spode was appointed potter to him.

The porcelain, stone-china, and ordinary earthenware manufactured were of the very highest character, and rank with the best of the period. Very fine underglaze blue prints were applied (Colour Plate V shows a typical tureen and stand from a large earthenware dinner service). In porcelain, tea services such as that shown in Plate 60 were produced in thousands of different patterns. A dessert service plate shown in Plate 61 illustrates the generally high standard of Spode porcelain.

In 1827, the second Mr. Spode died and was succeeded by his son, the third Josiah Spode,

[1]The exact date of the introduction of porcelain and of the stone-china body is still open to doubt, but for a full account of this ware the reader is referred to L. Whiter's well-illustrated *Spode, A History of the Family, Factory and Wares from 1733–1833* Barrie & Jenkins, London, 1970.

Colour Plate V. A fine Spode blue-printed
earthenware tureen, cover and stand from a dinner
service of c.1820. Stand, 17 inches long.
Godden of Worthing Ltd.

Plate 60. A Spode porcelain tea service of the
popular design number 967 (painted pattern-number
mark), c.1815. Teapot, $6\frac{3}{8}$ inches high.
Godden of Worthing Ltd.

Plate 61. A fine quality Spode porcelain plate painted with a view, of the Brighton seafront with the old chain-pier, c.1812. *Private collection.*

among the very highest in order of merit. Services were produced both in china and earthenware, and in every variety of ornamentation – in china from the simple gold or coloured lines and borders, and in earthenware from the commonest printed patterns, to the most profuse and lavish relief and painting. One of their highest efforts in the way of services was the dessert service made especially for H.R.H. the Prince of Wales in 1866. It consists of 198 pieces, comprising a centre (Fig. 21), eight compotiers, two cream-bowls, two ice-pails, twelve sweetmeat compotiers, seventy-two cups and saucers, and fifty plates.

One of the greatest improvements effected by the firm in ordinary earthenware was in the production of what they appropriately termed an 'Ivory body'. In this kind of ware, they produced all the usual services of every conceivable design and of various degrees of decoration. In the dinner and dessert services, the

Plate 62. Copeland earthenware vase decorated in the Etruscan-style – an 1851 Exhibition example. *Conservatoire National des Arts et Metiers, Paris.*

who, however, survived his father by only two years, dying in 1829. The business was then carried on by the executors of the third Josiah Spode (his only son, named Josiah, being a minor), and Alderman Copeland (son of William Copeland previously mentioned) until 1833, when the entire concern was purchased by Alderman William Taylor Copeland. He shortly afterwards took into partnership his principal traveller, Thomas Garrett, and the firm became Copeland & Garrett, and so continued until the partnership was dissolved in 1847. From that time, the style was W. T. Copeland, late Spode. In 1867, Mr. Copeland took his four sons into partnership, and from that time the firm continued under the name of W. T. Copeland & Sons. Mr. Alderman Copeland (1797–1868), who was Lord Mayor of London in 1835–6, was M.P. for Coleraine from 1828 to 1832, and for Stoke-upon-Trent from 1837 to 1852 and 1857 to 1865.

Of the productions of this firm it is manifestly impossible to give even a résumé. The bare enumeration of the different articles in porcelain and earthenware would occupy many closely printed pages. For breakfast, dinner, dessert, tea, and toilet services the firm ranked

110

Fig. 21. Centrepiece, Prince of Wales' Service,
made by Copeland's in 1866.

delicate, soft, warm tone of the ivory tint is peculiarly grateful to the eye, and has a charming effect when set out on the white linen cloth; it has all the softness of the finest examples of old Wedgwood cream-coloured ware. In this body, every variety of pattern – from the rich old Spode, with its Eastern brilliant combinations of gold and rich patches of colour, down to the most ordinary printed borders – was made. The vase shown in Plate 62, decorated in the Etruscan-style, is an example purchased from the Copeland display at the 1851 Exhibition. The attractive blue printed and gilt ewer and bowl shown in Plate 63 was also purchased at the Great Exhibition of 1851.

Plate 63. Copeland ewer and basin decorated with an underglaze blue print, enriched with gilding. 1851 Exhibition examples.
Conservatoire National des Arts et Metiers, Paris.

In porcelain, vases, tazzas, bottles and other articles of every conceivable form and decorated in an endless variety of ways in painting, in alto-relievo figures and flowers, and in massive jewelling, gilding, and enamelling, were produced and were of the most costly and elegant character. Services, of the most sumptuous as well as of severely simple character, were also produced in every style of art and on every scale of cost. Among Copeland's achievements

in colour were a new turquoise (which they christened 'Cerulean blue') which is remarkable for its brilliant intensity; Sardinian green, also very good; and vermilion of a finer and richer glow than has been produced elsewhere.

For a fuller review of Copeland's porcelain, the reader is referred to G. Godden's *Victorian Porcelain* (Herbert Jenkins, London, 1961).

Copeland's were also large producers of painted and enamelled tiles for internal decoration – and these, from the excellence they attained in the body and the skill displayed in the design and ornamentation, became a speciality of the firm. They were produced in endless variety and for every purpose, one of the most striking and attractive novelties in this kind of mural decoration being a continuous design for a whole room, first attempted by them for Mr. Macfarlane of Glasgow. Highly decorative tiles for flower-boxes, lily-pans, garden-seats, slabs for chimney-pieces, table-tops, fireplaces and for every other purpose were also highly produced, and are most decorative.

In Parian, statuary and busts, as well as other objects, were extensively made. This was another speciality of the firm, and one the discovery of which belongs to them. It was introduced by Copeland in about 1842[1] and from that time to the twentieth century was extensively manufactured. Among Copeland's finest works in Parian are the 'Infancy of Jupiter', 'Lady Godiva', 'Nora Creina', the 'Flute-player', the 'Reading Girl', busts of 'A Mother' and of 'Love' all by Monti; 'Young England' and 'Young England's Sister', a very charming pair by Halse; two admirable pairs, 'Before the Ball' and 'After the Ball', and 'Prosperity' and 'Adversity', and some flower-holders, by Owen Hall – a modeller of high repute and great power in design; a 'Shepherd-Boy', 'Spring' and 'Summer', by L. A. Malampre; and 'Master Tom' and 'On the Sea Shore', by Joseph Durham, R. A. Among their other special works, Foley's 'Ino and Bacchus', Durham's 'Chastity' and 'Santa Filomena', Monti's 'Night'

[1] For the full history of the Parian body, see Geoffrey Godden's *Victorian Porcelain*, Herbert Jenkins, London, 1961.

Fig. 22. Porcelain Centrepiece. Paris Exhibition of 1867.

and 'Morning', and a score or two others, are brilliant examples. Besides figures, groups and busts, a large number of other beautiful objects of various kinds were produced in Parian.

The more ordinary classes of goods for general use and consumption are all of good quality, whether produced in ordinary earthenware, stoneware, or any other kind of body, such as 'crown ware'.

Of the many talented Copeland artists, the principal ones were Hürten, who attained, and deservedly so, the distinction of being one of the best flower-painters in Europe (see Plate 64); Weaver, who after his death was worthily succeeded by his son and whose birds were equal to those of any other painter; Alcock, a figure-painter of great power and excellence (see Plate 65); F. Abraham, a figure-painter of much promise; and Brayford, whose productions were of a high order of merit. Besides these, a number of other talented artists were employed; and the staff of enamellers, ground-layers and gilders included some of the best obtainable in each department – Bale's speciality of jewelling being more perfect and beautiful than was usual. In these works, too, female talent had been highly cultivated, many of the productions of the paintresses evidencing pure feeling and cultivated taste. The art director of the establishment, Mr. R. F. Abraham, was formerly at Coalport with Mr. Rose. The softness of touch, purity and delicacy of feeling, sunny mellowness of

113

Fig. 23. Copeland's Parian figures at the 1871
Exhibition.

tone, chasteness of design, and correctness of
drawing produced on the best pieces of his productions proved him a thorough artist and
rendered him peculiarly fitted for the post to
which he had been called.

The marks successively used by this firm in
its various changes are as follows:

SPODE (Painted)	Sometimes impressed in the body, and at others painted on the glaze; also SPODE in larger capital letters, c. 1800–33.

Printed in blue or black on
the bottom of the goods of
that description, c.1805–33.

Spode printed marks employed prior to 1833

SPODE, SON & COPELAND or SPODE & COPE-
LAND, both impressed and printed. Prior to 1816

These marks with some variations in detail,
occur printed on the ware.

COPELAND
& GARRETT

C & G
with the name of
the pattern.

Various Copeland & Gar-
rett marks, c.1833–47, and,
below, Copeland marks
from 1847 onwards.

Copeland
Late Spode.

Copeland late Spode

COPELAND late SPODE.

COPELAND
LATE SPODE.

COPELAND

COPELAND
PATENT JASPER

COPELAND

Copeland

Copeland
Stone China

COPELAND

B

c.1875–89

c.1804–1910

TRADE MARK

COPELANDS CHINA
ENGLAND

Printed mark,
c.1875 onwards.

In recent years the new marks have incorporated the name 'Spode' and from 1970 the
former Copeland firm has been retitled SPODE
LIMITED.

The following are the approximate dates
when it is believed some of the most celebrated
printed patterns were first introduced: 'Castle',
1806; 'Roman', 1811; 'Turk', 1813; 'Milkmaid',
'Dagger-border', 'Tower', 'Peacock' and 'New
Temple', 1814; 'New Nankin', 'New Japan' and
'India', 1815; 'Italian' and 'Woodman', 1816;
'Blossom' and 'Pale Broseley', 1817; 'Waterloo'
and 'Arcade', 1818; 'Lucanao' and 'Ship', 1819;
'Panel Japan', 'Geranium' and 'Oriental', 1820;
'Font' and 'Marble', 1821; 'Bud and Flower',
'Sun', 'Bonpot' and 'Union', 1822; 'Double
Bonpot', 'Blue Border' and 'Filigree', 1823;
'Image' and 'Persian', 1824; 'Etruscan' and
'Bamboo', 1825; 'Blue Imperial' and 'Union
Wreath', 1826.

115

Plate 64. A pair of Copeland porcelain vases painted
by C. F. Hurten, the famous flower painter, c.1870.
19 inches high.   *Editor's collection.*

Plate 65. A fine Copeland porcelain plate painted by
Samuel Alcock, 'Court Costume of 1895'. c.1895.
                                Editor's collection.

For a good selection of Spode's various high
grade products, the reader is referred to A.
Hayden's *Spode and his Successors* (Cassell,
London, 1925); and for the many Spode blue-
printed patterns see S. B. Williams' *Antique Blue
and White Spode* (B. T. Batsford, London, 1943),
and, particularly, L. Whiter's *Spode, A History
of the Family, Factory and Wares from 1733–1833*
(Barrie & Jenkins, London, 1970).

Minton & Co.

Thomas Minton, the founder of this famous firm, was born in Wyle Cop, Shrewsbury, in 1765, and received his education at the Shrewsbury Grammar School. On leaving school, he was reputedly apprenticed as an engraver at the Caughley China Works, near Broseley, in Shropshire. On the expiration of his apprenticeship, he continued to be employed for a time at the Caughley China Works under Mr. Thomas Turner and then removed to London, where he reputedly engraved some patterns for Josiah Spode. From London, having married, he removed into Staffordshire in 1788 or 1789. In Staffordshire, he set up as a master-engraver at Stoke-upon-Trent, where the rapidly increasing demand for blue-printed earthenware gave promise of a good opening for so skilful a draughtsman and engraver as he had become. His residence and engraving shop was one of a block of buildings then called Bridge Houses, erected by Thomas Whieldon. Here he became very successful, one of his chief employers being Josiah Spode, for whom he engraved a tea-ware pattern called the 'Buffalo', which continued in demand for many years.

Plate 66. Selection of Minton porcelain teaware of the 1805–12 period. Marked only with pattern numbers. *Editor's collection.*

In 1793, having determined to commence the manufacture of earthenware, Thomas Minton purchased a plot of land – the site of the present manufactory – and commenced building on a very small scale. The following account of the early progress of the works was written by Mr. Stringer, Minton's historian, in the nineteenth century:

To start with, there was on 'Bisque' and one 'Glost' oven, with slip house for preparing the clay, and only such other buildings and appliances as were necessary to make a good working commencement. Mr. Minton formed an engagement with the brothers Poulson, who owned the works opposite to the land he had purchased, known as the 'Stone Works', and who were potters on a small scale and, as was then the practice, had houses on the works. Mr. Joseph Poulson was the practical potter and his brother Samuel was modeller, mould-maker and useful man-of-all-work. It was not until May 1796 that Mr. Minton's works were in operation. The next year's transactions showed a satisfactory advance in every respect, as did every subsequent year; and amongst the circumstances favouring Mr. Minton's prosperity may be named – first, that aided by Mr. Poulson's experience as a

potter, and his own good taste as an engraver and designer, he produced a quality and style of ware that commanded a ready market; and in his brother, Mr. Arthur Minton, who had established himself in the retail trade in the metropolis, a ready and devoted agent to extend the trade; so much so that the business done by him in 1800 amounted to nearly £2,000. He was also fortunate in having the acquaintance of Mr. William Pownall, a merchant of Liverpool, who aided him with capital to extend his operations and who was, for a few years, a sleeping partner in the business. Mr. Joseph Poulson was in a short time after the opening of the works admitted as a partner, and the firm traded as Minton & Poulson (c.1799–1801 and 1805–11).

From the first establishment of the pottery works at Stoke, their success was unbroken, and not only were great advances made in processes of manufacture but also they were so much enlarged that at the time of Mr. Minton's death in 1836 they were among the most important in the district. Herbert Minton, the second son, was born at the house erected at the works at Stoke-upon-Trent in March 1792. In 1808, when only sixteen, he became traveller and salesman and represented the house both in London and the provinces; and this he continued to do till more pressing engagements necessitated his more general attendance at the works. In 1817, Thomas and Herbert Minton were admitted into partnership with their father, the firm being Thomas Minton & Sons. In 1821, the elder brother, Thomas Webb Minton, quitted the works for the purpose of studying for the Church. In 1828, the partnership was dissolved, although Herbert Minton continued to devote his energies to the development of the concern.

On his father's death, in 1836, he again took up the business and shortly afterwards took into partnership John Boyle, under the style of

Plate 67 (facing). A superb Minton porcelain 'Wellington' vase, green ground, with flower painting probably by Thomas Steel, the famous Derby-trained flower painter, c.1830–5. 13½ inches high.
Editor's collection.

Minton & Boyle. In 1841, Mr. Boyle withdrew from the firm and, in about 1842, became a partner with the Wedgwoods. In 1845, Michael Hollins, nephew to Mrs. Minton, joined the firm under the style of Minton & Hollins, also known as Minton & Co. In 1849, a nephew of Mr. Minton's, Colin Minton Campbell, joined the firm. In 1858, Herbert Minton died, and Messrs Hollins and Campbell continued the manufactory, which was, in 1873, formed into an extended company, the trading style being simply Minton.

Up to the later part of 1797, white, cream-coloured and blue printed ware only was made at these works. In 1797, porcelain was introduced and continued until 1816, when it was abandoned and earthenware only again produced. Some pre-1816 tea-ware is shown in Plate 66. In 1824, porcelain was again made and has been a staple branch to the present day. A superb porcelain vase of the 1830s, shown in Plate 67, has a flower-painted panel by the Derby-trained artist Thomas Steel.

In the 1830s, some of the more skilled workmen from the Derby works found employment with Mr. Minton and brought their skill to bear on his productions. Among these were Steel, Bancroft and Hancock, as painters in fruit and flowers. John Simpson held the position of principal enamel-painter of figures and the highest class decorations from about 1837 to 1847, when he removed to London to take charge of the porcelain painting at Marlborough House. Simpson's painting is of superb quality, as is evidenced by his rare signed portrait miniatures. An example, of 1857, is shown in Plate 68.

Samuel Bourne, who had been apprenticed to Wood & Caldwell as an enamel-painter, entered the service of Mr. Minton in 1828 as chief designer and artist and continued until 1863, when the infirmities of increasing years necessitated his retirement. In 1848, Leon Arnoux, son of a manufacturer of hard porcelain at Toulouse, visited Stoke, and it was arranged that M. Arnoux should superintend and carry out the patent which, in 1839, Mr. Minton, in conjunction with Dr. Wilton George Turner, had taken out for an 'improved porcelain'.

Plate 69. A fine quality Minton porcelain plate with intricate pierced border, the centre painted with an interior view of the 1851 Exhibition.

Editor's collection.

Plate 68. A miniature on porcelain of the Princess Royal, signed by John Simpson, the Minton figure painter, and dated 1857.　　*Editor's collection.*

There was, however, so much risk in firing this 'Hard Paste' porcelain, in consequence of the difficulty of producing a sagger capable of withstanding the necessary heat, that the manufacture was abandoned, and M. Arnoux turned his attention to the artistic decoration of the ordinary manufacture. To his continual zeal and ability, combined with the enterprise which has always distinguished the firm, England is indebted for the highest honours in this branch of her national industries.

At the Great Exhibition of 1851, a council medal was awarded to this firm – an honour which each successive exhibition, whether English or foreign, has augmented. The open-work edged porcelain plate shown in Plate 69 is a typical example of this period and, in fact, shows an interior view of the 1851 Exhibition building.

In 1850, majolica was added to the other art productions of this manufactory, and in this the firm stood pre-eminent for sharpness of details, purity of colours, excellence of glaze, and artistic character of these goods. In 1851, Della Robbia and Palissy ware were also commenced. These types of earthenware, with their semi-translucent coloured glazes, proved exceedingly popular and the style was copied by most manufacturers from the 1850s onwards. None of them, however, reached the high standard of the Minton ware. An example, from the Victoria and Albert Museum, is shown in Plate 70. Colour Plate VI is typical of some superbly executed animal and bird models.

Of the variety of productions of Minton's works, it is impossible to speak in detail. So varied, so distinct, and so extensive are they in material, body, style, decoration and uses, that anything like a detailed account becomes impossible. In stoneware, all the ordinary articles – jugs, mugs, bottles etc. – were extensively produced; and in ordinary earthenware, dinner, tea, breakfast, toilet and other services were made in great variety, from the ordinary white and blue printed ware to richly enamelled and gilt patterns.

In china, besides all the usual services – dinner, tea, breakfast dessert, dejeuner, toilet, trinket – an endless variety of fancy and ornamental goods was produced. Notable among

120

Colour Plate VI. A Minton 'majolica'–glazed
cock, modelled by John Henk. Date mark for 1876.
13½ inches high.　　　*Godden of Worthing Ltd.*

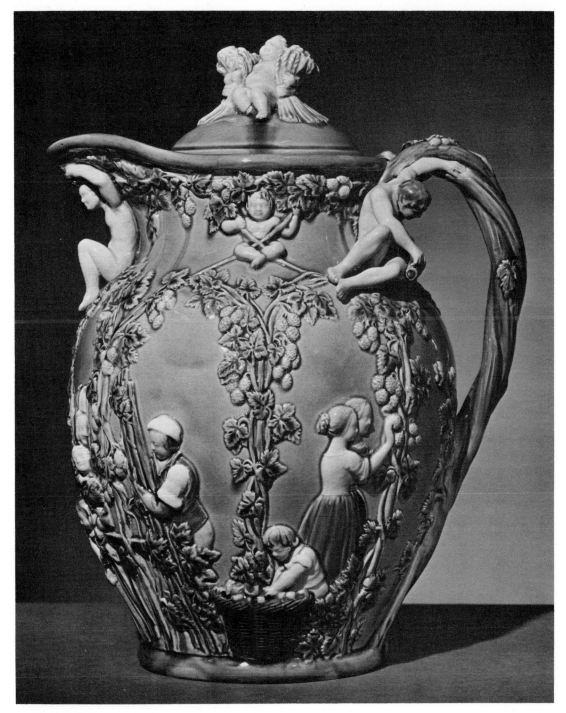

Plate 70. A Minton 'majolica'– glazed moulded
covered jug, designed by H. J. Townsend in 1847–
a popular model produced over several years, c 1847.
10½ inches high.
    Victoria & Albert Museum (Crown copyright).

Plate 71. A selection of rare Minton inlaid
earthenware copies of the very rare and early 'Henri
II' ware. The Minton examples normally bear the
signature of Charles Toft. c.1870–80. Central vase,
22 inches high.

City Museum & Art Gallery, Stoke-on-Trent.

these are vases, ewers, tazzae and other articles
of extreme beauty and of every style of decoration. For a period of about twenty years from the
late 1840s, some superb objects were made in
Sèvres-style (see Colour Plate VII). A marked
feature of the porcelain after 1863 is the embossed gilding of borders by a patented process. In
Parian, the statuary, busts, groups, vases, ewers
and other articles equal those of almost any
manufactory.

Of the many copies of earlier ceramic styles
attempted by Minton's, the rarest and most
interesting were the inlaid Henri Deux master-
pieces produced by Charles Toft in the 1860s
and 1870s. Such individual hand-made examples
were expensive and were made for the prestige
international exhibitions. A good selection of
the Henri Deux ware from the City Museum,
Stoke-on-Trent, is illustrated in Plate 71.

One of the processes successfully adopted by
Minton's was that of pâte-sur-pâte – a process in
which the artist, instead of using colour, em-
ploys liquid clay, in which he paints or, rather,
'lays on' his design, the whole being afterwards
glazed. In this process, Marc Louis Solon, formerly of Sèvres, was particularly successful, and
the trays, plaques, vases and other forms
produced by him are characterised by pure but
severe taste and masterly treatment.

For the full history and description of the
technique of 'pâte-sur-pâte', the reader is
referred to G. Godden's *Victorian Porcelain*
(Herbert Jenkins London, 1961). An engraving
of a Solon pâte-sur-pâte vase shown at the
1871 Exhibition is reproduced in Figure 24, but
the true beauty of this cameo-like ware is best
seen in Plate 72.

In contrast to these unique Solon master-
pieces, we have the mass-produced Minton tiles.
In 1828, Herbert Minton first turned his attention to the subject but was prevented by circumstances from fully developing his plans. In 1830,
Samuel Wright, of Shelton, took out a patent for

Colour Plate VII. A superb Minton porcelain vase
and cover, typical of this firm's Sèvres-styled ware.
c.1850–60. 18¾ inches high. *Godden of Worthing Ltd.*

the 'manufacture of ornamental tiles'. This, in January 1844, he supplemented by another patent for the 'manufacture of ornamental bricks and quarries for floor pavements and other purposes'. Mr. Wright's experiments were highly satisfactory; but from various causes, although he executed several orders, they were not commercially successful, and he sold his moulds and patent-rights to Mr. Minton, who agreed to pay him a royalty of ten per cent on all the tiles sold. Mr. Minton commenced the

Fig. 24. Minton pâte-sur-pâte vase by Solon. 1871 Exhibition.

manufacture in a single room next to the throwing-house at the earthenware works, and only three men were at first employed. He was much aided in his task by George Leason, a practical potter who had been brought up under him.

In June 1840, Richard Prosser took out a patent for making a variety of articles from clay in a powdered state, viz., buttons, tesserae, floor tiles, glazed tiles, tiles., etc., by pressure, by preference using screw presses of different powers for articles containing up to and including fifty square inches of surface in each piece; articles of larger surface and, of course, requiring a greater pressure being made by hydraulic presses, the pumps of which were worked by steam. Mr. Prosser sold the half part of the English patent to Mr. Minton.

In August 1845, Michael Daintry Hollins joined Mr. Minton in the general manufacturing business, and the tile department formed a separate concern under the style of Minton, Hollins & Co. The history of the manufacture of encaustic and other tiles by Minton, Hollins & Co. is the history of the entire trade in these useful and beautiful articles.

The marks used by Minton's are varied. The earliest to occur on porcelain is

A pattern number is often placed where the M is drawn here. The period of this mark is from about 1805–16. Earlier Minton porcelain normally bears only the pattern number, painted in a neat manner.

Numerous printed marks incorporating the initials of the various partnerships were then used, as follows:

M   – c.1822–36
M.&.B – c.1836–41
M.&.Co – c.1841–73
M.&.H – c.1845–68

From the late 1840s, a painted or gilt 'Ermine' mark was sometimes used. From 1842, small

123

Plate 72. A very fine Minton bottle-vase, decorated in the pâte-sur-pâte technique by M. L. Solon, c. 1900. 13¼ inches high.

Messrs. Sotheby & Co.

'year' marks were impressed into the ware; these show the year of manufacture.

MINTON YEARLY MARKS

1842	1843	1844	1845	1846	1847	1848	1849
1850	1851	1852	1853	1854	1855	1856	1857
1858	1859	1860	1861	1862	1863	1864	1865
1866	1867	1868	1869	1870	1871	1872	1873
1874	1875	1876	1877	1878	1879	1880	1881
1882	1883	1884	1885	1886	1887	1888	1889
1890	1891	1892	1893	1894	1895	1896	1897
1898	1899	1900	1901	1902	1903	1904	1905
1906	1907	1908	1909	1910	1911	1912	1913
1914	1915	1916	1917	1918	1919	1920	1921
1922	1923	1924	1925	1926	1927	1928	1929
1930	1931	1932	1933	1934	1935	1936	1937

1938	1939	1940	1941	1942

Impressed in the clay to show year of manufacture, 1842–1942 inclusive. The figures 43, etc., have been used for 1943 onwards. These cyphers occur in sets of three: month, potter's mark, and year cypher.

From 1862 to 1873, the name Minton was impressed in the body. This became Mintons after 1873.

Of the many printed marks employed, the staple one was the globe mark. This underwent changes over the years:

Uncrowned,
c. 1863–73

Crowned,
c.1873+
'England'
added below
from 1891

Twentieth-century
version with
'Made in England'

The reader is referred to G. Godden's *Minton Pottery and Porcelain of the First Period, 1793–1850* (Herbert Jenkins, London, 1968) for a full review of the Minton story up to 1850. Many other marks will be found, as well as numerous illustrations. After 1850, the story is continued in Godden's *Victorian Porcelain* in H. Wakefield's *Victorian Pottery* (Herbert Jenkins, London, 1961 and 1962 respectively).

It is virtually unnecessary to state that Messrs. Minton's still continue at Stoke. Their works Museum contains a magnificent collection of their ware.

Hollins

The history of the famous works of Messrs. Minton, Hollins & Co., and of the rise and development of their manufacture of encaustic, enamelled, majolica and other tiles, has already been given on page 123. In 1868, the partnership ceased and from that time the manufacture of tiles passed into the hands of Michael Hollins and was continued under the style of Minton, Hollins & Co. The productions of the works consisted of unglazed encaustic and tesselated or, rather, geometrical tiles for pavements; glazed encaustic tiles for fire-hearths; majolica and enamelled tiles for grate-cheeks, flowerboxes, wall-linings, etc.; and plain and painted tiles for various species of decoration. These were all made from the same moulds and were of precisely the same excellent quality, both in body and decoration, as under the old firm.

In majolica tiles for flower-boxes, many effective and appropriate designs were made in bold relief and richly coloured. Earthenware tiles, printed or painted, not in relief, were also largely produced for the same purpose. For wall decoration, fireplace cheeks and linings and other purposes, the variety of tiles was very extensive and embraced almost every class of design. In these were some with the patterns (notably the lily) all in very high relief, and colouring of the richest and most effective character. Others had their patterns painted by hand on the flat surface by skilled artists; and others, again, were transfer-printed or were a combination of printing and painting. Some formed a more or less rich diaper, some were separate or continuous patterns, and some formed borders of more than usual elegance. The fireplace and surround shown in Plate 73 formed part of the firm's display at the 1876 Philadelphia Exhibition.

Plate 73. A Minton Hollins tiled fireplace as shown at the 1876 Philadelphia Exhibition, from *The Art-Journal*, 1876.

The marks used were MINTON HOLLINS & CO. PATENT TILE WORKS, STOKE ON TRENT; MINTON & CO. Patent, STOKE ON TRENT; MINTON HOLLINS & CO. STOKE ON TRENT; M.H. & CO, etc., at the back of the tiles. Messrs. Minton Hollins Ltd. continued into the twentieth century, the Ltd.' being added in 1928.

The Trent Potteries

Established in 1861 by George Jones, who died in 1893, of the firm of George Jones & Sons. They produced all descriptions of earthenware, from the gaily-decorated articles required for Africa and South America, and white granite for the United States, to stoneware, and printed, enamelled, and gilt ware, for home use and for the Colonies. The firm also made both useful and ornamental articles in majolica, most of which are of a high order of art. Some of the productions exhibited in Paris in 1867 (when they obtained a medal), London in 1871, Vienna in 1873, and Sydney in 1876 are shown in Figure 26.

The imitation Palissy ware was highly successful, and in vases, candelabra, centre and side pieces, flower-shells and other articles many striking and good designs were produced. The manufacture of china in all its branches was added in 1876, and this was produced in great variety and of a high quality in body, glaze, and artistic finish. A flower-basket, formed like the curled leaf of a water-lily, has its double handle – which forms a support by passing beneath the leaf – composed of the long flower-stems of the plant twisted and plaited together, with exquisitely modelled flowers and buds at the sides. Another equally charming production is a quadruple flower-basket whose handles, crossing each other, loop up and give apparent support to the matted basket. These may be classed among the most elegant of novelties. They are produced in celadon and white china.

What we have said about these china flower-baskets will hold equally well with regard to the pâte colorée in vases – which, in the firm's finest body of earthenware, were introduced in about 1880. The delicate ground-colours of these, the

Fig. 25, Messrs. George Jones' majolica ware.

Plate 74. A George Jones pâte-sur-pâte vase by F. Schenck, c.1885. 14 inches high.
Godden of Worthing Ltd.

masterly way in which the groups of flowers and foliage are arranged, the judicious manner in which the relief decoration is managed, the purely artistic painting of the groups, the heightening of the rims and supports with gold, and the perfect harmony and unobtrusiveness of the whole render these productions of Messrs. Jones and Sons acquisitions to be sought and cherished. The pâte-sur-pâte style of decoration was employed c.1876–86. A fine example is shown in Plate 74.

George Jones' son, Horace, was trained at the South Kensington Art School and designed many of the firm's patterns and forms. Such pieces may bear his initials, H.O.J. The trade mark used by this firm was simply the initials G J joined together. A later version is the same monogram of G J between the horns of a crescent, on which are added '& Sons'. In about

127

Plate 75. Representative pieces from the Earl of
Shrewsbury's service made by Messrs. H. & R.
Daniel in 1827. Diameter of plate, 10 inches.
Godden of Worthing Ltd.

1907, the Trent Pottery was renamed the Crescent Pottery, and the word Cresent occurs under some late marks of the 1924–51 period.

Henry Daniel: H. & R. Daniel

Henry Daniel, who had earlier been responsible for all the enamelling and gilding at the Spode works, established his own porcelain factory at Stoke in 1823. Extremely fine work was carried out at this little-known manufactory. In about 1826, the style became H. & R. Daniel. Rare marked specimens show the quality attained. In 1827, the Earl of Shrewsbury ordered several services from this firm. A selection of pieces from one of the Earl's services is shown

in Plate 75, and these examples show well the fine quality of the Daniel products. Many pieces from these Shrewsbury services bear a large printed mark of flowers, a vase and a harp with the words H. & R. DANIEL, STOKE-UPON-TRENT, STAFFORDSHIRE. But most Daniel products are unmarked. The representative parts of a tea-set shown in Plate 76 are good examples of Daniel porcelain.

From about 1829, the firm's style was H. Daniel & Sons. Henry died in 1841. The Stoke pottery was continued by Richard until about 1854. The Daniels closely rivalled Spode and Minton, and their ware is unfortunately neglected by collectors, who as yet do not recognise Daniel porcelain.

Fig. 26. Messrs. George Jones' majolica ware.

129

Copeland Street Works

The business of this firm was established in 1859 at the Albert Works, Liverpool Road, by Turner, Hassall & Bromley as a Parian manufactory only. In 1863, the much larger Copeland Street Works were built. In 1865, Mr. Bromley having previously retired, Mr. Thomas Peake joined the firm, which continued as Turner, Hassall, & Peake until 1871, when the last-named was succeeded by Mr. Poole and the style became Turner, Hassall & Poole. In 1873, Mr. Hassall was succeeded by Mr. Stanway and the firm became Turner, Poole & Stanway. Later on, Mr. Turner also retired and, Josiah Wood having become a partner, the style was altered to Poole, Stanway & Wood and so continued until 1880, when it changed to Turner & Wood – being carried on by Josiah Wood and the executors of Mr. Turner until the closure in 1888.

At first, only Parian was made; but after a time, the decoration of china (bought in the white) was added. After about ten years, the manufacture of china was commenced, and it developed into a large branch of the business. The productions were principally Parian statuary of a good quality in body, colour and workmanship; china tea, breakfast, dessert, trinket and other services, vases, figures and groups; majolica in all the usual varieties of articles; and terra-cotta, in which were produced water-jugs, fern-stands, tobacco-jars, filters, candlesticks, flower-vases and teapots. A speciality of the works, introduced by Mr. Turner, was the novelty of decorating the Parian body with majolica colours, by which means a clearness and brilliancy as well as softness of colour was attained and a pleasing effect gained. The terra-cotta goods were produced in red and cane colour, and were richly enamelled. In statuary Parian, a large variety of groups, single figures, busts, animals and ornamental pieces were produced. The models have a high degree of excellence. In centre-pieces and compotiers, the firm was particularly successful. In 1886, this firm advertised 'over 5,000 special articles and designs'.

Albert Works

The works formerly carried on by the above firm were occupied in about 1882 by J. & J. Snow who here, as well as at the Pyenest Street Works, Hanley, manufactured terra-cotta, jet, majolica and other varieties of ware, both in the useful and ornamental classes. They continued at Stoke until 1895 and at Hanley until 1907.

Glebe Street Works and Wharf Street Works

These two manufactories belonged to Robinson & Leadbeater and were confined to the production of Parian goods, of which they were among the largest producers. The **Glebe Street Works** were commenced in 1850 by a clever Italian figure-modeller named Giovanni Meli, who produced fine groups and single figures till 1865, when he sold the business, plant, moulds and machinery to Robinson & Leadbeater and returned to Italy with the intention of commencing a terra-cotta manufactory. This he relinquished, mainly through lack of a suitable native clay or marl for the making of his saggers, and went to Chicago, where he succeeded in his wishes and established a manufactory of the kind he attempted in Italy.

The **Wharf Street Works** were commenced in 1858 by Leveson Hill, after whose death, in 1860, they were carried on by his executors until 1870, when they were sold to Robinson & Leadbeater, who thus became proprietors of both concerns. By them, the works were considerably enlarged and, as their business operations were rapidly extending, they soon ranked amongst the largest in the district.

They produced Parian figures, groups and busts in large variety – classical, portrait, and imaginative; vases of endless form and variety; centrepieces and comports; flower-stands; brackets and pedestals; bouquet-holders; trinket-caskets; cream-ewers, jugs and other articles. By giving constant and undivided attention to this one branch of ceramic art (Parian), the firm succeeded in so improving it, in fineness and purity of body and in tone of colour, as to render their productions of far higher than average merit. They studied excellence of body, originality of design and

Plate 76. A Daniel porcelain tea service of fine
quality, c.1835. Diameter of plate, 9 inches.
Godden of Worthing Ltd.

131

cleverness of workmanship as before that of marketable cheapness. In material, they ranked with the best productions of many competing firms, while in fineness of surface and careful manipulation they were scarcely excelled. Some examples are finished in a warm ivory tone (Plate 78).

Plate 77. Selection of Robinson & Leadbeater figures from an advertisement of 1896.

Among the designs produced by this firm, there were many of more than average merit and, in some instances, of large size. 'Clytie', a clever reproduction, is a bust of about twenty-two inches in height; 'Apollo' is twenty-six inches high; and several others (Gladstone, Disraeli, Cobden, Tennyson, Dickens and other Victorian celebrities) are of various heights. Among their principal groups are 'Innocence Protected', 'Penelope', 'The Power of Love,' 'Cupid Betrayed', 'Cupid Captive', 'Golden Age', 'Rock of Ages', 'Guardian Angel', 'The Immaculate Conception', 'Christ and St. John', 'The Combat', 'Lion Slayer', 'Dante and Beatrice', 'Hubert and Arthur', and 'Virgin and Child'. In single figures, there are many well designed and faultlessly produced. These are all good, and the same remark will apply to the remainder of the figures and busts. Among the latter, those of Abraham Lincoln, Charles Sumner, Governor Andrew, Garfield and Long-fellow had a very extensive sale in the United States – to which market, indeed, the greater part of their general statuary and other goods was sent.

Messrs. Robinson & Leadbeater continued into the twentieth century. The late nineteenth-century mark was R & L in an oval; but most examples are unmarked. Frederick Robinson established his own business at 55 Wharf Street in 1905, but the original firm retained the old title.

Copeland Street

At these works (formerly Billington & Co.), Messrs. Shorter & Boulton, who entered upon them in 1879, chiefly manufactured majolica for the American and Australian markets. Many of their designs in vases, flower-stands, jugs, trays, dejeuner- and tea-sets, etc., were strikingly original, and the quality was of more than average excellence. Messrs. Shorter & Boulton continued until 1905.

Plate 78. Two Robinson & Leadbeater figures, tinted in imitation of ivory. Initial marks. c.1890. 18 inches high.

Godden of Worthing Ltd.

Bridge Works

This manufactory was formerly worked by Davenport & Co., W. Adams & Co., Minton, Hollins & Co., Jones & Co., Grose & Son, and Hancock & Whittingham (1873–9). From 1879 to 1882, Messrs. B. & S. Hancock were working the Bridge Works, which was then carried on by S. Hancock for the production of the usual classes of earthenware from 1882 to 1891. From 1892 into the twentieth century, Messrs. S. Hancock & Sons were at Wolfe Street, Stoke.

Anchor Works

This manufactory formerly belonged to Thomas Wolfe, next to his son-in-law, Hamilton (as Wolfe & Hamilton, c.1800–11), and later was worked by Z. Boyle & Co., W. Adams & Co., and Minton, Hollins, & Co. In 1872, Messrs. Walker & Carter took over the works for the manufacture of ordinary earthenware. They continued to about 1889.

London Road (and Eastwood Vale)

The works of William Henry Goss (born in 1833; died in 1906) were commenced in 1858 for the production of Parian, ivory porcelain and terra-cotta, and their progress from that time was very marked. The most famous of the specialities of Mr. Goss's manufacture was jewelled porcelain, in which vases, scent-bottles, tazzae, and other ornaments were produced; also vessels to be filled with perfumes, including illuminated scent-vases, pomade-boxes, rice-powder jars, pastile and scented ribbon burners – the latter made largely for the great Paris and London perfume houses.

The process of modelling jewelled porcelain, which is of extreme richness and beauty, was the invention of Mr. Goss, who, observing that the enamel jewels on the old Sèvres porcelain frequently dropped off or were rubbed off, turned his attention to the subject. The process adopted at Sèvres was as follows: a gold foil was marked into circles, ovals and other required forms for the reception of the enamels, which were then pencilled-on and fired before applying them to the article they were intended to decorate. After being vitrified into imitations of uncut rubies, emeralds, etc., they were stuck on the surface of the porcelain with a flux and again fired. The adhesion was by this process often incomplete, and thus it frequently occurred that part of the design became rubbed away. The process invented by Mr. Goss for this mosaic jewellery was to indent the designs for the intended jewelled decoration in the dry or moist clay before baking, and in these to insert the jewels – which were all previously cut – and thus attain an increased brilliancy. Being inserted into the hollow or recess prepared for them, they were made secure. The process was an extremely delicate but very ingenious and beautiful one, and the effect produced was richer and finer than that attained by any other processes. Real pearls are said to have been also introduced by Mr. Goss with good effect.

The floral brooches and crosses are of great beauty, and in delicacy of modelling remind one of the famous old Bristol floral plaques. Some were produced in pure white bisque, others were tinted in the natural colours of the flowers represented, and others were in ivory porcelain prepared by a patented process.

In Parian – for which Mr. Goss ranked deservedly high – busts, statuary (notably an exquisite group of Lady Godiva), vases, tazzas, bread-platters and many other ornamental goods were made. Notable among these are admirable busts of Queen Victoria, the Earl of Beaconsfield, Mr. Gladstone, Lord Derby, etc. As portrait-busts, they rank far above the average and are, indeed, perfect reproductions of the original persons. It is not often that this can be said of portrait-busts, but it was a particular study of Mr. Goss and he succeeded admirably in it.

Another of Mr. Goss's specialities was ivory porcelain, which he produced in a full, soft, mellow tone which characterises the finest ivory. It possesses all the delicate beauty of ivory but with more durability; and, unlike ivory, it is unchanging. In this material, one of Mr. Goss's most successful productions was a pierced scent-bottle of the pilgrim-bottle or puzzle-jug

Fig. 27. Mr. Goss's productions at the 1862 Exhibition.

form. Its centre was double-pierced in a very elaborate pattern and judiciously heightened with lines of gold.

Another of Mr. Goss's achievements was in the production of egg-shell porcelain, in which he stood pre-eminent. The pieces produced in this are so light and thin; and yet the body is of such extreme hardness and firmness that it is as strong as thicker and more massive ware. It is a finer and purer body than Sèvres, thinner and far more translucent than Belleek, more delicate in tone than Worcester, and more dainty to the touch than any other.

In terra-cotta, of peculiarly fine quality and rich colour, water-bottles and all the usual articles were made. Many examples were decorated with fern motifs. All kinds of enamel colours and lustres were also made at these works. The name W. H. GOSS was generally stamped in the ware; and on the higher class goods, the crest – a falcon rising, ducally gorged – was used. Messrs. W. H. Goss continued into the twentieth century and became Goss China Co. Ltd. in 1934.

To present-day readers, the name Goss is almost entirely associated with small trinkets bearing the arms of various towns or cities. These pieces only became an important branch of the Goss products in the 1890s, continuing in high favour up to the period of the 1914–18 war.

[The reader is warned that the vases shown as Figures 1243 to 1249 in the 1883 edition are not of Goss manufacture.]

Empire Works

The Empire Porcelain Company was established in about 1896 at the Empire Works in Stoke Road. A wide range of pottery and porcelain was subsequently produced. The various marks include the initials E.P.C., E.P. or the word Empire. The firm continued to 1967.

London Road

In 1856, a valuable mine of red clay having been found on the London Road, a manufactory of floor, roof and ridge-tiles, etc., was commenced and was purchased by William Kirkham who, in 1862, built a manufactory for the production of terra-cotta and general earthenware for the home and foreign markets. To this, he added the making of brassfounders' fittings, chemists' goods and stoneware. The terra-cotta comprised water-bottles, ornamental flower-pots and stands, table-jugs, spill-cases and a variety of other articles a deep, rich, full red in colour, and close, hard and durable in texture. The ornamentation consisted of printed groups of Etruscan figures, borders and groups of flowers, enamelling in various colours, and dead and burnished gilding. Some of the fern decorations were graceful, natural and elegant; and those with Etruscan figures and enamelled borders were in good taste. William Kirkham continued to 1892.

London Road

Messrs. Steele & Wood commenced the manufacture of art-tiles in 1874 at their London Road pottery, and were very successful in producing decorated tiles of various classes for hearths, stoves, dados, pilasters, furniture and skirtings. The partnership was dissolved in 1884 but the old title was retained until 1892.

Railway Pottery

Established by S. Fielding & Co. in Sutherland Street in 1870 for the manufacture of majolica, terra-cotta, jet, Rockingham, green-glaze goods and general earthenware, in all of which the usual useful, ornamental, and fancy articles were made.

This firm introduced in the early 1880s a new feature in majolica goods, which they named 'Majolica argenta', in which they produced a vast variety of articles of a remarkably taking, pleasing and useful character. This, as its name implied, consisted of a white body and glaze with the proper majolica colouring liberally and judiciously used either on the body or on the embossed decorations. The effect was extremely pleasing. Some of the more popular and artistic patterns were 'Shell and Net', 'Ribbon and Leaf', 'Daisy', and 'Fan'; and in each of these, the idea of the pattern was fully carried out on an infinite variety of articles, ranging from large ice-dishes and bread-trays to cups and saucers and all the minutiae of the table.

One of the distinctive features of the majolica produced by Messrs. Fielding & Co. was the masterly and effective way in which they introduced, on some of their best pieces, hand-modelled flowers and foliage. Modelled and coloured true to nature in every minute detail, and thrown in graceful negligence around the bodies of the vases, they became such perfect reproductions that it was difficult to divest the mind of the idea that the roses were not fresh gathered from the tree and temporarily twined around the vase for its adornment.

In addition to majolica, which had been their staple trade, Messrs. Fielding & Co. extended their works, in about 1880, by adding the manufacture of a good quality of earthenware, in which they produced all the usual services and other articles. Among the novelties in toilet sets were the 'Spring' and 'Fruit' patterns, the underglaze decoration of which was of a highly satisfactory character; and another in which the handle of the ewer was formed of a riding-whip, the thong of which was brought round the sides, which were further decorated by a horseshoe in relief suspended from a ribbon. Their mark was FIELDING impressed, or the name of the pattern on a ribbon, with the initials S.F. & Co., printed. Messrs. S. Fielding & Co. (Ltd.) continue to the present day. Their well known trade name is Crown Devon. Hand-painted vases and other objects were produced in the twentieth century.

Victoria Pottery Company

The works of this company, in Lonsdale Street, were established in 1882 by Messrs. Robinson, Leadbeater & Leason for the manufacture of the higher classes of majolica and ivory or cream-coloured earthenware. In these, they produced all the usual varieties of useful and ornamental goods; the dessert services, game-pie dishes and other articles were of more than average excellence. The firm was of very short duration.

The Campbell Brick and Tile Company

The company was formed in 1875 for the purpose of carrying on at Fenton the business of Robert Minton Taylor (nephew to Herbert Minton and a partner in the firm of Minton,

Hollins & Co. till 1868, when a dissolution, consequent on effluxion of time, took place). A new manufactory, to which the Fenton business was transferred, was erected at Stoke in 1876. The productions, like those at Fenton, were encaustic, mosaic, geometrical, and majolica tiles. The encaustic tiles were produced not only in the usual simple red and buff colours but also in various combinations of buff, red, blue, green, yellow, white, black, brown, grey and every shade of compound colour. The geometric tiles were prepared with mathematical nicety, and produced remarkably rich and effective pavements. Some have the ornament exquisitely modelled in relief and in the representation of natural objects, such as the hawthorn, bramble, violet, primrose, anemone, lily and lilac.

The mark of the firm was a compass $\begin{smallmatrix} & N & \\ W & + & E \\ & S & \end{smallmatrix}$ encircled by the words CAMPBELL BRICK & TILE CO., STOKE-UPON-TRENT.

In 1882, the title was amended to the Campbell Tile Co. (Ltd), and as such continued into the twentieth century.

"Otago" Toilet.

"Osborne" Dinner Ware, "Kent pattern.

Fluted Toilet, "Delhi" pattern.

Fluted Sardine.

Fluted Dinner Ware, "Kew" pattern.

"Poppy" Stilton.

Desk Stilton, 3 Sizes.

Fluted Butter Stand.

Fig. 28. S. Fielding & Co.'s ordinary ware as advertised in 1892.

Keys & Mountford

Samuel Keys was originally a figure modeller at the Derby factory, and later at Minton's. He manufactured well designed Parian figures and groups, in partnership with John Mountford, in John Street from about 1849 to 1857. Several examples were exhibited by this firm at the 1851 Exhibition.

John Mountford, who claimed to have discovered the Parian body while employed by Copeland's, continued at John Street until about 1859. Signed examples are recorded.

Samuel Keys was in partnership with Briggs, as Keys & Briggs at Copeland Street, Stoke, from about 1860 to 1864. Examples of their earthenware were included in the 1862 Exhibition.

Fig. 29. 'Durham' Beer Set.

Winton Pottery

Messrs. Grimwade Brothers established their Winton Pottery in about 1886. A wide range of useful and decorative earthenware was produced. The Durham Beer Set illustrated in Figure 29 was made in several patterns and sold in the 1890s at a cost of from 1/11d to 3/9d per set. The style became Grimwades Ltd. in about 1890, and as such continues to the present day.

Alexander Pottery

George Thomas Mountford established this pottery in Wolfe Street in about 1880. Good-class earthenware was produced to 1898, when Messrs. Myott Son & Co. (Ltd.) succeeded. This later firm moved to Cobridge early in the twentieth century, and afterwards to their present factory at Hanley.

Carlton Works

Messrs. Wiltshaw & Robinson established their Carlton Works in Copeland Street, Stoke, in about 1890. They produced good quality china and earthenware, which is normally marked with their trade mark Carlton or the initials W. & R. In 1958, the firm was renamed Carlton Ware Ltd.

Colonial Pottery

Messrs. Winkle & Wood (formerly of the Pearl Pottery, Hanley) took the Colonial Pottery in 1889. In 1890, F. Winkle continued the Colonial Pottery as F. Winkle & Co. (while Wood continued the Pearl Pottery). General earthenware was produced. Marks incorporate the initials F W & Co. 'Ltd.' was added after 1910, and the firm continued to about 1931.

Potters working in Stoke in 1890 and not previously mentioned include:

Beech & Adams
Boulton & Floyd
Brough & Jones
C. R. Clark & Co.
Gaskell & Grocott
W. T. Gleaves
Thomas Hulse
Marsh & Co.
G. Mellor & Co.
J. & R. Plant
Pointon & Co. Ltd.
Shingley & Co.
Smith & Co.
C. Toft.

and in 1900:

Biltons Ltd.
L. A. Birks & Co.
Boulton & Floyd
J. W. Brough
J. F. Elton & Co.
J. F. Matthews
James Smith.

137

TUNSTALL

The Tunstall potters enumerated by Simeon Shaw in 1829 were John Mear, T. Goodfellow, Ralph Hall, S. and J. Rathbone, J. Boden, Bourne, Nixon & Co., Breeze & Co., and Burrows & Co. John Ward, in 1843, enumerated seventeen: china and earthenware – Hancock & Wright, Bill & Proctor, and Rathbone & Brummitt; earthenware only – Wood & Challinor, Thos. Goodfellow, John Meir & Son, Joseph Heath & Co., Hall & Holland, Wm. Adams, Jun. & Co. (Greenfield), Podmore Walker & Co. (two manufactories), James Beech (two), Thos. Bowley, and Mayer & Mawdesley; china toys and black ware – Michael Tunnicliffe and John Harrison. James Beech & Abraham Lowndes also had a manufactory here in 1829.

Unicorn Pottery and Pinnox Works

These large and important manufactories of general earthenware, situated in Amicable Street and Great Woodland Street, were, early in the nineteenth century, occupied by Edward Challinor, who was succeeded in 1825 by Podmore Walker & Co. (who also occupied the Swan Bank Pottery). They were succeeded by Wedgwood & Co, the head of the firm being Enoch Wedgwood. The works, which were very extensive and gave employment to six or seven hundred persons, occupied an area of about an acre of ground and were among the most substantially built and best arranged in the pottery district. The goods produced were the higher classes of earthenware, in which dinner, tea, breakfast, dessert, toilet and other services, and all the usual miscellaneous articles were made

to a very considerable extent, for the home, Colonial, Continental and American markets. The quality of the "Imperial Ironstone China' – the staple production of the firm – was of remarkable excellence, both in body and glaze.

The aim of the firm was to produce the best, most artistic, and most pleasingly effective designs and adapt them to ordinary purposes, so that they might become the everyday surroundings of the artisan as well as of the educated man. Thus they associated durability of quality in body and a perfect glaze with purity of outline in form, chasteness of decoration, and clearness and harmony of colour, adapting their designs and styles of decoration to the national tastes of the people in the various parts to which the goods were sent.

One of the most successful of their original ordinary printed designs was the pattern known as 'Asiatic Pheasants', which became so popular as to be considered one of the standard patterns of this country and the Colonies. It was, indeed, so popular that this blue-printed design was copied by nearly every Staffordshire earthenware manufacturer of the period. The Wedgwood & Co. version is shown in Plate 79.

Other equally effective designs were also introduced by Messrs. Wedgwood with great success. In the higher classes of decoration – painting, jewelling, and gilding – the productions ranked deservedly high, and the firm was particularly successful in services bearing monograms and armorial decorations. They also supplied large quantities of Ironstone china, specially made for the use of ships,

138

restaurants and hotels, which was considered to be exceedingly durable. The basic marks used by the firm were:

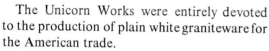

Plate 79. A Wedgwood & Co. (of Tunstall) blue-printed plate of the popular 'Asiatic Pheasants' design, c.1870. *Editor's collection.*

The Unicorn Works were entirely devoted to the production of plain white graniteware for the American trade.

Messrs. Wedgwood & Co. became a limited company in 1900 and continued using this old title until 1965, when the new style Enoch Wedgwood (Tunstall) Ltd. was adopted to avoid the confusion which often arose between the old title (and marks) and that of Josiah Wedgwood & Sons Ltd.

Greenfield Works

This business was originally established at Stoke by the grandfather of William Adams III, who carried on the business in his own name until about 1829, when it was changed to Wm. Adams & Sons – the second William Adams being head of the firm. In 1834, the works at Greenfield, Tunstall, were opened. In 1853, a dissolution took place and the works were carried on by William Adams (the second) until 1865, when he retired in favour of his sons, William and Thomas – the style then being W. & T. Adams. It is recorded that, in the 1860s, 73,000 dozen plates were made by this firm per week! The trade was entirely confined to foreign markets.

Their earthenware was noted for the richness and variety of its coloured and printed patterns, the bright fancy character of which was much admired. The goods consisted of tea, toilet, and table services, besides other articles. White granite (or Ironstone china) was also made for the American and other markets, some of the raised patterns – as, for instance, the 'Dover' – being remarkably good and the forms of the pieces faultless. Transfer-printing was much used, and was judiciously combined with 'sponged' patterns with good effect. Many marks have been used, and Messrs. William Adams & Sons (Potters) Ltd. continue to the present day.

William Adams was an apprentice to Josiah Wedgwood. He commenced business for himself at Tunstall, and there produced some fine works of art in jasper and other ware. He was succeeded in the Tunstall business by his son Benjamin Adams. 'About 1800', according to Shaw, 'Mr. Benjamin Adams, of Tunstall, was successful in the manufacture of jasper', in imitation of that of Wedgwood. Benjamin Adams continued until about 1819. For a full history of the Adams family of potters, and for illustrations of their ware, the reader is referred to William Turner's *William Adams – An Old English Potter* (Chapman & Hall Ltd., London, 1904).

139

Plate 80. An Adams granite-ware teapot bearing the impressed initial mark W.A. & S., c.1840. 8 inches high. *Editor's collection.*

The Newfield Works

Occupied in 1857 by William Adams, junr., these works were carried on by Messrs. W. H. Grindley & Co. from 1880 to 1891 for the same classes of goods. Messrs. W. H. Grindley & Co. (Ltd.) worked the Woodland Pottery, Tunstall, from 1891 to the present day.

George Street Pottery

Established in 1862. At these works, William Holdcroft (formerly Holdcroft & Wood, working period 1864–71) manufactured earthenware dinner, toilet, tea, and other services, and the usual varieties of useful articles, including jugs in great variety. The styles of ornamentation were hand-painting, transfer-printing, ground-colours and lustre-glazes. Connected with these works is the interesting fact that Mr. Holdcroft was the first to introduce into the Potteries the down-draught system of firing, which effected a great saving in fuel and a freedom from smoke. William Holdcroft worked at George Street from 1871 to 1896 and was succeeded by Holdcroft & Co. from 1896 to 1905.

Lion Works

These works in Sandyford were commenced for home trade goods by James Beech in 1838. In 1845, they passed to Thomas Walker, who made South American goods, and in 1856 to Broughton & Mayer. In 1862, Ford & Challinor became proprietors and continued the manufacture of general earthenware for the home and foreign markets to about 1880. Thomas Ford & Co. succeeded from 1880 to 1890.

Phoenix Works

These works were built in the eighteenth century by Anthony Keeling, one of the eminent potters of the district in the olden days. He married Ann, daughter of the celebrated Enoch Booth, to whose business he succeeded. At the commencement of the nineteenth century, he was the principal manufacturer in Tunstall. He was succeeded in 1810 by Thomas Goodfellow, from whom the works passed into the hands of Mr. Bridgwood, by whom (being joined in partnership by Edward Clarke in 1858) they were carried on under the style of Bridgwood & Clarke. Mr. Bridgwood dying in 1864, Mr. Clarke became sole proprietor and carried on the concern until 1877, when he removed to the New Bridge Works, at Longport, and later to the Churchyard Works at Burslem. The marks used were EDWARD CLARKE impressed on the body of the ware, and the royal arms with supporters, garter, motto, etc., above a flowing ribbon on which are the words EDWARD CLARKE, PORCELAIN OPAQUE, and beneath, TUNSTALL. Edward Clarke continued at Burslem until about 1887.

Victoria Works

Established in 1858 by John Tomkinson, then carried on under the style of Turner & Tomkinson from 1861 until 1873, when Mr. Tomkinson retired and the business was continued by George Turner and his sons under the style of G. W. Turner & Sons. The goods produced were ordinary printed and enamelled earthenware in dinner, toilet, and other services for the home and colonial markets. The mark used was simply the name or initials of the firm. Messrs. G. W. Turner & Sons continued until about 1895. They also owned the Alexandra Works at Tunstall.

The Swan Bank Works

One of the oldest manufactories in Tunstall, it belonged to Ralph Hall from about 1822 to 1848. Ralph Hall was succeeded by Podmore, Walker & Co., from whom, in about 1862, it passed into the hands of Beech & Hancock, and from 1876 to James Beech. The productions were the ordinary classes of earthenware and stoneware for the home trade, in which all the usual services were made in 'sponged', printed, painted, enamelled, gilt, and lustred styles. Stoneware jugs of excellent quality and other articles were also made, as were black ware and other jardinieres or flower vases. James Beech continued to 1889.

Black Bank and High Street Works

These works were carried on by Ralph Hammersley from about 1860 to 1888 – the latter for the production of ordinary earthenware, and the former for common jet, red and Rockingham ware articles. Ralph Hammersley (& Sons) potted at Burslem until 1905.

The Church Bank Works

Built in 1842 by Robert Beswick, by whom they were carried on until 1860, and since then by Beech & Hancock, Eardley & Hammersley (1862–8), Ralph Hammersley alone, and from 1870 by Thomas Booth & Son. The firm commenced business in 1864 at the Knowles Works, Burslem, as Evans & Booth, which in 1868 was altered to Thomas Booth & Co., and in 1872 to Thomas Booth & Son. In about 1876, Thomas G. Booth succeeded. In 1883, Messrs. T. G. & F. Booth took over and continued to 1891, when the style became Booths. 'Ltd' was added in about 1898. This firm continued to the 1940s. Various marks have been used incorporating the initials of the various firms – T B & Co., TGB., etc. All these firms produced good quality earthenware objects.

Messrs. Booths Ltd. became famous for their 'Royal Semi-Porcelain' and for their 'Silicon China'. An important twentieth-century development that should be noted here was in the large scale reproduction of eighteenth-century Worcester (and other 'collectable') porcelain.

Such pieces may bear the crescent-shaped mark (really the initials of C. Bowers) or copies of the old marks. Other specimens are unmarked and are often offered for sale as originals. It should be noted that the Booth copies are in opaque earthenware, not porcelain as were the originals.

Well Street Pottery or The Old Works

These works – of old foundation – were formerly carried on by Clive & Lloyd, and, after Mr. Lloyd retired, by Stephen Clive under the style of Stephen Clive & Co. from about 1875 to 1880. They were worked by Cumberlidge & Humphreys from 1880 to 1885 (and later at the Gordon Pottery). Their productions were the ordinary middle classes of earthenware goods for the home and foreign markets.

Woodland Pottery

Messrs. Hollinshead & Kirkham, formerly Edmund T. Wood (working period 1860–75), carried on this pottery, which was situated in Woodland Street. Earthenware for the home and foreign markets was produced in all the usual varieties from 1876 to 1890. From 1890 to 1956, Messrs. Hollinshead & Kirkham were at the Unicorn Pottery, Tunstall.

Greengate Pottery

Messrs. John Meir & Son manufactured earthenware here in all the usual services of the more ordinary classes. From 1812 to 1836, the style was John Meir; and from 1841 to 1897, it was John Meir & Son. Several initial marks were used. Often, the initial I is given instead of J.

Sandyford Works

Ordinary earthenware was made here by Jabez Blackhurst from 1872 to 1883.

Tunstall or Church Works

In 1857, Messrs. Blackhurst & Dunning commenced these works for the manufacture of ordinary earthenware for the home and South American markets. In 1867, Mr. Dunning died and the business was carried on by Richard Blackhurst alone till his death in 1877; then by Messrs. Goode & Kenworthy, who continued to about 1888. Messrs. Goode & Watton continued until 1894.

Highgate Pottery

Established by George Hood, who purchased the land from Mr. Randle-Wilkinson in 1831 and built the manufactory. The works were bought in 1846 by William Emberton, after whose death in 1863 they were carried on by his sons, Thomas Isaac and James Emberton, until 1882. The goods manufactured were all the usual varieties of earthenware for the home markets, and the firm was also a large producer of special goods for Ceylon, Calcutta, Bombay and other Indian markets. From 1882 to 1888, James Emberton continued the Highgate Pottery. George Hood is believed to have produced many earthenware figures during the first half of the nineteenth century.

Clay Hill Pottery

Messrs. Thomas Elsmore & Son manufactured ordinary earthenware here from about 1872 to 1887.

Royal Albert Works

Established in 1873. Alfred Meakin produced a large range of good Ironstone china and earthenware here during the later part of the nineteenth century. As Alfred Meakin (Tunstall) Ltd., the firm continues to the present day and has become one of Britain's foremost manufacturers.

Soho Works

George Guest manufactured common earthenware here from about 1875 to 1885. Rathbone Smith & Co. are listed at the Soho

Pottery from 1884 to 1897; then Smith & Binnall; and, from 1900, the Soho Pottery Company.

Gritten Street

J. & W. Selman produced earthenware figures here in the 1860s. Rare marked examples are recorded.

Brownhills

In about 1782, John Wood (son of Ralph Wood, of Brownhills, and Mary Wedgwood) built a manufactory, with house adjoining, on property which he had purchased from Thomas Lovatt but originally belonging to the Burslem and Wedgwood families. Here he carried on the potting business until his death in 1797. He was succeeded by his son, John Wood, who continued it until 1830, when he took down the manufactory, enlarged the house, and extended the grounds.

Brownhills Works

These works (formerly Marsh & Haywood's during the 1818–36 period) were from 1842 until 1860 carried on by George F. Bowers, who attained a fair reputation for china goods and gained a medal at the Exhibition of 1851. Subsequently, he commenced the manufacture of earthenware, which he continued until his death. He was succeeded by his son, Frederick F. Bowers, at whose failure in 1871 the manufactory was purchased by James Eardley. It was then carried on by Eardley's son and sons-in-law – Alfred J. Eardley, Edwin Meir, William H. Bratt, Robert H. Parker, and George Hammersley – under the style of The Brownhills Pottery Co.

The goods produced were of the useful classes of table, tea, toilet and other requisites in fine earthenware, stoneware, buff, turquoise, and cream-coloured ware; and in decorations of the fine earthenware services, improvements were effected by which the printing of enamel upon the glaze and lining on the bisque was carried out. In stoneware, some excellent designs in teapots and jugs were produced, as were also jugs and other useful articles in creamware. Adaptations of Japanese ornamentation in the former were very successful. In jet ware, teapots, jugs and other articles, highly decorated in enamel and gold, were made. The firm also had a process of printing in yellow upon the glaze of their jet goods, which produced a cheap and somewhat effective class of decoration. Another speciality was a rich full deep-red terra-cotta, highly glazed and elaborately decorated in a variety of effective patterns in enamel and gold. In this, toilet services of good design and novel appearance were made.

In ornamental goods, the company produced vases of various forms (notable among which are the 'Hindoo', 'Milan', 'Pekin' and other designs), scent-jars, flower-tubes and stands, and other articles. The marks used, besides the name of the pattern, bear the initials B.P.Co. with ribbon, etc., printed on the ware. The company continued until 1896 and was succeeded by Salt Bros.

Tunstall potters listed in 1890 and not previously mentioned include:

> Colclough & Lingard
> George Nixon
> John Procter
> Stevenson Bros.
> E. Swann
> Britannia Works
> Newfield View
> Madeley Street
> Well Street
> Globe Pottery.

In 1900, the following Tunstall potters were listed, in addition to those mentioned in the main text:

> Thomas Dean
> Gater Hall & Co.
> Johnson Bros. Ltd.
> Knight & Sproston
> Lea & Boulton
> Lingard & Webster
> Pitcairns Ltd.
> T. Rathbone & Co.

Shaw & Sons
Black Works
New Gordon Pottery
Alexandra Pottery
Keele Street
High Street (Tiles)
Swan Bank Pottery
Pinnox Pottery
Newfield Pottery
Sandyford Pottery.

NEWCASTLE-UNDER-LYME

Newcastle Pottery

Established by Harrison & Baker in 1866 for the production of red ware, ebony or jet ware, and terra-cotta, as well as ordinary horticultural goods. In red and jet ware and Rockingham ware, the usual useful and ornamental classes of articles were made up to about 1890.

PART II
OTHER NINETEENTH-
CENTURY POTTERIES

AIRTH (Stirlingshire, Scotland)

Dunmore Pottery Peter Gardner acquired this pottery in about 1860. Richly decorated useful earthenware – teapots as well as services – was produced. An advertisement of 1855 lists 'Vases, afternoon Tea Sets, Garden Seats, Flower Pots, Dessert plates, Leaves, Mantelpiece, Dining-room and Toilet table Ornaments, Etc'. A circular mark 'Peter Gardner. Dunmore Pottery' has been recorded. Rare green glazed figures bear the impressed mark DUNMORE (shown in Plates 258 and 259 in G. Godden's *Illustrated Encyclopaedia of British Pottery and Porcelain*, Herbert Jenkins, London, 1966). From 1903 to c.1911, the style was Dunmore Pottery Co.

ALLOA (near Stirling, Scotland)

Alloa Pottery These works were established in 1790 by James Anderson and were afterwards carried on by William Gardner. In 1855, they passed by purchase into the hands of W. & J. A. Bailey. At first, the works, under Mr. Anderson, produced common brown-ware pans and crocks, and by Mr. Gardner the addition was made of Rockingham-ware teapots. Later, this branch of manufacture was considerably improved and so greatly extended that, in the 1870s, no less than twenty-six thousand teapots could be produced by them per week. Majolica and jet ware goods were also largely made, and a speciality of the firm was its artistic engraving of ferns and other decorations on the finer qualities of teapots, jugs, etc. Glass was also made. The excellent quality of the Alloa goods arises from the nature of the clay got in the neighbourhood, and the density of colour and softness to touch of the glaze are highly commendable. Messrs. W. & J. A. Bailey continued until c.1908.

AYLESFORD (Kent)

Terra-Cotta Works Established here in about 1850 by Mr. Edward Betts, who discovered a valuable bed of plastic clay on his estate in the neighbourhood. At the Exhibition of 1851, Mr. Betts exhibited a terra-cotta vase (see Fig. 30) made at Aylesford from this native clay, from a design furnished by John Thomas the architect. The Aylesford Pottery Company ceased in c.1906.

BARNSTAPLE (North Devon)

C. H. Brannam's 'Barum Ware' This potter established his Litchdon Pottery in about 1879. Pottery jugs and vases will be found decorated with coloured slip or with incised motifs. Examples are normally signed 'C H Brannam. Barum' incised into the base, often with the date of manufacture. J. F. Blacker's *The ABC of XIX Century English Ceramic Art* (Stanley Paul, London, c.1911) illustrates, on page 443, a contemporary engraving of some 'Barum' vases.

Alexander Lauder Potting at Barnstaple from October 1876 to c.1914, his examples are marked 'Lauder Barum' and are similar to those of C. H. Brannam.

Fig. 30. Aylesford terra-cotta vase, 1851.

Fig. 31. View of the Belleek factory.

BELLEEK (Co. Fermanagh, Ireland)

The village of Belleek, County Fermanagh, is situated on the banks of the river Erne, near the borders of Donegal and Fermanagh. The manufactory – a view of which is seen in Figure 31 – stands on a small island in a bend of the river Erne, near whose bridge there was (in 1878) a large water-wheel, of over 100 horse-power, which gave motion to grinding-pans, lathes, turning-plates and all the varied and skilfully designed apparatus.

Before the establishment of the works by David McBirney and Robert Williams Armstrong in 1863, trials were made of the felspar of the Irish locality with ordinary Cornish china clay at the Royal Porcelain Works at Worcester. The results were so satisfactory that Mr. Armstrong, who at that time was architect to the

proprietor, laid the project for forming a manufactory at Belleek before his friend David McBirney of Dublin, and he embarked with him in the attempt to produce first-class ceramic goods in Ireland. The firm, composed of these two gentlemen, initially traded under the style of D. McBirney & Co. Mr. McBirney died in 1882, and Mr. Armstrong became the sole proprietor. At this period, about two hundred people were employed. Mr. Armstrong and his wife designed most of the novel marine forms. Skilled workmen were brought over from Staffordshire, mainly from the Goss works.

The chief peculiarities of the ornamental goods were lightness of body; rich, delicate, cream-like tone of colour; and glittering iridescence of glaze. Although the principal productions were formed of this white ware – which resembles either the finest biscuit (of Buen Retiro or Dresden) or almost the ivory of the hippopotamus, or shines with a lustre like that of nacre – local clays were found which yielded jet, red, and cane coloured ware.

Facsimiles of sea-shells and of branches of coral, which might well be supposed to be natural, are among the principal features.

'The reproduction of natural forms by Ceramic Art', states *The Art-Journal* of 1869, 'is not by any means a novelty. We are familiar with the fish, the reptiles, and the crustacea of Bernard Palissy, with the relieved and coloured foliage of Luca and of Andrea della Robbia. In England, we have seen the shells reproduced by the artists of the Plymouth china, and the delicate leaves and flowers of the old Derby ware. The designer of much of the Belleek ware has the merit, so far as we are aware, of being the first artist who has had recourse to the large sub-kingdom of the radiata for his types. The animals that constitute this vast natural group are, for the most part, characterised by a star-shaped or wheel-shaped symmetry; and present a nearer approach to the verticillate structure of plants than to the bilateral balance of free locomotive animals. . . . It would have been hardly possible to bring into the service of plastic art a more appropriate group of natural models. Again, in the fantastic and graceful forms of the mermaid,

Fig. 32. Belleek ware, 1872 Exhibition.

the nereid, the dolphin, and the sea-horse, the Belleek art-designer has attained great excellence of ideality; the graceful modelling is set off with the happiest effect by the contrast between the dead Parianlike surface of the unglazed china and the sparkling iridescence of the ivory-glazed ground.'

The productions of the Belleek works comprise all the usual services; and a large variety of ornamental goods, figures and groups of figures, animals etc., was also made, characterised by excellent modelling and judicious colouring. Among the choice examples of manipulative skill are some cabinet cups and saucers in 'egg-shell' china. The body is so thin, and worked to such a degree of nicety, as to be of little more than the thickness of writing paper. This delicate body – either plain or tinted and gilt, and then glazed with the iridescent glaze so characteristic of Belleek ware – is unique in its appearance and matchless in its extreme delicacy. Of the same filmy body, exquisitely tinted, cardium and other shells were also produced. A young artist, Mr. Sheerin, painted some Belleek vases during the 1880s.

Besides the speciality of these works ('Belleek China'), there were manufactured white graniteware services of every variety and of excellent quality in body and glaze, and in printed, painted, enamelled, and gilt decorations. Parian and ordinary white china, as well as ivory body, were also largely made in a vast variety of styles, as were also porcelain insulators for telegraph poles. Pestles and mortars, etc., and sanitary ware formed a staple part of the trade of these works.

The marks used by the Belleek company were the following:

BELLEEK.
CO. FERMANAGH.

149

Plate 81. Typical Belleek porcelain, reproduced
from the firm's 1904 catalogue.

150

The Belleek factory has continued (under various owners) to the present day. Many of the nineteenth-century marine forms are still in production, and if it were not for the evidence of the new form of mark it would be difficult to differentiate between ware made in 1880 and that made in the 1960s. From about 1890, 'Co Fermanagh. Ireland' has been added on a ribbon under the printed tower mark. This printed mark has also been simplified. The drawing is not as detailed as the earlier version – i.e., only one window is normally shown in the tower.

Magazine articles on Belleek occur in the *Antiques Magazine* of September 1946 and February 1953, and in *Country Life* of 21st November 1957. Illustrations of typical pieces are included in G. Godden's *Illustrated Encyclopaedia of British Pottery and Porcelain* (Herbert Jenkins, London, 1966) and in C. & D. Shinn's *The Illustrated Guide to Victorian Parian China* Barrie & Jenkins, London, 1971). The examples shown in Plate 81 are reproduced from the firm's 1904 illustrated catalogue – but in some cases, the same designs are being produced today.

BELPER (Derbyshire)

In about the middle or towards the latter part of the eighteenth century, a small manufactory of common coarse brown ware existed here; and

Fig. 33. Belper stoneware portrait bottle.

in about 1800, William Bourne took to the works carried on by Messrs. Blood, Webster & Simpson at Belper Pottery. William Bourne, sen., was, it appears, very much engaged in the business of the then new canal. Mr. Bourne carried on the manufacture of salt-glazed blacking, ink, ginger-beer and spirit bottles. The ordinary brown ware, produced from a less vitreous clay found on the spot, consisted of bowls, pans, dishes, pitchers and all the commoner varieties of domestic vessels, and these were of excellent and durable quality. The stoneware bottles, etc., were made from a fine and more tenacious bed of clay at Derby, a few miles distant. The finer or figured ware was made from clay produced from Staffordshire. By Mr. Bourne, all these descriptions of goods were made; but he principally confined himself to the manufacture of stoneware bottles of various kinds. A good antique-shaped hunting jug, and other similar articles, and figures in relief were also extensively made.

In 1812, Joseph Bourne (son of William Bourne) took to the Denby Pottery, then carried on by Mr. Jäger, and the two works were carried on simultaneously until 1834, when the Belper Pottery was finally closed, the workpeople, plant and business being removed to Denby and incorporated with those works, and the premises converted into cottages. From that time, no pottery has been made at Belper.

The mark used while these works were carried on in conjunction with those at Denby was this:

BELPER & DENBY

—

BOURNES
POTTERIES

DERBYSHIRE ✳

a similar mark was used on Bourne's stoneware made at Denby and Codnor Park, but with these place-names instead of Belper & Denby.

It may be well to remark that a series of political bottles, bearing representations of various Reform leaders, was made. On these, the head of the individual – the King, Sir Francis Burdett, Earl Grey, or whoever was intended – formed the neck of the bottle, and the arms and bust were the shoulder; political references, and the name of the political leader, were impressed on the clay. One of these, which represents the King (William IV), bears in front the words WILLIAM IV'S REFORM CORDIAL (see Fig. 33). Similar stoneware bottles were made at other potteries (see Plate 91).

BENTHALL (Broseley)

Benthall Works The manufactory of encaustic tiles, mosaics, and majolica which was carried on by Messrs. Maw at the Benthall works, near Broseley, was initiated at Worcester in 1850. Messrs. Maw commenced experimenting on the processes of manufacture on the premises formerly occupied by the Worcester Porcelain manufactory and afterwards used for the production of encaustic tiles by Mr. Fleming St. John and his partners, by whom the moulds and plant were sold to Messrs. Maw, who, in 1852, feeling the necessity for carrying on the manufacture, removed to these works at Benthall.

Another seven years was spent by them in a series of costly experiments upon the clays of the Shropshire coalfield as well as on the plastic materials found throughout the kingdom, many of which no one had before attempted to turn to economic account.

In 1851, Messrs. Maw began the manufacture of plain, geometrical, mosaic, and ordinary encaustic tiles; but after 1857 there was a continual grafting on of specialities and the production of new colours. In 1861, they commenced the manufacture of very small tesserae for the formation of pictorial mosaics. The production of coloured enamels for the surface decoration of majolica tiles next occupied their attention; and after years of experimenting, all the colours employed in the ancient tiles of Spain and Italy were successfully reproduced.

Messrs. Maw were the first in this country to produce the transparent celeste, or turquoise blue, employed in ancient Chinese enamels – specimens of which were exhibited in the Paris

Exhibition of 1867. Among the productions may be mentioned tesserae for mosaic work, decorated with rich enamels; embossed tiles; 'sgraffito' – a ware the decoration of which is produced by the cutting away of superimposed layers of different coloured clays, after the fashion of cameo carving; 'slip-painting' – the production of a pattern by the painting of liquid clay on a ground of another colour and the whole glazed over, after the first burning, with transparent coloured enamels; 'pâte-sur-pâte' – tiles in which the design in high relief is superimposed on a ground of a different colour; mixed coloured glasses and enamels for the decoration of pottery, by which the most subtle and brilliant effects were produced.

Another branch of ceramics – that of 'art pottery' – was added to Messrs. Maw's manufactory. This comprised the production in majolica of vases, tazzas, and other articles, more or less decorated with raised or surface ornamentation. They were of excellent design – the body light but compact and the decorations of remarkably good and artistic character. A selection of this decorative Maw ware is housed in the Shrewsbury Museum.

In 1882–3, Messrs. Maw entirely rebuilt their works on land purchased by them at Jackfield. This firm continued until 1970, with several changes in post-war years. Nineteenth-century marks incorporate the name Maw & Co. Broseley.

Salopian Art Pottery Company This pottery was in existence from c. 1880 to about 1912. An advertisement of 1883 mentions nearly three hundred shapes. Vases and plaques in enamel and slip-painting, raised fruit and flower work and incised decoration. Some examples bear the name SALOPIAN and could therefore be confused with Caughley work, which bears a similar mark, although this 'art' ware is of pottery, not porcelain.

BIDEFORD (North Devon)

Bideford was a famous pottery centre in the seventeenth century and its ware was exported to the early settlers in North America (see *Antiques Magazine*, July 1962).

The Bideford Old Pottery This pottery belonged to W. H. Crocker and had been in the possession of himself and his ancestors for some two centuries. Its productions, under W. H. Crocker, received a marked improvement. The works were almost entirely rebuilt and much extended in 1870.

Ornamental goods were made to some extent, and consisted of garden vases, edgings, jugs and other articles. Flower-pots, sea-kale and rhubarb pots and chimney tops were also made.

The great speciality of the productions were, however, fire-clay ovens, which were made in considerable numbers and of various sizes. The mark was the proprietor's name: W.H. Crocker – Bideford.

BIRKENHEAD (Cheshire)

'Della Robbia' Pottery Harold Rathbone established his pottery at Birkenhead (on the south side of the Mersey, opposite Liverpool) in about 1894. Designs were modelled on the old Italian maiolica ware, and the name 'Della Robbia' was adopted. The ware was very popular for a short period, but the works were closed in 1901. The Della Robbia Pottery and Marble Company Limited re-opened them and continued to c.1906. Some typical examples of Della Robbia pottery are illustrated in J. F. Blacker's *The ABC of XIX Century English Ceramic Art* (Stanley Paul, London, 1911) and H. Wakefield's *Victorian Porcelain* (Herbert Jenkins, London, 1962); and a selection of ware of the 1896 period is shown in Plate 208 of G. Godden's *Illustrated Encyclopaedia of British Pottery and Porcelain* (Herbert Jenkins, London, 1966).

BISHOPS WALTHAM (Hampshire)

The Bishops Waltham Clay Company Ltd. This was established in September 1862 to exploit the local clay, which was of fine quality. At first, the products were utilitarian; but in February 1866, the manufacture of art pottery was undertaken. These pieces are of terra-cotta body, of graceful and simple form. Most examples bear transfer-printed classical figure designs (see Plate 82). A dessert service was contemplated for presentation to Queen Victoria, but only a few plates were completed before the production of art pottery was discontinued, in 1867, after little more than a year's production. The mark is BISHOP WALTHAM within a double-lined oval; specimens are rarely seen.

BONESS (near Linlithgow, Scotland)

The Boness Pottery This pottery dates from about 1766. In about 1784, it was partly reconstructed by a Mr. Roebuck – an enterprising Englishman who, having left for England, sold the pottery to a Mr. McCowen. Afterwards, in 1799, it was continued by Alexander Cumming, who was succeeded by his nephew, James, and it became one of the largest potteries in Scotland; earthenware and brown ware were manufactured in all its branches. The firm had another manufactory called the South Pottery, where brown ware was made for the home market. On the death of James Cumming, the works passed into the hands of his nephew, William, and then to Shaw & Sons. In 1836, it was sold to James Jamieson, who carried on for a number of years under the title of James Jamieson & Co.

J. Arnold Fleming, in his *Scottish Pottery* (Maclehose, Jackson & Co., Glasgow, 1923), states that Jamieson & Co. employed about forty potters. The pottery was situated on both sides of the Main Street – two kilns on the north side and two on the south. Excellent blue printed earthenware was produced, one pattern – 'Bosphorous' – being particularly favoured. Skilled potters, printers and painters were brought up from Staffordshire to this Scottish pottery. The printed mark 'J. Jamieson & Co.' has been recorded. Jamieson died in 1854, and for a short period after this the factory was in the hands of a local coal company. But it soon reverted to the manufacture of pottery under John Marshall, who retained the old staff.

In 1867, William McNay was taken into partnership and the firm continued under the title John Marshall & Co. These works were the first in Scotland to adopt Needham's patent for manufacturing clay. The ordinary useful classes of earthenware, dinner, tea, toilet and other services and all the usual domestic articles were produced in white, sponged, printed, painted, enamelled and gilt styles and were supplied both to home and foreign markets. John Marshall & Co. continued until 1899.

Bridgeness Pottery Charles W. McNay worked the Brigdeness Pottery in Grange Road from about 1886. Earthenware has been produced to the present day. Animal models were produced early in the twentieth century.

Industrial Co-operative Pottery Society Ltd., Bo'ness This short-lived venture produced some printed earthenware from c.1887 to 1894. A marked mug decorated with a coloured overprint of children playing soldiers is in the Godden Collection. The mark is INDUSTRIAL POTTERY BO'NESS within an oval. The firm's title prior to 1892 was the Bo'ness Industrial Pottery and Manufacturing Society.

BOVEY TRACEY (Devon)

The Folly Pottery In 1835, the works were carried on by Messrs. John & Thomas Honeychurch. In an advertisement of sale, the pottery was thus described: 'To be sold by public auction, as directed by the assignees of John and Thomas Honeychurch, bankrupts, at the Union Inn, Bovey Tracey, on the 2nd May, 1836, the Folly Pottery, situate in the parish of Bovey Tracey, in the county of Devon. This may be designated one of the largest and most complete potteries in the West of England, 14 miles from Exeter and 28 from Plymouth; its situation being in the land of clay, from which nearly all the potteries in Staffordshire draw

their supply, with coal-mine and railroad, etc.'

The advertisement, after giving particulars regarding the processes, etc., speaks of a glost-kiln and a biscuit-kiln, capable of containing 1,600 saggers of ware; flint kilns; a quantity of Cornish clay and flints, copper-plates, moulds, etc.

In 1842, the pottery was purchased by two Devonshire gentlemen – Captain Buller and Mr. J. Divett – who enlarged the works and obtained the lignite from underground workings. The supply of this substance, however, proving insufficient for the increased requirements of the manufacture, ordinary coal was substituted in its stead; and after the opening of a railway to the works, Somersetshire coal was used to the entire exclusion of the lignite. The works were carried on by Messrs. Buller & Divett under the style of the Bovey Tracey Pottery Company. In general character, they were similar to those of the Staffordshire pottery district. On the average, five ovens were fired each week. The quality of the ware was about equal to the ordinary and commoner classes of Staffordshire goods. It consisted of all the ordinary services and articles in white, blue printed and coloured ware, and was principally supplied to the home markets in the West of England and to Mediterranean ports. The company ceased in c.1894. A new company – The Bovey Pottery Co. Ltd. – continued from c.1894 to 1956.

BOW (London)

Bow porcelain, being of the period c.1750–76, is not featured in this volume dealing, as it does, with post-eighteenth-century ware.

BRAMPTON (near Chesterfield, Derbyshire)

The Welshpool and Payne Potteries Belonging to Matthew Knowles & Son, these works embraced the old works carried on in the eighteenth century by Mr. Blake, and afterwards by his widow, and those of Luke Knowles. They came into the hands of Matthew Knowles in about 1835, and were considerably enlarged

Plate 82. Two typically decorated Bishops Waltham terra-cotta articles, c.1867. Jug 6¾ inches high.
Editor's collection.

by him. Having been joined in partnership by his son, under the style of Matthew Knowles & Son, the works were again, in 1875, much extended.

All the general descriptions of brown and stoneware goods were produced for the Australian, Russian, African and Jamaica markets, as well as for the home trade. Among these were stoneware spirit-bottles, and spirit-kegs and barrels, which were much esteemed for their hardness, durability and fine quality; ginger-beer bottles, both in stoneware and brown ware; jam-jars, for wholesale preserve manufacturers, in gallon and half-gallon sizes, in brown ware glazed inside – forming one of the staple productions of Mr. Knowles and of which, with one exception, he was the only maker in the district; stew and sauce pots; fruit and other jars; flat dishes; turtle and beef pots; bowls and

colanders; tobacco-jars, highly ornamented; 'Punch' jugs of striking design; 'hunting' jugs; 'game' jugs and other jugs designed and modelled with great taste; puzzle jugs; posset-pots; candlesticks of classical design and good execution; bread-baskets; toast-racks; tea-kettles; flower-pots and vases; foot and carriage warmers; grotesque tobacco-pipes; and a large variety of other goods, besides the usual domestic vessels, were made at these works.

The water filters made by Mr. Knowles, of which he produced a large number, were of excellent construction and good design. They were among the best produced and, being in the fine deep rich colour of the Chesterfield ware, were very effective and perhaps more pleasing in appearance than many others in the lighter Bristol ware, etc. In china clay ware, also, a large variety of articles of remarkably good quality were made. Messrs. M. Knowles & Son continued into the twentieth century.

155

The Pottery These works were established in 1810 by Oldfield, Madin, Wright, Hewitt & Co. After various changes and retirements, John Oldfield became sole proprietor of the works in 1838, and they continued under his name. They were, from time to time, considerably extended, and they became nearly the largest in the district. The goods manufactured were the usual descriptions known as 'New Brampton' or 'Chesterfield ware' or, as more frequently falsely called in the London and other markets, 'Nottingham ware' – a remarkably hard, compact and durable salt-glazed brown ware; and stoneware, which was dipped in different 'slips'.

In brown ware, the principal goods produced were dishes and bowls of various kinds; turtle, beef, butter, Dutch, stew, sauce and other pots; bottles and jars of all shapes and sizes and for all uses; pitchers and jugs in endless variety; churns; milkpans and pancheons; tea and coffee-pots; Welsh trays; carriage and feet warmers; hare-pans and dog-troughs; spirit and wine barrels and kegs; figured flower pots and stands; scent-jars; 'hunting', 'cottage', 'tulip' and other figured jugs and mugs, etc. of great beauty and of excellent design; and many other articles. In 'antique ware', Mr. Oldfield made remarkably effective and well-designed hunting, game, cottage, tulip and other jugs; figured Stilton-cheese stands; fruit-dishes and trays; tea and coffee pots; tobacco-pots, some of which, with goblet and candlestick, were very striking; watch-stands; 'Toby Fillpot' jugs; puzzle-jugs, etc. The impressed marks comprise the name Oldfield in various forms. Messrs. Oldfield ceased in about 1888.

The Walton Pottery Built by William Briddon in 1790 and, at his death, continued by his son, William Briddon, who, dying in 1848, was succeeded by his son, also William Briddon. The goods made were brown ware and stoneware in all their varieties. In these were produced stew, turtle, beef, and butter pots; jugs of every variety; preserve and pickle jars; pancheons, bowls and colanders; porringers and patty-pans; bottles of every conceivable size and shape;

filters; spirit barrels and kegs; foot-bottles and carriage warmers; tea and coffee pots; twisted and grotesque pipes; and many other articles. In quality, they were much the same as those of other Brampton manufactories. The Briddons ceased in c.1892.

Wheatbridge Pottery These works were in the Wright family for these generations. The staple trade of the manufactory was general brown ware for the Dutch markets. As E. Wright & Co. Ltd., this firm continued into the twentieth century.

The Alma Pottery This pottery was commenced by Samuel Lowe and his then partners in about 1852. After a few years, Mr. Lowe's two partners withdrew from the concern and it continued in his hands solely. The goods produced were the same general kinds, both of ware and articles, as the other Brampton potteries. In brown ware and in stoneware, Mr. Lowe produced filters, bottles of every kind and size, jugs and mugs, jars of various descriptions, and all the articles usually produced in this ware and of the same general quality as those of other works in the district. As S. Lowe & Sons, the firm continued into the twentieth century.

BRAMPTON (Lincolnshire)

At Brampton, near Torksey, in Lincolnshire, there was from about 1803 to 1807 a small porcelain manufactory which traded under the name Sharpe & Co. William Billingsley, of Derby fame, lent practical help; but apart from some very rare inscribed jugs (shown in Plates 75 and 76 of G. Godden's *Illustrated Encyclopaedia of British Pottery and Porcelain*, Herbert Jenkins, London, 1966), the products were unmarked and are as yet unidentified.

BRISTOL (Gloucestershire)

Bristol porcelain, being of eighteenth-century date, is not featured in this volume, which deals with post-eighteenth-century ware.

The Temple and St. Thomas's Street Works
The oldest stoneware pottery in Bristol – that of J. & C. Price & Brothers in St. Thomas's Street and Temple Street – was established in about 1735 or 1740 and was continued by succeeding generations of the same family. The 'Old Salt-Glaze' was used until about 1835 when, great improvements having been made through the experiments of Mr. Powell, it was found practicable to dip the stoneware into liquid glaze in its green or unfired state, instead of first burning and then 'smearing' as formerly practised. Messrs. Price, having adopted the new method, continued to improve their works, and built much larger kilns than usual in potteries of the kind. The superiority of Bristol stoneware over others became so well established that London makers bought their glaze from that city. The stoneware goods were of the highest quality, and some excellent imitations of the antique – of very fine body, faultless glaze and elegant form – were produced.

Among the useful goods were water filters of simple but excellent construction and elegant form; feet and carriage warmers; barrels and churns; bread, cheese and other pans; bottles, jugs and every other kind of domestic vessel. Messrs. Price also made all the other usual varieties of stoneware goods. In 1907, they became Messrs. Price, Powell & Co.

Powell's Temple Gate Pottery This stoneware pottery was established in the eighteenth century. The products were termed 'Bristol Ware' or 'Improved stone', introduced by Mr. Powell in about 1835. Its peculiarity consisted in its being coated with a glaze which was produced simultaneously with the ware itself, so that one firing only was needed. So great was Mr. Powell's success with his discovery that, shortly after its introduction at the Temple Gate Pottery, almost every other manufacturer of stoneware adopted it; and, in a large measure, it superseded the old salt-glazed ware.

The goods made were bread pans, filters, foot-warmers, bottles, jars and other domestic vessels. Vases and bottles of classic shape were occasionally made, as were enormous jugs – one of which, capable of holding twenty-five gallons, was exhibited by the firm. The firm's title during the latter part of the nineteenth century was W. Powell & Sons. In 1907, this firm merged with Messrs. Price and became Price, Powell & Co.

Wilder Street Pottery In about 1820, a pottery, on a small scale, was worked in Wilder Street, Bristol, by a family named Macken, descendants of the owner of the old pottery at St. Ann's, Brislington, where flower pots and other coarse brown ware was made. Macken afterwards went to America.

Messrs. Pountney & Co. Temple Backs Pottery This pottery was established in the eighteenth century. Various changes in the partnerships subsequently took place. In 1813, Pountney & Carter were the owners, trading under the title Elizabeth Ring & Co. In 1816, Carter retired and was succeeded by Edward Allies, the style being Pountney & Allies. Mr. Allies retired in 1835, and in the following year Mr. Gouldney entered into partnership. He retired in 1850. Mr. Pountney died in 1852 and the works were continued by his widow, until her death in 1872, under the style of Pountney & Co. They were then purchased by H. S. Cobden of the Victoria Pottery, by whom they were extended.

During Mr. Pountney's lifetime, some Parian figures, etc., were made, and some examples made by Raby (who moved to Staffordshire) were in the possession of Mrs. Pountney, as were also some excellent imitations of the Etruscan and other styles. Examples of the early productions of these works are scarce, and it is interesting to state that the old Bristol (porcelain) mark of the cross was used on some of the pieces of earthenware made here. The mark is sometimes in blue and sometimes impressed.

A name well known in connection with these works is that of William Fifield (and his son, John), who was a painter of merit. Examples sometimes bear the artist's initials and the date.

Messrs. Pountney & Co. continued potting at the Bristol Victoria Pottery until 1969; under the

Fig. 34. View of the Bristol Pottery in 1869.

new title Cauldon Bristol Potteries Ltd., they continue at Redruth, Cornwall. 'Ltd.' was added to the title (and marks) in 1889. Good quality earthenware was produced.

The reader is referred to W. J. Pountney's *Old Bristol Potteries* (J. W. Arrowsmith, Bristol, 1920) for a first-hand account of the Bristol potteries.

Smaller Bristol potteries of the 1880–90 period include: Albert Pottery Company; A. Ellis, of the Crown Potteries; J. G. Hawley; A. Niblett; J. T. Spokes and J. & J. White of the Baptist Mills Pottery.

It should be noted that, late in the nineteenth

century and early in the twentieth century, Messrs. S. J. Kepple & Sons were decorating porcelain in the old Bristol manner, and such reproductions bear the marks of the original. This porcelain is, however, very soft, the originals are of hard paste porcelain.

BROXBOURNE (Hertfordshire)

In 1843, Mr. Pulham succeeded in making terra-cotta of a good stone-colour and a rich pale red. Having done this, he began to produce various small objects for architectural purposes – bosses, angle-quoins, brackets, balustrades, small flower-pots and vases. He also

158

introduced what is termed granulated terra-cotta, having the appearance of stone.

In 1871, besides other of his productions, Mr. Pulham exhibited a small fountain, which was at play during the whole time of the Exhibition, and also several new vases. The fountain (for which a prize medal was awarded) and principal exhibits were very favourably noticed. At the Paris Exhibition, in 1867, were exhibited fountains, vases and architectural embellishments – amongst which may be named the Preston vase (a number of which were made for the People's Park, Preston), with medallions representing the staple commerce of the place; some rich columns; and novel window-jambs and dressings. Notable among the rest was the Mulready monument erected for the Science and Art Department, South Kensington, at whose instigation it was sent to Paris.

Fig. 35. Broxbourne terra-cotta vase.

CADBOROUGH (Sussex)

The Cadborough Pottery Near Rye, in Sussex, this pottery was first built in about 1807 and was carried on by James Smith, and afterwards by his son, Jeremiah Smith. In 1840, the business passed into the hands of William Mitchell (who had had the management of it, under Mr. Smith, since 1827), who carried it on in his own name until 1859, when he took one of his sons, Frederick Mitchell, into partnership and the firm became Wm. Mitchell & Sons. It so continued until 1869, when the partnership was dissolved. Mr. Mitchell, senior, continued the Cadborough business for common earthenware, and his son, Frederick Mitchell, took the fancy department – which was his own creation – to new premises: the Bellevue Pottery. In 1870, Mr. Mitchell, senior, died and the business at Cadborough was then taken for a short period by Henry Mitchell.

The goods produced were the ordinary common brown ware, glazed and unglazed, consisting of flower-pots, chimney-pots, pitchers, and crocks of various kinds; and all the usual domestic vessels, many of which were mottled or 'splashed' under the glaze.

At Crowborough, Chailey, and Burgess Hill, brown Sussex ware was also made – that of Chailey being of somewhat curious character with impressed ornaments. Other Sussex potteries were situated at Brede, Dicker, Hastings and Rye (q.v.). Some typical Sussex ware has been illustrated by Mr. George Savage in the *Apollo Magazine*, August 1956.

CARDIGAN (Wales)

The Cardigan Potteries Established in 1875 by Messrs. Miles & Woodward for the production of common coarse red earthenware goods for domestic and horticultural purposes. But the clay of the district being found suitable for other classes of goods, they were added to the operations. The productions were vases, jugs, flower-stands and other ornamental articles. These were decorated and glazed in a manner

159

Fig. 36. Castle Espie terra-cotta vases.

peculiarly their own, which gave to them a distinctive character over those of other manufactories. In some, quaint and well-designed patterns were impressed in the clay – and the whole being surface-coloured and highly glazed, they have a rich and peculiar appearance. The firm traded as The Cardigan Potteries and Woodward & Co., and their works were called the Patent Brick Tile & Pottery Works and Cardigan Potteries. This pottery was of short duration and closed before the end of the nineteenth century.

CASTLE ESPIE (Co. Down, Ireland)

In the middle of the nineteenth century, at Castle Espie, near Comber, county of Down, Samuel Minland established brick and tile works. Common pottery was manufactured there from the local red clay. The brown glazed ware consisted of dairy vessels, teapots, flower-vases and other plain household articles.

Captain Beauclerc, at the Exhibition of 1851, exhibited two terra-cotta vases of his own modelling, made in Ireland of Irish material, reproduced in Figure 36. They were in two tints – the body of each vase being of a deep red and the figures of a lighter and much yellower clay.

CASTLE HEDINGHAM (Essex)

Edward W. Bingham (born in 1829) established his small pottery at Castle Hedingham, Essex, in 1864. Bingham (see Plate 83), assisted by his family, produced a variety of earthenware articles decorated with applied relief motifs and coloured glazes. This ware has a decidedly medieval air. Edward Bingham specialised in the reproduction of German stoneware, Palissy ware and Greek and Roman pottery, as well as early English ware (see Plate 84). His products were marked with an applied castle above a scroll inscribed 'E. Bingham'. Examples were also marked with his name and 'Castle Hedingham Essex' incised into the clay.

By 1885, he had enlarged the concern to such

an extent that thirteen kilns were used. Nevertheless, Castle Hedingham ware retained the characteristics of a simple country pottery – although the motifs were more pretentious than most. In 1899, Edward Bingham transferred the pottery to his son, who had assisted him for many years. The son sold the pottery in 1901 but was retained as manager for a few years before he emigrated to America.

Three well-illustrated articles published in the *Connoisseur Magazine* in February, March and April 1968 give good information on the Castle Hedingham ware.

CASTLEFORD (Yorkshire)

Castleford Pottery Castleford, which lies about twelve miles from Leeds, was supported by its glass-houses, chemical works, and potteries – where common brown ware was made from an early period. The Castleford Pottery was established, towards the close of the eighteenth century, by David Dunderdale for the manufacture

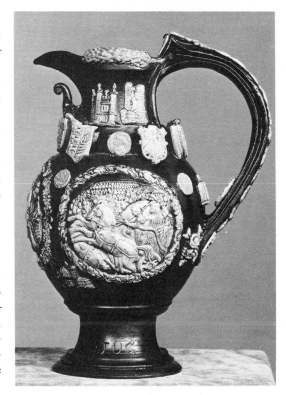

Plate 84. An ornate Castle Hedingham jug in an early style. *Private collection.*

Plate 83. Portrait of Edward W. Bingham of Castle Hedingham. *Dr. Pitman.*

of the finer kinds of earthenware – more especially Queen's or cream-coloured ware, which was then being made so largely at Leeds and other places as well as in Staffordshire. He took into partnership a Mr. Plowes and, in 1803, the firm was D. Dunderdale & Co. and consisted of these two persons. The partnership was not of long duration. Mr. Plowes, after the dissolution, removed to Ferrybridge, where he joined the proprietors of the pot-works there; and Mr. Dunderdale continued the Castleford works alone.

The next partner was Mr. T. E. Upton, a relative of Dunderdale's, and these two shortly afterwards took into partnership John Bramley (or Bramler) and Thomas Russell, a hotel proprietor at Harrogate – Dunderdale owning a half of the concern, Russell a fourth, and Upton and Bramley an eighth each.

In 1820, the manufactory was closed; and in 1821, a part of the works was taken by some of the workmen – George Asquith, William and Daniel Byford, Richard Gill, James Sharp, and David Hingham. They were succeeded by Taylor, Harrison & Co. – Harrison having been an apprentice of David Dunderdale's. The place was, for several years, carried on by the latter and the son of the former under the style of Taylor & Harrison, who gave up the manufacture of earthenware and continued it for stoneware alone.

The staple production in Dunderdale's time was the 'Queen's' or 'cream-coloured ware', which in appearance assimilated closely to the creamware made at the Herculaneum Works at Liverpool and was not so fine or so perfect in glaze as that made at Leeds. In this ware, dinner, dessert and other services, as well as open-work baskets, vases, candlesticks and a large variety of other articles, were made, both plain and painted, or enamelled and decorated with transfer printing.

The typical Castleford body is a type of white basalt. Many moulded designs were employed. Teapots are the most commonly found articles. A rare and decorative class of this type has coloured panels, normally hand-painted in an attractive manner. Black basalt ware was also made. Marks include D D & Co. or the name D. Dunderdale & Co. in various forms. It should be noted that the white-bodied ware was very seldom marked and some assumed examples were doubtless made by other manufacturers of the period (see *Apollo Magazine* of July 1948).

In 1825, the old works were again opened by Asquith, Wood & Co. They were joined in partnership by Thomas Nicholson – who had served his apprenticeship with Harley, Green & Co. of the Leeds Pottery – and carried on the business as Asquith, Wood & Nicholson, and afterwards as Wood & Nicholson. In 1854, Mr. Nicholson took into partnership Thomas Hartley, the style being Thomas Nicholson & Co. Later on, Mr. Nicholson having retired from the concern, it was carried on by Thomas Hartley alone, and afterwards with partners, under the old name of Nicholson & Co. In 1872, Mr. Hartley died and the Castleford Pottery was carried on by his co-partners, Hugh McDowell Clokie and

John Masterman, under the style of Clokie & Masterman until 1887, when the title became Clokie & Co. – a firm which continued until 1962.

The various firms used a variety of marks, most of which incorporate their initials: T N & Co (Thomas Nicholson & Co., 1854–71); C & M (Clokie & Masterman, 1872–87).

For further information on Castleford ware, see O. Grabham's *Yorkshire Potteries, Pots and Potters* (Yorkshire Museum, 1916).

The Eagle Pottery Established in 1854 by a company of workmen under the style of John Roberts & Co., it was afterwards continued by Pratt & Co. They sold it to Mr. H. McDowell, after whose death the buildings were converted into a glass bottle manufactory. This was prior to 1878.

Other small potteries at or near Castleford in 1890 include: Ford Bros., Victoria Pottery; W. Gill & Son, Providence Potteries; Nicholson & Masterman, Albion Pottery; and C. Phillips & Son of Whitwood Mere.

CAUGHLEY (Shropshire)

Caughley porcelain, being of the period c.1775–99, is not featured in this volume, which deals with post-eighteenth-century ware. For up-to-date information on Caughley products, and illustrations, the reader is referred to G. Godden's *Caughley and Worcester Porcelains, 1775–1800* (Herbert Jenkins, London, 1969). The Caughley works were taken over in 1799 by the partners in the nearby Coalport Porcelain Works (see page 164).

CHEAM (Surrey)

A pottery was worked here, in about 1840, by William Waghorn & Son of the Ewell Pottery (q.v.); but on their retiring in 1851, it was transferred to Mr. Baker, by whom it was worked until 1868, when he was succeeded by Messrs. Cowley & Aston. It was closed in 1869. In the same year, another pottery was opened by

Plate 85. Three typical De Morgan pieces. The right-hand vase was purchased for the South Kensington (Victoria and Albert) Museum in 1887. Ship vase, 12¾ inches high.
Victoria & Albert Museum (Crown copyright).

Henry Clark for the manufacture of ornamental and plain flower-pots, rustic fern-stands, vases, chimney-pots, drain-tiles, etc. The products were of a bright red colour. When a mark was used, it was simply 'Henry Clark, Cheam Pottery'.

CHELSEA (London)

Chelsea and Chelsea-Derby porcelain being of eighteenth century date are not featured in this volume, which deals with post-eighteenth-century ware. Typical production are featured in Godden's *Illustrated Encyclopaedia of British Pottery and Porcelain* (Herbert Jenkins, London, 1966). *British Porcelain, 1745–1840*, edited by R. J. Charleston (Ernest Benn, London, 1965) is also helpful, as are various specialist reference books on Chelsea porcelain.

De Morgan Pottery (Chelsea, Merton Abbey and Fulham) Toward the end of the nineteenth century, two famous potters were experimenting with the reproduction of the lustre and glaze effects of the Eastern potters. The first of these English potters was William De Morgan (1839–1917) who, after early training in painting at the Royal Academy Schools, turned his attention to stained glass and to tile painting. He was encouraged in this by his friend, William Morris. Due to his success in tile decoration, he established, in 1872, his own small pottery and showroom in Cheyne Row, Chelsea, where he was able to produce his own tiles instead of purchasing the undecorated tiles from outside sources as he had done previously. At this period, he was seeking the lost art of Moorish or Gubbio lustres.

De Morgan ware had all the breadth of the old Spanish work with a character of the artist's own and an exquisite iridescent colour. Fine vases and plaques (Plate 85) were made, as well as tiles. Due to the success of this venture, De Morgan was forced to find larger premises; and in 1882, he moved to Merton Abbey where he erected larger kilns. This sufficed until 1888, when he was again forced to move – this time to his Sands End Pottery in Fulham, London. From 1888 to 1908, he was in partnership with Halsey Ricardo. From then on, '& Co.' was added to the factory mark.

William De Morgan did not enjoy good health. He spent the winter months in Florence. While there, he employed local artists to draw suitable patterns, under his supervision. These patterns were sent back to England and used in the decoration of the pottery. The initials of his chief painters are found on many specimens: these include Charles and Fred Passenger (partners from 1898), Joe Juster and J. Hersey.

163

CLEVEDON

In 1907, ill health forced William De Morgan to retire from the pottery. Pieces were decorated by the remaining artists, however, until 1911. De Morgan then became a successful novelist.

The De Morgan pottery has a character and charm all its own. Although, perhaps, not always in accord with modern taste, the colours and lustre effects must command respect. An interesting article by Norman Prouting on De Morgan ware is contained in the *Apollo Magazine* of January 1953.

Among other potters experimenting with glaze effects during the closing years of the nineteenth century, the most interesting was Bernard Moore (see page 93).

CHISLEHURST (Kent)

The West Kent Potteries These potteries were opened in 1820, before which time other works were in operation and carried on by the steward of Lord Sydney – the owner of the estate – for the manufacture of ware for the use of the estate. At Christmas, 1822, the works were taken by Mr. Pascall, who continued to carry them on until January 1869, when he died aged ninety-two. After that, it was carried on by his sons, Messrs. Pascall Brothers. The productions were the ordinary red-ware flower and root pots, sea-kale pots, and other horticultural ware; building and paving bricks and tiles; roofing and ridge tiles; chimney tops; drain, socket and other pipes. Messrs. Pascall were patentees of the famous West Kent flower-pots with loose bottoms – celebrated for their convenience for changing and examining the roots – and of the patent sea-kale pots for growing sea-kale in hot-houses.

CLEVEDON (Somerset)

Elton Pottery Sir Edmund Elton started pottery experiments in 1879. In 1882, his Sunflower Pottery was in production and the products became known as 'Elton Ware'. A *Pottery Gazette* review of 1894 noted: 'The ware is made from native clay, apparently of a darkish colour, and is decorated in coloured slips. Some of the colours are very fine, more of the nature of

Plate 86. Sir Edmund Elton at work on a typical Elton-ware jug.   *Sir Arthur Elton.*

enamels than slips; the whole is coated with a brilliant transparent glaze...' Vases in many forms were produced. Most examples bear the name ELTON incised into the clay.

Sir Edmund Elton (Plate 86) died in 1920, but his son continued the pottery for about ten years.

Contemporary accounts of this pottery are contained in the *Magazine of Art*, 1883, and *The Art-Journal*, 1901. Over two thousand examples are retained at Clevedon Court, the family seat of Sir Edmund Elton, which is open to the public at certain times under the National Trust scheme.

COALPORT (near Broseley, Shropshire)

The Coalport Works At one time also known as Coalbrook Dale, these works were founded in or before 1796 by John Rose, to whom ceramic art is indebted for many important improvements. He was the son of a farmer and apprenticed to Thomas Turner of the Caughley China Works, by whom he was taken into the house and taught the art in all its branches. Ultimately, a difference arose between them, and Mr. Rose left Mr. Turner and commenced a small business on his own account at Jackfield, from whence he removed to Coalport (on the opposite bank of the river Severn).

John Rose had not long established himself at Coalport when other works were started on the opposite side of the canal, and only a few yards distant, by his brother Thomas Rose and partners, who commenced business under the style of Anstice, Horton & Rose. These works, however, did not continue long. They passed, in 1814, into the hands of John Rose and partners, who formed them into one establishment. By 1799, the Coalport works had become so successful that John Rose and his partners – Edward Blakeway and Richard Rose – were able to purchase the Caughley factory with all the moulds and other working material. They thus became proprietors of all three works, to which soon afterwards considerable additions were made.

Although many changes in the proprietary took place, the commercial style of the firm remained John Rose & Co.

The early nineteenth-century products were seldom marked and are often difficulty to identify with certainty, but a good range of the early ware is featured in G. Godden's *Coalport and Coalbrookdale Porcelains* (Herbert Jenkins, London, 1970), a work which also identifies the products of the Anstice, Horton & Rose partnership. Plate 87 illustrates some rare early documentary pieces, similar at first sight to Worcester or Derby ware of the period.

A colourful and expensive class of Coalport porcelain is that known as 'Coalbrookdale'. Examples are decorated with encrusted flowers, etc., in high relief (Plate 88). It should be noted that other manufacturers of the period made similar floral encrusted pieces during the period 1815–30.

In 1820, John Rose received the gold medal of the Society of Arts for the best porcelain glaze produced without lead. It was competed for by Copeland's, Davenport's and other

Fig. 37. Coalport china works at the beginning of the nineteenth century, from a painting by Muss.

Plate 87. Typical specimens of early Coalport
'Japan' pattern porcelain. The plate is marked
'Coalbrookdale'. c.1805.   *Editor's collection.*

principal manufacturers as well as by Mr. Rose,
but was honourably gained by him. It bears the
inscription: 'To Mr. John Rose, MDCCCXX,
for his improved glaze for porcelain.' Special
circular marks record this event.

Both at the Great Exhibition of 1851 and
that of 1862 – as well as at the French Exhibition
in 1855 – Messrs. Rose & Co. carried off medals
for their productions; and these recognitions of
excellence were continued at the later international exhibitions. The productions took rank
among the best porcelain of the kingdom, many
of the specialities of this firm being marvels of
beauty, the colours pure and full, and of extreme
richness. Sardinian green – a colour for the
extreme depth and richness of which these
works were celebrated – was introduced with
remarkable effect both in services and otherwise.

Rose du Barry was a speciality of the Coalport works, and a colour on the excellence of
which its proprietors always prided themselves.
This was used as a ground in every conceivable
variety of decoration. When enriched with
raised dead (matt) and burnished gold, and
with the exquisite painting by which it is usually

accompanied, it has a remarkably rich and chaste
effect. One of the finest and most massive pieces
in this colour is a claret jug with raised gold
vine-leaves and grapes and other decorations,
and spendidly painted on one side with the head
of a Bacchante and on the other with a bunch of
grapes. A pink or light Rose du Barry was also
much used as a ground for pilgrims' bottles,
vases, services, etc., where, for some kinds of
decoration, it harmonised better than the full
colour would.

A blue with a slightly purplish cast, which
gives it an additional richness and fullness, was
also introduced and formed a splendid ground
for Japanese decoration in vases, in which style
of decoration the Coalport artists excelled. In
these Japanese patterns, some of the designs are
unusually elaborate and intricate, and the
workmanship is characterised by extreme precision and regularity, while the gilding and
colour – especially the deep reds and blues –
are rich and full in the extreme.

The principal artists employed at that time
[c.1875] were Charles Palmere, William Cook,
John Randall, J. and W. Birbeck, A. Bowdler,
J. Hartshorne, Jabez Aston; formerly employed
was R. F. Abraham [c.1862], a student from
Antwerp and Paris and a successful follower of
the school of Etty. Modellers of a very high class

Plate 88. A 'Coalbrookdale' floral-encrusted Coalport porcelain vase, c.1825. 12½ inches high.
Godden of Worthing Ltd.

in their respective branches were also employed, and the excellence of their work is apparent in all the higher class productions of this establishment.

On some examples of the early part of the nineteenth century, the written name 'Coalport' or 'Coalbrookdale' appears; but these are of rare occurrence. Another mark adopted somewhat later, though only used very sparingly, was simply C D, for Coalbrookdale, or the same two letters enjoined thus:

At other times, the contraction 'C Dale', in similar writing letters, was used.

Another mark, of larger size, adopted in 1820, is a circle in which is a wreath of laurel surrounding the words 'Coalport Improved Felt Spar Porcelain' in four lines across. Encircling the wreath are the words 'Patronised by the Society of Arts. The Gold Medal awarded May 30, 1820'; while beneath and outside the circle is the name 'J. Rose and Co.' This mark (and slight variations) was adopted upon Mr. Rose obtaining the gold medal previously mentioned.

Other marks adopted by this firm are, first, a monogram of the letters C B D, for Coalbrookdale; (the same monogram, surrounded by a garter bearing the name of 'Daniell, London' – a firm which for many years, like Mortlock's and other leading houses connected with Coalport, have had that mark used for some especial orders); and second, the initials of the various manufactories which have from time to time

been incorporated with or merged into the Coalport establishment. Thus the scroll – which at first sight looks like a short 'and' (&) – will, on examination, be seen to be a combination of the script letters C and S, for Coalport and Salopian, enclosing within its bows the three letters C, S and N denoting respectively Caughley, Swansea and Nantgarw. This mark was used from about 1861 to 1875. From 1875 to 1881, the printed mark 'Coalport A.D. 1750' was employed. From 1881 into the twentieth century, the crowned mark was used:

'England' was added in 1891, and this became 'Made in England' after about 1920. The Company moved to Staffordshire in 1926 and there continues.

The reader is referred to *Coalport and Coalbrookdale Porcelains* by G. A. Godden (Herbert Jenkins, London, 1970).

CODNOR PARK (Derbyshire)

Codnor Park Works The pottery at Codnor Park was built in 1820 by the Butterley Iron

Fig. 38. Coalport vases shown at the 1871
Exhibition

Company, the owners of the iron works of Butterley and Codnor Park. At that time, the But-
terly works were under the management of
William Jessop, son of one of the partners and
afterwards senior partner of the firm.

William Burton, formerly an engine-fitter
with the iron company, was induced to commence the pottery and, having engaged a skilled
workman from the Brampton Potteries, near
Chesterfield, commenced operations in 1821.
The pottery, situated near the Codnor Park
Ironworks, from which it took its name, and
pretty close to the Butterley Canal, was successfully carried on for several years. Sir
Richard Phillips, in his *Tour*, in 1828, thus notes
the pottery:

Over near Codnor Castle I viewed a rough
and ill-built manufactory, where they turn
and bake those opaque bottles used for
ginger-beer, soda-water, liquid blacking, etc.
About 50 women and children finish 100 gross
per day, and they sell the half pints at 15d.
and 16d. per doz., and all pints at 2s., and
quarts at 3s. 6d. They are made of the clay
of the vicinity, and the agent for selling them
is Kemp, in Milk Street, London. They are
harder and less liable to burst than glass
bottles.

In 1832, William Burton having got into
pecuniary difficulties, the works were closed.
After remaining unworked for many months,
the pottery was, in 1833, taken by Joseph
Bourne of the Denby Pottery.

The Codnor Park Works, which gave employment to about sixty persons, were carried on by

Plate 89. A twentieth-century Coalport jewelled
porcelain vase bearing the crowned 'Coalport. A.D.
1750' mark. 7 inches high.   *Editor's collection.*

Joseph Bourne until 1861, when they were finally closed. The workmen and plant were transferred to the Denby works, where additional rooms had been erected for their accommodation.

The goods produced at Codnor Park were the usual class of household vessels, and stoneware bottles of various kinds (of sizes up to six gallons), and pans, bowls, jugs, pitchers and other articles. Besides these, however, a remarkably fine, compact, light and delicate buff-coloured terra-cotta was produced. In this were made butter-coolers, vases of various kinds, flower-baskets and pots, ewers, spill-cases and numberless other articles. Many of these were of excellent design and beautifully decorated with foliage and other ornaments in relief. Puzzle-jugs were also made of this material and surface-painted with a peculiar mottled effect.

The mark during William Burton's time was his name and 'Codnor Park' or simply the name 'Wm. Burton' impressed on the clay. The manufacture of ordinary housefold earthenware was discontinued when Joseph Bourne took the concern.

CHURCH GRESLEY (Derbyshire)

Church Gresley Pottery Established in about 1790 by a Mr. Leedham for coarse ware, this pottery was, in about 1816, bought by Mr. W. Bourne, who commenced the manufacture of Derbyshire Ironstone cane ware. He was succeeded by Mr. Edwards, Messrs. Shaw and Harrison, and Henry Wileman, at whose decease in 1864 they were taken by Mr. T. G. Green. Cane-coloured Ironstone, Rockingham, mottled, black lustre, buff and other ware was made; and at an adjoining manufactory, built by Mr. Green in 1871, the usual services and domestic articles in painted, lined, sponged, and cream-coloured earthenware were made. Mr. Green took out patents for a process of moulding earthenware, and for a bat-making machine.

Messrs. T. G. Green & Co. Ltd. continue to the present day.

'Gresley' China In 1794, a manufactory was established in Church Gresley by Sir Nigel Gresley, Bart., of Darkelow, and C.B. Adderley of Hams Hall, who died in 1826. In June 1795, William Coffee, one of the modellers at the Derby china manufactory, was engaged for these works, as is shown by a letter as follows:

> My being your debtor makes it my duty to inform you immediately of my arrival here, and likewise my engagement with Sir Nigel Gresley and Mr. Adderley, lest you should suppose I had forgot the obligation I lie under to you.

The works were situated within fifty yards of Gresley Hall, near the village and castle of Gresley, in the county of Derby, with also a place in Burton-on-Trent itself. From some cause or other, the project did not answer, and in about 1800 the works passed into the hands of William Nadin, who carried on the manufactory for four or five years, then discontinued it and was succeeded by Mr. Burton, of Linton, Derbyshire, who continued the works for a few years and then closed them.

By Mr Nadin, the usual classes of ordinary Staffordshire ware were made, as also was china. In the latter, one great speciality was boots, shoes and slippers, which were extensively produced and variously ornamented. His son, Mr. J. Nadin, wrote in reference to these: 'My father made a large number of china boots and shoes, and I well remember when about six years old, walking up to my ankles into a pond of water in a pair of these boots (Wellington in shape).' He also stated that when his father 'had these works, he received an order for a magnificent dinner-service – the price was fixed at £700 – for Queen Charlotte, through Colonel Desbrow, her Chamberlain, but he was never able to execute it, as the china always came out of the ovens cracked and crazed, though he employed the very best men he could obtain.'

The Duke of Kent is said to have paid the works a visit, accompanied by Colonel Desbrow. No examples of the production of these works are, as far as my enquiries go, now known to be in existence.

In about 1832, William Edwards, solicitor, of Derby, (brother-in-law of the second William Duesbury of the Derby china works), in conjunction with a Mr. Tunnicliffe, commenced a yellow ware manufactory at the Hay, Burton-on-Trent. Later on, the manufactory of china or 'artificial marble' was commenced in High Street, workmen having been brought from the Potteries and from Derby. They only continued in operation for a few years, and the productions were not marked. In ornamental ware, Mr. Edwards confined himself to the production of figures; but they were complete failures. 'Mr. Edwards' artificial marble gods and goddesses, made at the Burton-on-Trent works, came out of the oven with their limbs twisted into every conceivable form'. On his failure, the works were closed and he removed to Butt House, near Woodville – at that time known as Wooden Box. Mr. Edwards employed some really good workmen, amongst whom was a clever modeller named Wornell, some good examples of whose work were in the possession of Mr. Abraham Bass, by whom much of this information was supplied to me.

Commonside Pottery At these old-fashioned works, the commonest earthenware was first made; and afterwards, by Edward Grice, sanitary goods and chimney-pots were made. He was succeeded in 1873 by Mason, Gough & Till. In 1874, Mr. Mason left the firm, which became Till & Gough and then J. Till from about 1884 to 1895. Yellow, Rockingham, and buff ware was made, of the usual quality and in the same general variety of articles as in the other Derbyshire potteries.

Commonside Works Edward Grice, who, after leaving the Commonside Pottery, established these works in 1867, manufactured sanitary and terra-cotta goods of various kinds.

Plate 90. Bretby Art Pottery – an advertisement of c.1896.

Hill Top Works These works were established in 1810 by John Cooper, who, with partners, carried them on successively as John Cooper, Cooper & Massey and Cooper & Banks. They next belonged to Henry Ansell. The proprietor until about 1900 was Nehemiah Banks. The ware produced was the ordinary 'Derbyshire Ironstone Cane Ware', buff ware, Rockingham ware, and black lustre ware. Horticultural ware of superior quality was also largely made.

The Pool Pottery William Mason, formerly of the Waterloo Pottery, moved here in 1880. Yellow ware of utilitarian nature was produced into the twentieth century. Many very large 'Church Gresley Barge' teapots were made here.

Bretby Art Pottery In 1883, Henry Tooth, whose connection with the Linthorpe Pottery then ceased, commenced, in conjunction with a partner, some new works at Church Gresley for the production of a similar class of goods to those produced at Linthorpe. The works, carried on under the name of the Bretby Art Pottery produced a large variety of ornamental articles and all the usual classes of useful goods to which an art character could be imparted. The spot chosen was calculated for their full development – coal and clays, both the ordinary red and a fine yellow, being abundant. The pieces produced at these works are characterised by a firmness of body, a perfectness of glaze that is not given to 'craze', and a clearness of colour that is very refreshing. Simplicity – even, in some instances, carried to severity – of form, combined with richness, and at the same time harmony of colouring, and a softness and delicacy of blending, are among the characteristics of this art pottery. An advertisement of 1896 is reproduced in Plate 90. The mark is a sun with the word BRETBY.

This firm continues to the present time and has used the same mark, with the addition of 'England', from about 1891.

DENABY (Near Mexborough, Yorkshire)

The Denaby Pottery Established for the manufacture of fire-bricks, etc., this pottery was, in about 1864, taken by John Wardle (from Messrs. Alcock's of Burslem), who was joined in partnership by William Wilkinson, under the style of Wilkinson & Wardle, for the production of all the ordinary classes of printed earthenware, pearl body, and creamware. In these, all the more popular and favourite patterns were produced from entirely new copper plates. Dinner, tea, coffee, toilet and other services, and other articles of really good and effective design, were also produced. Yellow or cane-coloured ware was also made, as well as tiles for external decorative purposes, from clay found at Conisborough, where branch works were established. The mark adopted by the firm was the Staffordshire knot, with the words 'Wilkinson & Wardle, Denaby Potteries'. These works, after an existence of a few years only, were closed in 1869 or 1870, and the buildings were converted into bone and glue works.

DENBY (Derbyshire)

The Denby Pottery In the parish of Denby, seven miles from Derby and two from Ripley, this pottery is in the midst of the rich ironstone and coal-fields of Derbyshire, the former of which are said to have been regularly worked from the time of the Romans. The works were commenced in 1809 by a Mr. Jäger, on the estate of W. Drury Lowe, where, some time before, a valuable and extensive bed of clay had been found to exist. This clay, previous to the establishment of the Denby Works, was used at the Belper Pottery for the manufacture of stoneware ink, blacking and other bottles. The Denby clay was also supplied to the Derby China Works in considerable quantities, where it was used mostly for saggers.

In 1812, Joseph Bourne, son of William

Bourne, of the Belper Pottery, succeeded Mr. Jäger and the Belper and Denby works were carried on simultaneously until 1834, when the Belper works were discontinued and the plant and work-people were removed to Denby. The works, at this time, much increased and gradually extended their operations. In 1833, the Codnor Park Works passed into the hands of Mr. Bourne and were carried on by him, along with those of Denby, until 1861, when they were closed and the work-people and plant, as in the case of the Belper Works, were removed to Denby. The stoneware bottle dated 'August 19th 1836' shown in Plate 91 bears the double-address mark, Denby & Codnor Park, Bournes Potteries, Derbyshire'. In 1845, Mr. Bourne also became possessed of the Shipley Pottery and in 1856 removed those works to Denby. With the Denby Pottery were, therefore, incorporated those of Belper, Codnor Park and Shipley. Mr. Joseph Bourne, having taken his son Joseph Harvey Bourne into partnership, the business was carried on under the style of Joseph Bourne & Son (Ltd), and has so continued into the twentieth century. In 1851, a medal was awarded to Mr. Bourne for his stone bottles. He died in 1860, and his son died in 1869.

The great bulk of the stoneware produced by Bourne & Son was the kind known as salt-glazed stoneware, which, on account of its peculiar vitreous and non-absorbent qualities, was in great demand not only in the home market but in all parts of the world. In about 1836, a considerable change was made in the size and form of the salt-glaze kilns, and for these improvements Joseph Bourne obtained a patent.

Foot-warmers, carriage-warmers, medical appliances, mortars and pestles, pipkins, feeding-bottles, candlesticks, pork-pie moulds and every other variety of domestic and other vessels were made.

'Hunting-jugs' – a name by which a certain class of jug with raised ornaments consisting of hunting subjects is known – were made to a great extent (see advertisement, Fig. 39). Some of these were made with greyhound handles. Jars for preservatives, pickles, jellies and marmalades were a staple branch of the Denby

Plate 91. Denby stoneware bottle dated 1836. 8 inches high. *Editor's collection.*

manufacture.

In terra-cotta, of a warm buff colour, flower vases of various designs, lotus vases, garden and other vases, wine-coolers, water-bottles, ewers with snake handles, flower-stands, Stilton-cheese stands and trays, fern-stands, fonts,

Indian scent jars, butter-coolers, mignonette-boxes and many other articles of artistic excellence were made. A finer type of terra-cotta was introduced in c.1880; vases and plaques were produced.

The marks included the name Bourne in various forms. The firm of Joseph Bourne & Son Ltd. continues at the Denby Pottery to this day. The modern ware bears marks featuring the name Denby.

DERBY (Derbyshire)

For a detailed study of the history of the Derby factory during the eighteenth century, the reader is referred to F. Brayshaw Gilhespy's *Crown Derby Porcelain* (F. Lewis, Leigh-on-Sea, Essex, 1951) or his *Derby Porcelain* (Spring Books, London, 1961). The following account starts at the end of the eighteenth century.

In 1796, William Duesbury died and, not long afterwards, Michael Kean (who had for a time the management of the business for the widow and her young family) married the widow. But before long, for reasons into which it is needless to enter, he withdrew hastily from the concern and the works were then continued for, and afterwards by, the third William Duesbury. Mrs. Duesbury, by her marriage with Michael Kean, had a family of five children. She died in 1829.

The third William Duesbury (grandson of the founder of the works) was the eldest son of William Duesbury by his wife Elizabeth Edwards. He was born in 1787. On the 26th September 1808, he married Annabella, daughter of William E. Sheffield. For a time, the concern was carried on under the style of Duesbury & Sheffield. In 1815, Mr. Duesbury leased the premises to Robert Bloor, who had been a clerk to his father and had carried on the business during his minority. The entire concern ultimately passed into Bloor's hands, and for the first few years was carried on with judgment and skill.

Fig. 39. Bourne's advertisement of 1896.

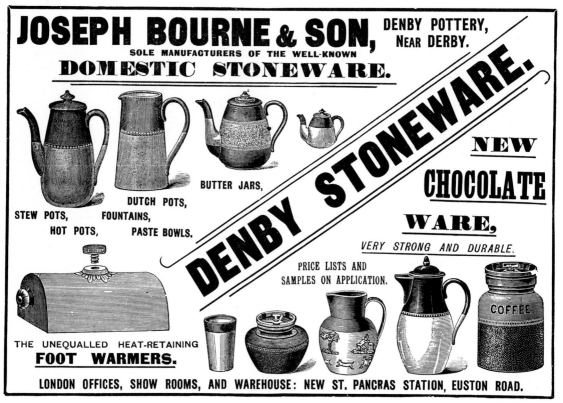

Before Mr. Bloor's time it had been the constant plan of the Duesburys – so worthily tenacious were they of their reputation and of keeping up the high and unblemished character of their works – to allow none but perfect goods to leave their premises. No matter how costly the article or how trivial the fault, all goods which were not perfect were stowed away in rooms in the factory and thus accumulated to an enormous extent. When Bloor took the concern, this stock of 'seconds' became to him an almost exhaustless mine of wealth. Having to pay the purchase money by instalments, he found the easiest method of doing so was to finish up these goods – sending them to different large towns, where they were sold by auction. One of the sales, in 1822, continued for twenty-five days. By this means, Robert Bloor amassed large sums of money, as the 'Derby-china' found ready and liberal purchasers wherever it was thus offered. But this system, though it had a temporary good effect, produced a lasting evil, as the standard of workmanship was allowed to degenerate. However, it must be stated that not all Bloor-Derby specimens are of poor quality. Some very fine examples were also made.

Robert Bloor was assisted in his works by his brother Joseph, by whom the 'mixing' was mainly done, and from 1828, when Robert Bloor's health began to fail, they were carried on for him by a manager named Thomason.

The two brothers died within a short time of each other. Robert, who lost his mind many years before his decease, died in 1845, and Joseph died the following year. The works then passed into the hands of Thomas Clarke (who had married a grand-daughter of Robert Bloor's), who discontinued them and sold most of the models to the Staffordshire manufacturers – the greater bulk going into the hands of Mr. Boyle, of Fenton. The final dissolution of the old works took place in 1848, when a number of the workmen naturally migrated into Staffordshire and Worcestershire.

At this time, however, several of the old hands – actuated by the laudable desire of securing the continuance of a business which for a century had been so successfully carried on, and of continuing it as one of the trades of their native town – 'clubbed together' and commenced business on their own account. They each and all threw into the common stock what knowledge, experience, money and tools they possessed, took premises in King Street (on the site of old St. Helen's Nunnery), and under the name of Locker & Co. commenced making 'Derby china'.

Mr. Locker (who was a native of Blackfordby and had been clerk and warehouseman at the old works in the latter part of their existence) died in 1859, and the works were next conducted under the style of Stevenson & Co., and then Stevenson, Sharp & Co. till the death of Mr. Stevenson, when the style was changed to Hancock & Co. and the works were continued by Mr. Samson Hancock. This small King Street porcelain works was continued by various owners until 1935. No printed decoration was done. All decoration was hand-painted.

Plate 92. Bloor-Derby porcelain of good quality, c.1825–35. Ewer, 11 inches high.
Godden of Worthing Ltd.

Plate 93. A good quality Bloor-Derby teapot of the
early 1830s. 4¾ inches high.   *Sotheby & Co.*

In 1862, a special mark was adopted comprising the old Derby crowned baton mark with
the addition of the initials S and H, placed one
each side of the device. This mark continued in
use until 1935.

**The Derby Crown Porcelain Company or
Royal Crown Derby** In 1877, Edward Phillips,
having severed his connection with the Worcester works, of which he was managing director,
formed a new limited liability company at Derby
and completed the purchase of the old Derby
workhouse, with land and extensive premises
comprising in all some fourteen or fifteen acres
of ground, and converted the buildings, to
which immense additions were made, into a
china factory. Three biscuit and three glost
ovens were erected, as well as every possible
requirement for the preparation of the whole
of the raw materials and the turning out of a
vast amount of finished goods of every class.
In 1878, the first goods, undecorated, were sent
away; and by 1880, the whole manufactory had,
in every department, been brought into full
working order. In the following year, 1881,
Edward Phillips – to whom the town and district
owed the establishment of this revival of the old
glory of Derby and who had been indefatigably
and unresting in every detail of its founding and
development – died, after a very brief illness, at
the age of sixty-five. Consequent on his death,
Mr. McInnes and Mr. Litherland were appointed
managing directors. Under their skilful management, the works were still further developed, the
business connections much increased, and a
more advanced and higher tone was given to
many of the productions. The works, in the
1880s, employed some three hundred hands.

Plate 94. Three examples of Stevenson & Hancock's porcelain decorated in the style of earlier Derby porcelain, c.1900.   *Godden of Worthing Ltd.*

The productions were porcelain and, rarely, a vitrified stoneware or hard earthenware. In porcelain, all the usual services – dinner, tea, breakfast, toilet, trinket, and déjeuner – and a variety of other useful articles were made, as were also vases of every conceivable design and of the most exquisite styles of decoration.

One of the main aims of the directorate – and in this they were eminently successful – was the revival of the old 'Crown Derby' shapes, colours and patterns in services and other useful classes of goods, and in vases and ornamental articles.

The specialities were the vases, principally of Persian and Indianesque character, decorated in the richest of styles with a profusion of raised gilt ornament and an elaborate colouring that was eminently effective. In this raised-gold decoration the works were markedly successful, the egg-shell china cups and saucers thus decorated being far beyond those of other houses.

In these examples, which are chefs d'oeuvre of the plastic art, the body is of a high degree of transparency, of marvellous thinness, and of extreme hardness and tenacity, and on some examples the raised-gold pattern is in the finest and most delicate of lines. In whatever style, indeed, the decoration of these choice cabinet specimens was done, there is a studied delicacy and beauty that is in keeping with the apparently fragile body of which they are composed.

The services, whether plain, printed, painted, or ornamented and gilt, were all of the better and higher class, and embraced patterns of great excellence and beauty. The productions met with signal success in the United States and Australia.

The chief artists employed in about 1883 were, in painting, James Rouse, Sen., (then nearly a nonagenarian, from the old Derby China Works, whose 'right hand has forgot none of its cunning') as a flower-painter; his son, a clever landscape-painter, whose productions emulate

177

Plate 95. A pair of Royal Crown Derby porcelain dwarfs, one of several reissues of early Derby models, c.1885. 6¾ inches high.
Godden of Worthing Ltd.

the father's; Count Holtzendorff, a landscape-painter whose productions have, as a rule, a soft dreaminess of colour and subdued tone that is very pleasing; W. H. Hogg, a talented modeller, two of whose busts found a place at the Royal Academy Exhibition of 1883; J. Platts, a painter of figures; and H. Deakin. The principal gilders (of whom there was a considerable staff) were A. Piper and S. F. Lambert.

The mark adopted by the company was the printed crown of the old Derby China Works surmounting the letter D (for Derby), repeated to form a monogram and conveying the idea of the name 'Crown Derby'.

Since the above account was written, in the early 1880s, the Crown Derby Company has gone from strength to strength. In January 1890,

the company was appointed 'Manufacturers of Porcelain to Her Majesty', and the title became The Royal Crown Derby Porcelain Company. From this date 'Royal Crown Derby' was added above the trade mark. The firm continues to this day.

For a table of year cyphers and other information on artists, see Godden's *Victorian Porcelain* (Herbert Jenkins, London, 1961).

George Cocker A figure modeller at the Derby factory, he established his own small works at Derby in c.1826, in partnership with John Whitaker at Friar Gate. An advertisement of 1826 reads: 'Ladies or Gentlemen may have figures, ornaments, etc. executed from models or drawings of their own ... a variety of Tea and Dessert services of modern and approved pattern ...'

Some figures bear Cocker's incised signature. In 1840, Cocker left Derby for London. He was later employed at Minton's and other Staffordshire potteries.

Derby marks are featured in Godden's *Encyclopaedia of British Pottery and Porcelain Marks* (Herbert Jenkins, London, 1964). Typical ware is shown in his *Illustrated Encyclopaedia of British Pottery and Porcelain* (Herbert Jenkins, London, 1966).

DITCHLING (Sussex)

At Ditchling, pot-works are said to have existed for 'several hundred years'. Be this as it may, some old pot-works for the coarsest brown ware, and bricks and tiles, were bought in 1870 by H. Johnson & Co., in the belief that from the superior quality of the native red clay they would be able to produce architectural terracotta of a more than ordinarily durable quality. By them, the Ditchling Works were much extended, and they succeeded in making terracotta of an excellent bright red colour and a fine, hard, durable and almost metallic surface. Ditchling terra-cotta was successfully used on many public buildings, and the firm received medals at the London and Philadelphia Exhibitions.

DUBLIN (Ireland)

Donovan Whether James Donovan of George's Quay, Poolbeg Street, Dublin, was a manufacturer or not is uncertain, but I believe not. He purchased both English and Continental ware in the white, and decorated it in his own place. He amassed a large fortune and purchased estate in Sussex. In this business, he was usually known in Dublin as 'The Emperor of China'. In about 1790, he had a glass manufactory at Ringsend, near Dublin, and he employed a painter to decorate pottery, and placed all sorts of fancy and imitation marks on the china and earthenware. His name sometimes occurs as DONOVAN only, and at other times as $\frac{\text{DONOVAN}}{\text{DUBLIN}}$. He continued to about 1829.

The first directory entry is in 1770: 'Donovan (James & Son), china and Glass-merch. George's Qu.'; the last, that of 1829, reads: 'Donovan (J), China and Glass Manufactory, Richard Street, Ringsend'.

EWELL (Surrey)

Nonsuch Pottery A pottery existed here in the early part of the eighteenth century; but in about 1790, or soon after, the bed of clay having been exhausted, it was discontinued. In about 1800, the steward of the Nonsuch estates, on which the pottery was situated, gave permission for a new pottery to be established wherever the clay could be found; and soon afterwards, the Nonsuch Pottery was opened in Nonsuch Park. It was founded by William Richard Waghorn, who was joined in partnership by his son.

This firm continued until 1851, when the works were transferred to Mr. Swallow, who had until that time been their foreman. By him and his partner, Mr. Stone, the business was continued under the style of Stone & Swallow, and by them a pottery – principally for the manufacture of fire-bricks – was established at Epsom. Mr. Swallow died in 1866 or 1867, and Mr. Stone continued the works alone; they were known as the Nonsuch Pottery or as Stone's Ewell and Epsom Potteries.

The goods manufactured by William Waghorn were 'Italian tiling', used very extensively in the buildings of the time and remarkable for their strength and durability; ornamental roof tiles; ridge tiles; 'Nonsuch fire-bricks'; 'Nonsuch fire-loam'; paving and other tiles; moulded bricks and the like for Gothic buildings; ornamental chimney-pots; pipes; flower-pots and vases. The mark was simply Stone & Co. The premises were still leased to Stone's in 1909. The manufacture ceased in c.1914.

FREMINGTON (North Devon)

The Pottery At Fremington, near Barnstaple, this pottery was established in the early part of the nineteenth century by George Fishley, who, in 1839, was succeeded by his son, Edmund Fishley. He continued it until his death in 1861, when it passed into the hands of his son, Edwin B. Fishley (1832–1912).

The goods produced were of glazed red ware, and consisted principally of pitchers and jugs; scalding-pans for milk for producing the world-famed 'Devonshire cream'; flower-pots and pans; washing pots, cauldrons, and pans; baking dishes and bread pans; salting vessels and chimney pots, and many other articles. Some of the water pitchers bear the peculiar names of 'Long Toms', 'Thirty Tales' or 'Gullymouths'. Yellow-ware jugs and other domestic vessels were also made.

In ornamental ware, some good designs in jars, beer jugs and vases were produced. These were formed of a body of red clay, with figures and flowers in white clay. They were sometimes coloured, with good effect. The beer jugs, which were a speciality of the works, were generally white with incised drawings showing the red colour of the underlying body.

The great speciality of the Fremington pottery, like that of Bideford, was in the manufacture of fire-clay ovens. The material of which they were composed was remarkably firm, hard and compact, and retained the heat for a considerable time. These ovens, a peculiarity of the West of England and of some of the Welsh districts, were simply enclosed in raised brickwork, leaving the mouth open to the front. They were heated inside with wood or gorse, and were remarkable for the small quantity of fuel required. The bread baked in them was stated to be of a peculiarly wholesome and sweet character.

The mark used on the ovens was simply the proprietor's name impressed in the clay while moist. On the ornamental ware, the name was written on the bottom of the ware:

E. B. FISHLEY
FREMINGTON

Edwin B. Fishley potted at Fremington until his death in 1912. His grandson, W. Fishley Holland (born in 1889), who had worked at this pottery from 1902 to 1912, has written a fascinating account of his career and of this type of West Country pottery. His book *Fifty Years a Potter* (Pottery Quarterly, Tring) was published in 1958.

W. Fishley Holland built a pottery at Braunton in 1912.

FULHAM (London)

Fulham Pottery Apart from the fact that the famous John Dwight worked this pottery in the late seventeenth century, little of note was produced until C. I. C. Bailey purchased the works in 1864. He then enlarged the manufactory and installed improved machinery.

The goods made at these works were glazed and unglazed stoneware, brown ware, porous ware, terra-cotta and china. In stoneware, or 'Bristol ware', all the usual domestic vessels were made very extensively; also drain, sanitary and chemical appliances of every description, including Field's syphon traps (of which they were sole makers), War-Office-pattern pipes and others. Works of art of a high order in stoneware, terra-cotta, china and other bodies were also produced.

For the stoneware department, M. Cazin (formerly Director of the School of Art at Tours, in France) was engaged to design figured and other fancy jugs and mugs. Some of these, with armorial bearings and other decorations in incised lines, or impressed, were good adaptations of the antique. A cannette, in my possession, bears the artist's name–CAZIN, 1872, STUDY– and was said to be remarkably good, as was another example, made expressly for me, with a finely modelled armorial medallion and other incised and relief ornaments, with the date '1873' and the artist's name, C. CAZIN, also incised. The coloured stone-ware or 'sgraffito' ware equals in many respects that made by Doulton (See Colour Plate VIII). In 1872, Mr. Bailey received a medal at the Dublin Exhibition for his stoneware and terra-cotta.

Mr. Bailey also introduced a marked improvement in the construction of filters – the water passing downwards at the back and then rising in zigzag direction by its own force to the tap at the top in front. Thus the water had to travel a much further distance through the filtering matter than by the old method and, having to be taken a far more circuitous course, it was brought more thoroughly in contact with the purifying medium.

Terra-cotta stoves of simple and effective construction were also made at these works.

In 'Sunderland Ware' – i.e. brown ware, white inside – cream pots, starch pans, milk bowls, dishes, trays and basins were manufactured. Chemical apparatus – receivers, retorts and evaporating dishes–was, as well as porous ware, a speciality in these works. In terra-cotta, the works produced vases, statues, architectural enrichments, chimney shafts and stoves of very good quality. In colour, the Fulham terra-cotta is a light pink and a rich red; and when these were combined, a peculiar delicacy and finished effect was produced.

The manufacture of china ware was, during 1873, very wisely and successfully added to this establishment and, with the aid of good workmen and artists, did much to establish a fresh fame for Fulham. The art direction of this branch was placed by Mr. Bailey in the hands of E. Bennet, a well-known sculptor, while the china body modelled flowers were undertaken by Mr. Hopkinson. I am the more particular in

Colour Plate VIII. A rare Fulham stoneware vase
from the Bailey Pottery, decorated by E. Bennett in
the Doulton-style, c.1880.
Victoria & Albert Museum (Crown copyright).

stating these arrangements as, being the beginning of a new manufacture, I am desirous of putting on record the circumstances of its commencement.

The body, it may be well to note, was made from Dwight's original recipe – the very body of which the first china ware made in England was produced – and therefore the new 'Fulham china' had an historical interest attached to it which was possessed by no other. It was a wise thought that induced Mr. Bailey to restore to Fulham the special manufacture which had rendered its name famous in the ceramic annals of Great Britain.

An interesting pair of figures in nineteenth-century Fulham porcelain are illustrated in the *Antique Collector*, October 1956. Two other figures in the Victoria and Albert Museum are shown in Godden's *Illustrated Encyclopaedia of British Pottery and Porcelain*, (Herbert Jenkins, London, 1966).

Porcelain is listed in Bailey & Co.'s advertisements up to 1887. Bailey's Fulham Pottery closed in about 1889. Most pieces bear marks incorporating Bailey's name.

The Martin Brothers (Fulham & Southall). The Martin brothers have a claim to be considered the first of the studio potters. The brothers, Robert Wallace Martin (1843–1923), Walter Martin (1859–1912), Edwin Bruce Martin (1860–1915) and Charles Martin (died in 1910), worked together in their studio (see Plate 96) as a team, producing salt-glaze stoneware of a unique and varied character. This Martin ware is now popular and can be quite costly.

Plate 96. Group photograph of the Martin Brothers at work in their studio, c.1900. Left to right: Walter, Wallace (R. W.), and Edwin Martin.
Editor's collection.

Plate 97. A selection of typical stoneware made by
the Martin Brothers. Face jug dated 1900, 8¾ inches
high. *Victoria & Albert Museum (Crown copyright).*

Robert, usually known as Wallace, Martin
was the mainstay of the partnership. He was
mainly responsible for the series of grotesque
bird models with moveable heads, as well as for
other animal forms.

Walter Martin received early training at
Doulton's pottery at Lambeth. He was responsible for 'throwing' all the large vases and was
also in charge of mixing the clays and of the
firing process.

The third brother, Edwin, decorated vases
and similar objects with incised and relief patterns – seaweed, fish and floral motifs.

Charles Martin took the responsibility of
management and administration off the
shoulders of his brothers and managed their
retail shop in Brownlow Street, Holborn.

The reader is referred to Blacker's *The ABC of
English Salt-Glaze Stoneware* (Stanley Paul,
London, 1922) and to *Country Life*, 23rd March
1961, for full accounts of the Martin brothers.
A detailed and well-illustrated work of reference
is Charles Beard's catalogue of the Nettlefold
Collection of Martinware (privately published,
1936), but this is now very scarce and expensive.

Four typical examples in the Victoria and
Albert Museum collection are shown in Plate 97.

The Martin brothers worked from 1873 to
1914. Their ware is marked with their name,
place of production ('Fulham' at first; later,
'London and Southall') and numerals signify-
ing the month and year of production – all incised into the soft clay before firing. The various
changes in the basic marks are:

182

R W Martin 84
Fulham

Fulham Period, c.1873–4

R W Martin 9
London

London mark, c.1874–8.
Note no letter prefix to number.

R W Martin 21
Southall

OR R W MARTIN SOUTHALL.

Southall Period, c.1878

R W Martin
London & Southall

London & Southall marks, c.1879–82

R W Martin & Brothers
London & Southall

'& Bros' or '& Brothers'
added to name from 1882 onwards,
with double address
"London & Southall".

GATESHEAD (Durham)

The Carr's Hill Pottery The first manufactory for white ware in the north of England. Painted, enamelled, and brown ware was also made. It was established in about 1750 by a Mr. Warburton, who removed to this place from Newcastle, and it was successfully carried on by him and his successors until 1817, when it was closed. A part of the premises was afterwards carried on by Messrs. Kendall & Walker, and later still by Messrs. Isaac Fell & Co.

GLASGOW (Scotland)

Verreville Pottery In 1777, the Verreville Works were built for a glass-house, as the name implies, by a Mr. Cookson of Newcastle and a Mr. Colquhon of Glasgow. In 1806, they were sold to the Dumbarton Glass Work Company, who immediately re-sold them to John Geddes, with this stipulation: that he was not to manufacture crown or bottle glass. Mr. Geddes carried on the manufacture of flint-glass until 1820, when he commenced making earthenware.

In 1827, the title became Geddes, Kidston & Co., and in the 1830s Kidston & Price. In 1838, the works passed into the hands of Robert Alexander Kidston, who added the manufacture of china to that of glass and earthenware. He began by bringing skilled workmen and artists from the principal seats of china manufacture. Figures, porcelain basket-work and flowers were produced by workmen who had acquired their skill in the old and celebrated porcelain works of Derby, while Coalport and several of the most famous Staffordshire china works supplied a general staff of potters, together with gilders, and flower and landscape painters. Mr. Kidston carried on the business to 1846 and produced a beautiful porcelain.

Robert Kidston also worked the Anderston Pottery. Designs registered in 1841 by Kidson & Co., of the Anderston Works, Glasgow, are reproduced in Godden's *British Pottery and Porcelain, 1780–1850* (Arthur Barker, London, 1963).

The firm of R. A. Kidston & Co. was sequestrated in January 1841. A subsequent partnership of Kidston, Cochran & Co. was dissolved in December 1846, and Robert Cochran & Co. continued.

In 1856, Robert Cochran ceased the manufacture of china and devoted the whole of the works to the manufacture of earthenware and white granite-ware. Mr. Cochran devoted great attention, and spared no expense, to promoting the introduction of labour-saving machinery. He also made great improvements in the kilns or ovens in which the earthenware was fired, by which he reduced the quantity of the coal used to nearly one half. They were applied successfully in his own works at Verreville and Britannia.

Mr. Cochran died in 1869 and was succeeded in the Verreville Pottery by his son, also named Robert Cochran, by whom the works were carried on. The goods manufactured consisted of white, sponged, printed and enamelled ware.

Messrs. R. Cochran & Co. continued to 1918. Various marks were employed incorporating the title or initials.

Heathfield Pottery At these works, Messrs. Ferguson, Miller & Co. produced the admirable terra-cotta vases shown at the 1851 Exhibition.

Fig. 40. Messrs. Ferguson, Miller & Co.'s vase, 1851.

One of these, a vase of large size and excellent modelling, bore a frieze of figures typical of the great gathering in 1851 (see Fig. 40). These figures were modelled with great accuracy and arranged in an artistic manner.

The works passed into the hands of Messrs. Young.

Glasgow Pottery These works, established in 1842 by J. & M. P. Bell & Co. in Stafford Street, Glasgow, for the manufacture of white and printed earthenware, soon rose to the first rank among the potteries of Scotland. Particular attention was from the first paid not only to the excellence of body of the ware but also to improvement in form and in style of decoration. In these particulars they were eminently successful, and in 1851 they received honourable mention at the Great Exhibition. Later on, the manufacture of china was commenced; and later still, the fine white and pearl granite ware, and white and decorated sanitary ware. The works were of great extent and produced all the usual varieties of goods in dinner, breakfast, tea, toilet, dessert and other services, as well as all the usual classes of articles, in every variety of style, from the plain white or cream colour to the most richly enamelled and gilt patterns.

The earthenware services were of more than average excellence of quality, and the china, both in body and glaze, was of superior class. Some of the dessert plates, with hand-painted

Fig. 41. J. & M. P. Bell & Co.'s tureen, 1851 Exhibition.

Fig. 42. Messrs. J. & M. P. Bell's exhibits at the
1862 Exhibition.

groups of flowers and open-work rims, equal
most English makes; and some of the tea services
are of tall classic form and of excellent taste in
colour and decoration. In Parian, admirable
vases, with figures in relief, and other ornamental goods were produced.

The old marks used by the Glasgow Pottery
were: an eagle holding a roll, on which is inscribed the name of the patterns, and underneath the initials of the firm – J. & M.P.B. & Co.;
the Warwick vase and the name J. & M.P. BELL
& Co. The later marks are: a garter bearing
the initials of the firm – J. & M.P.B. & Co. –
surrounding the trade-mark of a bell; the name
of the pattern below. These are all printed on
the ware. Another mark impressed in the body is
a bell with the initials J B; and another is a bell
only.

Some of Messrs. Bell & Co.'s exhibits are
shown in Figure 42. The original company
continued to 1910. 'Ltd' occurs on marks from
1881 onwards. From 1910 to 1940, the firm was
continued by Joseph Turner and John Weir.

North British Pottery James Miller worked this pottery from about 1869 to 1875. Earthenware was produced, including blue printed ware. Marks occur incorporating the initials J M & Co. From about 1875 to 1904, A. Balfour & Co. worked the North British Pottery.

Saracen Pottery The Saracen Pottery, established in 1875 by Bayley, Murray & Brammer, at Possilpark, produced Rockingham, cane-coloured, Egyptian black, jet, and mazarine blue ware on an extensive scale – mostly in teapots, jugs, and other useful domestic articles, both for the home and foreign markets. The mark used was the initials of the firm and the name of the works.

From about 1884, the firm was known as the Saracen Pottery Company. It ceased production in about 1900.

Kingfield Pottery John Anderson worked this pottery in the eighteenth and early nineteenth century. The Kingfield Pottery Company produced eighty dozen black earthenware teapots per week. The ware is unmarked.

Mount Blue Pottery James Brown (and then his widow) worked the Mount Blue Pottery at Camlachie (Glasgow) from the early 1880s to 1914. Earthenware was produced.

Goven Pottery Charles Purves produced good earthenware here from about 1869 to the 1890s. Rockingham and majolica glazed earthenware, as well as jet, were produced.

The Port Dundas Pottery Company These works were established for the manufacture of stoneware articles in about 1816. In the earlier years of its existence, there were several changes in the proprietorship; but from about 1845, it passed to the hands of James Miller, who traded as J. Miller & Co. and later as the Port Dundas Pottery Co. The works, in 1856, contained three salt-glaze ovens, in which were manufactured chemical vessels and apparatus of various kinds, spirit-bottles, jars and the like. At about this time, many of the towns in the north of Scotland,

finding the desirability of having a good water supply introduced, had recourse to high-pressure stoneware water-pipes for the purpose, which were manufactured in large quantities at these works. In the same year, a new glaze was introduced, giving to the ware a cream-coloured appearance; and a great demand having thus sprung up for stoneware beer-bottles, the works were greatly enlarged.

By far the greatest portion of ware made in Port Dundas was thrown on the potter's wheel, the motive power for which was supplied, until 1866, by girls who turned a large driving-wheel communicating with a pulley under the workman's wheelhead by a rope. The proprietor in that year endeavoured to introduce steam-power, but so strong was the opposition of the throwers that the machines and accompanying shafting lay aside for three years unused. They were then erected in a distant part of the works, and apprentices were all but forced to work on them. These, however, had not been long fitted up when the workmen, seeing the immense advantages to be derived from their use, gladly availed themselves of the offer of the proprietor to substitute steam machinery for hand-power throughout the whole factory – the immediate result of which was to raise the piece-work earnings of the workmen from thirty to forty-nine per cent. They had one attendant less to pay, a part of whose wages the workman kept for himself while a proportion of it was paid to the company for the use of the steam-power and up-keep of the machinery.

The speed of the wheel, requiring to be varied according to the different operations performed upon it, was now under the complete control of the workman's foot and not, as formerly, at the will or according to the strength of the assistant wheel-turner. In this way, complete revolution was quietly effected in the stoneware potting of Scotland. The incentive having been given, orders came from many potteries in England to the Scottish machine-maker for similar steam-machines.

With the introduction of the cream-coloured stoneware glaze, the ovens had to undergo extensive alterations. The old salt-glaze cupboard-kilns gave place to much larger sagger-ovens, in which the ware was burned. The improvement in the appearance of the ware having brought it into much greater demand, the works rapidly extended until, in the 1870s, in the Port Dundas Pottery, with its branch-works the Crown Pottery, there were fifteen ovens in regular operation.

The ware produced was beer, ink, and spirit bottles; preserve, acid, butter, and druggists' jars; chemical vessels and apparatus, and every kind of article made in stoneware; water-filters, Rockingham and cane-ware. All the goods were stamped with the name of the firm in an oval.

In about 1878, a process for printing on the unfired stoneware body was perfected and patented by this firm, who exhibited their manu-factures at the Chilean Exhibition at Santiago in 1875 and there received the first prize gold medal for the general excellence of their ware.

The Port Dundas Pottery Co. continued making stoneware at 66 Bishop Street, Port Dundas, Glasgow, until 1932. 'Ltd' was added to the firm's style in 1905.

Hyde Park Potteries This manufactory of ordinary stoneware bottles, jars, spirit-casks, feet- and carriage-warmers, pans of various kinds, and all the ordinary classes of stoneware goods, was established in about 1837 by John McAdam. In 1844, John McAdam moved to a new works in the Gallowgate district, and later to the Campbell Field Pottery.

Britannia Pottery These large works of Glebe Street, Glasgow, were established in 1857 by Robert Cochran, the senior partner of the Verreville Pottery Company, the succeeding partners being Alexander Cochran (son of Robert) and James Fleming. The works con-tained six biscuit and seven glost ovens and produced all the usual varieties of ordinary earthenware goods in granite and cream-coloured ware for South America, and printed, enamelled, painted, and gilt ware for the home markets. James Fleming's son stated that 12,000 plates were produced daily. Messrs. Cochran & Fleming continued to June 1920 (and were then succeeded by the Britannia Pottery Co. Ltd.). The seated figure of Britannia occurs on several marks.

Annfield Pottery Messrs. John Thomson & Sons, at the Annfield Pottery, Gallowgate, manufactured both china and earthenware goods for the home and foreign markets. The works closed in the early 1880s.

Bridgeton Pottery The Bridgeton Pottery was built in 1869 by Mr. F. Grosvenor (who for some years previously had been a partner in the Caledonian Pottery at Glasgow) for making the usual articles in stoneware, including chemical ware, bottles for various uses, spirit-jars, and Rockingham-ware teapots. In 1870, he took out a patent for the manufacture of bottles and jars by machinery. He also invented an improved bot-tle-stopper. The firm became Grosvenor & Son after 1899 and worked the Eagle Pottery from 1906. Their trade mark, from 1879, was an eagle.

Barrowfield Pottery Established by Henry Kennedy in 1866, these works produced all the usual classes of articles of glass-lined stoneware, including glass-lined bottles and jars for domes-tic and other purposes, both for home and foreign markets. The mark used was three bottles side by side beneath a ribbon bearing the words 'Established 1866'. As Henry Kennedy & Sons Ltd., the firm continued into the twentieth century.

Campbellfield Pottery The Campbellfield Pot-tery Co. was established at 60 Rochester Street, Gallowgate, Glasgow, in the 1870s. From about 1884, 'Limited' or 'Ltd' was added to the title and the address was changed to Flemington Street, Springburn, Glasgow. Earthenware was produced up to 1905. The mark used was C P C Ltd. on a ribbon, across a thistle; later, Spring-burn.

Wellington Pottery Established in 1797. A. C. Williamson succeeded his father, John William-son, in 1864, and made red-ware at this pottery up to about 1894.

GRANGEMOUTH (Stirlingshire, Scotland)

Fire-Brick Works These works belonged to the Grangemouth Coal Company and were established in 1842. The productions consisted of ornamental vases and tazzae of various patterns; statuary, both single figures and groups; fountains, vases and plinths; flower-stands and pots; chimney-shafts, some of which were highly decorated in relief; pedestals, brackets, salt-glazed pipes, grate-backs, bricks and tiles. The company received honourable mention for their goods at the Exhibition of 1851, and at the Hamburg Exhibition of 1866 had a gold medal awarded to them for their vases and ornamental figures. The works continued at least to the 1880s.

GREENOCK (Renfrewshire, Scotland)

The Clyde Pottery The Clyde Pottery works were established by James and Andrew Muir and others in 1816, the business then being carried on under the style of the Clyde Pottery Company, with James Stevenson as manager – although at one time the pottery traded under his name as James Stevenson & Co. He was succeeded by Thomas Shirley, to whom the business was transferred and who altered the style to Thomas Shirley & Co. In 1857, Messrs. Shirley were succeeded by the Clyde Pottery Company (Limited), with James Brownlie as manager. Having existed for five years, that firm was succeeded by John Donald, Robert Gibson Brown and John McLauchlan, under the old style of the Clyde Pottery Company.

The goods produced were the ordinary qualities of cream-coloured, sponged, painted, printed, pearl-white, enamelled, and gilt ware suitable for home trade, and also various kinds of ware to suit particular foreign markets. The mark was C.P. Co. (Clyde Pottery Company). The company ceased in about 1903.

The Greenock Pottery Established by James Stevenson early in the nineteenth century. Staffordshire-type earthenware was produced here under various managements. Messrs.

Minton supplied goods to James Stevenson & Co. between December 1809 and June 1816. The name Ladyburn Pottery was adopted in about 1850. The pottery closed in 1860.

The 1845 statistical account of Scotland states that the two (unnamed) Greenock potteries gave employment to 200 persons and produced 100,000 items a year, the work-people being employed for ten hours daily at wages from 10/- to £1 per week.

GREENWICH (London)

Ransome's Patent Stone Works These works were established at Ipswich in 1844 and removed to Greenwich in January 1866. Frederick Ransome, the inventor of a process for producing an artificial stoneware capable of being moulded – a member of the well-known Ipswich family – was in early life connected with the Orwell Works firm of Ransomes & Sims. It was while there, and noticing a workman engaged in dressing a millstone, that he conceived the idea of producing artificial stone capable of being moulded to any form, and to be a perfect imitation, both in appearance and substance, of the blocks taken from our best quarries. For ten years, the difficulties he had to encounter were very great; but he at length succeeded in making not only perfectly equable and homogeneous grindstones, with keen cutting powers and that needed no dressing, but also the decorative stonework which, among other places, was introduced in the Brighton Aquarium, London Docks, Albert Bridge, Whitehall and St. Thomas's Hospital. The demand for this artificial stone becoming much extended, the inventions were taken up by a company in 1871 and extensive works were erected at East Greenwich, to which the business was transferred. They were carried on by A. H. Bateman & Co. Ltd.

The material was, to all intents and purposes, a pure sandstone whose silicious particles were bound together by a cement of silicate of lime – a mineral substance well-known to be of the most indestructible nature. It could be moulded to any form while in a plastic state and worked with

Fig. 43. Ransome's vases.

the chisel the same as any natural stone. The process of manufacture was based upon one of the most beautiful of chemical reactions: flints were dissolved by means of caustic alkali under high pressure, so as to form silicate of soda – a kind of water-glass. This viscous and tenacious substance was then rapidly mixed with a proportion of very fine and sharp silicious sand in a pug mill, so as to form a soft plastic mass which could be moulded into any shape that was desired. The soft stone was next immersed in a bath of chloride of calcium solution, which was made to penetrate every pore by means of hydraulic or atmospheric pressure. Whenever this solution came into contact with the silicate of soda, the two liquids were mutually and instantaneously decomposed – the silica taking possession of the calcium and forming the hard, solid silicate of lime, and the soda uniting with the chlorine to form chloride of sodium in a small quantity. Instead, then, of the particles of sand being covered with a thin film of the liquid silicate of soda, they were covered and united together with a film of solid silicate of lime – one of the most indestructible substances known. The small quantity of soluble chloride of sodium – one of the results of decomposition – was then washed out of the stone by a douche of clean water or by hydraulic pressure, its complete removal being ensured by chemical tests. The stone was then dried and was fit for use.

The productions of these works embraced vases of admirable design, fountains, tazzas (in these three departments some two hundred different designs were produced), terminals, flower-boxes, flower-pots, tree-pots, garden edgings, figures, busts, chimney-pieces, balustrades, chimney-shafts and tops, window-heads, and plinths, capitals, memorial crosses and grave-stones. Filters, too, for reservoirs were made extensively and had the reputation of being among the most effective. Pavement tiles of various colours, and also with inlaid patterns, were made.

The trade mark of the company – the only mark used in this manufactory – was a winged genius grinding an arrow, from an antique gem at Rome.

GRESLEY – see *Church Gresley*

HIGH HALDEN (Kent)

High Halden A small pottery was working at Halden (near Tenterden, Kent) in the first half of the nineteenth century. G. Bemrose illustrates a marked money-box in his *Nineteenth Century English Pottery and Porcelain* (Faber & Faber, London, 1952).

HULL (Yorkshire)

The first distinct information I have been able to gather regarding pot-works at this place is that in 1802 (eighteen years earlier than the first date previously given by Chaffers), by a deed dated August 10th in that year, Thomas English of Hull, merchant, sold a plot of land on what is called the Humber Bank, in a part of what was then the outskirts of the town and known as Myton. The piece of land consisted of 3,718 square yards, and was conveyed to James Smith and Jeremiah Smith, both of Hull, potters; Job Ridgway, of Shelton, Staffordshire, potter; and Josiah Hipwood of Hull, blockmaker. The deed of partnership between these parties was dated 23rd November 1802. From the fact of two of the parties, James Smith and Jeremiah Smith, being described as 'of Hull, potters', while Job Ridgway was of 'Shelton, Staffordshire, potter', the probability is that the Smiths were already in business there as pot-makers and that Ridgway joined them for the purpose of increasing and improving their manufacture.

The partnership, however, was but of short duration; for in 1804, Mr. Ridgway, being desirous of retiring, agreed to sell to the remaining partners all his fourth part of the lands, works, stock-in-trade, debts, etc., for the sum of £1,000. Hipwood left the concern in the same year, when James Rose became a partner with the Smiths. In 1806, the proprietors assigned all their interest in the works to Messrs. Job and George Ridgway, who carried them on for some years. In 1826, they were succeeded by William Bell, who became the proprietor in that year by deed of conveyance from the brothers Ridgway.

By Mr. Bell, the manufactory, now called the Belle Vue Pottery, was very much extended and the operations were carried on on a large scale, chiefly for export – the principal part of the trade being with Hamburg, where his brother, Edward Bell, was in business. A large German and Dutch trade was done through his means. The works were closed in 1841, when the plant and stock were disposed of by auction.

At this sale, Charles Johnson of Hull acted as auctioneer for Mr. Stamp, and stated that the copper-plates – the stock of which weighed about three hundred-weight, and amongst which were some of the 'willow pattern' –'were sold to a pottery works at or near Rotherham', which are presumed to be either the Swinton or the Don works.

The ware produced was cream-coloured, green-glazed, ordinary white, and blue printed; and in them, the usual classes of useful goods, consisting of services of various kinds and miscellaneous articles, were made. One notable dinner-service was made to commemorate an exploit in connection with the noted pirate Paul Jones, and was, it would appear, made for the owner, or family of the owner, of the *Crow Isle*, a Baltic trading ship. In the centre is represented the *Crow Isle* successfully beating off Paul Jones on its homeward voyage, when off the Yorkshire coast, in 1779.

Another example of the Belle Vue Pottery is a butter-pot in form of a cow, with moveable lid, in yellow ware. Mr. Johnson had also in his possession a portion of a remarkably fine green-glazed dessert service of very artistic design, in embossed leaves, with basket-work centres to the plates, which was bought at the Hull works from Mr. Bell in 1838. It has the impressed mark of two bells surrounded by the words BELLE VUE POTTERY, HULL; but sometimes the bells appear without the lettering. It would seem that the bell mark and the Belle Vue title date only from 1826, when William Bell succeeded the Ridgways.

ILKESTON (Derbyshire)

The Ilkeston Potteries Established by George Evans in 1807, these works were carried on by him until his decease in 1832, when they passed to his son, Richard Evans. During the lifetime of George Evans, Derbyshire stone bottles alone were made. The buildings were then considerably increased, and a general pottery was added for the production of useful articles in stoneware and ornamental terra-cotta goods. The productions in stoneware were bottles, jars and pans of all sizes and of every usual form; water filters of an improved construction; carriage, foot, and other warmers; sanitary pipes, and ware of every kind; and in terra-cotta, vases, pedestals, flower and tree boxes and pots, garden-edgings, chimney-tops of various designs, and all the more usual productions of fire-clay goods.

KILNHURST (near Rawmarsh, Yorkshire)

At Kilnhurst, a place which one would naturally say took its name from pot-works, there was a manufactory of earthenware known as the Kilnhurst Old Pottery.

Established in about the middle of the eighteenth century, on the estate of the Shore family, it was held at the beginning of the nineteenth century by a potter named Hawley, who had also a pottery at Rawmarsh and who was succeeded by George Green (one of the family of the Greens at Leeds) from whom, in 1832, it was purchased by Brameld & Co. (subject to Mr. Shore, the owner, accepting them as tenants) at a valuation, Green retaining the manufactured goods, copper-plates, moulds, etc. In 1839, it came into the hands of Twigg Brothers and was carried on by the surviving partner, John Twigg, who produced the usual varieties of earthenware and made some unsuccessful trials in china. This pottery ceased in about 1884. Various marks incorporating the name Twigg were employed.

KIRKCALDY (Scotland)

Sinclairtown Pottery Messrs. George MacLachlan & Son were manufacturers of ordinary earthenware at this place. The works were continued by Kirk Bros., and then by L. Buist & Sons into the twentieth century.

Other manufactories were the Kirkcaldy Pottery, belonging to David Methven & Sons, who made a large quantity of 'Mocha' and other earthenware, and the Gallatown Pottery, belonging to Robert Heron & Sons. D. Methven & Sons continued to about 1930; Robert Heron & Sons continued to about 1929, but from 1884 onwards their address is listed as the Fife Pottery. Their freely painted 'Wemyss' ware

proved very popular (see J. A. Fleming's *Scottish Pottery*, Maclehose, Jackson & Co., Glasgow, 1923).

KNOTTINGLEY (Yorkshire)

The Ferrybridge Pottery This pottery was established in 1792 by William Tomlinson, who had for partners Mr. Seaton, a banker of Pontefract; Mr. Foster, a shipowner of Selby; Timothy Smith, a coal proprietor; and Mr. Thompson, an independent gentleman residing at Selby. The firm was styled William Tomlinson & Co. until 1796, when, the proprietors having taken into partnership Ralph Wedgwood of Burslem, it was changed to Tomlinson, Foster, Wedgwood & Co. Ralph Wedgwood was the eldest son of Thomas Wedgwood of Etruria (cousin and partner of Josiah Wedgwood), and was brought up at that place under his uncle and father. [In his *Life of Josiah Wedgwood* (Virtue & Co., London, 1865). Jewitt gave for the first time, as the result of considerable research, a notice of this remarkable man, Ralph Wedgwood, and of his inventions, and of his family and connections. Ed.] He had carried on business as a potter under the style of Wedgwood & Co. at the Hill Works, Burslem, and while there prepared and presented to Queen Charlotte some fine examples of his manufacture on the occasion of the restoration of health to the king. His partnership with Tomlinson & Co. of Ferrybridge was not of long duration. His partners being dissatisfied at the large amount of breakage caused by his experiments and peculiar mode of firing, the partnership was dissolved and he retired from the concern, having succeeded in getting a thousand pounds awarded to him as his share of the business.

After the dissolution, which took place in about 1800 or 1801, the style of Tomlinson & Co. was resumed and so continued until 1834, when it changed to Tomlinson, Plowes & Co. – Mr. Plowes, of the Castleford Works, having joined the proprietary. In 1804, the name of the manufactory, which up to that period had been called the Knottingley Pottery, was changed to that of the Ferrybridge Pottery.

Mr. Tomlinson was succeeded by his son, Edward Tomlinson, who continued the works under the style of Edward Tomlinson & Co. until 1826, when he retired from the concern. A part of the premises was then worked by Wigglesworth and Ingham, and afterwards the whole place was again taken by Reed, Taylor & Kelsall; and after the retirement of Kelsall, by James Reed and Benjamin Taylor.

Mr. Reed, father of John Reed of the Mexborough Pottery, was a man of great practical skill. In his time, many improvements in the ware were made and the manufacture of china was introduced. He, in conjunction with his partner, took the Mexborough Pottery and carried on the two establishments conjointly. Ultimately, Mr. Reed gave up the Ferrybridge works and confined himself to those at Mexborough, while Mr. Taylor carried on the Ferrybridge works alone.

The ware principally made was cream and cane-coloured; green glazed, in which dessert services and other articles were made, and which were of a lighter colour than what Wedgwood produced; Egyptian black, of the usual quality; and fine white earthenware, in which was produced all the usual kinds of goods in enamelled or blue printed decoration.

In the time of Reed and Taylor, china of a very fine quality was reputedly made, but the manufacture was not of long duration. Tea and coffee services, dessert services, scent bottles and a variety of articles were made of this body, and were remarkably good in form and in style of decoration.

Cameos, medallions and other ornamental articles, in the time of Ralph Wedgwood's connection with the works, were made in imitation of those of Josiah Wedgwood – to which they were, however, very inferior both in body and finish.

After Mr. Taylor gave up the works, Lewis Woolf entered upon them as tenant for a few years and in 1856 became the purchaser. In 1857, the Australian Pottery, closely adjoining – and, indeed, connected with the Ferrybridge Pottery – was built by the sons of Lewis Woolf. The proprietors of the joint works, The Ferrybridge

192

and Australian Potteries, were Lewis, Sidney and Henry Woolf, who traded under the style of Lewis Woolf & Sons until 1884. Subsequent owners were Poulson Bros. (1884–97); Sefton & Brown (1897–1919); and T. Brown & Sons (Ltd.), who continue to the present day.

The marks used at the Ferrybridge Pottery have been but few. So far as my knowledge goes, those which will be of interest to the collector are the following: TOMLINSON & CO., impressed upon the bottom of the ware; WEDGWOOD & CO, impressed on cameos, creamware, etc., made during the time of Ralph Wedgwood's connection with the work (c.1796–1800); FERRYBRIDGE, also impressed – one variety of which mark is peculiar through having the letter D reversed thus: FERRYBRIᗡGE. Another is a shield with the words OPAQUE GRANITE CHINA in three lines, supported by a lion and unicorn and surmounted by a crown. The mark from about 1880 was the lion and unicorn with the shield and crown, and the words 'Ferrybridge and Australian Potteries'. From 1884, the marks have incorporated the title or initials of the various owners.

LAMBETH (London)

The Lambeth Pottery In 1815, John Doulton established his stoneware works at Vauxhall. Soon afterwards, he was joined in partnership by John Watts, the business being carried on under the style of Doulton & Watts. Some eleven years after this, the works were removed to High Street, Lambeth. In 1858, Mr. Watts died and the manufactory was carried on by Mr. Doulton, in co-partnership with his sons, under the style of Henry Doulton & Co. In 1854, Henry Doulton took out a patent for 'improvements in kilns used in the manufacture of stoneware, earthenware, and china'. In 1859, he took out another patent for 'improvements in earthenware jars and bottles'; and in 1861, the same gentleman also patented his 'improvements in the construction of vats and similar vessels for containing liquids'. At the exhibitions of 1851 and 1862, medals were awarded to this firm, as

Plate 98. View of the Lambeth foreshore, showing the rear of the Doulton works (middle, left) and the large Stiff factory (extreme right) in the 1860s.
Photo: Messrs. Doulton.

they were also at other exhibitions. At the international exhibitions of 1871 and 1872 they also received the highest commendation, as at those of Vienna, Philadelphia and Paris.

The goods manufactured by Messrs. Doulton & Co. included chemical vessels of large size (up to 500 gallons) and all kinds of stoneware suitable for the laboratory and works of the manufacturing chemist, and articles of domestic use; terra-cotta for architectural and gardening purposes; sanitary ware of all kinds; plumbago and other crucibles, muffles, furnaces, etc. In addition to Lambeth, the firm had fire-clay and tile works at Rowley-Regis, Smethwick and St. Helen's. The production of their stoneware and terra-cotta goods gave employment to about six hundred men and the consumption of coals was over ten thousand tons per annum in the 1870s.

In stoneware, Messrs. Doulton produced every possible variety of household vessel.

Decorative ware may be said to date from about 1870 onwards. Many of the salt-glazed stoneware productions were of extremely artistic character and evince a purity of taste. Some of the jugs and tankards from antique examples, in brown, blue, claret and fine white stoneware, are remarkably elegant. The forms are admirable, and the decorations, whether in repoussé or incised or other style, are well considered and especially adapted to the material, the mode of production, and the use of the object.

In terra-cotta, Messrs. Doulton's work ranked high for the beauty of their productions, the variety of designs they introduced and the durability and excellence of their material. In vases for gardens, pedestals, fountains, garden-seats, flower boxes, and pendants, brackets, etc., they produced a large number of exquisite patterns. In statuary and architectural decoration, the productions consisted of figures, busts and medallions, keystones, arches, trusses and string-courses; capitals, bases and finials; rain-water heads of marvellously bold and effective design. Some of the highest achievements in art,

193

Fig. 44. A selection of Doulton ware.

as applied to original conceptions modelled in the most masterly manner in terra-cotta – the creations of George Tinworth – were also produced in this way. Painting on pottery was also introduced into this manufactory with very good results. Many of the artists were young female students from the Government Schools of Art.

One especially noteworthy class of objects consists of loving cups, jugs, flower vases, candlesticks, pitchers and other vessels on which the ornament is principally executed in sgraffito or incised outline. This was sometimes effected as soon as the vessel left the wheel, but more generally after it had been allowed to dry to a consistency which would permit of its being worked upon. To the designs thus incised in outline, especially to the leafage, colour was

applied with an ordinary water-colour brush and burnt in (Plate 99). This ware was called 'Doulton ware' or 'sgraffito ware'. No two pieces were formed alike. The principal exponent of this spontaneous form of decoration was Hannah B. Barlow (worked 1872–1906). Her designs are of animal life, and are signed on the base with her monogram (see page 196). Her sister Florence did similar work but mainly depicted bird life. Mary Mitchell incised figure motifs.

These decorative pieces were made of Doulton's traditional highly fired stoneware – a body which made the firm famous earlier in the nineteenth century when it specialised in the manufacture of utilitarian objects such as pipes.

194

George Tinworth, mentioned in connection with the terra-cotta body, modelled some charming and amusing animal groups from about 1880 onwards (Plate 100). Tinworth, who was employed at Doulton's from about 1866 to his death in 1913, was mainly known during his lifetime for a long series of religious plaques modelled in high relief. These were commissioned for churches and private chapels. All Tinworth's work bears his incised conjoined initials; TG.

Another Doulton speciality was 'Impasto' ware, in which the colour was applied to the raw clay and was, moreover, so thickened by the vehicle by which it was incorporated that it modelled the form as well as painted it. The

Plate 99. A pair of Doulton sgraffito vases, with animal subjects incised by Hannah B. Barlow, c.1900. 13½ inches high.   *Editor's collection.*

Plate 100. Three examples of George Tinworth sculpture in Doulton's stoneware, showing two typical animal groups, c.1890.   *Editor's collection.*

slight amount of relief obtained by the artist gave a surpassing richness to the work and imparted a reality to the design that is eminently pleasing.

One of the later Doulton achievements, after about 1881, was the silicon ware – a body of such extreme hardness that, like Wedgwood's agate and basalt ware, it was sometimes polished by the lapidary after leaving the kiln. In this ware, vases of good design and finish were delicately perforated and the floral, arabesque or other designs with which they are profusely covered literally carved in the most elaborate manner and then worked up by the pâte-sur-pâte process with the richest, softest and most harmonious effects. In the same silicon body were also produced graceful designs of foliage, hand-modelled in alto-relievo and enamelled on the unglazed body of the ware.

Doulton ware won wide praise during the second half of the nineteenth century, and the production was large and varied. All pieces are fully marked and bear the initials of the decorator.

A branch factory was established at Burslem, in the Staffordshire potteries, in 1882 (see page 12). Production ceased at Lambeth in 1956, but has continued at Burslem to the present day.

The standard Lambeth marks are:

DOULTON & WATTS   Doulton & Watts marks, in
LAMBETH POTTERY   various forms, c.1826–54.

DOULTON
LAMBETH   Doulton mark, c.1854–69.

Oval impressed mark, c.1869–77. The year of production could occur in the centre of this mark after 1873.

Circular impressed mark, c.1877–80.

Impressed mark, c.1880–1902. Year of production might appear on examples up to 1888. 'England' added below from 1891.

Incised monograms of Doulton artists:

Hannah B.
Barlow
c.1872–1906

Florence
Barlow
c.1873–1909

George
Tinworth
c.1867–1913

Arthur B.
Barlow
c.1872–9

The reader is referred to Blacker's *The ABC of English Salt-Glaze Stone-Ware* (Stanley Paul, London, 1922), H. Wakefield's *Victorian Pottery* (Herbert Jenkins, London, 1962) and D. Eyles's *Royal Doulton 1815–1965* (Hutchinson, London, 1965).

The London Pottery In 1840, this manufactory in High Street, Lambeth, came into the hands of James Stiff, subsequently the head of the firm of James Stiff & Sons. At that time, the works consisted only of two small kilns and covered an area of probably less than a quarter of an acre of ground. By about 1880, however, it comprised fourteen kilns (some of them more than twenty feet in diameter) and covered two acres. It had a very extensive frontage on the Albert Embankment, overlooking the River Thames. By means of a private dock, with entrance under the Embankment, it was enabled directly to carry on a very extensive export trade and also to import the coals, clay and other raw material used in the production of brown and white stoneware and terra-cotta. Until 1860, when fresh buildings were erected, a delft-ware signboard existed in the front of this pottery.

The five principal kinds of pottery manufactured by Messrs. Stiff & Sons were:

Colour Plate IX Doulton stoneware vase decorated
in the art nouveau style by Eliza Simmance and
signed with her 'E S' monogram mark, c.1910. $17\frac{3}{4}$
inches high.   *Editor's collection.*

1. Brown salt-glazed stoneware, in which tubular socket drain-pipes were produced; telegraph insulators, battery jars (with which they supplied the Post Office, Government of India, Colonial telegraphs, railways, etc); water filters, jugs, bottles, jars and all kinds of chemical apparatus.

2. White stoneware, or 'double glazed' ware or 'Bristol ware', in which salt was not used, but the glazing was obtained by the application of a liquid glaze to the interior and exterior of each article before it was placed in the kiln. This ware – which was generally made in a rich yellow ochre on the upper parts, with the lower part of a creamy-white colour – was only introduced into Lambeth about a quarter of a century before but had, to a considerable extent, superseded the old brown stoneware by about 1875.

3. Buff and red terra-cotta, in which were made garden vases, pedestals, chimney-tops, window arches, string courses, groups of figures, coats of arms, enormous statuary ten or twelve feet in length, lions and every description of architectural decoration for buildings. This terra-cotta, being thoroughly vitrified, was invaluable for all purposes where durability was of importance. Another great advantage was that, in it, the choicest and most elaborate patterns, either raised or counter-sunk, could be obtained at little more than the cost of perfectly plain stone.

4. Porous ware, in which porous cells, plates, etc., of every shape and different degrees of porosity were extensively made.

5. Plumbago and fire-clay crucibles for every conceivable purpose, and of the very highest quality.

The quality of the stoneware or 'Bristol ware' was remarkably good, being extremely hard and covered with an excellent clear and firm glaze. The artistic execution of terra-cotta goods was of a high order of excellence.

Messrs. Stiff & Sons produced a large number of water filters of excellent construction and artistic design. Some of these had Gothic arches, with figures or armorial decoration, and others were decorated with elegant foliage. The 'Popular' filter, intended for use among all classes, purified eight gallons of water per day, was sold complete and was fitted for a mere trifle.

The potteries of Messrs. Stiff & Sons were among the largest in London. They employed about two hundred hands; their annual import of raw material, clay and coals was about fifteen thousand tons; and they had business relations in almost all parts of the world. It is well to add that at this pottery vases, tankards and water-jugs of excellent design and clever manipulation were made.

Messrs. Stiff & Sons' works were taken over by Doulton's in 1913. Self-explanatory impressed marks were used on some decorative ware.

An old photograph showing the Stiff factory in about 1866 is reproduced in Plate 101.

Fore Street A manufactory of various kinds of pottery existed here in Lambeth at the beginning of the nineteenth century and was carried on by Richard Waters who, in June 1811, took out a patent for 'a new method of manufacturing pottery ware'. First, 'in the fabrication of various articles of considerable magnitude', 'instead of throwing or moulding them on a revolving table, the clay is made into sheets and then applied upon moulds and finished by beating or pressure, or by turning while in a revolving state'; second, forming 'delf-ware pots and other articles by compression of the clay between suitable moulds', third, 'making or clouding the Welsh ware by using a number of pipes instead of one in distributing the colour'; fourth, 'making earthenware jambs, tiles for facing houses, and for paving hearths, balustrades, balconies, and bricks vein-coloured, variegated either by the last process or by putting together masses differing from each other', and in the admixture of stony or metallic or other mineral substances, so as to differ in their colours and appearance when baked; fifth, by this process making 'figures, statues, ornaments, armorial bearings, and the like'; sixth, by this process making 'stone mortars and pestles, cisterns, coffins, worms for

197

distillers' use, tiles, with a hook on the back instead of a knob, also with a higher edge and deeper return than usual'.

Imperial Pottery Another pottery at Lambeth was that of Stephen Green (from c.1830) which in 1858 passed, by purchase, into the hands of John Cliff, by whom it was considerably enlarged. Mr. Cliff here brought into use, in about 1862, his own 'patent kiln for what is known as double glaze or Bristol glaze kiln, and a circular bag for the salt glaze and pipe kiln, since adopted generally'. Here, also, under his own eye, Siemens' gas furnace was tried on pottery. Here, also, Mr. Cliff brought out and into work his patent wheel and patent lathe (c.1863) – two most important improvements in the potter's art, and said to be the most perfect and convenient machines existing at that time. The works were closed in 1869 through the site being required by the Metropolitan Board of Works for improvements, and Mr. Cliff removed to Runcorn in Cheshire.

The works were originally established for the manufacture of common red ware; but after a time, Mr. Green added a little salt-glazed ware; and then, as the double–glazed 'Bristol ware' gained favour, added it and made it his principal business, giving up the red ware entirely. Later still, he manufactured drain-pipes and a good deal of chemical stoneware; and, besides all the usual articles, water filters were extensively made here.

A stoneware bottle, in the form of Queen Victoria, is in the Victoria and Albert Museum and is inscribed 'S. Green Lambeth – 20th July 1837'. The old works were many times much injured by fire – being nearly destroyed just before passing into Mr. Cliff's hands in 1858.

Union Pottery William Northern established his Union Pottery for the production of Lambeth-type stoneware in 1848. He continued to about 1892. Some pieces with impressed marks are recorded, including some interesting shaped bottles – fish, etc. William Northern took out several patents relevant to his pottery.

Canal Potteries Messrs. Thomas Smtih & Co. worked this pottery in Old Kent Road from about 1879 to 1893. Their ware was similar to the stoneware of Doulton and Stiff. Impressed or incised marks are self-explanatory, being 'Smith & Co. Old Kent Road London' in various forms. This firm was succeeded by Hosea Tugby & Co., who ceased in about 1904.

Blackfrairs Road The terra-cotta works of Blanchard & Co., formerly carried on here, were established in 1839 by H. M. Blanchard, who served his apprenticeship with Coades & Sealy at Lambeth. The productions consisted of vases, tazzas, statues, busts, groups of figures, brackets, pedestals, terminals, crosses, fountains, balustrades, trusses, and every specimen of architectural enrichment. In 1851, and again in 1862, the firm was awarded medals for terra-cotta goods, considered to be among the best produced (Fig. 45). Among the most successful of the works executed may be named the terra-cotta for the Brighton Aquarium, the Victoria and Albert Museum, and the columns of the arcades in the Royal Horticultural Gardens.

After continuing in Blackfriars Road for upwards of forty years, Messrs. Blanchard, in 1880, removed their works to Bishop's Waltham, in Hampshire, where they covered an extent of some twenty acres of ground and possessed some of the finest beds of clay in the kingdom. The productions were terra-cotta, as before, and roofing and blue-ware paving tiles, and other goods.

LANGLEY MILL (Derbyshire)

Langley Mill Pottery This pottery was established in 1865 by James Calvert, and was the first in the neighbourhood. The productions were vitrified stoneware of similar character and quality to that of Messrs. Bourne at Denby (see page 172). In this ware, a large trade was done in ginger-beer, ink, beer and other bottles, and all the usual domestic vessels – jars, pitchers,

Plate 101. Photographic view of the Stiff stoneware factory in about 1866. *Photo: Messrs. Doulton.*

Fig. 45. Messrs. Blanchard's terra-cotta vases.

hot-water bottles, foot-warmers, jugs and mugs – produced from clay found in the neighbourhood. In the 1880s, the firm was Calvert & Lovatt, subsequently Lovatt & Lovatt. It was Lovatt's Potteries Ltd. from 1931 until 1967, when the new title Langley Pottery Ltd. was adopted. Their trade mark is 'Langley Ware'.

LARNE (Co. Antrim, Ireland)

Larne Pottery Pottery works were built close to the small seaport of Larne, county of Antrim, by James Agnew, proprietor of the estate, and were worked under the management of his agent, Mr. Walker, from about 1850 to 1855. Afterwards, for two or three years, they were worked by the Greenock Pottery Company, since which time the works have been closed.

The goods produced were white and printed earthenware, cane ware, Rockingham teapots, brown pans, and crocks and dairy and kitchen utensils of various kinds. Some of the latter-named were made from clays and were very good of their kind.

The firm's rubbish-heaps were on the borders of Larne Lough, and the beach was strewn with fragments of pottery.

LEEDS (Yorkshire)

Leeds Pottery For the eighteenth-century history of Leeds Pottery, the reader is referred to D. Towner's *English Cream-coloured Earthenware* (Faber & Faber, London, 1957), and especially to Mr. Towner's *The Leeds Pottery* (Cory, Adams & Mackay, London, 1963).

At the commencement of the nineteenth century, Messrs. Hartley, Greens & Co. (or, slightly later, Messrs. Greens, Hartley & Co.) were operating the Leeds Pottery. A large export trade was carried on with the typical Leeds creamware. Shortly after the death of William Hartley, in 1820, the firm became bankrupt. In 1825, the works were acquired by Samuel Wainwright, who carried it on in the name of Samuel Wainwright and Company, engaging as confidential cashier Stephen Chappell. At Wainwright's death, in 1832, the trustees carried on the business with Stephen Chappell under the style of the Leeds Pottery

200

Company until 1840, when the trustees transferred the whole concern to Chappell, who took it at his own valuation. Shortly after, his brother James became a partner in the concern, the firm consisting of Stephen & James Chappell until 1847, when they became bankrupt.

The pottery was then carried on for about three years, for the benefit of the creditors, by the assignees under the management of Richard Britton, who had for some time held a confidential position with Mr. Chappell. In 1850, the concern passed, by purchase, into the hands of Samuel Warburton and Mr. Britton and was by them carried on under the style of Warburton & Britton until 1863, when, on the death of Mr. Warburton, Richard Britton became sole proprietor. On 1st July 1872, he was joined in partnership by his two eldest sons, John Broadbent Britton and Alfred Britton, the firm consequently becoming Richard Britton & Sons.

The ware manufactured at different periods at these interesting works consisted of the coarse brown earthenware made on its first establishment; delft-ware, produced only in small quantities and for a short period; hard and highly vitrified stoneware, with a strong salt glaze; cream-coloured, or 'Queen's' ware; Egyptian black ware; Rockingham ware; white earthenware and yellow ware. The great speciality of the works was the perforated 'Queen's' or cream-coloured earthenware, for which they became universally famed and successfully competed with Wedgwood. It is this kind of ware which, among collectors, has acquired the name of 'Leeds Ware'. In colour, the old Leeds ware – i.e., the cream-coloured earthenware – is of a particularly clear rich tint, usually rather deeper in tone than Wedgwood's Queen's ware, and of a slightly yellowish cast. The body is particularly fine and hard, and the glaze is of extremely good quality.

In the early part of the nineteenth century, white earthenware or pearlware was made at these works. It was a fine, hard, compact body, and had, like the cream-coloured, a remarkably good glaze. In this ware, services – especially dinner and tea – were produced, and were decorated with transfer printing, painting, lustre, and tinsel. 'Tinselling', it must be understood, is the peculiar process by which a part of the pattern is made to assume a metallic appearance by being washed here and there over the transfer or drawing.

Lustre, both gold and silver, was used occasionally in the decoration at Leeds, and excellent examples of lustre ware were also produced. In about 1800, black basalt ware was introduced at Leeds. This was of the same character as the Egyptian black, then so largely made in Staffordshire by Wedgwood, Mayer, Neale, and others. The body was extremely compact, firm and hard, but had a more decided bluish cast than was usual in other makes. In this ware, tea and coffee-pots, cream ewers and other articles were made. I have been able to ascertain that, up to 1812–13, probably from ninety to a hundred distinct patterns and sizes of teapots alone were produced in black basalt at these works. The patterns of the teapots were very varied in form, style of ornamentation, and size. In form, there were round, octagonal and other shapes, including some of twelve sides. In ornamentation, some were engine-turned in a variety of patterns, and others were chequered or fluted. Others, again, were formed in moulds elaborately ornamented in relief with flowers, fruits, borders or festoons; and yet others had groups of figures, trophies, and medallions in relief on their sides. The knobs of the lids were seated figures, lions, swans, flowers and such like. The lids were made of every variety – inward and outward fitting, sliding and attached with hinges. In speaking of engine-turning, it may be well to note that 'engined' mugs and jugs were made at these works as early as 1782, if not at an earlier date. For Leeds ware of the early nineteenth century, the reader is referred to an article by D. C. Towner in the *Apollo Magazine*, May 1957.

The Leeds Pottery in the 1870s produced the ordinary descriptions of earthenware for domestic use, consisting of dinner, tea and coffee, toilet and other services, jugs and mugs, bowls and basins, and all the other usual articles mainly for the London market – which took nearly one half of the whole production of the works.

White earthenware, the same as the ordinary Staffordshire ware, was produced in the usual styles, and pearl white was also manufactured in toilet ware and tea and breakfast services. Rockingham ware, tea and coffee pots and other articles were also made, as were Egyptian black glazed ware and yellow earthenware.

The marks used before the 1860s and 1870s were an English letter ⚜ within a Gothic quatrefoil in a circle, impressed in the body of the ware; or the name of the pattern within an ornamental circle and, below it, the initials of the firm – R.B. & S. – printed on the surface. These initials relate to the period 1872–5.

From about 1878, the works were carried on by Messrs. Taylor Bros., but they ceased after a few years and the works closed.

REPRODUCTIONS OF OLD LEEDS WARE

From 1880 to about 1916 a local firm produced close copies of old Leeds pierced creamware, and these pieces bear the old mark 'Leeds Pottery' impressed into the clay. Such pieces normally have a very crazed glaze. See Godden's *Illustrated Encyclopaedia of British Pottery and Porcelain* (Herbert Jenkins, London, 1966), Plates 346 to 348.

Other potters working at Leeds have also produced copies of antique creamware in the Leeds tradition.

Leathley Lane Pottery This was established in the early part of the nineteenth century by, I believe, a Mr. North, for the manufacture of black ware, but was afterwards used for ordinary white earthenware. From Mr. North, the works passed into the hands of a Mr. Hepworth, who made the ordinary brown salt-glazed ware. It was next worked by Mr. Dawson, one of the trustees of the Leeds pottery, who took into partnership Mr. Chappell. It was carried on by Dawson and Chappell, and afterwards by Chappell alone. Then, till 1851, it was worked by Shackleton, Taylor & Co., and next by Taylor & Gibson and Gibson & Co. The premises were small, and produced white ware of the commonest kind, yellow ware made from

the Wortley clays, and Rockingham ware.

In the early 1880s, the owners were Taylor Bros., who ceased in about 1890.

Burmantofts These works, established by Messrs. Wilcox & Co., at Leeds, sprang rapidly into repute and produced many works of a high order of merit. In terra-cotta, the productions embraced architectural details and enrichments of every kind – including panels, tiles and dados – in immense variety and of the most masterly and finished styles in design and decoration. In pottery, which Messrs. Wilcox & Co. named 'Yorkshire Art-Pottery', a large number of articles more or less decorative were produced. Vases of every conceivable variety and of a large range of sizes (Plate 102), flowerstands and holders, pot-pourris, rose-leaf bowls, dessert services, comports, cake-stands, waterbottles and other articles were produced; and the coloured glazes are, in many instances, clear

Plate 102. Two Burmantofts colour-glazed vases, c.1890. Large vase, 19 inches high.
Editor's collection.

and effective, and the flown varieties extremely pleasing. The introduction on some pieces of sgraffito and of stipple decoration under the rich glaze was attended with satisfactory results: also the adoption of hand-modelled flowers, foliage, and examples of animal life. The faience tiles, panels and other productions of the firm were of a high standard of excellence.

The company was established in about 1880. The manufacture of pottery was discontinued in 1904 and subsequently only terra-cotta ware was produced. Apart from the name in full, a monogram of the initials B.F. was used as a mark.

For further information, see Grabham's *Yorkshire Potteries, Pots and Potters* (Yorkshire Museum, 1916).

The *Pottery Gazette Diary* for 1885 lists the following Leeds potters, not previously mentioned: Robinson & Sons, Jack Lane Pottery; Sykes & Dickinson (Black Ware); Joseph Taylor, Petty Pottery; J. Wainwright (Black Ware), Pontefract Lane Pottery.

The 1900 list includes: T. Kay & Son, Holbeck Moor Pottery; Leeds Art Pottery & Tile Co., Leathley Road; W. Lupton, Hunslet Hall Pottery; and Sykes & Dickinson, Lane End Pottery.

LIVERPOOL (Lancashire)

The Herculaneum Pottery This pottery, the largest ever established in Liverpool, was founded in 1796 on the site of some old copper-works on the south shore of the River Mersey at Toxteth Park. The pottery had originally been established in about 1793–4 by Richard Abbey, who took into partnership a Scotsman named Graham. Abbey, who was born at Aintree and was apprenticed to John Sadler as an engraver, produced many very effective designs for mugs, jugs, tiles, etc. Of these, one of his best productions was the well-known group of the 'Farmer's Arms'. After leaving Sadler's employment, Abbey removed to Glasgow, where he was an engraver at the pot-works, and afterwards served in a similar capacity in France

before he began business in Liverpool. Messrs. Abbey & Graham, who had been successful in their factory at Toxteth Park, sold it to Worthington, Humble & Holland, and Abbey retired to his native village, where he died in 1801.

On taking to these works, Messrs. Worthington, Humble & Holland engaged as foreman and manager Ralph Mansfield of Burslem. Besides Mansfield, the new company engaged about forty hands – men, women and children – in Staffordshire and brought them to Liverpool. As Wedgwood had chosen to call his new colony Etruria, the enterprising company determined on christening their colony Herculaneum, which name they adopted and stamped on their ware. The buildings acquired from Richard Abbey were considerably enlarged, the arrangements remodelled, new ovens and workshops erected, houses for the workmen built. The little colony was peopled in the middle of November 1796; the works were opened on the 8th December.

The first productions of the Herculaneum works were confined to blue-printed ware, in which dinner, toilet, tea, and coffee services, punch-bowls, mugs and jugs were the principal articles made; and cream-coloured ware, which was then so fashionable. At a later date, terra-cotta vases and other articles were produced. Of their cream-coloured or Queen's ware, the examples which have come under my notice are of remarkably fine quality and are as well and carefully potted as those of any other manufactory.

The Herculaneum works also produced some remarkably good jugs of a fine hard body, with bas-relief figures and foliage. These pieces, which rival Turner's celebrated jugs, are sometimes marked with the name HERCULANEUM in small capitals, impressed. A special jug of this type is shown in Plate 103.

In 1800 and again in 1806, the manufactory was considerably increased, as was the number of proprietors. Early in the nineteenth century, porcelain was made and continued to be produced to the time of the close of the works. In 1833, the company was dissolved and the property sold for £25,000 to Ambrose Lace, who

Plate 103. A marked 'Herculaneum' Liverpool stoneware jug with enamelled inscription, c.1800. 20 inches high. *Godden of Worthing Ltd.*

leased the premises to Thomas Case and James Mort, who are said to have carried on the business for about three years only. By these gentlemen, it is said, the mark of the 'Liver' was introduced. In about 1836, the firm of Case, Mort & Co. was succeeded by that of Mort & Simpson, who continued the manufactory until its close in 1841.

During the time the works were carried on by Case, Mort & Co., a fine dinner service was made for the Corporation of Liverpool. It was blue-printed, and had on each piece the arms of Liverpool carefully engraved and emblazoned. Another service of somewhat similar description was made; this had the earlier mark of HERCULANEUM impressed. The marks used at the Herculaneum works at different periods appear to have been the word HERCULANEUM (the same name also occasionally occurs in

blue printing); a crown, with the word Herculaneum in a curve above it, impressed; a crown within a garter bearing the word Herculaneum, impressed or printed;

the crest of the borough of Liverpool, a bird called the Liver, or Lever, with wings expanded and bearing in its beak a sprig of the plant liverwort. Of this mark of the crest, three varieties are shown:

they are all impressed in the ware. Another and more imposing-looking mark has the name of the pattern (PEKIN PALM, for instance) within a wreath of foliage, surmounted with the crest of Liverpool on a heraldic wreath.

Much recent research on this important but hitherto neglected factory has been carried out by Mr. Alan Smith and is incorporated in his *Illustrated Guide to Liverpool Herculaneum Pottery* (Barrie & Jenkins, London, 1970), a work which includes very many illustrations of documentary examples of Herculaneum ware.

LLANELLY (Carmarthen)

South Wales Pottery These works, which were, in about 1883, the only blue and white earthenware manufactory in the principality, were established in 1839 by William Chambers, junior, of Llanelly House, who carried them on up to the end of 1854. The general classes of goods manufactured were white or creamcoloured, edged, painted, and printed ware. Other descriptions of goods – viz., coloured bodies, figured, enamelled – and Parian were tried and worked for a time, but were soon discontinued. It was also intended to commence the making of china, and a kiln was built specially for that purpose; but the idea was then abandoned, and porcelain was never made at these works.

In about 1850, white granite and underglaze printed ware was made for the United States. At the end of 1854, the business of the South Wales Pottery was transferred to Coombs & Holland, who carried them on till 1858, when the partnership was dissolved. Mr. Holland continued the business alone till 1869, when he was joined in partnership by Mr. D. Guest, under the style of Holland & Guest. In 1877, the firm changed to Guest & Dewsbury.

The goods produced consisted of table, tea, and toilet services and other ordinary articles in printed earthenware of average quality, and the usual classes of white, cream-coloured, sponged, and painted ware. The copper-plates formerly in use at the other earthenware potteries in South Wales – viz., the Landore, the Ynisymudw, and the Cambrian Pottery, Swansea – were purchased for the South Wales Pottery and were introduced in their patterns and shapes. Messrs. Guest & Dewsbury continued to 1927. A. Smith's *Liverpool Herculaneum Pottery* (Jenkins, London, 1970) gives fuller information.

LOWESBY (Leicestershire)

In 1835, Sir F. G. Fowke, Bart., commenced some terra-cotta works at Lowesby, in Leicestershire, and produced vases of good character and of remarkably hard and fine body from the clays of the neighbourhood. He had previously, in about 1833, made some garden-pots for his own use; and finding the clay good and tenacious, he determined upon utilising it. In colour, the terra-cotta was a full rich red, and in some cases the articles were decorated with Etruscan figures and ornaments in black enamel. Vases, ornamented flower-pots, butterpots and other articles of domestic use were produced, and these were mostly decorated with patterns in black or occasionally in colours and gilt.

A shop for the sale of the Lowesby ware was opened in King William Street, London, under the management of a Mr. Purden. The ornamental vases, made of different sizes, were sent up to London as they came from the kiln, and many of the antique shapes were there painted and enamelled under Mr. Purden's superintendence. The manufacture was only continued for a few years, and then, not being found to answer, died out. The place was later used as a brick and tile works.

The mark is a fleur-de-lis beneath the name LOWESBY in a curved line. Occasionally, the name LOWESBY occurs without the fleur-de-lis.

The arms of Sir Frederick G. Fowke, Bart., the founder of the works are: vert, a fleur-de-lis, argent; so the mark represented the armorial bearing of the family and the name of the estate.

LOWESTOFT

Lowestoft porcelain, being of the approximate period 1757–99, is not featured in this volume, which is concerned with post-eighteenth century ware.

[The reader is warned that the account given in the 1878 and 1883 editions of Jewitt's *Ceramic Art of Great Britain* is in several respects incorrect and that some of the engravings are of Chinese (not Lowestoft) porcelain. For a good selection of true Lowestoft porcelain and an up-to-date account of the factory's history, the reader is referred to Godden's *Illustrated Guide to Lowestoft Porcelain* (Herbert Jenkins, London, 1969). Ed.]

MADELEY (Shropshire)

A small manufactory of china was established and carried on for about a quarter of a century at Madeley by Martin Randall, who served his apprenticeship at the Coalport works – his elder brothers, Edward and William Randall, having been reputedly apprenticed at Caughley. From Coalport, Martin Randall went to the Derby China Works, where he remained for some time and became the friend of two of their painters, Phillip Clavey and William Pegg. From Derby, he removed to London and entered into business with a Mr. Robins, at Islington. Upon dissolution of the partnership, he went down to Madeley in about 1825 and established himself in Park Place, where for a few years he confined himself to redecorating Sèvres china, which was procured by agents, chiefly in Paris. White china was obtained where feasible; but when that could not be had, dessert, tea and breakfast services, vases, wine coolers, jardinières and other articles, ornamented simply with blue and gold lines, dots or sprigs of flowers, were purchased – the latter of which were removed by fluoric acid, the glaze being so blended with the body that it gave back a new surface on being passed through the enamelling kiln, which he put up at a larger house to which he removed at the bottom of Madeley.

His want of experience in the processes of making led to frequent errors and losses, the latter being the greater from his constant desire to produce a body which would equal Nantgarw and Sèvres. He at length succeeded, however, in producing the nearest approach to the old Sèvres of any at that time made in this kingdom. It had all the mellow transparency and richness, and the same capability of receiving the colours into the glaze, of that famous ware – and had this to such an extent that experienced connoisseurs found it impossible to distinguish between them excepting by the mark, which no bribe would induce them to imitate.

From Madeley, Mr. Randall removed his business to Shelton in the Staffordshire Potteries in about 1840; and here it was that Herbert Minton was so struck with the beauty of his productions that he made overtures to him to join his firm – which, however, he did not do. He soon afterwards retired from business and went to live at Barlaston, where he died in 1859.

A porcelain lion is recorded with the mark

TMR
MADELEY; apart from this specimen, shown
S
in Plate 368 in Godden's *Illustrated Encyclopaedia of British Pottery and Porcelain* (Herbert Jenkins, London, 1966), no marked Madeley porcelain is recorded.

Details of the artists reputedly employed to decorate porcelain in the Sèvres-style at Madeley are given in the *Connoisseur Magazine* of December 1908.

MANSFIELD (Nottingham)

William Billingsley This Derby painter established a small decorating establishment at Mansfield in about 1799. This was a short-lived venture as Billingsley left in June 1802. Signed examples are very rare: 'William Billingsley – Mansfield'. A marked teapot is in the Victoria and Albert Museum. This and other examples are shown in Plates 50–2 in Godden's *Illustrated Encyclopaedia of British Pottery and Porcelain* (Herbert Jenkins, London, 1966).

MEXBOROUGH (Yorkshire)

The Rock Pottery or Mexbro' Pottery Situated at Mexborough, a town near Swinton, the works – at first very small – were, I believe, established for the manufacture of brown and yellow ware, and for common red garden-pots, by a person named Beevers, who, with a partner named Ford – trading as Beevers & Ford – carried on the business for some years. The workrooms, at this time, were built close up to the rock, which, indeed, formed the back wall of the manufactory; and from this circumstance the place was called the Rock Pottery.

The goods at this time and subsequently, during the proprietorship of Ford, Simpson & Beevers, were made entirely from native clays and were confined to cane or yellow ware dishes and jugs for household use, garden and root pots of red ware, and pitchers of a brown ware. The works next passed into the hands of Reed & Taylor – who also owned the works at Ferrybridge – by whom they were enlarged, and the manufacture of finer kinds of earthenware was introduced.

In 1839, the pottery passed into the hands of James Reed, who, in 1849, was succeeded by his son, John Reed, who continued it until his decease in 1870. It was then carried on by his executors under the management of Mr. C. Bullock. During the time of Reed's proprietorship, and that of his father, considerable alterations and additions were made to the works, and new kilns were erected. The character of the productions was also much improved, and several new varieties of ware were introduced.

In 1873, Messrs. Sydney Woolf & Co., the owners of the Australian Pottery at Ferrybridge, became the purchasers of this manufactory and carried it on conjointly with their other works at Ferrybridge under the management of Bowman Heald. By Messrs. Woolf & Co., the works were considerably extended and several new varieties of shapes and patterns were introduced.

The goods were, in ordinary white earthenware, all the most marketable varieties of painted, printed, enamelled, and gilt dinner, toilet and other services. Rockingham ware was also produced. In terra-cotta, Mr. Reed manufactured large-sized flower-vases for gardens and other decorative purposes; pendant flower-vases for conservatories and entrance halls, root-pots of tasteful design, butter-coolers, and similar objects. In green-glazed earthenware, dessert services were made in which the plates, centres and comports were embossed with leaves, flowers and other patterns, many of them from the original moulds of the Swinton works, which passed by purchase to the Mexborough pottery; and others of equally elegant design from moulds expressly belonging to Mexborough. In this ware, garden seats, both plain and foliated, of the same designs as those produced in the old days of the Rockingham works, and also root-pots and flower-vases were made. The mark used by Mr. Reed was simply 'Reed' impressed in the ware. The works closed in about 1883.

Mexborough Old Pottery At Mexborough was formerly another pot-work, known as the Mexborough Old Pottery. This was established at the end of the eighteenth century by Messrs. Sowter & Bromley, who held the works until 1804, when they came into the possession of Peter Barker. Peter Barker was the son of Joseph Barker, who came out of Staffordshire as manager of the Swinton Pottery. He became partner with Mr. Wainwright at the pot-works at Rawmarsh (afterwards Hawley's) and ultimately took to the works at Mexborough. These were continued by the brothers Peter and Jesse Barker (who were succeeded by Samuel Barker, the son of the latter) until 1834, when they acquired the Don Pottery. By Samuel Barker, they were continued until 1844. The Mexborough Old Pottery was then discontinued and converted into iron-works.

At these works, the commoner descriptions of earthenware, including blue printing, were produced.

MIDDLESBROUGH (Yorkshire)

The Middlesbrough Pottery Established in 1834, this was the first public works established in that place. From 1824 to 1844, the firm traded as The Middlesbrough Pottery Company; from that time until 1852 as The Middlesbrough Earthenware Company, and from then to about 1887 as Isaac Wilson & Co. The works, with the wharf, occupied an area of about 9,702 square yards.

The goods produced were the ordinary opaque china, cream-coloured ware, and lustre enamelled ware in dinner, tea and toilet services and all the general classes of domestic vessels, enamelled flower-pots and bread-trays. Some of these were of very good quality, and the printed services are equal to the more ordinary Staffordshire goods.

The printed marks indicating the pattern have, in addition to the name of the pattern, the initials of the firm as M.P.Co. for Middlesbrough Pottery Company; and I.W. & Co. for Isaac Wilson & Co. O. Grabham illustrates some specimens in his *Yorkshire Potteries, Pots and Potters* (Yorkshire Museum, 1916).

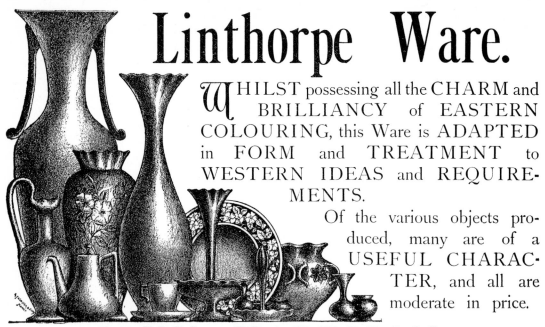

Linthorpe Ware.

WHILST possessing all the CHARM and BRILLIANCY of EASTERN COLOURING, this Ware is ADAPTED in FORM and TREATMENT to WESTERN IDEAS and REQUIREMENTS.

Of the various objects produced, many are of a USEFUL CHARACTER, and all are moderate in price.

JOHN HARRISON,
LINTHORPE ART POTTERY, Middlesbrough-on-Tees.

Plate 104. A Linthorpe advertisement of 1884, reproduced from the *Pottery Gazette*.

Linthorpe Pottery These works, which were established at Middlesbrough in 1879, and whose productions, from the smallest and simplest objects up to the larger and more pronounced achievements, were characterised by a purity of art-treatment not found elsewhere, were situated on the outskirts of the important town of Middlesbrough.

Originally a brick-yard, known as the 'Sun Brick Works', it was conjectured that the extensive beds of fine clay upon which they were erected were capable of being utilised for much higher purposes. Their owner, John Harrison, having put himself in communication with others, entered upon a series of experiments, caused trial-pieces to be made, and became so fully impressed with the capabilities of his raw material that he wisely determined upon entering on the manufacture of high-class pottery, and to give to it a distinctive character that

should at once assert itself and take up a position in ceramics unknown to and untried for by other manufacturers. In this, he was so eminently successful that 'Linthorpe' mottling, flowing, and blending of colours and glazes became sufficient of a speciality to form of itself a distinctive feature in decoration of plastic ware.

At the first starting of the works, in 1879, Mr. Harrison called in the services of Dr. Dresser, who supplied numbers of the forms and designs for pieces then and afterwards produced. His name was, for a time, impressed in the body of the ware. Collectors will, from this hint, know that pieces bearing the stamp 'Chr. Dresser' date back to the first three or four years of the history of these works. Later, the works – untrammelled by the former conventionalities, and casting off the rigid severity of angular outlines on the one hand and grotesque combinations and distortions on the other – entered on another, newer, and far more graceful and effective phase of art, with the result that

Linthorpe ware took its stand among the very highest productions of any locality.

The peculiarity of this ware lies, of course, in the marvellous and never-ending variety and effect of the 'Linthorpe glaze', and the peculiar mode of treatment adopted in the preparation and arrangement of the colours. No two pieces ever made could be alike. The general colour will be the same in any number of pieces of a service, the form will be strictly identical, and the whole will harmonise together; but the accidental pattern, so to speak, which the peculiar glaze assumes in the firing varies in its minute details in such an endless and, at the same time, lovely variety as only nature herself could produce.

In other branches of decorative art, though totally distinct from the Linthorpe speciality of flowing glazes, these works were equally successful. Whether in underglaze painting, sgraffito, or the perhaps more beautiful process of pâte-sur-pâte, the vases produced by Mr. Harrison were all characterised by a strict adherence to the highest and truest principles of art. An advertisement of 1884 is reproduced in Plate 104.

The works at Linthorpe employed from eighty to a hundred hands, and were arranged with a marked attention to the comfort – in abundance of room, light, air and ventilation – of all employed: the ladies painting-room, presided over by a trained lady artist and in which many were engaged in the various processes of decorating, being a model.

The marks used were simply the word LINTHORPE, or the same word across the outline of a flat urn ('Number One' pattern of the works) impressed in the body of the ware. On some pieces, the signature of Dr. Dresser, the designer, occurs; on others, the monogram 'H.T.' of Henry Tooth.

The Linthorpe Pottery closed in 1889.

Blacker's *The ABC of Nineteenth Century English Ceramic Art* (Stanley Paul & Co., London, 1911) includes a contemporary review, with illustrations, of the Linthorpe Pottery. Examples of its productions can be seen in the Dorman Memorial Museum, Middlesbrough.

MILL WALL (London)

Mr. Blashfield, afterwards of the Stamford Terra-cotta Works, who had previously been engaged in the plastic, scagliola, and cement business, commenced the manufacture of terra-cotta vases, statues and chimney-shafts, turning to good account the models he had used in his former business and those he had aquired from Coades. These works he carried on until 1858, when he removed to Stamford.

MORTLAKE (London)

Joseph Kishere produced stoneware at Mortlake during the first quarter of the nineteenth century. Marked examples are in the Victoria and Albert Museum (see *Godden's Illustrated Encyclopaedia of British Pottery and Porcelain* (Herbert Jenkins, London, 1966, Plate 33). William Kishere succeeded his father, and the pottery was known to be still operating in 1831.

MUSSLEBURGH (near Edinburgh, Scotland)

The Mussleburgh Pottery This pottery produced good quality earthenware from 1820 to about 1840. Marked plaques and a toby jug (with crown mark in relief) are recorded, and a porcelain jug dated 1827 and bearing the place-name MUSSLEBURGH is shown in Godden's *Illustrated Encyclopaedia of British Pottery and Porcelain* (Herbert Jenkins, London, 1966, Plate 430).

NANTGARW (Glamorgan, Wales)

These short-lived works, whose history is so mixed up with that of Swansea, Derby, Coalport, Pinxton and other places, were commenced on a small scale in 1813 by William Billingsley, the famous flower-painter of Derby, and his son-in-law, Samuel Walker. Shortly afterwards, having applied to the Board of Trade for patronage and Government aid, Mr. Dillwyn, of the

Cambrian Pottery at Swansea, went over to examine and report upon the ware; and this examination resulted in his entering into an agreement with Billingsley and Walker by which they, with their recipes, moulds and appliances, removed to Swansea.

In about two years, this engagement was brought to a close and Billingsley and Walker returned to Nantgarw, where they again commenced the manufacture of china of the same excellent and peculiar kind for which they had become so famous. The whole of the money subscribed is said to have been expended in little more than two years. This, in great measure, appears to have been caused by experiments and trials and alterations in buildings, and by the immense waste in 'seconds' – which were invariably broken up, instead of being disposed of at a cheaper rate.

The productions of Nantgarw were – as far as beauty of body decoration, as well as form, are concerned – a complete success, and the works gradually but surely made their way in public estimation. The London houses – especially, it is said, Mortlock's – found it to their advantage to support the manufactory, and there was thus no difficulty in finding a good and profitable market. A service was made and presented to the Prince of Wales (afterwards George IV): 'the pattern was a green vase, with a single rose on every piece, and every rose different'. This beautiful service was believed to have been painted by Pardoe. It helped materially to make the works fashionable, and it is said that they were visited by numbers of the nobility and gentry, 'as many as forty gentlemen's carriages having been known to be there in one day'. A considerable quantity of the Nantgarw ware was sold in the white to Mortlock, who had it painted in London and fired at the enamel kiln of Robins & Randall, of Spa Fields. Moses Webster, one of the painters of the Derby China Works, also decorated much of this ware in London. The manufacture of china at Nantgarw ceased in 1820. Billingsley and Walker reputedly removed to Coalport, but there is no evidence available now to show that Walker was at Coalport or that either of them painted Coalport

porcelain. Walker ultimately sailed for America, where he established a pottery. In 1823, the greater portion of the Nantgarw china works was pulled down.

In about 1835, William Henry Pardoe of Bristol, a good practical potter, took the remaining part of the premises and commenced a red-ware pottery in connection with an extensive tobacco-pipe manufactory. To this he afterwards added Rockingham ware and stoneware departments, in each of which he produced goods of excellent quality. Mr. Pardoe died in 1867, and the Nantgarw works – those works around which such a halo of interest exists – were continued by his widow and family. The goods included red and brown earthenware, made from clay found in the neighbourhood – many of the pitchers being of purely mediaeval form – stoneware bottles of every kind, jugs, butter-pots, cheese and bread pans, foot and carriage warmers, snuff-jars, hunting jugs and mugs, tobacco-jars and other goods. Tobacco-pipes, which experienced smokers declared to be equal to those from Broseley, were also made. This pottery closed in 1920.

The only porcelain marks used at Nantgarw which can be considered to be marks of the works are the following, impressed in the body of the china:

NANT-GARW

C W .

and the single word NANTGARW in red colour. This mark has been used on reproductions.

The goods produced were tea, dinner, and dessert services, vases, cabinet cups, pen and wafer trays, inkstands, and a large variety of other articles.

The Nantgarw porcelain body is of the finest quality. Like that of Swansea, it is very translucent. No true picture of the Nantgarw form and styles could be formed from the one or two illustrations it might be possible to reproduce in a general reference book. The reader is therefore referred to specialist works such as W. D. John's *Nantgarw Porcelain* (Ceramic Book Company, 1948) and E. M. Nance's *The Pottery and Porcelain of Swansea and Nantgarw* (Batsford, London, 1942).

NEWCASTLE-UPON-TYNE (Northumberland)

The following brief account of the earthenware works of Newcastle-upon-Tyne and its district was drawn up for the British Association by one of the manufacturers, Mr. C. T. Maling, in about 1863, and it will serve well as an introduction to this section.

The manufacture of white earthenware was introduced into this district by Mr. Warburton, at Carr's Hill Pottery, near Gateshead, in about 1730 or 1740. These works were very successfully carried on for seventy years, when they gradually declined, and in 1817 were closed. A small portion of the building is still used as a brown ware pottery. The next manufactory was built by Mr. Myers, at Newbottle, in the county of Durham, about 1755, where brown and white earthenware still continue to be made. In 1762, Messrs. Christopher Thompson and John Maling erected works at North Hilton, in the county of Durham; their successor, Mr. Robert Maling, in 1817 transferred his operations to the Tyne, where his descendants still continue the manufacture. St. Anthony's, Stepney Bank, and Ouseburn Old Potteries were commenced about the year 1780 or 1790. Messrs. A. Scott & Co., and Messrs. Samuel Moore & Co., erected potteries at Southwick, near Sunderland, the former in the year 1789, the latter in 1803. The pottery carried on by Messrs. John Dawson & Co., at South Hylton, was built by them in 1800. The works of Messrs. John Carr & Sons, at North Shields, were erected in 1814. Messrs. Thomas Fell & Co., built St. Peter's Pottery in 1817. The establishment of Messrs. Skinner & Co., Stockton-on-Tees, dates from 1824.

There are now [1863] about twenty-five potteries in this district, of which, on the Tyne, six manufacture white and printed ware; four white, printed, and brown ware; and three brown ware only . . . On the Wear there are two potteries manufacturing white and printed ware; two white, printed, and brown ware; and two brown ware only . . . On the Tees there are four potteries manufacturing white and printed ware . . . Two at Norton manufacture brown ware . . . The potteries in this district, being situated upon navigable rivers, have great advantages over their inland competitors, Staffordshire and Yorkshire.

The description of goods manufactured is that used by the middle classes and working classes, no first-class goods being made. The principal markets, in addition to the local trade, are the Danish, Norwegian, German, Mediterranean, and London, for exportation to the colonies.

The potteries of the Tyne are:

Newcastle Pottery or **Forth Banks Pottery** commenced in about 1800 by Addison and Falconer, from whom it passed into the occupation of Redhead, Wilson & Co., and from c.1838 to J. Wallace & Co. This company continued to 1893.

The Stepney Bank Pottery Established in about 1780 or 1790, this pottery was, in 1801 occupied by Messrs. Head & Dalton; in 1816 by Messrs. Dryden, Cockson & Basket; in 1822 by Messrs. Davies, Cockson & Wilson; in 1833 by Messrs. Dalton & Burn, who were succeeded by G. R. Turnbull, by whom the character of the ware was considerably improved. In about 1872, the works passed into the hands of John Wood. Messrs. J. Wood & Co. (Ltd.) continued to about 1910.

Ouseburn Bridge Pottery Commenced in 1817 by Robert Maling (see North Hylton Pottery), who manufactured white and printed ware, chiefly for the Dutch market. He was succeeded in 1853 by his son, Christopher T. Maling, who, in 1859, built Ford Pottery and discontinued his old works. They were reopened under the name of the Albion Pottery by Bell Brothers in about 1863; next worked by Atkinson & Galloway (it is possible that this partnership was styled Galloway & Atkinson, as pottery of the period is known bearing an impressed mark 'G & A

C. T. MALING & SONS,

A AND B FORD POTTERIES, NEWCASTLE-ON-TYNE.

B FORD POTTERY.

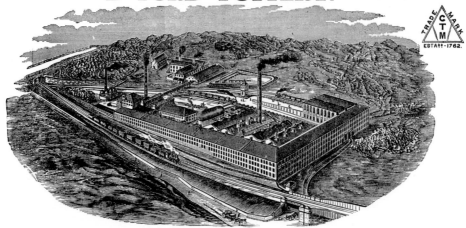

Manufacturers of EVERY DESCRIPTION of SUPERIOR EARTHENWARE
FOR HOME AND EXPORT TRADES.

GOVERNMENT STAMPED MEASURE JUGS AND MUGS.

EXETER SHAPE
In quarts and pints.

YACHT PATTERN — **BETA SHAPE**
WITH OR WITHOUT RIM FOOT
In quarts, pints, and ½-pints.

GOOD CODE PATTERN — **PEAR SHAPE**
In quarts, and pints.

TALL MUC
With or without Spout.

LOW MUC
WITH OR WITHOUT FOOT
In quarts, pints, and ½-pints.

HALF PINT — **DRINKING HORN**
In ½-pints.

DURHAM SHAPE

EASTFIELD PATTERN

JARS FOR WHOLESALE JAM MANUFACTURERS.
SANITARY WARE.
Extracts of Meat Pots and Bottles.   Potted Meat Pots and Bottles.

Registered "Britannic" Photographic Frame

Albion Pottery'); and lastly, by W. Morris. They were finally closed in 1872.

Ford Pottery Built in 1859 by Christopher T. Maling (son of Mr. Robert Maling, who in 1817 removed the Hylton pottery to Newcastle) for manufacturing by machinery marmalade, jam, and extract-of-beef pots. These are of a very fine and compact white body, with an excellent glaze made from borax without any lead. It is said that at least ninety-five per cent of such pots used by wholesale manufacturers in Great Britain were made at this establishment. The pots, being entirely made by machinery, are necessarily much more uniform in size and weight and thickness than those made by any other process. The main mark is simply the name MALING impressed in the clay, with sometimes the initial of the house for whom they were made, such as $\begin{smallmatrix} MALING \\ K \end{smallmatrix}$ for Keiller, and so on. A triangle-shaped mark also occurs. Messrs. C. T. Maling & Sons (Ltd.) continued into the twentieth century.

From about 1890, a mark depicting a castle was employed on their varied ware. The firm closed in July 1963. An interesting advertisement of 1895 is reproduced in Plate 105. It shows a mocha jug ('Moco') and various stamped measures.

Ouseburn Pottery Built at about the same date as Stepney Bank Pottery (about 1780 or 1790) by Mr. Yellowley, who was succeeded by T. & J. Thompson, then by I. Maling, it was finally closed in about 1864. White, printed, and brown ware were its productions.

Another Ouseburn Pottery was established at the latter end of the eighteenth century or the early part of the nineteenth century by Ralph Charlton, who carried on the business on a small scale for the manufacture of brown ware. On his death, he was succeeded by his son, John Charlton, who after a few years was succeeded

Plate 105. A Maling advertisement of 1895, showing typical products and the standard mark (top, right). Reproduced from the *Pottery Gazette*.

by George Gray, who was followed by Morrow and Parke, and then Mr. Rogers, who extended the buildings. It was next worked by William Blakey until 1860, when it passed into the hands of Robert Martin & Co.

Another Ouseburn Pottery passed in 1860 into the hands of John Hedley Walker, its productions being flower-pots, chimney-pots and horticultural vessels of various kinds, as well as the lead-pots and lead-dishes which were so extensively used in the lead-works of the district. J. H. Walker continued until about 1896.

The Phoenix Pottery Built by John Dryden & Co. in about 1821, this pottery at first produced brown ware, and afterwards white and printed ware. In about 1844, it passed into the hands of Isaac Bell & Co., and was afterwards carried on successively by Carr & Patton (who at the same time had North Shields Pottery); John Patton; and Cook Brothers, who discontinued manufacturing earthenware in 1860 and converted the premises into a chemical factory.

St. Peter's Pottery Established in 1817 by Thomas Fell and Thomas Bell, this pottery was carried on under the style of Thomas Fell & Co. until 1869, when it became a limited liability company. The productions were the ordinary classes of earthenware in white, printed, and sponged varieties. Rare figures are recorded. The mark was formerly an anchor with the letter F (for Fell) on one side and the workman's mark or number on the other, impressed

in the body of the ware. Later on, this mark was discontinued and the name FELL was substituted, and later FELL & CO. The company ceased in about 1890. Several printed marks were employed, incorporating the name Fell or the initals T F & Co.

St. Anthony's Pottery This was one of the oldest potteries for fine eartheware on the Tyne, being established in about 1780, but nothing is known of its early history. In 1803 or 1804, it passed into the hands of a Mr. Sewell, in whose family (c.1820–52) it was continued under the styles of Sewell & Donkin and Sewell & Co. (1852–78), the principal productions being cream-coloured, painted, and blue-printed goods (the cream-coloured ware, to imitate Wedgwood's table ware, being made in considerable quantities for Holland and other Continental markets). The fact of printing on pottery from wood engravings being practised at these works is highly interesting, as I have been enabled to ascertain that engravings by Bewick were thus brought into use. Specimens are, however, very rare. Silver and gold lustre was also made. Several forms of marks were used: SEWELL; SEWELL & DONKIN; SEWELLS & DONKIN, AND SEWELLS & CO.

In 1882, the works were reopened by Mr. Lloyd. In 1883, the title was Lloyd & Hedges. Production was limited to about two years. In 1891–2, Messrs. Patterson & Parkinson worked this pottery and were succeeded by T. Patterson & Co. (1893–1908). The potters T. Patterson, Patterson & Parkinson, and then Patterson & Scott also worked the Carr's Hill Pottery, Newcastle-upon-Tyne.

Sheriff Hill Pottery These works were carried on from 1850 by George Patterson, as the successor to the firm of Jackson & Patterson (c.1833–47). His chief production was white ware, which he supplied largely to the Norwegian markets. In 1903, the Sheriff's Hill Pottery Co. (Ltd.) was formed.

Messrs. Lewins & Parsons are also stated to have had a pottery here for the manufacture of the commoner kinds of earthenware.

Tyne Main Pottery At South Shore, on the opposite side of the River Tyne to St. Peter's, this pottery was built by Messrs. Richard Davies & Co. in the year 1833 and carried on by them, manufacturing white, printed, and lustre ware, chiefly for the Norwegian market. It was closed in 1851. Mr. R. C. Wilson, the managing partner, then commenced manufacturing at Seaham Harbour. A plate in the Godden Collection,

dated 1847, bears the impressed mark DAVIES & CO.

The local directories also list R. C. Wilson of the Tyne Main Pottery in the 1830s and up to 1851; but on the evidence of the marked 1847 plate, it would appear that the title Davies & Co. was retained.

There was also a pottery at Jarrow for a few years which manufactured brown ware only.

A recent work, *Tyneside Pottery* by R. C. Bell (Studio Vista, London, 1971), gives a good and full account of this little-known ware and illustrates many typical examples.

NEWTON ABBOT (South Devon)

The Aller Pottery Near Newton Abott, this pottery was commenced for the manufacture of common brown ware in 1865, and three years later came into the hands of Messrs. John Phillips & Co. for the production of architectural pottery, consisting of tiles, sanitary and sewage ware, garden edgings, ornamental chimney pots, decorative bricks, flower vases and like articles. The markets principally supplied were those of Devonshire, Somersetshire, and Cornwall.

The mark was a horse's head, couped, with the Greek words ΦΙΛΕΩ ΙΙΙΙΙΟΝ, being a playful allusion to the name of the proprietor, Phillips. This firm continued into the twentieth century and amalgamated with the Watcombe Company in 1903. Its new title was The Royal Aller Vale and Watcombe Art Potteries.

Other potteries near Newton Abbot include that of Candy & Co. Ltd., a firm incorporated in 1882 which continues to this day.

A wide range of earthenware has been produced. The ware is seldom marked. The initials N^{C}A are, however, recorded on some specimens.

NORTH SHIELDS (Northumberland)

The Low Light Pottery Established in 1814 by Nicholas Bird, and afterwards passed from him, in or about 1829, to Messrs. Cornfoot, Colville & Co. The firm was, in about 1832, changed to

Cornfoot, Carr & Patton; and on the withdrawal of Mr. Cornfoot, in about 1835, the style was changed to Carr & Patton. Next, in about 1850, the firm was John Carr & Co. And when the concern became the property of the first of these partners, John Carr, he and his sons carried it on from 1854 under the style of John Carr & Son, and from 1860 onwards as John Carr & Sons.

Originally, brown and black ware of the usual common kinds were made, in addition to the ordinary earthenware; but in 1856, these were discontinued and the ordinary white earthenware in cream-coloured, printed, painted, and lustred varieties was substituted. These goods were exported principally to the Mediterranean ports and to Alexandria, for transport to Cairo, and by the Red Sea to Bombay.

The mark – which, however, was seldom used – is a stag's head. A rare printed plate with moulded floral pattern border of about 1850 in the Godden Collection has the impressed mark J. CARR & CO. J. Carr & Sons continued to c.1900.

NUNEATON (Warwickshire)

The works here were established in about 1830 by Peter Wager Williams, upon the site of what evidently had been very old pot-works but of which no record appears to exist. At first, there were two distinct manufactories, of which one was worked by his eldest son, John Williams, who sold it to his three brothers, Peter, Charles and James, by whom it was carried on under the style of Caroline Williams. It afterwards passed by purchase into the hands of J. Rawlins and was taken by Messrs. Broadbent & Stanley Brothers, by whom it was considerably extended. The other manufactory was carried on by Walter Handley, at whose death it passed to his son-in-law, David Wheway, at whose decease it was incorporated with the other and carried on jointly by Broadbent & Stanley Brothers. In 1871, Mr. Broadbent retired from the concern.

The goods included terra-cotta vases,

chimney-pots, coloured paving-tiles for geometric designs; garden-edging, ornamental, ridging, plain building and ornamental bricks; and sanitary and other pipes.

The marls from which the various goods were made, on the ground worked by this firm, comprised about twenty different measures of several colours and qualities. The works occupied nearly ten acres of ground.

Messrs. Stanley Bros. continue to the present day.

PAISLEY (Renfrewshire)

Paisley Earthenware Works Messrs. Robert Brown & Son established these works in 1876 and produced white enamelled earthenware goods of a similar quality to those of Staffordshire. Their principal productions were sanitary appliances, baths of every kind (a speciality being the larger baths, five feet six inches in length). This firm continued into the twentieth century.

Crown Works At the Crown Crucible Works, also belonging to Messrs. Robert Brown & Son, plumbago crucibles and kindred goods were manufactured. The marks were a crown and

BROWN   PAISLEY,

name and a crucible within an oval border surmounted by a crown. This firm continued until about 1933.

PINXTON (East Derbyshire)

Having an idea that some clays found on the family estates near Pinxton might be available for the manufacture of china ware, John Coke entered into a correspondence with William Duesbury, of the Derby China Works, and sent him samples of his clays for trial and experiment. Whatever encouragement or otherwise he received from Mr. Duesbury, the result of his own convictions and his own trials determined Mr. Coke on starting the works. He ultimately made an engagement with William Billingsley, of the Derby China Works, and, having built a very conveniently arranged factory, commenced the manufacture of china ware in 1796.

Here, Billingsley succeeded in producing that beautiful warm-feeling body which he afterwards perfected at Nantgarw and at Swansea. And here, too, stimulated by Mr. Coke's good taste, he introduced faultless forms in his services and a high style of excellence in decoration. He brought with him several experienced workmen and artists from the Derby works and took them into the factory, and instructed several young people of Pinxton.

Through a misunderstanding, the arrangement between Messrs. Coke and Billingsley was not of long duration. In April 1799, Billingsley left the place and removed to Mansfield, where, it is said, he occupied himself in decorating and finishing china ware which he bought in the white state in Staffordshire and elsewhere. He afterwards moved to Worcester, Nantgarw, Swansea and, reputedly, to Coalport.

The group of porcelain shown in Figure 46 is a selection of pieces made during Billingsley's time at Pinxton. They are remarkable for the beauty of the body and of the glaze, and some of them are noticeable for the excellence of the gilding. The coffee pot is one of a set bearing views of different places in Derbyshire or elsewhere. These landscapes were excellently painted – of a special brownish effect which pervades

the whole colouring – by James Hadfield, who was the best landscape-painter at the works. The views on the pieces which have come under my notice are Pinxton Church, Darley Hall, Hartington Bridge, Ashwood Dale, Buxton, Wingerworth Hall, Tong Castle, Saltram, Menai Straits, Wanstead Church, Frog Hall, Caerphilly Castle, and others. The teapot and stand are of elegant shape, unusually narrow, and carefully gilt; the stand is of a peculiar form. The cup and saucer have the 'Derby Sprig' (Tournay sprig), as it is frequently called.

After the close of Billingsley's connection with the Pinxton works, they were carried on by Mr. Coke with the assistance of a Mr. Banks. Afterwards, Mr. Coke took John Cutts (a talented landscape painter) to manage the concern, and he became a partner in the works. In the later part of the time, the manufactory was carried on by Cutts alone. At the close of the Pinxton Works, which took place in 1813, Cutts removed into Staffordshire – settling himself at Lane End – where he commenced business, at first buying ware in the white and finishing it for sale. In 1811, Davies stated: 'There is a considerable porcelain factory at Pinxton, which finds employment for several hands.'

After Billingsley's removal from Pinxton, the character of the ware underwent a change. The granular body, of which I have spoken as produced and afterwards brought to such perfection by him, was his own secret and he zealously kept it. On leaving Pinxton, this secret naturally went with him; and there is some doubt if porcelain was made at Pinxton after Billingsley

Fig. 46. Selection of Pinxton porcelain.

Plate 106. A Pinxton porcelain teapot of typical form, c.1800. 10 inches long.
Victoria & Albert Museum (Crown copyright).

left. Certainly the subsequent owners continued to decorate the available stock of white porcelain; and they could also have purchased porcelain from other factories, such as Coalport, so avoiding the many risks incurred in making and firing their own porcelain.

Among the workmen brought from Derby along with Billingsley were Thomas Moore, a clever thrower; Ash, also a clever thrower and turner; and many others of repute. Among the painters were James Hadfield, a good landscape painter; Edward Rowland, a landscape painter; Morrell, who painted landscapes and flowers; Richard Robins, from London; William Alvey and others, including Slater and Marriott. Alvey commenced in 1803 and left in about 1808. He became master of Edingley School, near Southwell, where he died in 1867 aged about eighty-three. Alvey, who was held in high respect at Edingley, was an excellent musician, a clever draughtsman and colourist, a first-rate mathematician, a splendid penman,

a very fair land-surveyor, and a poet of no mean order. He was fond of drawing and painting to the last.

No especial mark was at any period used at the Pinxton Works. The number of the pattern was occasionally given, and sometimes a workman's mark was added; and although other marks were used, none seems to have been adopted as distinctive of the works. A writing letter P and impressed Roman capital letters have been noticed as occurring on specimens (such impressed letter marks also occur on Derby porcelain). A tea service bears inside the lid of the teapot the word PINXTON written in gold letters; this is rare. This service is of a beautifully clear white china, with broad edges of burnished gold – a handsome arabesque border of red, blue and gold ornamenting each piece. The porcelain and style are very similar to Derby.

The reader is referred to C. L. Exley's *The Pinxton China Factory* (published privately, 1963). Typical examples of Pinxton porcelain are also featured in Godden's *Illustrated Encyclopaedia of British Pottery and Porcelain*, (Herbert Jenkins, London, 1966).

PLYMOUTH

PLYMOUTH (Devon)

Plymouth Pottery Company Mr. William Alsop
(who had earlier made coarse earthenware)
built a manufactory for fine earthenware of the
ordinary quality but afterwards removed to
Swansea, his works passing into the hand of
Messrs. Bryant, Burnell & James. Subsequently,
Mr. Alsop returned from Swansea and formed
a limited liability company, in 1856, for the carrying on of this concern, and produced large
quantities of pottery and printed ware. On the
death of Mr. Alsop, a Mr. Bishop, from the
Staffordshire pottery district, took the management of the works; but the manufacture gradually died out, and in about 1863 the plant was
sold off.

The mark used by this company was the
Queen's Arms, with the initials P.P. Coy. L.
(Plymouth Pottery Company Limited) Stone
China. The quality of the ware was of the normal
description of white earthenware, blue printed
in various patterns.

Plymouth porcelain is, of course, of the eighteenth century period and is therefore not included in this volume dealing with the later
ware.

POLESWORTH (New Tamworth, Warwickshire)

Terra-Cotta Works This manufactory of terra-
cotta by the Midland Brick & Terra-Cotta
Company was established in 1875 under the
directorship of Mr. J. Joiner, for many years
principal manager at the Stamford Terra-cotta
Works. The productions consisted of fountains; garden, conservatory, and other vases of
various designs; architectural details and enrichments; chimney-tops, chimney-pieces,
capitals and columns, crestings and finials,
tomb-stones, monuments, memorial tablets and
urns; moulded and plain bricks; roofing-tiles,
garden-edgings, drain-pipes and other useful
goods. The terra-cotta was both red and buff,
and was of fine hard and durable quality, with a
clean, good surface.

218

POLLOKSHAWS (Glasgow)

Victoria Pottery David Lockhart and Charles
Arthur established this factory at Cogan Street
in 1855 under the style Lockhart & Arthur.
General earthenware was produced. In 1865,
the title became Lockhart & Co. (later, David
was added to the style); and in 1898, it became
David Lockhart & Sons. Printed marks are
recorded with the relevant initials D L & Co.,
D L & S. The works continued until 1953.

POOLE (Dorset)

The Architectural Pottery Company These works
were established in 1854 by Messrs. Thomas
Sanders Ball, John Ridgway (china manufacturer of Cauldon Place, Hanley), Thomas
Richard Sanders, and Frederick George Sanders. In 1857, John Ridgway retired, as did
Thomas Ball in 1861, and the works were continued by the Sanders alone.

The productions were patent coloured and
glazed bricks and mouldings, semi-perforated
and pressed; patent mosaic, tessellated, encaustic, vitreous and other glazed wall tiles;
embossed and perforated tiles, quarries and
fireclay goods. The clays used were Purbeck
clay, Cornish china clay and Fareham clay.
The encaustic paving tiles were of good design,
many being carefully copied from mediaeval
examples. A speciality of these works was the
tessellated tiles. Under Bale's patent process,
these were literally formed of thin tessserae of
various colours. The marks comprise the title
in full or the initials A.P. & Co.

In 1873, Messrs. Carter managed the Poole &
Hamworthy Potteries. Apart from the production of high grade and decorative tiles, various
forms of art pottery were made. Examples may
be found marked 'Carter.Poole' (in various
forms). In 1921, this firm became Carter, Stabler
& Adams (Ltd.). Their Poole Pottery has won
world-wide renown. In February 1963, the
firm's title was changed to Poole Pottery
Limited.

PORTOBELLO (near Edinburgh, Scotland)

Midlothian Potteries The Midlothian Stoneware Potteries at Portobello and Musselburgh, near Edinburgh, were established in about 1857 by Mr. W. A. Gray for the manufacture of general stoneware goods. But they had been in existence as earthenware works for upwards of a century before that time. (Late eighteenth century and early nineteenth century Portobello ware is illustrated by G. B. Hughes in *Country Life*, 28th August 1958). They were carried on under the style of W. A. Gray & Sons. The goods produced were all kinds of stoneware and the more ordinary descriptions of earthenware. This firm continued until about 1932.

Portobello Pottery These works were established in 1770. From about 1867, they were carried on by Murray & Buchan, and from about 1877 by A. W. Buchan & Co. For a number of years, they turned out ordinary white earthenware and Rockingham ware; but from 1842, the manufacture was entirely confined to stoneware bottles, jars, jugs, feet and carriage-warmers, spirit-bottles and the usual classes of such goods. The mark of the firm was a star. This firm continues to the present day. The modern mark is a thistle with the name Buchan. Decorative and useful stoneware is produced today.

Rosebank Pottery John Hay worked this pottery from the mid-1880s to about 1896. Then J. & T. Hay continued into the twentieth century.

PRESCOT (Lancashire)

The Moss Pottery Thomas Spencer, who established delft ware works at the bottom of Richmond Row, Liverpool, in the eighteenth century, removed them to Prescot, where he founded the Moss Pottery and made coarse brown ware from the native clays of the district. At his death, the works passed into the hands of his son who, in turn, was succeeded by his son, Thomas Spencer. White stoneware was afterwards manufactured to a large extent, but later the operations were principally confined to ordinary stoneware and sanitary ware – one of the most notable features of which were socket drain-pipes, for which Mr. Spencer held a patent dated 10th April 1848. Sugar-moulds for sugar refiners were at one time a staple production of the Moss Pottery, but these were superseded by iron moulds.

PRESTONPANS (near Edinburgh, Scotland)

Prestonpans Pottery There were two old pot-works, each more than a century old, in Prestonpans until 1838. In that year, they were both closed. In about 1836, Charles Belfield established his Prestonpans Pottery, where Rockingham–glazed teapots, cane jugs, etc., were produced. This firm continued until 1940. The old style was Charles Belfield & Sons.

Gordon Pottery Interesting and decorative earthenware was made here prior to its closure in 1832.

Watson Pottery John Fowler & Co. worked the Watson Pottery at Prestonpans from 1800 to the 1840 period.

READING (Berkshire)

Coley Avenue Works or **Groveland Works** These works were established in 1861 by Messrs. Collier & Son, and were continued under the style of S. & E. Collier. Brown terra-cotta, glazed and unglazed brown ware, and roofing and other tiles were the products of these works. The mark is two Rs superimposed by a larger letter C. This firm continued until 1957.

ROCKINGHAM – see *Swinton*

ROTHERHAM (Yorkshire)

North Field Pottery This pottery was established in 1851 by Joseph Lee, a working potter, who had previously carried on a small manufactory in the town of Rotherham. In 1855, it was purchased by George Hawley, of Rawmarsh, who on his death was succeeded by his son, William Hawley, and his two brothers. The firm was for a time carried on as W. & G. Hawley, and then Hawley Brothers. The goods manufactured were the commoner descriptions of earthenware. In 1903, this firm became Northfield Hawley Pottery Co. Ltd. The Hawley mark, from 1903 to 1919, was a lion rampant with the right paw on a globe.

Holmes Pottery These works were built on part of the Holmes Hall Estate – the kitchen garden, in fact – formerly belonging to the Walker family, who owned the large ironworks there. The pottery was at first extremely small but gradually extended itself until it was of considerable extent in the 1870s.

It was first worked by Earnshaw & Greaves, who were succeeded by Dickinson & Jackson, then by Thomas Jarvis, and later still by John Jackson & Co. The goods produced were the commoner class of white and blue printed earthenware. An attempt at china manufacturing was made here but abandoned. Messrs. G. Shaw & Sons succeeded J. Jackson & Co. in about 1888. The marks are J J & Co., prior to 1888, and subsequently G S & S; but examples are rarely marked. George Shaw & Sons (Ltd.) continued until 1947.

RUNCORN (Cheshire)

Old Quay Pottery These works were carried on in 1869 by John Cliff, who in that year removed from the Imperial Pottery, Lambeth, to this place. Utilitarian stoneware was the main product.

RUTHERGLEN (Lanarkshire, Scotland)

Caledonian Pottery The Caledonian Pottery at Rutherglen, near Glasgow, was first established at Glasgow in about 1780 by a joint-stock company, and was acquired in about 1825 by Messrs. Murray & Co. In 1870, the works were removed from Glasgow to Rutherglen, about a couple of miles from that city. At first, fine porcelain and china were made; then cream-coloured printed

ware, with Rockingham and salt-glazed ware. In 1851, the demand sprang up for stoneware ale and other bottles, and this became one of the staple trades of Glasgow and the surrounding district. The goods produced were the usual classes of 'Bristol' glazed stoneware, cane ware, and Rockingham and Egyptian black ware. A speciality of Murray & Co. was their patent 'spongy iron filter'. The mark used was a lion rampant.

From about 1895 to 1898, the firm was W. F. Murray & Co. Ltd., then the Caledonian Pottery Co. Ltd. until 1928.

RYE (Sussex)

The Bellevue Pottery This pottery is Ferry Road, Rye, Sussex, was established in 1869 by Frederick Mitchell (son and partner of William Mitchell of the Cadborough Pottery) for the manufacture of 'Sussex Rustic Ware'. This ware was of peculiar but highly pleasing character, and in it was made a large variety of fancy articles such as flower-baskets, candlesticks, jugs, vases and pilgrims' bottles. The clay was peculiarly light, of tolerably close texture, and was capable of being worked into any form. The glaze, of equal richness with that of Rockingham ware, was of exceedingly good quality, and it had a rich effect over the mottling or 'splashing' which characterised this ware. Some of the vessels were decorated with the leaf and head of the hop plant or with other excellent copies of leaves and flowers, etc. The peculiarity of this Sussex Rustic Ware was its lightness, and the richness of its mottling and glaze. Similar ware was produced at the Bellevue Pottery up to 1939.

The normal mark on Sussex Rustic Ware is the initials S.R.W. with 'Rye' within the segments of a cross.

Several potters today produce good studio-type pottery in this interesting little town.

SEACOMBE (Cheshire)

John Goodwin, a potter of Lane End in Staffordshire, established a pottery at Seacombe, on the opposite shore of the Mersey from Liverpool, in 1851. He brought his workmen from Staffordshire, and fired his first oven in June 1852. At this pottery (which closed before 1872), blue and coloured printed ware and Parian was made. A large export market was built up, and the works were amongst the most advanced of their period. Two printed marks are reproduced in Godden's *Handbook of British Pottery and Porcelain Marks* (Herbert Jenkins, London, 1968). These marks incorporate the name J. Goodwin or Goodwin & Co. and that of the Seacombe Pottery.

SEAHAM HARBOUR (Durham)

A brown-ware manufactory was built here in about 1836 by Captain Plowright, of Lynn. In 1838, it was altered into a white and printed ware manufactory by a number of workmen from Messrs. Dawson & Co. of Hylton. It was closed in about 1841, reopened in 1851 by R. C. Wilson, and finally closed in 1852.

SHIPLEY (Derbyshire)

These works were commenced in about 1825 on the estate of Edward Miller Mundy of Shipley Hall, by whom the buildings were erected in consequence of the discovery of valuable beds of clay. They were first carried on by some working potters from the Staffordshire district, and the ordinary classes of goods in cane or yellow ware were produced, as were also Rockingham-ware teapots and other articles. These were made to a considerable extent, and of good quality, but the works did not answer. They were next taken by a Mr. Waite – a blacking manufacturer from London – who commenced making stoneware bottles for his own blacking, and other articles of general use. Eventually, in 1845, the works passed into the hands of Mr. Bourne of the Denby Pottery (see page 172) and were carried on by him.

In 1856, the Shipley pottery was closed. The workmen and plant were removed to and incorporated with the Denby pottery.

SOUTH SHIELDS (Durham)

The Tyne or **Shields Pottery** Established in about 1830 by a Mr. Robertson, from whom, in 1845, it passed into the hands of John Armstrong, by whom the works were considerably enlarged. In 1871, the concern was purchased by Messrs. Isaac Fell and George Shields Young, by whom it was carried on under the style of Isaac Fell & Co. until 1878. The goods manufactured were 'Sunderland' and brown ware, of which large quantities were shipped to the Continent as well as supplied to the London, Scottish and other home markets.

STAMFORD (Lincs.)

That pottery was made in Stamford in mediaeval times was incontestably proved in the latter end of 1874 by the discovery of a kiln during the course of excavations in the rear of a house occupied by the Rev. E. F. Gretton; but from that early time, pottery was not made there until 1858. In that year, terracotta works were established by J. M. Blashfield. Previous to this time, Mr. Blashfield had been, until 1851, engaged in Southwark Bridge Road, Albion Place, Blackfriars, and Millwall in the Italian marble trade and the manufacture of cements and scagliola, and the making and laying down of tessellated pavements. In 1851, he commenced the manufacture of terra-cotta at Millwall, London, having previously purchased a number of moulds and models from Coades when that manufactory was closed. In 1858, Mr. Blashfield (whose name is intimately connected with the subject of encaustic paving-tiles, having been associated with Herbert Minton in their revival) removed his moulds and plant to Stamford, where a suitable clay was found to exist. In 1874, the works merged into a limited liability company under the style of the Stamford Terra-Cotta Company, which failed and was wound up in 1875, when the plant and stock were sold by auction, but afterwards to some extent revived.

The productions of this manufactory were terra-cotta as applied to every purpose – glazed

221

or enamelled tiles and bricks for wall-facings, hard ordinary paving-tiles, enamelled architectural enrichments for internal use, and red and buff moulded bricks.

Among the public buildings which were enriched by the art-works of Mr. Blashfield's manufactory are the urns, antifixa, and pavements in the royal mausoleums, Windsor; vases and terminals at Buckingham Palace; vases, tassas, borders at Kew and Hampton Court Gardens and Dairy Farm, Windsor; chimney shafts, etc., Sandringham; vases and pedestals, Marlborough Houses; the entire red, buff, grey and black terra-cotta details and enrichments for Dulwich College and, indeed, for most of the public buildings and private mansions of this country and abroad. The marks were the names impressed: J.M. Blashfield or Blashfield, Stamford or Stamford Terra Cotta Co. Ltd.

considerable skill. The firm commenced under the style of William Smith & Co. in January 1826. In 1829, a further partnership was entered into with William and George Skinner – sons of Mr. Skinner, banker, of Stockton – and continued for some years when George Skinner, having purchased the interest of his brother and of Mr. Smith, changed the style to that of George Skinner & Co.

By Mr. Skinner and Mr. Whalley it was thus carried on for some years. When the latter retired, the management devolved upon Ambrose Walker, who, shortly after the death of Mr. Skinner in April 1870, succeeded to the business and carried it on in connection with the executors of Mr. Skinner under the style of Skinner & Walker until 1880. It was then continued as Ambrose Walker & Co. until 1893.

The goods manufactured were principally

Fig. 47. Blashfield's Stamford Terra-Cotta.

STOCKTON-ON-TEES (Durham and Yorkshire)

Stafford Pottery Several earthenware manufactories have been carried on at this place. The largest, called the Stafford Pottery, at South Stockton or Thornaby, was established for brown ware in 1825 by William Smith, a builder, of Stockton, who shortly afterwards added general earthenware to its productions. To this end, he engaged and ultimately took into partnership John Whalley, a Staffordshire potter of

'Queen's ware'; a fine white earthenware; and a fine brown ware, which were shipped in large quantities to Belgium, Holland and some parts of Germany. The marks used include:

W.S. & Co.   S. & W.
QUEEN'S WARE   QUEEN'S WARE
   STOCKTON   STOCKTON
or STOCKTON impressed in the body.

In 1848, the firm consisted of William Smith, John Whalley, George Skinner and Henry Cowap, and in that year an injunction was granted restraining them from using, as they had illegally done, the name of WEDGEWOOD &

CO or WEDGEWOOD stamped or otherwise marked on goods produced by them. Many printed children's plates bear this form of mark.

Stockton-on-Tees is in the county of Durham but the Stafford Pottery is on the south bank of the Tees and may be regarded as a Yorkshire Pottery (see O. Grabham's *Yorkshire Potteries, Pots and Potters*, Yorkshire Museum, 1916).

North Shore Pottery The North Shore Pottery was established in about 1840 by James Smith and was carried on by his nephew, William Smith, junior (son of the William Smith to whom I have alluded as the founder of the Stafford Pottery), under the style of William Smith, Jun. & Co. Subsequently, it was carried on as G. F. Smith & Co., G. & W. Smith, and then William Smith.

The classes of goods made at this pottery were both in white and cream-coloured ware, the principal markets for which were – besides the home trade – Holland, Germany and Denmark. Large quantities of ware were also exported to Constantinople and other Mediterranean markets. In white earthenware and printed and coloured goods, dinner, tea, toilet and other services; bread, cheese and other trays of good designs; mugs, jugs, basins and all the usual varieties of domestic vessels were made.

The 'sponge-patterns' for foreign markets were extensively used, and green-glazed ware in flower-pots were also made. The impressed mark was W.S. Stockton; and the printed marks, besides an ornamental border and the name of the pattern, incorporated the initials W.S., used from about 1870 to 1884.

Messrs. W. H. & J. H. Ainsworth worked the Stockton pottery until about 1901.

Other Stockton potteries have been Mr. Harwood, The Norton Pottery at Norton, for Sunderland and yellow ware; Clarence Pottery Company for Sunderland and brown ware; and John Harwood for brown ware.

SUNDERLAND DISTRICT

For fuller details of the many Sunderland potteries than are included here, the reader is referred to an interesting booklet, *The Potteries of Sunderland and District*, edited by J. T. Shaw and published by the local Library and Museum (revised edition, 1961).

A type of 'splashed Lustre' is associated with Sunderland pottery, typical examples of which are illustrated in Plates 7 and 107.

Plate 107. A selection of Sunderland pottery made at the Southwick Pottery and bearing 'Scott' name-marks. *Sunderland Museum.*

South Hylton or Ford Pottery Erected by John Dawson & Co. prior to 1800, these works were carried on by that firm until 1864 when, on the death of the last of the family, Charles Dawson, they were closed and converted into bottle houses, which were destroyed by fire. The flint-mill was taken by Mr. Ball of the Deptford Pottery. A part of the premises was, several years afterwards, used as a brown-ware manufactory, and later still was worked by Messrs. Isaac Fell & Co.

Dawson employed some two hundred workmen and produced good printed earthenware. One mark was simply the name DAWSON impressed in the ware.

The Southwick Pottery Built in 1788 by Anthony Scott, who had previously carried on a small pot-work at Newbottle. The pottery was carried on by various members of the Scott family – A. Scott & Sons (1829–44), Scott Brothers & Co. (1844–54), A. Scott & Son (1872–82), A. Scott (1882–97). At these large works, the usual classes of white, coloured, and brown earthenware were produced for foreign markets. This firm closed in 1896. Various marks were used. A firm of Scott Brothers also potted at Portobello, Scotland but Scott Bros. marks probably relate to the Sunderland firm.

The Wear Pottery Founded by Brunton & Co. in 1789 and carried on by Samuel Moore & Co. from 1803, this pottery passed in about 1861 into the hands of R. T. Wilkinson, who carried it on under the style of Samuel Moore & Co. The works closed in 1881. The goods manufactured were the ordinary descriptions of white, sponged and printed earthenware, and brown ware. Marks included S. Moore & Co., Moore & Co. and SM & Co.

The High Southwick Pottery This pottery was carried on for Sunderland ware by Thomas Snowball from about 1850 to 1885.

DEPTFORD

Deptford Pottery These works were established at Diamond Hall in 1857 by William Ball for the manufacture of flower-pots, in which he effected many improvements – one of the principal of which was 'making them hollow-footed, or with concave bottoms, with apertures for drainage and air, and kept free from the attacks of worms'. In 1863, the manufacture of 'Sunderland ware' was introduced and was carried on very largely for the London and Scottish markets. Frog mugs and ship bowls were made in large numbers. At these works, too, suspenders, highly decorated, and other flower-vases and seed-boxes were extensively made. From 1884 to the closure in 1918, the title was Ball Brothers.

MONKWEARMOUTH

The Sheepful Pottery This pottery for Sunderland ware was established in 1840 by Thomas Rickaby, subsequently Rickaby & Blakelock, Rickaby & Co., then Messrs. T. J. Rickaby & Co. from 1865 to about 1910. The works were closed in about 1910.

The Sunderland Pottery or the Garrison Pottery Also established by Mr. Phillips in about 1807, and carried on by Dixon, Austin, Phillips & Co., these works produced white and Queen's ware, in all the usual variety of articles. Sponged, printed and painted, and lustred earthenware were also produced. The works were discontinued in c.1865. The marks include PHILLIPS & CO.,

PHILLIPS & CO.
SUNDERLAND POTTERY

Among the examples in the Sunderland Museum is a printed, coloured and lustred jug, bearing on one side the common view of the bridge over the Wear and on the other the Farmer's Arms, while in front are the words 'Forget me not' within a wreath. It bears the name DIXON AUSTIN & CO., SUNDERLAND. Figures were also produced, and marked examples might be seen. The name occurs in various ways apart from those above. Thus, among others, are W. DIXON, DIXON & CO., DIXON & CO., SUNDERLAND POTTERY,

DIXON AUSTIN & CO
Sunderland Pottery

DIXON & CO
SUNDERLAND POTTERY

DIXON & CO
SUNDERLAND.

SWADLINCOTE (Derbyshire)

Swadlincote Potteries The works of Messrs. Sharpe, Brothers & Co. were established by Thomas Sharpe in 1821 and were carried on by him alone until his death in 1838. They were then continued by his brothers as Sharpe, Brothers & Co., under which style they were carried on by the last surviving brother, Edmund Sharpe.

The productions were the same as those of the district generally – viz. Derbyshire Ironstone cane (or yellow) ware (the speciality of the district), buff drab ware, fire-proof ware, Rockingham ware, mottled ware, and black lustre ware. In Derbyshire Ironstone, every description of household vessel was made (see the engraving of the typical mixing bowl shown in the 1891 advertisement, Figure 48), as also in buff drab ware.

Fig. 48. Messrs. Sharpe Bros.' advertisement of 1891.

In Rockingham, mottled and black lustre ware, tea and coffee-pots in an endless variety of patterns, pressed and plain jugs and mugs of good designs and other useful articles were made as well as blue printed goods. Among the specialities of these works can be named the 'Toby Fillpot' jugs, which are made in both coloured and Rockingham ware on much the same model as the antique jugs of that name. The mark first used was simply the name THOMAS SHARPE, or T. SHARPE, impressed in the ware. That of Sharpe Bros. & Co. from about 1870 was the monogram 'S.B. and Co.' within a wreath of oak and ivy, and the words SHARPE'S PATENT. From 1895, Messrs. Sharpe Bros. & Co. Ltd.'s output mainly comprised sanitary ware.

Swadlincote Pottery These works, established in 1790 by John Hunt of Swadlincote, were, after his death, continued by Thomas Woodward and his son, James Woodward; they were the first of the kind in the place. Fire-bricks, fire-clay for Sheffield steel-works crucibles, and iron-furnaces were the sole productions till 1859, when the manufacture of sewage pipes, terra-cotta chimney-pots and vases was added.

SHARPE BROS. & CO.,

Established 1821.]   MANUFACTURERS OF THE   [Established 1821.

DERBYSHIRE IRONSTONE, CANE WARE, ROCKINGHAM, BUFF, AND BLACK LUSTRE, &c.

FOR HOME AND FOREIGN MARKETS.

SWADLINCOTE POTTERIES, Near BURTON-ON-TRENT.

LIST OF PRICES FREE ON APPLICATION.

MANDARIN.

SWADLINCOTE

After that, marble, white, and cane-coloured sanitary earthenware was introduced. Majolica and Rockingham ware were also at one time made. The mark was the anchor, with a portion of cable twisted round it, forming a monogram of J.W. From about 1888, the firm continued as Woodward & Rowley and produced only sanitary ware.

Ault Faience William Ault (born in 1841) established his pottery at Swadlincote in 1887. He had previously worked in the Staffordshire potteries, and with Henry Tooth at the Bretby Pottery. Many interesting glaze effects and impasto paintings were produced by William Ault, whose two daughters – Clarissa and Gertrude – assisted him. The Ault ware was very popular during the 1890s and early part of the twentieth century. Several forms were designed by Christopher Dresser. The mark at this period was a tall vase-shaped vessel with the name Ault on a ribbon below. The firm today is Ault Potteries Limited.

Swadlincote Mills Established by Messrs. Cartwright in about 1837 and carried on by Edward Grice, who produced all the usual sanitary and terra-cotta goods of the district.

The Waterloo Pottery Established in 1815 by Robinson & Rowley, and subsequently worked by Mr. Robinson alone, James Staley, Staley Brothers, and Mason & Adcock. Mr. Adcock died in 1879, and in 1880 Mr. Mason removed

Plate 108. A selection of Ault pottery, reproduced from a *Pottery Gazette* advertisement of 1898.

to the Pool Pottery. Mr. R. C. Staley, one of the former proprietors, carried on the manufactory and produced the usual descriptions of Derbyshire cane ware, yellow Ironstone, and buff, Rockingham, and mottled ware to about 1891.

Old Midway Pottery Established by a Mr. Granger, these works passed from him to Richard Staley, senior, and were carried on under the style of Richard Staley & Sons for the production of Derbyshire fireproof cane ware, Rockingham ware and buff ware, in which all the usual domestic and other articles were made. The mark is the name, often with 'Fireproof' added. This concern continued into the twentieth century.

J. C. Staton & Co. and James Toft also had small potteries at Swadlincote late in the nineteenth century.

SWANSEA

Cambrian Pottery In the middle of the eighteenth century, a small manufactory of earthenware belonging to William Coles – who afterwards took into partnership George Haynes – appears to have existed at Swansea. The buildings were originally copper-works, and were converted into a pottery. In February 1783, the works were offered for sale and were described as 'a very capital Set of Works, well calculated for the Pottery, Glass, or any other Business, wherein well constructed Cones are necessary' . . . as having 'been built within these few Years, and have been employed in a very extensive Pottery and Earthenware Manufacture'; . . . that 'There are two excellent Water Mills included in the Premises for grinding the Flints', and that 'Teignmouth Clay is to be had delivered at the works at 12s per ton, and Flints for 20s'.

[1]For illustrations of the varied products of the Swansea potteries, and their detailed histories, the reader is referred to E. M. Nance's monumental work *The Pottery and Porcelain of Swansea and Nantgarw* (Batsford, London, 1942).

The pottery was continued by Messrs. Coles & Haynes until 1800, when John Coles died and George Haynes continued under the style Geo. Haynes & Co. By him, the works were much enlarged and called the Cambrian Pottery. In 1800, according to Dr. Donovan, the works, then carried on by G. Haynes & Co., of which he gives an extended account, were extensive, and producing ware of a superior class, the buildings being said to be arranged on the same plan as those of Josiah Wedgwood at Etruria. In June 1802, Haynes sold his works, moulds, models and stock to Lewis Weston Dillwyn, and by him the buildings were very greatly enlarged and the business considerably extended. Haynes was retained as manager.

At first, only the ordinary descriptions of earthenware were made; but the manufacture was greatly improved by George Haynes, who produced a refined cream-coloured ware, an 'opaque china' and other varieties, as well as a very good kind of biscuit ware.

Upon the works passing into the hands of Mr. Dillwyn in 1802, the opaque china was much improved and the decorations assumed a more artistic character. The principal painter was William Young, who was particularly skilful in painting flowers but more especially natural history subjects – birds, butterflies and other insects, and shells on earthenware. These he drew from nature, and was remarkably truthful and free in his delineations. Young had his own muffle kiln and decorated on his own account. He afterwards became one of the proprietors of the Nantgarw China Works. Pieces decorated with his painting are of rare occurrence, especially those having his name, YOUNG PINXIT or YOUNG f. In the Victoria and Albert Museum are some interesting examples of this 'opaque china' or 'opaque porcelain'. The decorations consisted – we are told by Dr. Donovan in 1800 – of 'emblematical designs, landscapes, fruit, flowers, heraldic figures, or any other species of ornamental devices' – so several artists must have been employed at that time.

From 1811 to 1817, the firm traded as Dillwyn & Co.

Plate 109. An impressed marked 'Dillwyn & Co.'
Swansea earthenware plate with lustre decoration.
The basic shape of plate was made at several
potteries.   *Mr. & Mrs. Breeze.*

In 1814, Mr. Dillwyn received a communication from Sir Joseph Banks that a specimen of
china had been submitted to the government
from Nantgarw, and he was requested to examine and report on those works. This matter
is thus spoken of by Mr. Dillwyn himself: 'My
friend Sir Joseph Banks informed me that two
persons, named Walker and Beeley (alias Billingsley) had sent to Government from a small
manufactory at Nantgarw (ten or twelve miles
north of Cardiff) a specimen of beautiful china,
with a petition for their patronage; and that,
as one of the Board of Trade, he requested me to
examine and report upon the manufactory.
Upon witnessing the firing of a kiln at Nantgarw,
I found much reason for considering that the
body used was too nearly allied to glass to bear

the necessary heat, and observed that nine-
tenths of the articles were either shivered or
more or less injured in shape by the firing. The
parties, however, succeeded in making me
believe that the defects in their porcelain
arose entirely from imperfections in their small
trial kiln; and I agreed with them for a removal
to the Cambrian Pottery, at which two new
kilns, under their direction, were prepared.
While endeavouring to strengthen and improve
this beautiful body, I was surprised at receiving
a notice from Messrs. Flight & Barr[1] of Worcester, charging the parties calling themselves
Walker and Beeley with having clandestinely
left an engagement at their works, and forbid-
ding me to employ them.'

In 1814, then, William Billingsley and Samuel
Walker commenced for Mr. Dillwyn at the

[1] This should be Messrs. Flight, Barr & Barr. The
Flight & Barr period was from 1792 to 1807.

Cambrian Pottery the manufacture of china of the same body and glaze as they had produced at Nantgarw. For this purpose, some new buildings and kilns were erected on a place that had previously been a bathing-place, and the utmost secrecy was observed. Mr. Dillwyn – or, rather, Billingsley and Walker for him – succeeded in producing a beautiful china; but the loss of time in building and altering the kilns, and the losses and disappointments attending numerous experiments and trials, prevented it being made to more than a limited extent. Soon after the receipt of Flight & Barr's letter, Mr. Dillwyn dismissed Billingsley and Walker (who returned to Nantgarw) and continued the manufacture of china, but of a somewhat different body. In about 1817, the manufacture was discontinued by Mr. Dillwyn and for a time carried on by Mr. Bevington.

The Cambrian Pottery passed successively from Mr. Lewis Weston Dillwyn to T. & J. Bevington & Co. (1817–21) and then to T. & J. Bevington (1821–4), and back again, ultimately, to L. W. Dillwyn (1824–36) and then to his son, Lewis Lewellyn Dillwyn – by whom, in 1840, negotiations were entered into with Mr. Brameld of the Rockingham Works for the letting of the Glamorgan Pottery to the latter firm for the purpose of manufacturing china ware. The negotiations, however, fell through.

In about 1847, Mr. Dillwyn commenced the manufacture of imitations of Etruscan vases. This ware, which was called 'Dillwyn's Etruscan Ware', was a fine rich red body. On this was printed, in black outline, Etruscan figures and borders. The general surface was then painted over and up to the outlines with a fine black, leaving the figures of the original red of the body. The effect was extremely good, and some remarkably fine examples were made. A handled comport-bowl is engraved above with the standard mark.

The forms were all taken either from vases in the British Museum or from Sir William Hamilton's *Antiquités Etrusques, Grecques, et Romaines* (1766–7). But little was produced, as it was not a ware to command a ready sale. It was made from clay found in the neighbourhood, which, when not too highly fired, burned to a good red colour. Productions of these patterns ceased in about 1850.

In about 1851, Mr. Dillwyn retired from the concern and it passed into the hands of David Evans, who carried it on under the style of Evans & Glasson or Evans, Glasson & Evans (1850–62). Subsequently, it became D. J. Evans & Co. (1862–70).

The manufacture consisted of the ordinary classes of white, blue and white, and agate earthenware, the markets being principally Wales, Ireland, West of England and Chile. At about the end of 1869, earthenware was rather suddenly discontinued at the Cambrian Pottery, and the bulk of the work-people were discharged, the site having become more valuable for other commercial purposes. The engraved copper-plates were sold to the South Wales Pottery, Llanelly.

Among the artists at one time or other employed at Swansea – besides Young, of whom I have already spoken – were Pardoe, an excellent flower-painter (afterwards of the Nantgarw Works); Baxter, a clever figure-painter, who came to these works from Worcester, to which place he afterwards returned; Bevington, a flower-painter also from Worcester; Reed, a modeller of considerable repute; Wood, also a clever modeller; Morris, a flower and fruit-painter; Colclough, a painter of birds; David Evans who was a talented wild-flower painter;

and Beddow, who was a heraldic and landscape painter. To these, of course, must be added Billingsley, who was the best flower-painter of the day.

The principal marks used at these works appear to have been the following:

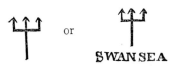

Cambrian Pottery.   CAMBRIAN POTTERY.

Various pottery marks incorporate the words CAMBRIAN POTTERY. On the porcelain made by Billingsley and Walker for Mr Dillwyn, the mark appears to have simply been the name SWANSEA printed in red; or the name sometimes occurs simply impressed. Sometimes, DILLWYN & CO. appears impressed in the body of the ware; all other times, SWANSEA with the addition of a tirdent 'which', Mr. Dillwyn says, 'denotes a supposed improvement which was not ultimately found to answer'.

SWANSEA   SWANSEA

or

SWANSEA

Other marks are:

DILLWYN &   DILLWYN & CO
COMPANY   CAMBRIAN POTTERY
OPAQUE CHINA
SWANSEA   HAYNES, DILLWYN &
                   CO. CAMBRAIN
                   POTTERY SWANSEA.

For further information on Swansea ware, and illustrations, see W. D. John's *Swansea Porcelain* (Ceramic Book Company, 1957) and E. M. Nance's *The Pottery and Porcelain of Swansea and Nantgarw* (Batsford, London, 1942).

The Glamorgan Pottery Situated to the west of the Cambrian Pottery, on the opposite side of the road leading to the North Dock Bridge. In extent, it was about two-thirds of the Cambrian; and it produced similar ware. It was discontinued in about 1840. The kilns were taken down, and part of the building was converted into iron warehouses. It was built in about 1814 by a Mr. Baker, who was soon after joined in partnership by Mr. Bevan and Mr. Irwin. The business was carried on under the style of Baker, Bevans & Irwin until 1839, when it seems to have been purchased by Mr. Dillwyn, who in the following year offered it unsuccessfully to Messrs. Brameld of the Rockingham China Works. Mr. Baker also at one time held another small pottery for a finer kind of earthenware, near the River Tawe, in another part of Swansea. The plant was transferred to Llanelly.

Various marks incorporate the initials B B & I.

Rickard In Swansea, there was also a small pot-work at Dyvatty Street belonging to Mr. Rickard (formerly belonging to William Mead, in about 1840), who produced black and Rockingham ware, teapots, jugs, and similar articles; also hardware jugs of mixed local clay and Dorset clay (principally for the home markets), ornamental flower-pots and garden-vases. The works closed in about 1892.

Landore Pottery In about 1852, John Forbes Calland, of Swansea district, built a pottery on the Swansea Canal, near the River Tawe at Landore, about a mile from Swansea. This was worked for a few years by Mr. Calland, who produced printed and common earthenware from white clays in dinner, tea and toilet ware for the home trade under the styles (and marks) of:

J. F. CALLAND & CO.,   CALLAND
LANDORE POTTERY.   SWANSEA

CALLAND & CO
LANDORE, SWANSEA

Not being commercially successful, Mr. Calland discontinued the manufacture in about 1856, when the engraved copper-plates were transferred to the South Wales Pottery at Llanelly, and the Landore Pottery ceased to exist.

SWINTON (Yorkshire)

The Rockingham Works In 1778, Thomas Bingley became a principal proprietor of the Swinton works and had for partners, among others, John and William Brameld and a person named Sharpe. Mr. Bingley was a member of a family of that name which had been resident at Swinton for more than four hundred years. The firm, at this time, was carried on under the style of Thomas Bingley & Co. Being thriving – indeed, opulent – people, the works were greatly enlarged and conducted with much spirit. An extensive trade was at this time carried on; and besides the ordinary brown and yellow ware, blue and white dinner, tea, coffee and other services were made, as also a white earthenware of remarkably fine and compact body, and other ware of good quality.

From about 1787 to 1800, the firm – consequent on some of the Greens of the Leeds Pottery having become partners – traded under the style of Greens, Bingley & Co., and John Green became acting-manager of the Swinton works and afterwards founded the Don Pottery. A peculiar kind of brown or Rockingham ware was made.

This Rockingham ware, which was of a fine reddish-brown or chocolate colour, was one of the smoothest and most beautiful types ever produced. The body was of fine hard and compact white earthenware, and the brown glaze – by which the peculiar shaded and streaky effect of this class of goods was produced – was as fine as it is possible to conceive, and required to be 'dipped' and passed through the firing process no fewer than three time before it arrived at perfection. In this ware, tea, coffee and chocolate services, jugs, drinking-cups and such like were produced and continued to be made to the close of the works in 1842.

Plate 110. A Rockingham-glazed coffee-pot of the type made at this Yorkshire factory. But the glaze effect was copied by many other firms and the name is still used today, although the colour is darker than the original. c.1820. 6 inches high.
Godden of Worthing Ltd.

After that time, similar 'Rockingham ware' – in every instance falling far short of the original in beauty and in excellence – was made by almost every manufacturer in the kingdom and always, especially for tea and coffee pots, met a ready and extensive sale.

One special article produced in this ware was the curious coffee or tea pot which is usually known to collectors as the 'Cadogan pot' (see Plate 14). It was constructed with a small opening in the bottom, to admit the liquid, but none at the top and no separate lid. From the hole in the bottom, a tube – slightly spiral – was made to pass up inside the vessel to within half an inch of the top so that, after filling, on the pot being turned over into its proper position for table use the liquid was kept in without chance of spilling.

In 1806, the firm of Greens, Bingley & Co. was dissolved. At this time, as appears from a memorandum of resolutions passed at a meeting held on 22nd January 1806, preparatory to the dissolution the partners (present)

231

were 'William Hartley for himself, and others (this was William Hartley, principal proprietor of the Leeds Pottery), Ebenezer Green for himself and others (this was another of the partners in the Leeds Pottery), George Hanson, Thomas Bingley, John Brameld, and William Brameld'. At this dissolution, the concern fell into the hands of John and William Brameld who, with partners, continued the works as Brameld & Co. until their death. The old price-lists continued to be used but had 'Greens, Bingley' erased with the pen and 'Brameld' substituted, so that the heading commenced 'Brameld & Co., Swinton Pottery'. They were later on joined in partnership by younger members of the family, who eventually became proprietors of the manufactory.

By John and William Brameld, by whom additional buildings were erected, cream-coloured ware was made very extensively; and a remarkably fine white earthenware – 'chalk-body', as it was technically called – was successfully produced. But owing to its costliness through loss in firing, this body was made only to a small extent.

In about 1813, the sons – Thomas Brameld, George Frederick Brameld, and John Wager Brameld – succeeded to the concern of the old proprietors, and to them the great after-success of the works was due. They considerably enlarged the manufactory, made many improvements in the ware, and erected a flint mill on the premises. Thomas Brameld, the eldest of the partners, a man of taste, laboured hard to raise the character of the productions of the Swinton Works to a high standard of excellence, and he succeeded to an eminent degree. In 1820, he turned his attention to the production of china ware, and made many experiments in bodies and glazes. Having expended large sums of money in the prosecution of this his favourite project, and in making art-advances in his manufactory, the firm became slightly embarrassed, which was increased by great losses sustained through the war.

In 1825, a year of great commercial difficulties, the firm succumbed to the embarrassments that had affected it. At a meeting with its creditors, etc., held at Rotherham, Thomas Brameld produced some remarkable examples of his china ware, the result of long and patient labour on his part. These being highly approved by all who were present, and appearing likely to succeed, Earl Fitzwilliam, the owner of the property at Swinton, agreed to assist in the prosecution of the work by the advance of capital and by taking an active part in the scheme.

This being done, Mr. Brameld set himself to his task with renewed spirit and with a determination to make his porcelain at least equal to any which could then be produced. In this, he certainly succeeded. The works were altered and enlarged; modellers and painters – the most skilful that could be procured – were employed; and every means taken to ensure the success, artistically and manipulatively, which quickly followed. In this porcelain, dinner, dessert, breakfast and tea services, vases, groups of figures and flowers, and numberless articles, both of utility and ornament, were produced. They were characterised by pure taste and an excellence of design and workmanship which told much for the skill and judgment of the mind that governed the whole of the manufactory.

George Frederick Brameld, the second of the partners, devoted himself to the strictly commercial part of the business on the Continent. He resided for some time at St. Petersburg, a large trade with Russia being carried on by the firm.

John Wager Brameld, like his eldest brother, was a man of pure taste. He was an excellent artist, and some exquisite paintings on porcelain by him have come under my notice. He was a clever painter of flowers and of figures and landscapes. In flowers, Mr. Brameld went to Nature herself, collecting specimens wherever he went and reproducing their beauties on the choice ware of the works.

Earthenware of various kinds – 'Brown China' or 'Rockingham Ware', green-glazed biscuit figures and ornaments, hard fine white stoneware, cream-coloured ware – and other varieties of goods were also still made; and the works, which at this time (c.1826) assumed the name

Plate 111. A fine marked Rockingham porcelain
tray painted by Thomas Steel, c.1830.
Godden of Worthing Ltd. (Rotherham Museum Coll.)

Rockingham Works, began to use the crest of
the Fitzwilliam family as the mark of the firm.

In 1826, on November 17th, Messrs. Brameld
& Co. secured the services of Mr. John Cresswell, painter on china, and articles of agreement
were drawn up by which Cresswell engaged
himself to them for five years at 7s. 6d. a day for
the first three years; 9s. 3d. a day for the fourth
year; and 10s. 6d. a day for the fifth year.

In 1830, the firm received orders for services
from the Duchess of Cumberland, the Duke of
Sussex, and others of the Royal Family. Also
in 1830, the Rockingham Works received an
order for a splendid dessert service for King
William IV, which was executed in the most
ornate style and gave intense satisfaction. The
original sketches for this service are named
'Original Designs for His Majesty's Dessert,

12th Nov., 1830, per J. W. B.' (John Wager
Brameld). They are pen-and-ink sketches by
Brameld himself. At this time, the works assumed the name of Royal Rockingham Works,
and the proprietors called themselves China
Manufacturers and Potters to the King, Queen,
and the Royal Family.

In 1838, the manufacture of china and earthenware bed-posts and cornices was added to the
other productions of the Rockingham Works.
In that year, a patent was taken out in the name
of William Dale for 'certain improvements in
constructing columns, pillars, bed-posts, and
other such-like articles', 'consisting of several
ornamental pieces or compound parts of china
or earthenware', 'united, strengthened and supported by a shaft or rod passing through the
whole length of the same, and furnished with
screw nuts or other description of fastenings,
and collars', etc. These bed-posts and other
similar things were made at the Rockingham

233

Plate 112. A four-poster bed, the two front columns being made of sections of Rockingham earthenware, c.1838–42.   *Godden of Worthing Ltd.*

noble owner but also the absolute proprietors in a loss of very many thousands of pounds. Only sixteen years had elapsed since the introduction of the china manufacture to the works, but those had been sixteen years of beauty and of artistic and manipulative success. No man better understood his art than Thomas Brameld; no man laboured harder and more disinterestedly in the ennobling of that art than he did; and few men, either before his time or since, succeeded in accomplishing greater or more honourable things.

Thomas Brameld, who resided at Swinton House, Swinton, died in 1850; John Wager Brameld died in 1851; and George Frederick Brameld died in 1853.

At the close of the works in 1842, the stock was sold off and dispersed, and the manufactory was discontinued. A small portion of the building was, however, taken by an old and experienced workman, Isaac Baguley (formerly employed at the Derby China Works), who was one of Brameld's best painters and gilders. Here he commenced business in a small way on his own account, and so continued until his death in about 1855. Mr. Baguley did not manufacture the ware himself, but purchased what he required in the white state from other makers and then painted, gilt, and otherwise ornamented them for sale. At his death, his son, Alfred Baguley, succeeded him and for a few years (until 1865) carried on this decorative branch of the business at the old premises. Mr. Baguley decorated earthenware and porcelain with commendable taste, and produced some extremely good and effective designs. One of his specialities was the old Rockingham-glaze ware, which he produced of a far purer and better quality than any other house. To this branch he paid particular attention, and produced the Rockingham chocolate or brown glaze on a china body. In this Rockingham china, breakfast and tea services, tea and coffee pots of the good old designs, drinking-horns and jugs were made, and, being gilt in the same manner as the old Rockingham ware, had a remarkably pleasing appearance, while in touch they were all that could be desired. He also made the famous old

Works, though never to any extent. They are now of very great rarity. An example is reproduced in Plate 112.

Another of these interesting examples is white, with an effective chintz pattern in colours. Others have small groups and sprigs of flowers, the outline in transfer printing and filled in with colour. An elegant work-table of this description of ware, of simple but effective design and excellent workmanship, was in the possession of Mr. Wilson of Sheffield. It was 2 feet 6 inches high, and 1 foot 6 inches in diameter at the top. Among the designs to which I have alluded was one representing a small and remarkably elegant table, of somewhat similar but much more ornate character, on which was a fish-globe stand of corresponding design.

Although the Rockingham Works were eminently successful from an artistic point of view, they were not so commercially. In 1842, they were closed, after involving not only their

'Bishopthorpe' and 'Wentworth' jugs. His mark was similar to that of the old works – the griffin crest of Earl Fitzwilliam with the name:

Baguley
Rockingham Works.

In 1852, a small portion of the works was tenanted by some earthenware manufacturers who traded as P. Hobson & Son, but their occupation was of only short duration.

The 'brown china' or 'Rockingham ware' services made at these works before 1842, though not all marked, usually bore the impressed words ROCKINGHAM, BRAMELD or BRAMELD & Co., or the name MORTLOCK.

In fine hard white stoneware and in fine cane-coloured ware, jugs of remarkably good design were made and were decorated with groups in relief in the same manner as – indeed, strongly resembling, both in body and in design – those

Plate 113. A marked 'Brameld' earthenware bowl with white relief motifs – a tasteful Rockingham essay in the Wedgwood-style. c.1820.
Godden of Worthing Ltd.

of Turner, which are so well-known to collectors. An attractive marked Brameld bowl is shown in Plate 113. Some noteworthy jugs have their handles formed of the leg and tail of a horse.

In green-glazed earthenware, dessert services, flower vases, garden seats and all the usual varieties of articles were made. The green, as a rule, was a somewhat lighter colour and not so good in quality as Wedgwood's. The pieces were generally marked with the usual impressed mark – BRAMELD.

In fine earthenware, services of every kind were produced – white, blue-printed, painted and gilt. The glaze on the earlier pieces, it should be remarked, was of a decided blue tint and somewhat inferior in quality. Some of the dessert services produced in the early part of the nineteenth century were particularly interesting. On each piece was painted some flower, as large as life and coloured true to nature in every particular.

There was in the Brameld family's possession a service of this same kind in which the flowers were beautifully painted by Collinson, the best flower-painter at the Swinton Works, and it was made between 1810 and 1815. The ware is particularly light and has a remarkably pleasant feeling in handling.

I have been somewhat particular in speaking of this variety of goods, because similar services were produced far more extensively at the Don Works, at Swansea, and at other places.

At Wentworth House, the Earl and Countess Fitzwilliam had, along with a large number of choice examples of Chelsea, Chelsea-Derby, etc., several other notable pieces of Rockingham china. Among these were a set of three Canova-shape vases, painted with groups of flowers; a dessert-service of white and gold seaweed pattern, each piece bearing the crest and the date 1838; three of the pattern-plates submitted to William IV in competition for the royal service; a number of sample plates of different designs; a breakfast service painted in flowers, each flower named; an elegant tray with raised flowers and a view of Arundel Castle; a pair of monkey beakers (vases with knobs in the form of a monkey), nineteen inches high; and a pair of fine biscuit scent bottles, sixteen inches high, decorated with exquisite raised flowers.

The chef-d'oeuvre of the Rockingham China Works was the gorgeous dessert service made for William IV, which is still preserved at Buckingham Palace. This service, which cost no less a sum than £5,000, consists of one hundred and forty-four plates and fifty-six large pieces, and is one of the finest produced in this or any other country. The plates have raised oak borders in dead and burnished gold running over a raised laced pattern, also in gold, and the centres are splendidly painted with the royal arms. The comports, which were all designed by Thomas Brameld, are emblematical of the use to which each piece has to be put. For instance, the comports for biscuits are supported by ears of wheat; the fruit pieces have central open-work baskets of fruit; the ice pails are supported by holly berries and leaves; and in each case the landscapes are also in unison with the uses of the pieces, which are of exquisite design, and have also oak leaf and lace decorations, so massively gilt in dead and burnished gold as to have the appearance of ormolu laid on the porcelain; and each piece is decorated with views of different seats – the sketches for which

were taken expressly for the purpose – and by groups of figures, etc.

There was in a Mrs. Reed's possession a unique example, being one of the specimen plates submitted for royal approval in a competition with the principal china manufacturers of the kingdom for the royal order. In this competition, twelve plates of different patterns were specially prepared and submitted by the Rockingham Works. In the centre of the one referred to are the royal arms, and the rim is decorated with oak-leaves and acorns. Another unique pattern-plate which belonged to the Brameld family is of the most delicate and exquisitely beautiful character. In the centre are the royal arms and on the rim are three compartments, two of which contain groups of flowers and the third a view, while between these the 'garter' is repeated. The cost at which, in the estimate, it was calculated these plates could be produced was twelve guineas each. The dessert service made for William IV was first used on the occasion of the coronation of Queen Victoria, and has only since been used on very special state occasions.

In biscuit, figures, busts, and groups as well as vases (of which splendid examples belonged to Earl Fitzwilliam) were produced. Among other specimens that have come under my notice are a Swiss boy and girl, a fine bust of Earl Fitzwilliam, Chantrey's 'Sleeping Child' and Chantrey's full-length statue of Lady Russell.

Among the artists employed at the Rockingham works were Collinson, who painted flowers; Llandig, who was a charming fruit and flower painter; Bailey, who was the principal butterfly painter, and who also painted landscapes and crests (landscapes and views formed an important branch of decoration on Rockingham porcelain); Speight, father and son – the latter of whom painted many of the finest subjects, both landscapes and figures, on the royal service, and who also painted the heraldic decorations on the same; Brentnall, who was a clever flower painter; Corden, who executed landscapes and figures; Thomas Steel, a famous flower and fruit painter (see Plate 111); Tilbury, who painted landscapes and figures; Mansfield, who was the principal embosser and chaser in gold; Aston, who was clever as a modeller of flowers; and Cowen, who was an artist of much repute, and who for many years enjoyed the patronage of the Fitzwilliam family. William Eley, too, was employed as modeller, and he executed some admirable works, including the bust of Earl Fitzwilliam.

Marks were seldom used on the early productions of these works. They are, therefore, only to be ascertained by a knowledge of the body, the glaze, and the style of ornamentation used. The following are the marks which have come under my notice:

Rockingham

This rare incised mark occurs on one of the famous 'Brown China' high-shaped teapots of which I have spoken. ROCKINGHAM occurs in capital letters, impressed in the body of the ware. These occur on early examples of 'Rockingham ware'. The retailer's name MORTLOCK also occurs on examples of this ware. BRAMELD in capital letters, impressed, occurs on green-glazed ware, etc. Brameld or BRAMELD & Co. also in small capital letters, impressed. The Brameld marks are of the period 1806–25. Various numbers, or crosses, occur after 'Brameld'.

An embossed mark in an oval, stuck on the ware, from which it generally differs in colour, being usually in blue.

ROCKINGHAM
WORKS
BRAMELD

in small capitals, in three lines, impressed. This mark occurs on biscuit figures, etc., with or without the griffin crest.

This griffin mark, the crest of the Earl Fitzwilliam, was adopted in about 1826 on the commencement of the manufacture of china under the assistance of that nobleman. It was at first printed in red. From 1830, 'Manufacturers to the King' occurs on these griffin marks, also the word 'Royal'. These later forms of marks are printed in purple.

Three recent reference books give reliable further information on Rockingham ware and feature illustrations of typical ware. They are: *The Rockingham Pottery* by A. A. Eaglestone & T. A. Lockett (Rotherham Museum, 1964), *Rockingham Ornamental Porcelain*, by D. G. Rice (Adam Publishing Co., 1965) and the *Illustrated Guide to Rockingham Porcelain* by D. G. Rice (Barrie & Jenkins, London, 1971).

The Don Pottery Closely adjoining the canal at Swinton, on which it had a wharf, this pottery was established in a very small way in about 1790. It was considerably increased in 1800 by John Green of Newhill. He was one of the Greens of Leeds, of the same family as the proprietors of the Leeds Pottery and a proprietor of the Swinton Pottery, who, in about 1800, purchased a plot of land at Swinton and, with the aid of partners, set about the erection of the new works. At this time, a person named Newton had an enamel kiln at the back of his house at Swinton, where he used to burn such ware as he decorated. To this man, for the first twelve months, Green of the Don Pottery brought his pattern pieces to be fired as he prepared them.

In 1807, other members of the family united with John Green, who also had partners named Clarke, the firm trading as Greens, Clarke & Co. In 1831, Mr. Green was proprietor of the Don Pottery. In 1834, the Don Pottery passed by purchase to Samuel Barker, of the Mexborough Old Pottery, which latter works he closed in 1844 and confined his operations entirely to the Don manufactory. In 1851, the firm became Samuel

Barker & Son, under which style it continued until 1882, when the surviving proprietor, Edward Barker, retired from the business, which he transferred in November of that year to his successors, Messrs. E. T. Smith, J. Adamson, J. Wilkinson and C. Scorah, who continued it under the old style of Samuel Barker & Son. As such, it continued until 1893.

Of the ordinary fine earthenware made soon after the opening of the works, some specimens, whose actual date can be satisfactorily ascertained, have come under my notice and show to what perfection in body and glaze, in manipulation, and in decoration the manufacture had already arrived. The most remarkable of these early specimens is a jug, commonly called the 'Jumper Jug'. On either side is the figure of a very uncouth, coarse, and slovenly-looking man in red coat, pink waistcoat, striped green and white under-waistcoat, orange neckerchief, orange breeches above which his shirt is seen, top-boots, and spurs. In his hand, he holds his hat – orange, with red ribands – on which is a card bearing the words 'Milton for ever'. They are marked 'Don Pottery', pencilled in red on the bottom.

An engraved pattern-book was issued by the firm, in the same style and of the same size as that of Hartley, Greens & Co. of the Leeds Pottery. A careful comparison of the two books reveals the fact that wheras in the latest edition of that of Leeds two hundred and sixty-nine patterns were engraved, in that of the Don Pottery two hundred and ninety-two were given. It also reveals the important fact that many of the Don patterns were identical with those of Leeds – the engraver of the former having evidently traced from those of the latter (Leeds) in preparing his plates. Many of the remaining patterns were slightly altered from Leeds, while others do not appear in the book of those works at all. In this pattern-book, Figures 1 to 8 are covered tureens; 10 to 12 are leaves; 13 to 18, covered vegetable dishes; 19 to 23, sauce-tureens with covers, stands, and ladles; 24, a two-handled drinking cup; 26 to 30, butter boats; 31 to 49, dishes and plates, etc.; 50 to 69, fruit bowls, side dishes, etc.; 70 to 76, perforated, open-work, and embossed baskets and stands, some of which have covers and are precisely of the same kind as those of the Leeds works; 78, also perforated and embossed; 79 to 83, perforated dishes and plates; 84 to 91, covered sugar-bowls, etc.; 111, a melon bowl of the same kind as those made at Leeds; 113 to 116, egg-cups and stands; 118 to 130, cruets, etc.; 131, an asparagus-holder, like the Leeds; 139 to 145, mugs and jugs; 146, a toast-rack; 147, an invalid's feeding-cup; 148 to 159, dishes, tureens, etc; 160 and 161, vegetable trays in compartments; 163 to 176, ice pails and domestic vessels; 177 to 183, inkstands; 184 and 185, flower-pots; 186 to 202, toilet services and shaving basins; 201, a scaphium; 206, a quintal flower-horn; 207, a pastille-burner. And then come candlesticks, egg-cups, flower-vases, flower-stands, vases, crosses with cup for holy water, etc. Another series of plates, the figures numbered from 1 to 54 and from A to K, are devoted to tea equipages, consisting of a remarkable and very striking variety of teapots,

Fig. 50. Selection of Don pottery.

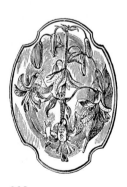

coffee-pots, milk-jugs, sugar-bowls, cake-trays, tea-canisters, basins or bowls, tea, coffee, and chocolate cups and saucers. On each plate throughout the series, the name 'Don Pottery' is engraved in a scroll.

Open-work baskets, tureens, twig baskets, in which the 'withies' were of precisely the same form as those of Leeds and Wedgwood, perforated plates, dishes, tureens, spoons, ladles, and other articles, ice-pails, salt-cellars, flower-vases, cruets and stands, inkstands, seals, bird-fountains, smelling-bottles and, indeed, every variety of articles, as well as services of all descriptions, and ornamental vases of several designs, were made in this ware, and such as were adapted for the colour were made in green-glazed ware. Of teapots, many patterns with raised groups, trophies, etc., and others for loose metal 'kettle-handles' are also engraved.

In cream-coloured ware, and also in the fine white earthenware, excellent dessert and other services were made, and were painted with flowers, with a truth to nature which has seldom been equalled.

From about 1810 to 1812, porcelain of an excellent quality was, to a very small extent indeed, made at the Don Pottery, and examples of this are of extreme rarity. In Mr. Manning's possession was a coffee-mug marked 'Don Pottery' in red. This interesting specimen is the only marked one which has come under my notice.

In fine cane-coloured ware, tea-services, jugs, etc., were made, and were ornamented with figures, borders and other designs in relief. Of this kind of ware, the sugar-box shown in Figure 50 serves as an example. It is ornamented with figures, trophies in black relief, and is marked 'Greens Don Pottery'. In green-glazed ware, flower-vases of large size, root-pots, dessert and other services; in red-ware, scent jars of bold and good design, large-sized mignonette vases, and many other articles; and in Egyptian black, teapots, cream ewers and jugs were made.

The marks adopted by these works have been but few, and only very occasionally used. They are, so far as I have been able to ascertain, as follows: 'Don Pottery' painted in red on the bottom of the vessel, or DON POTTERY GREEN impressed on the bottom of the pieces. Also DON POTTERY impressed.

The first of the crest marks shown below was impressed; the second example was printed and transferred on the ware. It was the first mark used by Samuel Barker, and was adopted by him on purchasing the Don Pottery on its discontinuance by the Greens.

Samuel Barker (& Son), from about 1834 to 1889, produced all the usual varieties of ordinary earthenware to a large extent, the works giving employment to between two and three hundred hands. In toilet services, many excellent patterns were produced, enamelled, gilt, and lustred as the dinner, tea, dessert and other services, and all the usual varieties of goods for home and foreign consumption.

Messrs. Barker's mark from about 1850 onwards was an eagle displayed rising out of a ducal coronet, and was adopted by the firm when it became Samuel Barker & Son, at which

SB&S.

time the old mark was discontinued. The eagle displayed was only used for a short time, the firm having adopted the old mark of the demi-lion rampant holding in his paws the pennon, enclosed within a garter, beneath which are the initials of the firm, S.B. & S. On the ribbon of the garter is usually given the name of the pattern.

TAMWORTH (Staffordshire)

The Terra-Cotta Works Established at Tamworth by Gibbs & Canning in 1847, these works produced architectural, horticultural and other useful and ornamental goods; Della Robbia ware, sanitary goods, tiles and bricks, etc. In terra-cotta, for architectural purposes, were made trusses and cornices, bosses and paterae, brackets and corbels, capitals and bases, balustrades and parapets, window and door-heads, terminals and finials, diaper work and every other detail, of a quality for sharpness, hardness and durability scarcely to be surpassed. Among ornamental goods, fountains, vases, tazzas, pedestals, garden-seats, brackets, figures and groups, and every variety of articles for the lawn, the garden, and the conservatory. The Della Robbia ware – a fine terra-cotta effectively enamelled in brilliant and flat colours on the surface – was produced in endless variety in plaques, etc., for ceilings and walls, garden and flower-vases, jardinières, mignonette-boxes and other articles.

TORQUAY (Devon)

Watcombe Pottery The works at Watcombe, about two miles from Torquay, in Devonshire, were established in 1869 and owe their origin to the discovery by G. T. Allen of a bed of the finest plastic clay of considerable extent and depth. This discovery was made while excavating behind his residence, and Mr. Allen took immediate steps to have its qualities tested for ceramic purposes.

A company was immediately formed for the getting and sale of the terra-cotta clay to various potters; but after experiments had been made, and its unique beauty discovered, it was wisely resolved to erect a pottery on the spot and convert the clay immediately from the pits into art-manufactures and architectural enrichments. Shortly afterwards, the company was fortunate enough to secure the services of Charles Brock, of Hanley in Staffordshire – a gentleman of the most enlightened taste, and of the most extensive practical knowledge – to

become the manager and art-director of the concern. Mr. Brock at once turned his attention to the development of the resources of the clay thus discovered; and having brought together a number of skilled workmen and workwomen from the Staffordshire potteries, and procured the best possible models and modellers, soon produced art-works which were unequalled in works of this character and material. In the 1870s, about one hundred persons were employed at the Watcombe works.

The Watcombe clay was remarkably fine, clean and pure, and it was eminently adaptable for most decorative purposes. Many of the borders and pressed ornaments have almost the sharpness of those made of Wedgwood's jasper body. Indeed, many of the productions bear a very strong and marked resemblance to those of jasper ware; and they are superior in many respects to the much vaunted terra-cotta of France and Germany.

The art productions of the Watcombe pottery were extremely varied. Among the more notable productions were statuettes and busts, for which the clay was peculiarly suitable. Of these, the figure of 'The Disc Thrower' was one of the most successful; and among other statuettes was a sweetly pretty figure of a barefooted country girl. In some, a charming effect was produced by leaving the figure itself of the natural red of the body and introducing a lighter tinted clay for the drapery in which it is partly enveloped – this, again, being lighted up and relieved here and there with a touch of colour.

Among the busts were a pair of Byron and Scott, of full life-size, being about two feet six inches in height, and two feet in width. In modelling, these busts were among the most easy, graceful and life-like we had ever seen, whether in marble, in Parian, or in any other material, while as productions in warm-tinted terra-cotta they surpassed anything to that time produced. They were not only life-like portraits of these two great and widely different types of men, as regards features and figure and pose, but they conveyed an actual reflex of the mind of each in the expression which the modeller had caught and perpetuated.

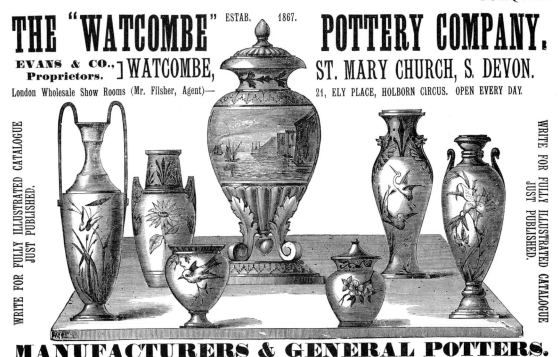

Fig. 51. A Watcombe advertisement of the 1880s.

The vases, which were made in great variety, were characterised by extreme chasteness and elegance of outline and by excellent taste in decoration, whether that decoration consisted in festoons of handsome modelled flowers, in pressed work, in printing, or in painting. Many of them in form and in ornamentation, although of so different a body, bore comparison with the better specimens of Wedgwood-ware, and exhibited a purity of taste which was quite refreshing. For tea or déjeuner services, the insides of the teapots and cream ewers were simply but judiciously glazed; while the cups were, as in some old Oriental examples, lined with celeste, which colour was also occasionally introduced on the handles and mouldings. Brackets of charming design, candlesticks, jugs, medallions, tobacco-jars, spill-cases, flower-stands – and, indeed, all the articles produced – bore the same stamp of care and elegance. The turning was done with admirable precision; the moulding with a refreshing delicacy of finish;

and the gilding and enamelling (only sparsely introduced, by the way, and then only as an accessory to the general design) were executed with a pure taste and by a master mind. Besides these, it is necessary to mention that architectural decorations and enrichments, statues, garden and flower-vases, pedestals, and garden edgings, besides other articles, were made – the commoner strata of clay being remarkably well adapted, from its hardness and durability, for these purposes.

Of the later departures [of the 1880 period] are some that are especially noteworthy. These are vases, water-bottles, and other elegant articles formed of buff or other delicately tinted clay and coated on the surface with a thin covering of other coloured clay. On these, the pattern or design was literally carved, the outline being traced through the coating of darker clay and the surface then entirely cut away down to the lighter body beneath. The pattern was thus left more or less in relief, of a darker tint than the body upon which it appeared. The effect of this

241

process, which was entirely done by hand and the work of skilled artists, was charming in the extreme. Another class of productions was the introduction of painting, in exquisite groups of flower buds, upon glazed vases of elegant form and of different coloured clays, the painting evincing a purity of taste and a delicacy and softness of finish that was eminently refreshing. The introduction of enamel decoration upon the unglazed surface was also accomplished with success. For this type of painted decoration, see the contemporary advertisement reproduced in Figure 51.

The works were carried on by a company under the style of The Watcombe Terra Cotta Clay Company, consisting of seven proprietors. They were situated about two miles from Torquay, on the Teignmouth Road. The marks used by the company were impressed in the body of the ware or printed on its surface. The usual mark is simply 'Watcombe, Torquay' or 'Watcombe'; but another was also adopted – a woodpecker on a branch of a tree, with a distant landscape and a ship on the sea, within a garter on which were the words WATCOMBE, TORQUAY. In 1903, the Watcombe company was combined with the Royal Aller Vale Company.

Terra-Cotta Works The terra-cotta works at Hele Cross, Torquay, were established in 1875 by Dr. Gillow – who that year discovered the bed of clay – and were worked by a limited liability company of which he was chairman and general director. The clay, which was of a remarkably fine, tenacious and durable quality, was of a rich full red colour, and its surface was almost metallic in its hardness and fine texture. It was almost identical in quality and beauty of tone to that of Watcombe, to whose productions those of Torquay bore a marked resemblance.

The company started with the aim of producing works of a high standard of excellence, and thus expressed their intention: 'They [the company] believe that they have at Hele Cross the best deposit of clay yet discovered, and their one aim and object is to improve the artistic standard by persevering energy. One year's

existence has given grounds for hope and encouragement; much has been done, but much more remains to be done. They trust to improve year by year, until they place terra-cotta in its old proud position as a favoured branch of Ceramic Art, and until Devonshire productions stand unrivalled throughout Europe.'

The productions of the Torquay Terra-Cotta Company were statuettes, single figures and groups, busts, groups of animals or birds, vases, ewers, bottles, jugs, and tazzas; butter-coolers, spill-cases and other domestic appliances; plaques of various sizes; candlesticks, toilet-trays, water-bottles and tobacco-vases. Many of these were painted and enamelled in good taste; and the ornamentation, whether in colour or gilding, was characterised by clever workmanship and judicious arrangement. Artists mentioned in a *Pottery Gazette* review of 1878 include Fisher, Birbeck and Miss Levin.

The company supplied not only the home but the foreign markets, and received high recognition. The marks used by the firm were: an oval garter bearing the words TORQUAY TERRA-COTTA CO. and, in the centre, LIMITED, printed on the ware; the name TORQUAY impressed in the clay; the words within a single oval line; and the monogram shown above, which is a combination of the letters T T C for 'Torquay Terra-cotta'. This firm worked into the twentieth century.

Messrs. Ridley & Taylor also made terra-cotta ware at Torquay late in the nineteenth century.

VAUXHALL (London)

The Vauxhall Pottery Carried on towards the close of the eighteenth century by a Mr. Wagstaff, this pottery, on his death in about 1803, passed into the hands of his nephew, John Wisker, who carried it on until his decease in

1838 – he having taken out a patent in 1833 'for certain improvements in machinery or apparatus for grinding covers or stoppers for jars, bottles, and other vessels made of china, stone, or other earthenware', such as are described in the patent of Robert Burton Cooper, taken out in 1831.

On the death of Mr. Wisker, the works were purchased from his executors by Alfred Singer but were discontinued and pulled down, and the site was built over. At these works, Mr. Singer, in conjunction with Henry Pether, manufactured small tiles, or tesserae, for tesselated pavements. In 1839, they took out a patent 'for certain improvements in the preparation and combination of earthenware or porcelain, for the purpose of mosaic or tesselated work', 'by cutting clay or other plastic material into rectilinear figures, by means of intersecting wires stretched in a frame' and 'the forming of ornamental slabs of mosaic work by cementing together small pieces of porcelain or earthenware of various figures and colours, on slabs of slate, stone, or other suitable material'.

There was another pottery at Vauxhall where coarse red or brown ware was made and where also, later on, a fine stoneware was produced.

WARRINGTON (Lancashire)

Warrington Pottery These works, in a locality where older ones had long existed, were established in Dallman Lane in 1850 by John Welsby, who manufactured stoneware, Rockingham and black teapots, coarse red ware, terra-cotta, chimney tops, ornamental garden vases, flower-pots and such like. On his death, in 1863, the works passed into the hands of Thomas Grace who, in 1871, removed them to the Winwick Road.

WATH-UPON-DEARNE (north of Rotherham, Yorkshire)

The Newhill Pottery Established in about 1822 by Joseph Twigg (who up to that time had the management of the Swinton Old Pottery), by whom – in partnership with his sons, John, Benjamin, and Joseph Twigg – it was carried on

until about 1866, when it passed into the hands of Binney & Matthews, who were succeeded by Dibb & Coulter. In 1872, the works were sold to Bedford & Richmond. The goods produced were the ordinary useful classes of earthenware, in which the usual services and articles of everyday use were made in white, printed, sponged and coloured varieties. The works closed in about 1880 and the buildings were converted into cottages.

WEST SMETHWICK, BIRMINGHAM (Warwickshire)

The Ruskin Pottery Established at West Smethwick by Edward & W. Howson Taylor in 1898. Many fine glaze effects and lustres were produced. The standard mark was 'Ruskin Pottery' impressed, with the year of manufacture. The pottery continued to December 1933.

WESTON-SUPER-MARE (Somerset)

The Royal Pottery Established in 1836 by Charles Phillips as a brick and tile manufactory. In the following year, glazed ware for domestic vessels was introduced, as was also, to a small extent, the manufacture of flower-pots and similar articles. In 1840, the production of glazed ware was discontinued; and the clay of the locality being found to be admirably adapted for horticultural vessels, vases and statuary, special attention was directed to them – with such marked effect that, at the Great Exhibition of 1851, medals and certificates of merit were awarded for them.

In 1870, Mr. Phillips retired from the business, which was purchased by John Matthews, by whom it was very considerably extended. Several new branches were added, and a new and better taste was infused into the art decorations. Notable among these introductions were rustic-work, baskets of artificial flowers, busts and vases. Flower-pots, of which from 20,000 to 30,000 were made weekly of all sizes, from $1\frac{3}{4}$ inches to 30 inches in diameter, were a staple production of the Royal Pottery and were supplied to the royal gardens at Windsor Castle,

243

to Kew Gardens, Hampton Court and numerous parks. They had the reputation of being the best, the most compact, and the most durable of any manufacture. Two specialities were the 'Oxford Pot', with perforated rim for training pelagoniums, azaleas, roses, etc., without the aid of sticks, and the 'Alpine-plant pot'.

The more notable ornamental productions were figure, shell and other fountains; figures, and groups of figures; statuettes and busts; eagles, lions and other gigantic figures on artificial rocks and pedestals; flower and other brackets; vases and tazzas, pedestals and garden-seats; fern stands and flower and fern baskets decorated with wicker-work, fern leaves and other ornamentational crocus pots, suspenders for flowers, orchid pots; window-boxes for flowers; arborettes for architectural decorations. The general colour was a delicate red. The greatest achievement in terra-cotta was the production of baskets of flowers – each individual leaf or flower modelled from nature – and vases decorated in the same manner.

The clay from which the various objects were made was the native clay of the place. The first six or eight feet in depth was fine plastic clay, from which the vases, statuary, fern stands, flower baskets and other finer goods were made.

Matthews would seem to have ceased in about 1888. Subsequent directories list only Conway G. Warne, who succeeded John Matthews.

JOHN MATTHEWS,
LATE PHILLIPS,
ROYAL POTTERY,
WESTON-SUPER-MARE.

WHITTINGTON (near Chesterfield, Derbyshire)

The Whittington Potteries Of very old establishment, these works were in existence from about the middle or latter end of the seventeenth century, if not longer. Here, the ordinary brown ware of the period was manufactured, the ware being of extreme hardness and closeness of texture and having a rich warm reddish-brown colour. In about 1800, and for some years later, the works, which were near the race-course, were held by William Bromley who, in addition to the ordinary brown ware, made also a white or cream-coloured earthenware of fine quality. In this fine body, he manufactured dinner, tea and other services, principally decorated, in the prevailing manner, with transfer printing in blue. He also practised bat-printing for some of his goods.

Mr. Bromley also made some experiments in, and succeeded in producing, a very good china ware but did not prosecute this branch of manufacture to any extent. At that time when Mr. Bromley was making the fine earthenware and was experimenting on porcelain bodies, my late father, Arthur Jewitt, then a young man, was residing at Brampton and was in habits of close intimacy with him. My father, being a man of scientific as well as of high literary attainments – and being, moreover, a good artist – took considerable interest in his friend Mr. Bromley's manufacture, and at his own house at Brampton entered with spirit into a series of experiments in enamelling and enamel-printing and in other processes for decorating the ware. For this purpose, he caused to be erected in his own house two enamel kilns – one of which he had constructed on the ordinary simple principle of heating, and the other on the spiral principle. He also fitted up, for the purpose of these private experiments, a small printing-room, and here, being, as I have said, a good artist, he tried various processes for transferring aquatints and etchings (which he etched and prepared himself) by the bat-process, both on to the biscuit and on to the white glazed ware.

The works afterwards belonged to Robert Bainbrigge & Co.

Stone Bottle Works These works, at Whittington Moor, were established in 1818 by Aaron Madin and continued by his son-in-law, Samuel Lancaster. The goods produced were stoneware, brown ware, and coarse black ware. The stoneware was made of fireclay, found underneath the Tupton coal measures at Brampton and elsewhere, and glazed. It was of good quality, and very hard and durable. The stoneware was, as was usual in the district, salt-glazed; and the black ware, made of the common brick-clay, was glazed chiefly with lead-ore. The goods produced were the usual domestic and other articles made in the neighbourhood, and their quality was equal to most others. Trading as A. Madin, this pottery continued into the twentieth century.

Whittington Pottery At these works, established in 1805, belonging to James Pearson, the usual classes of goods as made at the other potteries of the district were produced. Pearson & Co. worked into the twentieth century and continue at the present time at Brampton.

Whittington Moor Pottery Mr. S. Lancaster (late A. Madin) had a manufactory of coarse ware at this place – the body, as usual, coarse red outside and lined with a black glaze inside. The firm continued into the twentieth century.

Newbold There was a manufactory of coarse brown ware – pancheons, bread-pans, pots and the like – carried on by W. Sharratt at this place. The productions were of much the same character as those of Whittington Moor. Sharratt's name does not appear in the directories of the 1880s.

WILNECOTE (Staffordshire)

The Wilnecote Works Near Tamworth, these works were established in 1860 by George Skey, who purchased the coal-mines at this place and, in the course of sinking shafts, discovered important and valuable beds of fire and other clays well adapted for pottery purposes. He determined at once to erect kilns and workrooms, which he fitted up with suitable machinery, steam-presses and lathes, and the manufactory was opened in 1862. The goods produced were so well received that the works had very shortly to be enlarged and fresh workrooms and kilns were erected.

In 1864, Mr. Skey having found the concern grown to more than his own personal care could, single-handed, control, formed it into a limited liability company with a capital of £60,000, under the style of the Wilnecote Company Limited, afterwards altered to George Skey & Company Limited. The goods produced were fountains, vases, tazzas, brackets, pedestals, terminals, flower-vases, mignonette-boxes, fern-stands, garden-seats, balustrades, cornices, chimney-pots and every description of architectural enrichment. Game-pie dishes and other domestic articles were also produced, as were vases, garden-seats, flower-pots, brackets, fern-stands and a variety of other articles in 'rustic ware' – which was a fine-buff coloured terracotta, glazed with a rich brown glaze and sometimes heightened with a green tinge, just sufficient to give it a pleasing effect. In stoneware or Bristol ware, and sanitary ware, all the usual and many additional articles were made. Terracotta gas-stoves were extensively made and were of admirable construction.

The mark used was GEORGE SKEY WILNECOTE WORKS NR TAMWORTH, in an oval, impressed in the ware.

Messrs. Skey continued into the twentieth century but concentrated on the production of sanitary ware.

WOODVILLE, or WOODEN BOX, HARTSHORNE (Derbyshire)

Woodville, the name given to the village of Wooden Box, is five and a half miles from Burton-on-Trent. It was noted for extensive manufactories of Derbyshire Ironstone ware, cane-coloured, Rockingham, black, buff and brown ware, sanitary goods and terra-cotta. Its inhabitants were principally potters and colliers.

The Hartshorne Potteries Established in 1818 by Joseph Thompson, father of Richard and Willoughby Thompson, who succeeded him as Thompson Brothers and were in turn succeeded by Holland & Thompson, who failed in 1882. Derbyshire Ironstone ware, brown, cane, buff, and yellow Ironstone ware, black and Rockingham ware, terra-cotta goods and sanitary goods were made; and, by the last firm, all the usual kinds of white ware, china, and decorated goods were produced.

J THOMPSON

JOSEPH THOMPSON
WOODEN BOX
POTTERY

DERBYSHIRE

The Hartshorne Pottery Established in about 1790 by James Onions, who was succeeded by Luke Copeland. It was next carried on successively by Read, Malkin & Co., Read & Malkin, and G. S. Read. Mr. Read died in 1860, when the concern passed into the hands of J. B. Rowley. The goods produced were Derbyshire Ironstone or cane-coloured ware, Rockingham ware, mottled ware, buff ware, and black lustre ware. In these, all the usual articles for domestic use were made. J. B. Rowley ceased production in about 1895.

The Woodville Pottery Established in 1833 by Thomas Hall and William Davenport, this pottery in 1858 passed into the hands of Thomas Betteridge and Thomas Nadin, who in 1863 retired from the concern, which after that was carried on by Mr. Betteridge. The goods produced were the usual classes of Derbyshire cane-coloured Ironstone, Rockingham, mottled, and buff ware of the district. Thomas Betteridge continued into the twentieth century.

The Woodville Potteries Established in about 1810 by Mr. Watts, who was joined in partnership by his relative, Mr. Cash, in whose family it remained to about 1895 and was carried on under the style of Watts & Cash. The productions were the Derbyshire Ironstone or yellow ware, buff-coloured ware and Rockingham ware of the ordinary qualities in all the usual varieties of domestic vessels and services.

The Rawdon Pottery Built by the fourth Marquess of Hastings, on whose estate it was situated, this pottery was first worked by John Hall, who was succeeded, on his failure, by John Brunt. At his death, he was succeeded by his son, Thomas Brunt, who, however, did not succeed in the business. In 1861, the works passed to Smith, Dooley & Co. The goods produced were the usual varieties of articles in Derbyshire Ironstone or cane-coloured ware, Rockingham ware, buff ware, and cream-coloured ware. From about 1883 to 1896, the firm was T. C. Dooley (& Sons).

Wooden Box Pottery Established by Thomas Hallam in 1817, this pottery was successively worked by Mr. Robinson; Harrison & Cash; Hallam & Co.; Watts & Cash; and, later, Thomas Nadin, who manufactured Ironstone, cane, buff and Rockingham ware of the usual kinds and qualities up to about 1900.

Coleorton Pottery Established in 1835 by Messrs. Wilson & Proudman. The latter partner having retired, the works were carried on by John Wilson from 1844. Thomas Wilson succeeded and continued to 1880. Wilson Bros. continued until about 1895. The productions were yellow, buff or cane, and Rockingham ware, in which all the usual domestic articles were made.

Littlethorn Pottery George Smith produced ordinary earthenware here from about 1882 to about 1896, from which period 'Bros.' was added to the title.

WORCESTER

The history of Worcester porcelain dates from 1751 and the early history is outside the scope of this work. The partners from 1792 to 1807 were Messrs. Flight & Barr. Examples of their highly finished and fine quality porcelain may be marked with the incised B mark or with Flight & Barr in various forms. In 1807, Messrs. Barr, Flight & Barr succeeded and, until 1813, their ware was marked B.F.B. or Barr Flight

Plate 114. A pair of Barr, Flight & Barr Worcester cachepots showing a typical written mark and the superb quality of the painting, c.1810.
Godden of Worthing Ltd.

& Barr in many forms (see Plate 114). The Worcester porcelain of this period was of the finest quality, of a neat compact body decorated in the most tasteful and painstaking manner. The firm was 'manufacturers to their Majesties, Prince of Wales and Royal Family'. The title was again changed in 1813 to Messrs. Flight, Barr & Barr. Marks bearing this title or the initials F.B.B. can be dated 1813 to 1840. A similar high standard was attained and the Worcester porcelain of the period was probably the most highly finished of any English manufacturer.

Good examples are displayed in the Victoria and Albert Museum, and some are illustrated in the *Illustrated Encyclopaedia of British Pottery and Porcelain* by G. Godden (Herbert Jenkins, London, 1966).

Chamberlain's In 1786, Robert Chamberlain, who was apprenticed to the old Worcester Porcelain Company and who had continued with the different proprietors up to that period, commenced business for himself in premises at Diglis – the same which are now carried on by the Royal Worcester Porcelain Company. Chamberlain was a painter. On the first establishment of his business, he bought his porcelain from the Caughley Works (page 162) and painted it at Worcester. In a short time, however, he made his own, and his works soon grew into public favour and eminence. His son was an excellent artist. A portrait of Princess Charlotte, which he painted, is said to have given the highest satisfaction to Prince Leopold and others.

During the early part of the nineteenth century, Messrs. Chamberlain produced a large assortment of highly decorative porcelain, including bold 'Japan' patterns and cabinet pieces in the tradition of Messrs. Barr, Flight &

247

Fig. 52. Chamberlain & Co.'s exhibits at the 1851 Exhibition.

Barr. Various marks were employed (and are listed in sequence in Godden's *Encyclopaedia of British Pottery and Porcelain Marks* (Herbert Jenkins, London 1964). All include the name Chamberlain in various forms.

Typical examples of Chamberlain's Worcester porcelain are featured in Godden's *Illustrated Encyclopaedia of British Pottery and Porcelain* (Herbert Jenkins, London, 1966).

The manufactories of Flight, Barr & Barr and Chamberlain continued separately until 1840, when they amalgamated and formed one joint-stock company. The plant and stock were removed to Chamberlain's premises, and the works were there carried on under the style of Chamberlain & Co. From 1840 to 1847, the managing directors were Walter Chamberlain, John Lilly, Martin and George Barr, and Fleming St. John. From 1848 to 1850, the proprietors were Walter Chamberlain and John Lilly; and in 1850, Walter Chamberlain and Edward Lilly. In 1850, W. H. Kerr joined the concern, which was for a short time carried on under the style of Chamberlain, Lilly & Kerr; but on 1st January 1852, Chamberlain and Lilly retired and R. W. Binns entered into partnership with Mr. Kerr. The firm was then carried on under the style of Kerr & Binns and

W. H. Kerr & Co. In 1852, the works were considerably increased and rebuilt by Mr. Kerr, who retired from the concern in 1862. It was then carried on by a company of shareholders, R. W. Binns, F.S.A., holding the position of art director. From this date (June 1862), the present Worcester Royal Porcelain Company was born.

The products of Messrs. Kerr & Binns and, subsequently, of the Royal Worcester Company were extremely varied and of the highest quality. Concerning the Worcester enamels, the productions of the works were brought to a wondrous state of perfection, both as to body, glaze, form and decoration. Certainly neither in ancient nor in modern (1880s) specimens of ceramic art had such exquisitely beautiful works been produced as some of the enamels which, under the fostering hand of Mr. Binns, had been made. The body, unlike the works of Limoges or the Sèvres imitations, was pure porcelain, not a coating of porcelain or enamel over sheets of metal; and the effect was produced by the partial transparency of the white laid on the blue ground instead of by heightening. The tone was peculiarly soft and delicate, and the colours were pure and intense (an example is shown in Plate 115). Thomas Bott, an artist of

Plate 115. A Royal Worcester ewer and stand enamelled in the Limoges-style by Thomas Bott, shown at the 1871 Exhibition.
Dyson Perrins Museum, Worcester.

the very highest eminence, was brought up by Mr. Binns specially for the production of these enamels. Through his early death, in 1870, examples became very scarce.

To Mr. Binns was due the introduction and carrying out of the Worcester enamels in the style of Limoges; the ivory porcelain, a soft glaze body of an ivory tint; the Raphaelesque porcelain; jewelled porcelain, of a totally different and far higher character than that of Sèvres; and Japanese decoration on porcelain and pottery.

In Parian, the Worcester works produced figures, busts, groups and ornamental articles of a remarkably clean and pure body. Ivory porcelain – an improvement upon Parian, and capable of greater development – was a speciality of these works, and was first introduced for the Exhibition of 1862. Besides being used for busts, figures and ornamental pieces in its

simple state – when it had all the softness, beauty, and natural tint of ivory itself – it formed the basis of many of the ornamental decorations, especially the Raphaelesque ware, which is the colouring of the surface in relief in the style of the old Capo di Monte and Buen Retiro porcelain.

The jewelled porcelain, for which Worcester is famous, was totally different from that at any time made at Sèvres or Tournay. The French jewels were made by enamellers – each colour being fused on a small plate of metal, which formed the setting, and stuck on the vase or plate with gum if it was not required to pass through the fire. These jewels could be bought by the dozen or hundred in any variety; but the work decorated by them was essentially French

249

Fig. 53. Worcester Japanese-style ware, 1872
Exhibition.

and tinselly. The English jewelling, though
perhaps not so brilliant, was of higher and
purer character, and more legitimate as a decoration. Each of the jewels was formed of colour
melted on to the china and occasionally raised
higher and higher by repeated firings. Thus it
became a part of the material itself. One of the
most elaborate pieces of work produced at
these works, in this style, was a déjeuner set
made for presentation from the City of Worcester to the Countess of Dudley on her marriage in 1865. It is powdered all over with turquoise, but so arranged in geometric lines that
only the different sizes of the jewels are noticed
(see Godden's *Victorian Porcelain*, Herbert
Jenkins, London, 1961, Plate 53).

In Japanese-styled porcelain, Worcester
produced vases, spill-cases, jardinières, toilet
ornaments, trays, and an infinite number of
other elegancies. These productions were not
servile imitations but were Japanese art and

250

art-characteristics adapted and rendered subservient to the highest aims of pure design of our
country. Mr. Binns, in the introduction of this
style, caught the very spirit of Japanese art, and
so grafted it upon English productions that the
one became a component part of the other.
Among the more characteristic of the vases was
a set on which the designs, in relief (modelled
by Mr. James Hadley), represent the processes
of the potter's art as followed in the East; and
these were minutely painted and gilded by
Callowhill.

Messrs. Kerr & Binn's standard marks of the
period 1852–62 were:

Colour Plate X. A fine Royal Worcester vase,
modelled by James Hadley and painted by W.
Powell, 1909. $19\frac{1}{2}$ inches high.
Godden of Worthing Ltd.

The standard Royal Worcester marks from 1862 were:

(the second example, with the wording, dates from 1891).

For a full account of the Royal Worcester ware, artists and marks, the reader is referred to Godden's *Victorian Porcelain* (Herbert Jenkins, London, 1961).

Grainger The porcelain works of Messrs. Grainger & Co., in St. Martin's Street, were established in 1801 by Thomas Grainger, nephew to Mr. Chamberlain, to whom he served apprenticeship as a painter and later assisted in the general management of the works. When Thomas Grainger started a manufactory on his own account, he took into partnership a Mr. Wood, a painter of considerable skill, whose productions were characterised by a peculiar mellowness of shade and who excelled in mezzo-tint drawing. The works were carried on under the style of Grainger & Wood.

In 1812, Mr. Grainger took into partnership his brother-in-law, Mr. Lee, and the style was then changed to Grainger & Lee.

Grainger Lee
&co
Worcester.

About two years before this time, the works – having been destroyed by fire – were rebuilt on the opposite side of the street and then considerably enlarged. After Mr. Lee retired from the business, it was carried on by Thomas Grainger until his decease in 1839, when his son, George Grainger, succeeded him and carried on the works under the style of G. Grainger & Co. Up to 1848, porcelain alone was made, but in that year Mr. Grainger invented a new

body, which he named 'Semi-Porcelain', which was first made public at the Birmingham Exhibition of 1849. There, because of its peculiar qualities of durability, hardness and freedom from cracking with heat, it attracted considerable attention. The surface of the semi-porcelain bears every characteristic of the finest china; and in colour, painting, and gilding it could be made quite equal to it. But it had the additional advantage of being so completely vitrified that the inside, in case of being chipped or broken, remained of its original whiteness. It was peculiarly adapted for dinner services through not flying or cracking with heat so readily as the ordinary china does, and because of its power of retaining heat for a much longer time.

Many good artists were employed during the first half of the nineteenth century. These included the floral artist David Evans. Typical specimens of Grainger's Worcester procelain are featured in Godden's *Illustrated Encyclopaedia of British Pottery and Porcelain* (Herbert Jenkins, London, 1966). They also produced some admirable Parian vases, figures, and ornaments. Another variety of goods was perforated Parian; (Fig. 54) and another perforated porcelain, in which some exquisite articles were produced and decorated in the very highest style of art. Decorative examples of the pâte-sur-pâte style of decoration were also produced.

The mark from about 1889 was:

At this period, the Grainger company was incorporated with the Royal Worcester firm, but production continued until 1902.

Hadley James Hadley (formerly chief modeller to the Royal Worcester Company) established his own small works at Worcester in 1896. His 'Hadley Ware' normally has moulded ornamentation in tinted clay. James Hadley died in December 1903 and his sons sold the business to the Royal Worcester firm in July 1905. For a first-hand account of the works and illustrations of the marks, see Godden's *Victorian Porcelain* (Herbert Jenkins, London, 1961).

Locke Edward Locke established his own small works at Shrub Hill, Worcester, in 1895. His ware closely follows the styles used at the Royal Worcester works. This firm ceased production in 1904. The mark is Locke & Co. within a globe device. An advertisement of 1899 (Plate 116) shows typical products.

Sparks George Sparks decorated on his own account a quantity of Chamberlain porcelain and Coalport porcelain at Worcester from 1836 to 1854. Many examples are signed. Doe and Rogers also signed porcelain decorated by them during the first half of the century, and Messrs. Padmore & Co. decorated ware at Worcester late in the nineteenth century.

Mr. St. John's Encaustic Tile Works After the removal of Flight, Barr & Barr's works to the present site of the Royal Porcelain manufactory in 1840, Mr. Barr for a time continued making encaustic paving tiles on the old premises. In this, he was joined by Mr. Fleming St. John – one of the managing directors of the Royal Porcelain works – and some excellent patterns, of good colour and material, were produced. The tile works were, however, sold in 1850 to Messrs. Maw, who carried on the manufacture until 1852, when they removed to Broseley (see page 152).

Worcester Tileries These works were established in Rainbow Hill in 1870 by Henry C. Webb, the tiles produced being black, red, buff, grey, and chocolate geometrical tiles; the same with patterns in cream, fawn, blue, white and green; and encaustic or inlaid tiles. The mark is HENRY C. WEBB, WORCESTER in raised letters, in a small circle impressed in the clay.

This firm ceased early in the twentieth century.

Fig. 54. Messrs. Grainger's perforated china, 1862 Exhibition.

Plate 116. A selection of Locke's Worcester porcelain, reproduced from an 1899 advertisement.

YARMOUTH (Norfolk)

Although 'Absolon, Yarmouth' occurs on pieces of ware in different collections, it must not for one moment be taken for granted that the pottery was produced there. The Absolons were china and glass decorators and dealers in Yarmouth, and one of the family appears to have erected a kiln called the Ovens and there to have 'burnt-in' the flowers and other designs which he employed himself in painting upon ware procured from other places. His plan appears to have been to buy the undecorated cream-coloured ware and paint upon it flowers and views in the manner of those produced at the Swinton and Don potteries, and in the same manner to write their names on the back and then to burn them in his oven.

William Absolon worked at Yarmouth from about 1784 to about 1815. Several examples bear '25' or 'No 25' after the basic name mark.

This addition refers to the address – 25 Market Row – and is subsequent to 1790.

Absolon Yarm

Typical specimens are illustrated by A. J. B. Kiddell in an interesting paper contained in Volume 5, Part 1, of *The Transactions of the English Ceramic Circle* (1960); see also Godden's *Illustrated Encyclopaedia of British Pottery and Porcelain* (Herbert Jenkins, London, 1966).

YORK

York China Manufactory In 1838, Mr. Haigh Hirstwood, formerly of the Rockingham china works, established a china manufactory in York, and by the succeeding spring had so far progressed that the following paragraph appeared in the York papers:

253

YORK CHINA MANUFACTORY. Mr. Hirstwood, of Stonegate, is erecting a kiln, extensive warehouses, &c., in the Groves, for manufacturing, gilding, and burnishing china, which has not previously been attempted in this city.

The works were established in Lowther Street, Groves, and were continued until about 1850, when the concern was wound up. Mr. Haigh Hirstwood was born at Royd's Hall, near Huddersfield, in 1778, and learnt the art of china making and decorating under the Bramelds at the Rockingham works, as did also afterwards his sons and son-in-law. He continued at the Rockingham works upwards of forty years, leaving them only towards their close, when he removed to York and commenced business as a china-dealer. In 1839, as I have stated, he erected kilns at York and commenced business in the decorating and finishing departments, buying his china in the white from manufacturers in Staffordshire.

In this business he was assisted by his son-in-law, William Leyland, also from the Rockingham works, who became his managing partner. Disagreements having arisen, however, the business was broken up, Mr. Hirstwood remaining in York, where he died in 1854, and Mr. Leyland removing to London – when he took to painting and decorating lamps – where he died in 1853.

Mr. Leyland, who was a painter, gilder and enameller, understood all the practical details of the potter's art. Mr. Hirstwood was a painter of flowers, and was considered the best fly-painter at the Rockingham works. In 1826, he copied, for use in the decoration of Rockingham china, upwards of five hundred insects at Wentworth House, which had been arranged by Lady Milton, the daughter-in-law of Earl Fitzwilliam. He and his sons, Joseph and William (who were brought up at the Rockingham works) were engaged upon the chef-d'oeuvre of that manufactory – the services for King William IV and for the Duchess of Cumberland. He was succeeded in his business in Coney Street by his son, William Hirstwood, but the manufactory was entirely discontinued from 1850.

The goods principally produced were dinner, tea, dessert and other services, vases and figures. The style reputedly closely assimilated that of Rockingham china. No mark was used. Floral plaques said to have been painted by Joseph Hirstwood and by William Leyland are illustrated in O. Grabham's *Yorkshire Potteries, Pots and Potters* (Yorkshire Museum, 1916).

YNYSMEDW (Near Swansea, Wales)

Terra-Cotta Works This manufactory, about ten miles from Swansea, on the Brecon road, was commenced as a fire-brick works (there having been a small common brick-works there previously) in 1840 by Mr. Williams and his brother.

Terra-cotta was made in buff of good quality. In about 1850, Messrs. Williams added the manufacture of earthenware in table, tea, toilet and other services, etc., in common white painted and printed ware. This was continued till about 1859, when the blue-and-white branch was discontinued (the engraved copper-plates being purchased for the South Wales Pottery, Llanelly) and the works were transferred to Charles Williams. He disposed of them to Griffith Lewis and John Morgan of Pontardawe, who carried it on under the style of the Ynysmedw Brick Company, Ynysmedw Pottery Company and Lewis & Morgan, who also manufactured Rockingham teapots, glazed stoneware bottles and similar goods. In 1870, the works were transferred to W. T. Holland of the South Wales Pottery, Llanelly, by whom they were continued for some years.

Several marks have been recorded. These include one of the following distinguishing features: YNISMEDW POTTERY, YMP, YP, L & M, or Williams.

A creamware oval basket and fragments from the pottery site are shown in Plates 569 to 571 of Godden's *Illustrated Encyclopaedia of British Pottery and Porcelain* (Herbert Jenkins, London, 1966).

N.B. Various spellings of the place-name occur: Ynismedw, Ynysmedwy and Ynysmedw.

APPENDIX

MARKS AND DATING

It would be quite impossible to list here all the marks used by the thousand different firms mentioned in this book, although many marks are given in the text.

My comprehensive mark book, *The Encyclopaedia of British Pottery and Porcelain Marks* (Herbert Jenkins, London, 1964), contains over four thousand British marks. The gathering of material for it has enabled me to draw up some general rules for dating English marks of the nineteenth century. These may be summarised as follows:

1. Examples bearing the diamond shaped Patent Office Registration mark are subsequent to 1842 (see page 258 for full details of this mark).
2. The use of 'Limited' or the abbreviations 'Ltd.' or 'Ld.' after a firm's title indicates a date after 1855; and in the Potteries district, a date subsequent to 1860.
3. The word 'Royal' in the firm's title or trade name suggests a date after the middle of the nineteenth century.
4. The words 'Trade Mark' incorporated in a mark signify a date after 1862.
5. The occurrence of 'Rd.No.' followed by a number indicates a date after 1884 (see page 259 for full details).
6. The word 'England' occurring in marks signifies a date after 1880. The year 1891 has previously been given for this, but the 1883 edition of the present work includes several marks which include the word ENGLAND. It should be noted that 'Made in England' is a twentieth century term.
7. The words 'Bone China', 'English Bone China' and the like denote a twentieth-century date.

Many nineteenth-century printed marks are based on stock designs – variations of the royal arms, a garter-shaped mark (crowned or uncrowned) or the Staffordshire knot.

The garter-shaped mark (B) was extensively

A.

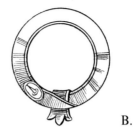

B.  C.

used from about the 1840s onwards; and the Staffordshire knot (C) can occur from about 1845. It was much used in the 1870s and 1880s and continues, in some instances, to the present day. These marks might be found with the initials or names of the relevant manufacturers. The royal arms (A) were employed from the early part of the nineteenth century but clear impressions which show the quartered arms *without* a central inescutcheon are subsequent to 1837 (see A above).

Many English marks consist of or incorporate the firm's initials, which often appear in triangular form: $\frac{F\&R}{B}$ or $\frac{H\&G}{B}$. In these cases, the bottom letter denotes in which town in the Staffordshire Potteries the factory was situated. The first example given here is Ford & Riley of Newcastle Street, Burslem, the second is Heath & Greatbatch, Union Pottery, Burslem. Serious confusion can arise in cases where the town's initial letter was placed directly after the firm's initials – as with Edwards & Brown of Longton, who used the initials E. & B.L. The main town and initials are Burselm (B), Cobridge (C), Fenton (F), Hanley (H), Longton (L) and Tunstall (T).

A selection of mark books is given in the Bibliography on page 263. *The Encyclopaedia of British Pottery and Porcelain Marks* will be found to contain over twice the number of English marks hitherto published and emphasis is placed on the accurate dating of each mark.

PATENT OFFICE DESIGN
REGISTRATION MARKS

These marks are of diamond shape and appear (impressed, moulded or printed) on a variety of Victorian ware from 1842 to 1883. The purpose of this mark was to show that the design or shape had been registered with the Patent Office in London and was protected from copying by other manufacturers for an initial period of three years. It should be noted that this mark will therefore show the *earliest* date that an object bearing it could have been manufactured.

Two slightly different forms of arrangement were employed. The first, from 1842 to 1867, gives the year letter in the top section. The second, from 1868 to 1883, has the year letter at the right. The Roman numerals at the top denote the class of object: pottery and porcelain was Class IV.

This form of mark was discontinued in 1883. Subsequently, a simple progressive system of numbering was employed in which the registration numbers were usually prefixed 'R^d N^o'. See page 259 for the key to this system.

Below are the two patterns of Design Registration Marks that were in current use between the years 1842 and 1883. Keys to 'year' and 'month' code-letters are given below.

The left-hand diamond was used during the years 1842 to 1867. A change was made in 1868, when the right-hand diamond was adopted.

INDEX TO YEAR AND
MONTH LETTERS

YEARS
1842–67
Year Letter at Top

A	= 1845	N	= 1864
B	= 1858	O	= 1862
C	= 1844	P	= 1851
D	= 1852	Q	= 1866
E	= 1855	R	= 1861
F	= 1847	S	= 1849
G	= 1863	T	= 1867
H	= 1843	U	= 1848
I	= 1846	V	= 1850
J	= 1854	W	= 1865
K	= 1857	X	= 1842
L	= 1856	Y	= 1853
M	= 1859	Z	= 1860

1868–83
Year Letter at Right

A	= 1871	L	= 1882
C	= 1870	P	= 1877
D	= 1878	S	= 1875
E	= 1881	U	= 1874
F	= 1873	V	= 1876
H	= 1869	W	= (Mar. 1–6)
I	= 1872		1878
J	= 1880	X	= 1868
K	= 1883	Y	= 1879

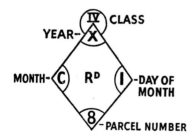

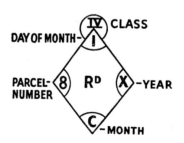

MONTHS (BOTH PERIODS)

A = December G = February
B = October H = April
C or O = January I = July
D = September K = November (and
E = May December
1860)

M = June
R = August (and
September 1st–19th
1857)
W = March

REGISTRATION NUMBERS

TABLE OF DESIGN REGISTRATION NUMBERS FOUND ON WARES FIRST REGISTERED BETWEEN JANUARY, 1884 AND 1909.

R^D No.   1 registered on 1st January 1884.
R^D No. 19754 registered on 1st January 1885.
R^D No. 40480 registered on 1st January 1886.
R^D No. 64520 registered on 1st January 1887.
R^D No. 90483 registered on 2nd January 1888.
R^D No. 116648 registered on 1st January 1889.
R^D No. 141273 registered on 1st January 1890.
R^D No. 163767 registered on 1st January 1891.
R^D No. 185713 registered on 1st January 1892.
R^D No. 205240 registered on 2nd January 1893.
R^D No. 224720 registered on 1st January 1894.
R^D No. 246975 registered on 1st January 1895.
R^D No. 268392 registered on 1st January 1896.
R^D No. 291241 registered on 1st January 1897.
R^D No. 311658 registered on 1st January 1898.
R^D No. 331707 registered on 2nd January 1899.
R^D No. 351202 registered on 1st January 1900.
R^D No. 368154 registered on 1st January 1901.
R^D No. 385088 registered on 1st January 1902.
R^D No. 402913 registered on 1st January 1903.
R^D No. 425017 registered on 1st January 1904.
R^D No. 447548 registered on 2nd January 1905.
R^D No. 471486 registered on 1st January 1906.
R^D No. 493487 registered on 1st January 1907.
R^D No. 518415 registered on 1st January 1908.
R^D No. 534963 registered on 1st January 1909.

SOME ERRORS IN THE 1883 EDITION

It is not surprising that some errors occurred in the 1878 edition and in the 1883 revised edition of Jewitt's original work. In fact, it is surprising that discoveries during the subsequent period of nearly ninety years have not proved more of Jewitt's original beliefs to be wrong. This section is not meant to descredit the original. Far from it – for I have the utmost admiration for Jewitt's painstaking research. But at the same time, especially now that unedited reprints may be offered to collectors, it is reasonable to draw attention to the few errors that do occur.

We have two basic points to remember when reading the original version. Firstly, many references are made to objects in the Museum of Practical Geology – articles which were transferred many years ago to the Victoria and Albert Museum (to use the modern name) and most of which can now be seen in this London museum. Secondly, one must bear in mind that when Jewitt referred to a factory established or working in the 'last century', he was, of course, referring to the eighteenth century. Similarly, when he wrote the 'present century', he was referring to the nineteenth century.

We can now turn to errors of fact. The page references relate to the 1883 edition or to straightforward reprints of that edition.

Page 115. A printer's error occurs nineteen lines up from the bottom, where the incorrect date 1799 appears for the correct date of 1769.

Page 124. Under the 'Bow' heading, eleven lines down, the date of Thomas Frye's Patent should read 1749, not 1748.

Page 129. Some of the marks attributed to Bow are suspect. In particular, the triangle marks are now known to relate to the Chelsea factory.

Page 159. Eight lines up from the bottom of the page, a printer's error has turned the correct date of 1776 into 1756, giving a completely false impression that by 1756 good-class porcelain was made at Caughley, whereas none was made until the 1770s.

Page 160. Eleven lines up from the bottom, it is suggested that John Rose established his Coalport factory in 1798 or 1799. Modern research shows that the works were in existence by at least 1796, for the Prince and Princess of Orange visited Coalport in August of that year and 'bought some pieces of Mr. Rose'. Furthermore, jugs occur bearing the date 1796 (see G. A. Godden's *Coalport and Coalbrookdale Porcelains*, Herbert Jenkins, London, 1970).

Page 162. Recent excavations on the Caughley and Worcester factory sites have shown that the series of Chinese-styled numeral marks, of which four examples are engraved, denote a Worcester origin, not Caughley as stated. For further information on this subject, the reader is referred to G. A. Godden's *Caughley and Worcester Porcelains 1775–1800* (Herbert Jenkins, London, 1969).

Page 162. In the second paragraph, Jewitt noted: 'I have already shown that transfer-printing was used on Worcester porcelain as early as 1757, and I have little doubt that quite as early, if not a few years before that period, it was practised at Caughley.' This statement is puzzling and must be incorrect, for porcelain was not made at Caughley before the 1770s. Earlier shards found on the site are of typical heavily-potted domestic earthenware decorated with simple coloured glazes or with slip decoration. One could not print on such pottery.

Page 196. Reference is made to a Plymouth porcelain bust of George II, and to figures of Henry Woodward and Kitty Clive. Known examples are not of Plymouth make; and the two famous actor figures occur in Bow and, rarely, in Derby porcelain.

Page 256. In this section on Lowestoft porcelain, the most serious errors occur – for parts relate to Chinese hard-paste porcelain of a well-known type made for the European market. Jewitt's engravings, Figures 841 to 843, relate to such ware which was formerly believed to have been made, or at least decorated, in Lowestoft. Of the articles shown in Figure 842, only one odd cup is of true Lowestoft make, although Jewitt notes that this group contains 'some very characteristic examples of the higher class make of Lowestoft works . . .' The 'Owl'-crest service and the 'Wilkes and Liberty' bowl are likewise of Chinese manufacture. Jewitt was perhaps in two minds regarding the Lowestoft products, for he also wrote: 'Let me again utter a word or two of caution to collectors against placing too implicit a reliance upon what has been written concerning Lowestoft china, and against taking for granted that all which is nowadays called Lowestoft china is really the production of that manufactory . . . The great bulk of the specimens now unblushingly ascribed to Lowestoft I believe never were in that town, much less were ever made there.' Since Jewitt wrote these words, spoilt factory-wasters and moulds have come to light showing the typical homely porcelain which was made at Lowestoft. The reader is referred to G. A. Godden's *Illustrated Guide to Lowestoft Porcelain* (Herbert Jenkins, London, 1969).

Page 302. Three lines down, the printed marks show that the spelling of Jewitt's 'Coxon' should be 'Cockson'.

Page 393. Figures 1111 to 1118, which are described as Copeland's productions, appear to be of Minton manufacture.

Page 394. Figures 1119 to 1124, which are described as Minton's productions, are Copeland.

Page 395. Figures 1125 to 1128, which are described as Minton's productions, are Copeland – mainly being engravings of pieces included in the 1867 Exhibition.

Page 425. The group of ornate vases which Jewitt attributes to the Goss factory in the engraving (Figures 1243 to 1249) are, in fact, French – the products of the famous Sèvres works.

Page 485. Jewitt notes that 'In 1825 the entire stock of the (New Hall) concern . . . was sold off . . .' This appears to be an error for 1835. Near the bottom of this page, Jewitt includes an engraving of an N mark and notes 'sometimes there is an incised letter N as here shown'. Although this statement has been copied by later authors, I do not know of this mark occurring on any specimen of New Hall porcelain.

Page 508. One line up, the name 'Meachin' should be 'Meakin'.

Page 555. In the short entry relating to Lane Delph Pottery, the names 'Wallis & Genison' should read 'Wallis Gimson & Co.' Wallis is the Christian name.

Page 561. The last paragraph, referring to William Littler and the Longton Hall porcelain factory, is very meagre; and the date of establishment, given as 'about 1765', is some fifteen years too late. For a good account of the Longton Hall factory and its products, the reader is referred to Dr. B. Watney's *Longton Hall*

Porcelain (Faber & Faber, London, 1957).

Page 566. The marks engraved at the bottom of this page are now believed to relate to Hilditch & Son of Lane End, Staffordshire (1822–30), not to Heath & Son.

Page 573. In the top paragraph, relating to the Glamorgan Pottery, the name 'Herwain' is twice given. This should be 'Irwin'. The original Jewitt volumes contain several spelling errors in names. These perhaps arose because Jewitt was depending largely on the memory of former work-people, and perhaps because spoken names were mispronounced or misheard and were written down as they sounded. This is the probable explanation for Irwin appearing as Herwain.

Page 619. The group of Bell products listed as Figures 1801 to 1807 and described as being shown at the 1851 Exhibition were, in fact, included in the 1862 Exhibition.

SELECTED
BIBLIOGRAPHY

GENERAL AND MARK BOOKS

Blacker, J. F. *The A.B.C. of Nineteenth Century Pottery and Porcelain*, Stanley Paul & Co., London, N.D., c.1911.

Blacker, J. F. *The A.B.C. of English Salt-glaze Stoneware*, Stanley Paul & Co., London, 1922.

Chaffers, W. *Marks and Monograms . . .* William Reeves, London, 15th revised edition, 1965.

Charleston, R. J. *British Porcelain, 1745–1850*, E. Benn, London, 1965.

Fisher, S. W. *English Ceramics*, Ward Lock, London, 1966.

Godden, G. A. *Victorian Porcelain*, Herbert Jenkins, London, 1961.

Godden, G. A. *British Pottery and Porcelain, 1780–1850*, Arthur Baker, London, 1963.

Godden, G. A. *Encyclopaedia of British Pottery and Porcelain Marks*, Herbert Jenkins, London, 1964.

Godden, G. A. *Illustrated Encyclopaedia of British Pottery and Porcelain*, Herbert Jenkins, London, 1966.

Godden, G. A. *Handbook of British Pottery and Porcelain Marks*, Herbert Jenkins, London, 1968.

Haggar, R. G. *English Country Pottery*, Phoenix House, London, 1950.

Haggar, R. G. *Staffordshire Chimney Ornaments*, Phoenix House, London, 1955.

Haggar, R. G. and Mankowitz W., *The Concise Encyclopaedia of English Pottery and Porcelain*, A. Deutsch, London, 1957.

Honey, W. B. *English Pottery and Porcelain*, A. & C. Black, London, 5th revised edition, 1962.

Honey, W. B. *Old English Porcelain*, Faber & Faber, London, 1948.

Hughes, B. & T. *English Porcelain and Bone China, 1743–1850*, Lutterworth Press, London, 1955.

Hughes, G. B. *Victorian Pottery and Porcelain*, Country Life, London, 1959.

Jewitt, L. *The Ceramic Art of Great Britain*, Virtue & Co., London, 1878 (revised 1883).

Morley-Fletcher, M. *Investing in Pottery and Porcelain*, Barrie & Rockliff, London, 1968.

Rhead, G. W. & F. A. *Staffordshire Pots and Potters*, Hutchinson & Co., London, 1906.

Sandon, H. *British Pottery and Porcelain for Pleasure and Investment*, J. Gifford, London, 1969.

Shaw, S. *History of Staffordshire Potteries*, Privately printed at Hanley, 1829.

Towner, D. *English Cream-coloured Earthenware*, Faber & Faber, London, 1957.

Wakefield, H. *Victorian Pottery*, Herbert Jenkins, London, 1962.

Ward, J. *History of the Borough of Stoke-upon-Trent*, W. Lewis & Sons, London, 1843.

Watney, B. *English Blue and White Porcelain*, Faber & Faber, London, 1963.

Wills, G. *English Pottery and Porcelain*, Guinness Signatures, London, 1968.

SPECIALIST WORKS ON
INDIVIDUAL FACTORIES OR TYPES

Adams

Adams, P. W. L. *The Adams Family*, St. Catharine Press, London, 1914.

BIBLIOGRAPHY

Peel, D. *A Pride of Potters*, Arthur Barker, London, 1959.

Turner, W. *William Adams, An Old English Potter*, Chapman & Hall, London, 1904.

Bristol

Mackenna, F. Severne, *Champion's Bristol Porcelain*, F. Lewis, Leigh-on-Sea, 1947.

Owen, H. *Two Centuries of Ceramic Art in Bristol*, Bell & Daldry, London, 1873.

Poutney, W. J. *The Old Bristol Potteries*, J. W. Arrowsmith, Bristol, 1920.

Caughley

Godden, G. A. *Caughley and Worcester Porcelains, 1775–1800*, Herbert Jenkins, London, 1969.

Chelsea

Lane, A. *English Porcelain Figures of the Eighteenth Century*, Faber & Faber, London, 1961.

Mackenna, F. Severne, *Chelsea Porcelain, The Triangle and Raised Anchor Wares*, F. Lewis, Leigh-on-Sea, 1948.

Mackenna, F. Severne, *Chelsea Porcelain, The Red Anchor Wares*, F. Lewis, Leigh-on-Sea, 1951.

Mackenna, F. Severne, *Chelsea Porcelain, The Gold Anchor Period*, F. Lewis, Leigh-on-Sea, 1952.

See also:

Charleston, R. J. *British Porcelain, 1945–1840*, E. Benn, London, 1965.

Godden, G. A. *Illustrated Encyclopaedia of British Pottery and Porcelain*, Herbert Jenkins, London, 1966.

Coalport

Godden, G. A. *Coalport and Coalbrookdale Porcelains*, Herbert Jenkins, London, 1970.

Copeland

Godden, G. A. *Victorian Porcelain*, Herbert Jenkins, London, 1961.

Hayden, A. *Spode and his Successors*, Cassell & Co., London, 1924.

Derby

Gilhespy, F. B. *Crown Derby Porcelain*, F. Lewis, Leigh-on-Sea, 1951.

Gilhespy, F. B. *Derby Porcelain*, Spring Books, London, 1961.

Godden, G. A. *Victorian Porcelain*, Herbert Jenkins, London, 1961.

Haslem, J. *The Old Derby China Factory*, G. Bell & Sons, London, 1876.

Doulton

Blacker, J. F. *A.B.C. of English Salt-glaze Stoneware*, Stanley Paul, London, 1922.

Eyles, D. *Royal Doulton, 1815–1965*, Hutchinson, London, 1965.

Wakefield, H. *Victorian Pottery*, Herbert Jenkins, London, 1962.

Leeds

Towner, D. *The Leeds Pottery*, Cory, Adams & Mackay, London, 1963.

Liverpool

Smith, A. *The Illustrated Guide to Liverpool Herculaneum Pottery*, Barrie & Jenkins, London, 1970.

Lowestoft

Godden, G. A. *The Illustrated Guide to Lowestoft Porcelain*, Herbert Jenkins, London, 1969.

Mason's

Godden, G. A. *The Illustrated Guide to Mason's Ironstone China*, Barrie & Jenkins, London, 1971.

Minton

Godden, G. A. *Victorian Porcelain*, Herbert Jenkins, London, 1961.

Godden, G. A. *Minton Pottery and Porcelain of the First Period*, Herbert Jenkins, London, 1968.

Wakefield, H. *Victorian Pottery*, Herbert Jenkins, London, 1962.

Nantgarw

John, W. D. *Nantgarw Porcelain*, Ceramic Book Co., Newport, Mon., 1948 and 1956 Supplement.

Nance, E. M. *The Pottery and Porcelain of Swansea and Nantgarw*, Batsford, London, 1942.

New Hall

Charleston, R. J. *British Porcelain, 1745–1850* (Chapter by G.E.A. Gray), E. Benn, London, 1965.

Holgate, D. *New Hall and its Imitators*, Faber & Faber, London, 1971.

Stringer, G. E. *New Hall Porcelain*, Art Trade Press, London, 1949.

Parian

Shinn, C. & D., *The Illustrated Guide to Victorian Parian China*, Barrie & Jenkins, London, 1971.

Pinxton

Exley, C. L., *The Pinxton China Factory*, Mr. & Mrs. Coke-Steel, Sutton on the Hill, 1963.

Rockingham

Eagleston, A. & Lockett, T. A., *The Rockingham Pottery*, Rotherham Library and Museum, 1964.

Rice, D. G. *Ornamental Rockingham Porcelain*, Adam Publishing Co., London, 1965.

Rice, D. G. *The Illustrated Guide to Rockingham Porcelain*, Barrie & Jenkins, London, 1971.

Scottish Pottery

Fleming, J. A. *Scottish Pottery*, Maclehose, Jackson & Co., Glasgow, 1923.

Spode

Hayden, A. *Spode and his Successors*, Cassell & Co., London, 1924.

Whiter, L. *Spode, A History of the Family, Factory and Wares from 1733–1833*, Barrie & Jenkins, London, 1970.

Williams, S. B. *Antique Blue and White Spode*, Batsford, London, 1943.

Swansea

John, W. D. *Swansea Porcelain*, Ceramic Book Co., Newport, Mon., 1957.

Nance, E. M. *The Pottery and Porcelain of Swansea and Nantgarw*, Batsford, London, 1942.

Wedgwood

Honey, W. B. *Wedgwood Ware*, Faber & Faber, London, 1948.

Kelly, A. *Wedgwood Ware*, Ward Lock, London, 1970.

Mankowitz, W. *Wedgwood*, Dutton & Co., New York, 1953.

Very many general reference books give a good outline of the Wedgwood story and illustrate typical ware. Such books include G. Godden's *Illustrated Encyclopaedia of British Pottery and Porcelain* (Herbert Jenkins, London, 1966). Several books by Harry Buten (of the Buten Museum of Wedgwood, U.S.A.) are particularly helpful in featuring the nineteenth and twentieth century ware.

Worcester

Barrett, F. A. *Worcester Porcelain*, Faber & Faber, London, revised edition, 1966.

Binns, R. W. *A Century of Potting in the City of Worcester*, Quaritch, London, second edition, 1877.

Binns, R. W. *Worcester China, 1852–1897*, Quaritch, London, 1897.

Godden, G. A. *Victorian Porcelain*, Herbert Jenkins, London, 1961.

Hobson, R. L. *Worcester Porcelain*, Quaritch, London, 1910.

Marshall, H. Rissik, *Coloured Worcester Porcelain of the First Period*, Ceramic Book Co., Newport, Mon., 1954.

Sandon, H. *The Illustrated Guide to Worcester Porcelain*, Herbert Jenkins, London, 1969.

G. Godden's *Caughley and Worcester Porcelains, 1775–1800* (Herbert Jenkins, London, 1969) will be found to contain much information on the Worcester ware of this period and is particularly helpful in assisting to distinguish between the similar ware of these two factories.

Apart from the standard reference books, several art magazines will be found to contain articles on various ceramic subjects. From the china collector's point of view, the most helpful magazines are:

Antiques An American monthly, published in New York.

Antiques Collector A British bi-monthly.

Apollo A British monthly.

Collectors' Guide A British monthly.

Connoisseur A British monthly.

Country Life A British weekly magazine of general interest containing, on occasions, interesting articles on china collecting.

EDITOR'S CLOSING NOTE

It is probable, if not inevitable, that in a work such as this – with notices of nearly five hundred factories and over a thousand different firms – some small errors in dating have occurred.

I would therefore be most grateful to hear from anyone who may be able to correct any dates or supply information on nineteenth-century firms not listed in this revised edition of Jewitt's *Ceramic Art of Great Britain*.

Geoffrey A. Godden
17 Crescent Road,
Worthing,
Sussex,
England.

INDEX

Bailey, C. I. C., *Col. Pl.* viii; 180–1
Bailey, W. & J. A., 147
Bailey & Batkin, *Pl. 49*; 83
Bailey & Bevington, 69
Bainbrigge, R. & Co., 244
Baker, 230
Baker, C. G., 23
Baker, W. & Co., 48
Baker, Bevans & Irwin, 230
Baker & Roycroft, 29
Balfour, A., & Co., 186
Ball, 79
Ball Bros., 224
Ball, J., 107
Ball, T. S., 218
Ball, W., 224
Bamford, J., 70
Bancroft, 119
Banks, 82, 216
Banks & Co., 78
Banks, E., 78
Banks, Sir, E., 228
Banks, N., 172
Banks & Thorley, 78
Barge teapots, 172
Barker Bros., 98, 107
Barker, E., 238
Barker, H. K., 54
Barker, J., 29, 207
Barker, P., 207
Barker & Son, 22
Barker, S. (& Son), 207, 237–8
Barker & Batty, 107
Barker, Sutton & Till, 25
Barkers & Kent Ltd., 107
Barlow, A. B., 196
Barlow, F., 194, 196
Barlow, H. B., *Pl. 99*; xxvii, 194, 196
Barlow, T., *Fig. 18*; 87
Barlow, T. W. & Son, 107
Barlow, W. (& Son); 87
Barnes, G., 98
Barnes & Wood, 98
Barnstaple, 147
Barr, Flight & Barr, *Pl. 114*; 246–7
Barratts of Staffordshire Ltd., 20
Barum ware, 147
Basalt, *Pl. 1*; xvi
Bat-printing, *Pl. 2*; xvii
Bateman, A. H. & Co., 188
Bates & Bennett, 35
Bates, Brown-Westhead & Co., 64
Bates, Elliot & Co., 14
Bates, Gildea & Walker, 14
Bates, Walker & Co., 14–16
Baxter, T., 229
Bayley, Murray & Brammer, 186
B & B., 23
BB & I., 230
B & C, 9
Beardmore, T., 101
Beardmore & Birks, 98
Beauclere, Capt., 160
Beddow, 230
Bedford & Richmond, 243

Beech, F. & Co., 36
Beech, J. (& Son), 10, 104, 140, 141
Beech, W., 10
Beech & Adams, 137
Beech & Hancock, 22, 141
Beech & Jones, 10
Beech & Morgan, 78
Beech & Podmore, 10, 25
Beech & Tellwright, 36
Beeley, 228
Beevers, 206
Beevers & Ford, 206
Belfield, C. (& Sons), 219
Bell device, 185
Bell Bros., 211
Bell, I. & Co., 213
Bell, J. & M. P. & Co., 184–5
Bell, T., 213
Bell, W., 190
Bell, Deakin & Proctor, 90
Belle Vue Pottery, 190
Belleek, *Pl. 81*; 148–50
Belleuse, C., 34
Belper, 150
Bennett, E., *Col. Pl. 8*; 180
Bennett, W., 81
Bennett & Shenton, 81
Benson, B., 29
Benthall, 152
Bentley, G. L. & Co., 107
Beresford, Bros., 107
Beswick, J. W., 107
Beswick, R., 141
Bettany, T., 90
Betteridge, T., 246
Betts, E., 147
Bevan, 230
Bevington, 229
Bevington, A., 70
Bevington, A. & Co., 58
Bevington, J., *Pl. 42*; 69, 70, 74, 76
Bevington, J. & T., 70
Bevington, S., 76
Bevington, T., 70
Bevington, T. & J. (& Co.), 229
BF (joined), 203
B.F.B., 246
B. G. & W., 16
BHB (joined), 196
Bideford, 152–3
Bill & Procter, 138
Billingsley, W., 206, 209–10, 215–6, 228–30
Billington & Co., 132
Biltons Ltd., 137
Bingham, E. W., *Pl. 83*; 160–1
Bingley, T. (& Co.), 231–2
Binney & Matthews, 243
Binns, R. W., 248
Birbeck, 242
Birbeck, J., 166
Birbeck, W., 166
Birch, 61
Birch, E. J., 61
Bird, N., 214
Birkenhead, 153

Birks, L. A., & Co., 137
Birks, T., & Co., 97
Birks Brothers & Seddon, 36
Bishop & Stonier, 55
Bishops Waltham, 153
B.L. & Co., 21
Blackhurst, J., 142
Blackhurst, R., 142
Blackhurst & Bourne, 23
Blackhurst & Dunning, 142
Blackhurst & Hulme, 107
Blackhurst & Tunnicliffe, 23
Blair & Co., 104
Blairs Ltd., 104
Blairs (Longton) Ltd., 104
Blakeway, E., 165
Blakey, W., 213
Blanchard & Co., 198
Blanchard, H. M., 198
Blashfield, 209
Blashfield, J. M., *Fig. 47*; 221–2
Blood, Webster & Simpson, 150
Bloor, J., 175
Bloor, R., 174–5
Boden, J., 138
Bodley, E. F. (& Co.), 21, 22
Bodley, E. F. & Son(s), 22, 38
Bodley, E. J. D., *Pl. 20*; 21
Bodley & Son, 21
Bodley & Diggory, 21
Bodley & Harrold, 22
Boness, 153
Boote, T. & R., *Fig. 1*; 11, 25
Booth, A., 97
Booth, E., 56, 141
Booth, R., 75
Booth, T. & Co., 141
Booth, T., & Son(s), 58, 78, 141
Booth, T. G. (& F.), 141
Booths (Ltd.), 141
Bott, T., *Pl. 115*; 248–9
Boughey, M. (& Co.), 97
Boughey, Shaw & Martin, 97
Boulton & Co., 107
Boulton & Floyd, 137
Bourne, 221
Bourne, C., 52
Bourne, E., 37
Bourne, J., 150, 168–9, 170, 172–4
Bourne, Joseph & Son (Ltd.), 173–4
Bourne, S., 119
Bourne, W., 10, 150
Bourne & Brown, 51
Bourne & Cormie, 10
Bourne, Nixon & Co., 138
Bovey Pottery Co. Ltd., 154
Bovey Tracey (Pottery Co.), 154
Bowdler, A., 166
Bowers, C., 142
Bowers, F., 143
Bowers, G. F., 143
Boyle, J., 119
Boyle, S., 49
Boyle, Z. & Co., 133
B. P. Co., 143

Bradbury, J., 107
Bradbury & Son, 91
Bradley, F. D., *Pl. 56*; 99, 104
Bradshaw, W., 101
Brameld (& Co.), *Pl. 113*; 191, 229, 232–7
Brameld, G. F., 232–4
Brameld, J., 231
Brameld, J. W., 232–4
Brameld, T., 232–4
Brameld, W., 231
Brammall, W., 99
Brammall & Dent, 99
Brammall & Repton, 99
Brampton (Derbyshire), 154–6
Brampton (Lincs.), 156
Brannam, C. H., 147
Brayford, 113
Breeze & Co., 138
Brentnall, 236
Bretby, *Pl. 90*; 172
Briddon, W., 156
Bridgeness Pottery, 154
Bridgett & Bates, 104
Bridgett, Bates & Beech, 104
Bridgwood, 87, 141
Bridgwood, J., 9
Bridgwood, R., 107
Bridgwood, S., 98
Bridgwood, S., & Sons (Ltd.), *Pl. 59*; 104
Bridgwood & Clarke, 9, 141
Brindley, J., 37
Bristol, 156–8
Britannia Pottery Co. Ltd., 187
British Anchor Pottery Co. Ltd., 107
Britton, A., 201
Britton, J., 201
Britton, R. (& Sons), 201
Broadbent & Stanley Bros., 215
Broadhurst & Sons, 103
Broadhurst, J., (& Sons Ltd.), 51, 103
Brock, C., 240
Bromley, W., 244
Brough, J. W., 137
Brough & Blackhurst, 101
Brough & Jones, 137
Broughton & Mayer, 141
Brown, C., 51
Brown, J., 186
Brown Paisley, 215
Brown, R. & Son, 215
Brown, T. & Sons, 192
Brown-Westhead, Moore & Co., *Fig. 16*; 64–7
Brownfield, W. (& Son), *Pl. 26–8, Figs. 5, 6*; 30–2
Brownhills, 143
Brownhills Pottery Co., 143
Brownsword, H., *Pl. 30*
Broxbourne, 158
Brunt, J., 246
Brunt, T., 246
Brunton & Co., 224
Bryant, Burnell & James, 218
B & T., 23
Buchan, A. W. & Co., 219
Buckley Heath & Co., 23
Buckley, Heath & Greatbatch, 23

270

271

T. & L., 98
TMR., 206
T N & Co, 162
Toft, C., *Pl. 71*; 122, 137
Toft, J., 227
Toft & Keeling, 74
Toft & May, 74
Tomkinson, J., 141
Tomlinson & Co., 192
Tomlinson, E., (& Co.), 192
Tomlinson, (W.) & Co., 191
Tomlinson, Foster, Wedgwood & Co., 191
Tomlinson, Plowes & Co., 191
Tooth, H., 172, 209, 226
Torquay, 240–2
Torquay Terra-Cotta Co. Ltd., 242
Townsend, G., 98
Townsend, H. J., *Pl. 70*
'Trade Mark', 257
T & R B, 11
T.R. & P., 22
T T C monogram, 242
Tundley, Rhodes & Procter, 22
Tunnicliffe, 171
Tunnicliffe, M., 138
Tunstall, 6, 138–44
Turnbull, G. R., 211
Turner, (& Co.), 82
Turner, G. W. (& Sons), 141
Turner, J., 55, 56, 82, 185
Turner Jasper Ware, 16
Turner, W., 82
Turner, W. G., 119
Turner & Banks, 108
Turner, Hassall & Bromley, 130
Turner, Hassall & Peake, 130
Turner, Hassall & Poole, 130
Turner, Poole & Stanway, 130
Turner & Tomkinson, 141
Turner & Wood, 130
Turner's Patent, *Pl. 48*; 82
Twigg, B., 243
Twigg, Bros., 191
Twigg, J., 191, 243

U
Underglaze-blue, xxviii
Unwin, 101
Unwin, J. (& Co.), 101
Upper Hanley Pottery Co., 81

V
Vauxhall, 242–3
Venables, H., 79
Vernon, J. (& Sons), 22, 27
Vernon, J. & G., Bros., 27
Victoria Pottery Co., 81
Victorian Ware, 70

W
Wade, J., & Co., 23
Waghorn, W. R., 179
Waghorn, W., & Son, 162
Wagstaff, 242
Waine, C., 107

Waine & Bates, 107
Wainwright, J., 203
Wainwright, S., (& Co.), 200
Waite, 221
Walker, A., & Co., 222
Walker, J., 91
Walker, J. H., 213
Walker, S., 209–10, 228–9
Walker, T., 140
Walker & Carter, 133
Wallace, J., & Co., 211
Walley, E., 35
Walters, T., 93
Walton, (J.), *Pl. 18*; 18
Warburton, 35, 183, 211
Warburton, J., 55–7
Warburton, S., 201
Warburton & Britton, 201
Wardle & Co., 81
Wardle, J., 172
Warne, C. G., 244
Warrilow, G., & Sons, 107
Warrilow & Cope, 99
Warrington, 243
W.A. & S., *Pl. 80*
Watcombe Terra-Cotta Clay Co., 242
Watcombe (Torquay), *Fig. 51*; 240–2
Waters, R., 197
Wath-upon-Dearne, 243
Watts, J., 192
Watts & Cash, 246
W B, 31
W & B, 22, 31
W B & S, 31
Weatherby, 80
Weatherby, J. H., & Sons, 80
Weaver, 113
Webb, H. C., 252
Webb, S., & Co., 90
Webb & Walters, 90
Webberley, W., 101
Webster, M., 210
Wedgewood, (& Co.), 222–3
Wedgewood, *Pls. 1, 3, 6, 30–2; Col. Pl. 3; Figs. 8–12*; xvi, xviii, xxi, 39–47
Wedgwood & Co., 191, 192
Wedgwood & Co. (Ltd.), *Pl. 79*; 138–9
Wedgwood, E., 138–9
Wedgwood, Enoch (Tunstall), Ltd., 139
Wedgwood, J., (& Sons), 39–47
Wedgwood, Sons & Byerley, 39
Wedgwood, T., 19
Wedgwood's Stone China, 39
Weir, J., 185
Welsby, J., 243
Wemyss, 191
West Kent Potteries, 164
West Smethwick, 243
Weston-super-mare, 243
W.E.W., 10
Whalley, J., 222
Whieldon, T., 108
White, G., 13
White, J. & J., 158
Whitehead, 58